INTERNATIONAL COURTS AND TRIBUNALS SERIES

General Editors:
Ruth Mackenzie, Cesare P.R. Romano, and Philippe Sands

In Whose Name?

INTERNATIONAL COURTS AND TRIBUNALS SERIES

General Editors:
Ruth Mackenzie, Cesare P.R. Romano, and Philippe Sands

A distinctive feature of modern international society is the increase in the number of international judicial bodies and dispute settlement and implementation control bodies; in their case-loads; and in the range and importance of the issues they are called upon to address. These factors reflect a new stage in the delivery of international justice. The International Courts and Tribunals series has been established to encourage the publication of independent and scholarly works which address, in critical and analytical fashion, the legal and policy aspects of the functioning of international courts and tribunals, including their institutional, substantive, and procedural aspects.

In Whose Name?

A Public Law Theory of International Adjudication

Armin von Bogdandy and Ingo Venzke

Translated from the German by Thomas Dunlap and revised by the authors

OXFORD
UNIVERSITY PRESS

OXFORD
UNIVERSITY PRESS

Great Clarendon Street, Oxford, OX2 6DP,
United Kingdom

Oxford University Press is a department of the University of Oxford. It furthers the University's objective of excellence in research, scholarship, and education by publishing worldwide. Oxford is a registered trade mark of Oxford University Press in the UK and in certain other countries

First Edition published in 2014

Published in the United States of America by Oxford University Press
198 Madison Avenue, New York, NY 10016, United States of America

British Library Cataloguing in Publication Data
Data available

Library of Congress Control Number: 2014937260

ISBN 978-0-19-871746-1

Acknowledgements

The present book explores the phenomenon of the exercise of public authority by international courts. It aims at a strong conceptual grasp, a nuanced political–philosophical assessment, and the development of the pertinent law. It forms part of a larger research project on that matter, the first phase of which focused on the most evident form of international public authority, namely international territorial administration. The second phase dealt with the manifold exercise of public authority by international bureaucracies. The book at hand now concludes the third phase, which zoomed in on international courts' public authority.

We thank Simon Hentrei, Matthias Kottmann, and Frauke Sauerwein for their excellent support in finalizing the book. Not only did they complete the bibliographical data with the help of Friederike Ziemer, but they also helped strengthen many passages through their critique. We are also grateful for the suggestions we received from Matthias Goldmann, Marc Jacob, András Jakab, Christoph Krenn, Christoph Möllers, Karin Oellers-Frahm, Mateja Steinbrück Platise, Stephan Schill, Dana Schmalz, and Nele Yang.

We further tested arguments of the book in the framework of events at the University of Amsterdam, the Hebrew University in Jerusalem, the University of Copenhagen, New York University School of Law, the École de Droit de la Sorbonne, the Universities of Tel Aviv and Zurich, Jawaharlal Nehru University in New Delhi, and Yale Law School. The Straus Institute for the Advanced Study of Law & Justice and the Amsterdam Center for International Law provided the framework for completing the German manuscript. Thomas Dunlap translated it into English before we revised it for publication. We thank the anonymous reviewers for their efforts and appreciate OUP's dedicated editorial work.

Amsterdam and Heidelberg in March 2014

Unless noted otherwise, translations from non-English references have been provided by Thomas Dunlap. Furthermore, earlier versions of parts of our book have been published as articles or book chapters, especially: 'In Whose Name? An Investigation of International Court's Public Authority and Its Democratic Justification' (2012) 23 European Journal of International Law; 'Beyond Dispute: International Judicial Institutions as Lawmakers' (2012) 12 German Law Journal (2011); 'On the Democratic Legitimation of International Judicial Lawmaking' (2011) 12 German Law Journal 1341; 'On the Functions of International Courts: An Appraisal in Light of Their Burgeoning Public Authority' (2013) 26 Leiden Journal of International Law 49; 'The Spell of Precedents: Lawmaking by

International Courts and Tribunals' in Karen Alter, Cesare Romano, and Yuval Shany (eds), *The Oxford Handbook of International Adjudication* (OUP 2014) 503; 'International Judicial Institutions in International Relations: Functions, Authority and Legitimacy' in Bob Reinalda (ed), *Routledge Handbook of International Organizations* (Routledge 2013) 461. By Armin von Bogdandy: 'The European Lesson for International Democracy: The Significance of Articles 9 to 12 EU Treaty for International Organizations' (2012) 23 European Journal of International Law 315; 'How to Conceptualize the Democratic Legitimacy of International Courts' (2013) 14 Theoretical Inquiries in Law 361. By Ingo Venzke: 'The Role of International Courts as Interpreters and Developers of the Law: Working out the Jurisgenerative Practice of Interpretation' (2011) 34 Loyola of Los Angeles International and Comparative Law Review 99; 'Antinomies and Change in International Dispute Settlement: An Exercise in Comparative Procedural Law', in Rüdiger Wolfrum and Ina Gätzschmann (eds), *International Dispute Settlement: Room For Improvements* (Springer 2012) 235; 'Understanding the Authority of International Courts and Tribunals: On Delegation and Discursive Construction' (2013) 14 Theoretical Inquiries in Law 381.

Table of Contents

Table of Cases

AD HOC AWARDS

CONSTITUTIONAL CHAMBER OF THE SUPREME TRIBUNAL OF JUSTICE OF VENEZUELA

CONSTITUTIONAL COURT OF COLOMBIA

CONSTITUTIONAL COURT OF ITALY

COURT OF JUSTICE OF THE EUROPEAN UNION

EUROPEAN COMMISSION OF HUMAN RIGHTS

EUROPEAN COURT OF HUMAN RIGHTS

FEDERAL ADMINISTRATIVE COURT OF GERMANY (BUNDESVERWALTUNGSGERICHT)

FEDERAL CONSTITUTIONAL COURT OF GERMANY (BUNDESVERFASSUNGSGERICHT)

FEDERAL COURT OF CANADA

GENERAL AGREEMENT ON TARIFFS AND TRADE

INTER-AMERICAN COURT OF HUMAN RIGHTS

INTERNATIONAL CENTRE FOR SETTLEMENT OF INVESTMENT DISPUTES

INTERNATIONAL COMMISSION OF INQUIRY

INTERNATIONAL CRIMINAL COURT

INTERNATIONAL COURT OF JUSTICE

INTERNATIONAL CRIMINAL TRIBUNAL FOR RWANDA

INTERNATIONAL CRIMINAL TRIBUNAL FOR THE FORMER YUGOSLAVIA

INTERNATIONAL TRIBUNAL FOR THE LAW OF THE SEA

IRAN-UNITED STATES CLAIMS TRIBUNAL

NORTH AMERICAN FREE TRADE AGREEMENT/UNITED NATIONS COMMISSION ON INTERNATIONAL TRADE LAW

PERMANENT COURT OF ARBITRATION

PERMANENT COURT OF INTERNATIONAL JUSTICE

SPECIAL COURT FOR SIERRA LEONE

TRIBUNAL OF ARBITRATION ESTABLISHED BY ARTICLE I OF THE TREATY OF WASHINGTON OF 8 MAY 1871

TRIBUNAL OF THE VATICAN CITY STATE

UK SUPREME COURT

US SUPREME COURT

WORLD TRADE ORGANIZATION

Table of Instruments

EUROPEAN COURT OF HUMAN RIGHTS

EUROPEAN UNION

INTERNATIONAL CENTRE FOR SETTLEMENT OF INVESTMENT DISPUTES

INTERNATIONAL COURT OF JUSTICE

INTERNATIONAL LAW COMMISSION

INTERNATIONAL TRIBUNAL FOR THE LAW OF THE SEA

UNITED NATIONS

WORLD TRADE ORGANIZATION

List of Abbreviations

AG	Advocate General
AJIL	American Journal of International Law
Art/Arts	article/articles
BCE	Before Common Era
BVerfGE	Decisions of the Federal Constitutional Court of Germany (Entscheidungen des Bundesverfassungsgerichts)
BVerwGE	Decisions of the Federal Administrative Court of Germany (Entscheidungen des Bundesverwaltungsgerichts)
CJEU	Court of Justice of the European Union
CML Rev	Common Market Law Review
Const	constitutional
Crim	criminal
CUP	Cambridge University Press
Diss Op	dissenting opinion
Doc	document
DSB	Dispute Settlement Body
DSU	Dispute Settlement Understanding
ECHR	Convention for the Protection of Human Rights and Fundamental Freedoms
ECtHR	European Court of Human Rights
ed/eds	editor/editors
edn	edition
EU	European Union
Eur	European
FAO	UN Food and Agriculture Organization
fn	footnote
GAL	Global Administrative Law
GATS	General Agreement on Trade in Services
GATT	General Agreement on Tariffs and Trade

IACtHR	Inter-American Court of Human Rights
ICC	International Criminal Court
ICCPR	International Covenant on Civil and Political Rights
ICI	International Commissions of Inquiry
ICJ	International Court of Justice
ICLQ	International and Comparative Law Quarterly
ICSID	International Centre for Settlement of Investment Disputes
ICSID Convention	Convention on the Settlement of Investment Disputes between States and Nationals of Other States
ICTR	International Criminal Tribunal for Rwanda
ICTY	International Criminal Tribunal for the former Yugoslavia
IFAD	International Fund for Agricultural Development
ILC	International Law Commission
ILO	International Labour Organization
ILOAT	International Labour Organization Administrative Tribunal
Intl	international
ITLOS	International Tribunal for the Law of the Sea
ITO	International Trade Organization
IUSCT	Iran–United States Claims Tribunal
J	journal
L	law/legal
NAFTA	North American Free Trade Agreement
NGO	non-governmental organization
No	number
OECD	Organisation for Economic Co-operation and Development
Op	opinion
OUP	Oxford University Press
para/paras	paragraph/paragraphs
PCA	Permanent Court of Arbitration
PCIJ	Permanent Court of International Justicc
PL	Public Law
Rep	report/reports
Res	resolution
Rev	review
RUF	Revolutionary United Front
SCSL	Special Court for Sierra Leone
Sep Op	seperate opinion

SPS	Agreement on Sanitary and Phytosanitary Measures
TBT	Agreement on Technical Barriers to Trade
TEU	Treaty on European Union
TFEU	Treaty on the Functioning of the European Union
tr/trs	translator/translators
TRIPS	Trade-Related Aspects of Intellectual Property Rights
U	university
UN	United Nations
UNCIO	United Nations Conference on International Organization
UNCITRAL	United Nations Commission on International Trade Law
UNCLOS	United Nations Convention on the Law of the Sea
UNCTAD	United Nations Conference on Trade and Development
UNGA	United Nations General Assembly
UNSC	United Nations Security Council
UNTS	United Nations Treaty Series
UP	University Press
US SC	United States Supreme Court
v	versus
VCLT	Vienna Convention on the Law of Treaties
vol	volume
WHO	World Health Organization
WTO	World Trade Organization
YB	yearbook

1

Agenda and Objectives

A. FRAMING THE PROBLEM

Viewed in light of an important and once even dominant understanding of international law, international courts are mere instruments of dispute settlement whose activities are justified by the consent of the states that created them and in whose name they decide.[1] Along with many other authors, we see this understanding as far too narrow. It eclipses other important judicial functions, underrates problems of legitimacy, and stands in the way of a full assessment of international adjudication. It poses obstacles to international courts' further development.[2] But what to put in its place? We propose a public law theory of international adjudication, which sees international courts as actors who exercise public authority.[3] The theory's three main building blocks are: *multifunctionality, international public authority,* and *democracy.*

The starting point of our inquiry is the impressive development of international adjudication over the past two decades.[4] Since 2002, international courts have rendered more judicial decisions every single year than was the case from time immemorial up to 1989. This holds true even if we exclude the supranational Court of Justice of the European Union (CJEU)

[1] Our notion of international courts encompasses also international arbitral tribunals. It excludes the supranational Court of Justice of the European Union. On our reasons see section C 2 of this chapter.

[2] For the state of the debate see the contributions in Cesare Romano, Karen Alter, and Yuval Shany (eds), *The Oxford Handbook of International Adjudication* (OUP 2014); Benedict Kingsbury, 'International Courts: Uneven Judicialization in Global Order' in James Crawford and Martti Koskenniemi (eds), *Cambridge Companion to International Law* (CUP 2012) 202–28; Geir Ulfstein, 'The International Judiciary' in Jan Klabbers, Anne Peters, and Geir Ulfstein, *The Constitutionalization of International Law* (OUP 2009) 126.

[3] Our work forms part of the International Public Authority research network: <www.mpil.de/red/ipa/ > accessed 28 January 2014.

[4] Yuval Shany, 'No Longer a Weak Department of Power? Reflections on the Emergence of a New International Judiciary' (2009) 20 Eur J Intl L 73.

and the most prolific international court, the European Court of Human Rights (ECtHR).[5] This change in quantity has gone hand in hand with a change in quality. Many international courts are today part of institutional approaches to finding solutions for urgent problems of world society. They are supposed to help pursue common goals effectively and overcome problems of cooperation on the international level.[6] Like few other institutions, they serve the promise of international law to contribute to justice in the global community. But this generally welcome development entails new problems. Within the mantle of interpreting the law, international courts have strengthened into actors whose activity should be qualified as an exercise of international public authority beyond their traditional role as mere dispute settlers. Their decisions stabilize and generate normative expectations. They also control and legitimize the authority exercised by other institutions. This multifunctionality can in principle advance international order. But it comes with new problems, which are famously addressed as a possible *gouvernement des juges*.[7] Any concrete legal interpretation, any proposal for further development, and any theory about international courts should bear in mind both the promise and the challenge.

This new take on courts, however, is not yet widely shared in international legal scholarship. Many accounts of international courts still proceed from the assumption—almost as though it were self-evident—that they should be understood as institutions for settling disputes. This is already evident from the fact that the courts are often dealt with under the heading *Dispute Settlement*,[8] along with good offices, mediation, and conciliation. In important textbooks and larger works on international law, they continue to appear as one instrument of resolving disputes among others,[9] with a particularly close connection with negotiation processes.[10] This understanding may be inspired, not least, by positive law. Article 33(1) UN Charter lists arbitration and judicial settlement among mechanisms for the 'pacific

[5] Karen J Alter, 'The Evolving International Judiciary' (2006) Northwestern Public Law Research Paper No 11–50 <http://ssrn.com/abstract=1859507> accessed 17 September 2013.

[6] On some of the difficulties on the way see André Nollkaemper, 'International Adjudication of Global Public Goods: The Intersection of Substance and Procedure' (2012) 23 Eur J Intl L 769.

[7] See Edouard Lambert, *Le gouvernement des juges et la lutte contre la législation sociale aux États-Unis* (Giard 1921).

[8] Malcolm N Shaw, *International Law* (6th edn, CUP 2008) 1010; Patrick Daillier and others, *Droit International Public* (8th edn, Librairie Générale de Droit et de Jurisprudence 2009) 923.

[9] Karl Doehring, *Völkerrecht* (2nd edn, CF Müller 2004) 470–502; Ian Brownlie, *Principles of Public International Law* (7th edn, OUP 2008) 701–25; Pierre-Marie Dupuy and Yann Kerbrat, *Droit International Public* (10th edn, Dalloz 2010) 613–56; Luzius Caflisch, 'Cent ans de règlement pacifique des différends interétatiques' (2001) 288 Recueil des cours 245, 442–60.

[10] John G Merrills, *International Dispute Settlement* (5th edn, CUP 2011) 1–25.

settlement of disputes' (Chapter VI UN Charter), alongside negotiation or mediation. This may have been plausible in 1945, when the UN Charter entered into force, and maybe even still in 1990; today, international courts are much better positioned as part of the law of international institutions.[11]

The traditional account of legitimacy is as deficient as its functional analysis. It justifies the international judiciary out of the consent of states and out of the consent of disputing parties to submit to a court's jurisdiction.[12] This construction of legitimacy is indebted to the cooperative, private law-inspired foundation of international law.[13] It continues to be important and as international courts have spoken about the foundations of their legitimacy, they have often espoused this viewpoint. For example, the Appellate Body of the World Trade Organization (WTO) declared: 'The WTO Agreement is a treaty—the international equivalent of a contract. It is self-evident that in an exercise of their sovereignty, and in pursuit of their own respective national interests, the Members of the WTO have made a bargain.'[14] We do not deny that the consensus of the states continues to constitute an important resource of legitimacy; however, it alone no longer sufficiently sustains many of the decisions made in recent decades.

We are not the first to raise the deficits of this narrow understanding of international courts. For a long time the state-oriented understanding has been challenged and paralleled by a community-oriented approach, which conceives of international courts as organs of the international community.[15] More recently, a regime-oriented understanding has emerged, which presents a view on international courts from the perspective of their contribution to global governance.[16] Important insights and developments have come about due to these two conceptions, which compete with the idea of international courts as instruments of dispute settlement in a state-centred

[11] See José E Alvarez, *International Organizations as Law-Makers* (OUP 2006) 458–520.

[12] Elihu Lauterpacht, 'Principles of Procedure in International Litigation' (2009) 345 Recueil des cours 387, 444–5, 453–4; differently Andrea M Steingruber, *Consent in International Arbitration* (OUP 2012) 12.

[13] Seminal Emer de Vattel, *Le droit des gens ou principes de la loi naturelle: Appliqués à la conduite et aux affaires des Nations et des Souverains*, vol 1 (Rey et Gravier 1838) 276–93; on Vattel see Emmanuelle Jouannet, *Vattel and the Emergence of Classic International Law* (Gina Bellande and Robert Howse trs, Hart 2012).

[14] *Japan: Taxes on Alcoholic Beverages—Appellate Body Report* (4 October 1996) WT/DS8/AB/R, WT/DS10/AB/R, and WT/DS11/AB/R, para 14.

[15] Hersch Lauterpacht, *The Development of International Law by the Permanent Court of International Justice* (Longmans, Green and Co 1934) 45–68; Antônio A Cançado Trindade, 'International Law for Humankind: Towards a New *Jus Gentium* (II)' (2005) 317 Recueil des cours 9, 21–3.

[16] Tomer Broude, *International Governance in the WTO: Judicial Boundaries and Political Capitulation* (Cameron May 2004); Garry P Sampson, 'Introduction and Overview: Future Directions' in Garry P Sampson (ed), *The WTO and Global Governance: Future Directions* (United Nations UP 2008) 1; Rudolf Dolzer and Christoph Schreuer, *Principles of International Investment Law* (OUP 2008) 18.

world order. But they too come with significant shortcomings, as our analysis will continue to show.

Questioning the legitimacy of international courts is not only of academic interest but also responds to public debates. In particular, investment arbitration enjoys increased visibility and attention. More than a small number of voices opine that such arbitration sometimes appears biased and has overreached—for example, when it constrains domestic administrators to prevent economic hardship or to protect the environment.[17] At issue here are not only weak states at the receiving end of power relations: the vote for a new Senate in the German city-state of Hamburg, for example, could have cost 1.4 billion euros. That is the sum which the Swedish energy firm Vattenfall claimed as damages when the new city government implemented its electoral promise and, contrary to promises by its predecessor, increased the ecological requirements for a future power plant.[18] Also, judgments of the European Court of Human Rights show problems finding acceptance, for instance when they prohibit preventive custody of dangerous criminals or give them a right to vote.[19] When it comes to decisions of the World Trade Organization (WTO), the supranational CJEU deliberately allows room for non-compliance.[20] The efforts of the International Criminal Court's Prosecutors to finally lead their costly Court to a first conviction have helped little to pull the Court out of a legitimacy crisis.[21]

A fresh and critical scholarly engagement with international courts is more necessary than ever. We do not share all of the noted critiques and would even see some of them as ill-guided or misconceived. Arguing about legitimacy in any event needs a more refined perspective: 'Whatever its pedigree, it is high time that "international adjudication" were made the object of critical analysis instead of religious faith.'[22] We therefore ask the question that cuts to the core of debates about legitimacy: in whose name

[17] Michael Waibel and others (eds), *The Backlash Against Investment Arbitration: Perceptions and Reality* (Kluwer 2010).

[18] *Vattenfall AB, Vattenfall Europe AG, Vattenfall Europe Generation AG v Federal Republic of Germany* (Award) ICSID Case No ARB/09/6 (11 March 2011). The case was finally settled.

[19] *M v Germany* ECHR 2009 (on preventive custody). In fact, the UK push for a reform of the ECtHR was triggered by a series of decisions on prisoner voting; see Joshua Rozenberg, 'Leaked Proposals Set out Britain's Tough Line towards Strasbourg' *The Guardian* (London, 28 February 2012).

[20] On the refusal to follow decisions by the WTO see Joined Cases C–120/06 P and 121/06 P *FIAMM et al v Council and Commission* [2008] ECR I–06513, paras 105–34.

[21] *Prosecutor v Thomas Lubanga Dyilo* (Judgment) ICC-01/04-01/06-2843 (14 March 2012) 7–9. Sara Anoushirvani, 'The Future of the International Criminal Court: The Long Road to Legitimacy begins with the Trial of Thomas Lubanga Dyilo' (2010) 22 Pace Intl L Rev 213.

[22] Martti Koskenniemi, 'The Ideology of International Adjudication and the 1907 Hague Conference' in Yves Daudet (ed), *Topicality of the 1907 Hague Conference, the Second Peace Conference* (Nijhoff 2008) 127, 152.

do or should international courts decide? Is it in the name of the parties to a concrete case, in the name of the international community, or in the name of a functional regime? We will argue that international courts speak in the name of the peoples and citizens whose freedom they ultimately shape, however indirectly. That is a far-reaching and demanding argument that requires hefty work. Bear with us.

There is another reason why we regard a public law theory of international adjudication as urgent. A new, multipolar order is emerging; one in which state and regional associations outside of the political west are gaining importance and exerting a growing international influence. In this context, the project of judicializing international relations must assert itself anew.[23] Along the way, it would not be a good strategy to avoid criticism so as not to weaken the project itself. That would be a step toward an outright ideologization of the international judiciary. We believe that a public law theory of international adjudication, based on a critical reconstruction with help of the three core concepts of *multifunctionality, international public authority*, and *democracy*, will be more appropriate, more persuasive and, in the final analysis, more promising.

B. NEW BASIC CONCEPTS FOR INTERNATIONAL COURTS

I. Multifunctionality

Our first concern is to lay out international adjudication as multifunctional and thereby transcend the one-dimensional fixation on dispute settlement.[24] International judicial activity should not be understood on the basis of a *single* dominant function.[25] Most decisions are better understood if one interprets them as multifunctional. When a court 'decides a case' and 'applies the law', this usually has a series of legal and social consequences that one can regard as functions. By 'functions' we mean the contributions an actor renders to a whole.

The use of functional analysis in the humanities and social sciences is indebted to the nineteenth century, when many theories, turning away from contract theory, interpreted society with the help of biological categories.

[23] Kingsbury, 'International Courts' 203.

[24] See also José E Alvarez, 'Rush to Closure: Lessons of the Tadic Judgment' (1997–1998) 96 Michigan L Rev 2031.

[25] A theoretical approach in which an institution or a system always performs only a single function seems to us implausibly narrow and can be explained only by specific theoretical constraints. Illustrative in this sense is Niklas Luhmann, *Law as a Social System* (Klaus A Ziegert tr, Fatima Kastner and others eds, OUP 2004) 142–7. Luhmann identifies only one function of the legal system as a whole, but then finds himself compelled to introduce a number of other *Leistungen* (contributions) to keep his theory sufficiently plausible, 167–72.

Society is described as a body whose organs make specific contributions to its existence.[26] The potency of this view is evident not least in the fact that institutions of a legal system and a political community are usually referred to as *organs*.[27] On the international level, the metaphor is especially virulent in the personification of the state.[28] However, functionalist thinking is not invariably organistic in the nineteenth-century sense. While theorists such as Talcott Parsons and Niklas Luhmann continued to be inspired by biological categories, they prepared the path toward new ways of understanding.

To avoid being misunderstood as functionalists, we stress at this point that a function does not by itself justify an institution.[29] There is indeed an apologetic temptation in functional arguments. We see that apologetic potential and decidedly gear our functional analysis toward a thorough normative assessment. Just as not every scholar who uses the concept of the institution is an institutionalist, the fact that we accord the concept of function an important role does not make us functionalists. We employ this concept without being adherents of a social science functionalism, with its specific approach to the world. Part of our ambition, then, is to transcend functional narratives of legitimacy.

It is common practice to approach a legal phenomenon in one of two ways: through its *concept* and its *function*. Work concerned with the concept includes capturing characteristic elements and thereby conventionally settled meaning.[30] In this sense we define courts as institutions whose central activity consists of making binding decisions on legal questions through independent and non-partisan individuals following established legal criteria and an orderly process.[31] International courts are called upon

[26] Thus Léon Duguit following Durkheim; on this Luc Heuschling, 'Frankreich' in Armin von Bogdandy, Pedro Cruz Villalón, and Peter M Huber (eds), *Handbuch Ius Publicum Europaeum*, vol 2 (CF Müller 2008) 491, 502–4.

[27] Ernst-Wolfgang Böckenförde, 'Organ, Organisation, Juristische Person: Kritische Überlegungen zu Grundbegriffen und Konstruktionsbasis des staatlichen Organisationsrechts' in Christian-Friedrich Menger (ed), *Fortschritte des Verwaltungsrechts: Festschrift für Hans J Wolff zum 75. Geburtstag* (CH Beck 1973) 269, 270–2.

[28] Reinhart Koselleck, 'Staat und Souveränität III' in Otto Brunner, Werner Conze, and Reinhart Koselleck (eds), *Geschichtliche Grundbegriffe*, vol 6 (Klett-Cotta 2004) 25, 26.

[29] Also Luhmann was adamant about this; see Niklas Luhmann, *Legitimation durch Verfahren* (2nd edn, Suhrkamp 1989) 6–7.

[30] Hans-Joachim Koch and Helmut Rüßmann, *Juristische Begründungslehre: Eine Einführung in die Grundprobleme der Rechtswissenschaft* (CH Beck 1982) 24, 73–7.

[31] The standard definition using the example of the state also contains the quality of 'permanence', which we forego. See Martin Shapiro, *Courts: A Comparative and Political Analysis* (University of Chicago Press 1981) 1–37; Cesare PR Romano, 'A Taxonomy of International Rule of Law Institutions' (2011) 2 J Intl Dispute Settlement 241, 251–4; Cesare PR Romano, 'The Proliferation of International Judicial Bodies' (1998–1999) 31 NYU J Intl L and Politics 709, 711–23; on the understanding from a German perspective see Ernst-Wolfgang Böckenförde, *Verfassungsfragen der Richterwahl* (Duncker & Humblot 1974) 86–99 and Christoph Degenhart, 'Gerichtsorganisation' in Josef Isensee and Paul Kirchhof (eds),

to determine what the law is and apply it to a concrete case. Article 38 ICJ Statute indeed states explicitly that the Court's 'function is to decide in accordance with international law such disputes as are submitted to it'. This is as trivial as it is apt.

When looked at in the functional way, the issue is mostly to identify the contribution of this institution or its characteristic activity to a larger whole. Now, it would be possible, following the established doctrines of the state functions,[32] to say that this was deciding a case in the just described manner and in this sense: 'adjudication', singular. This is in line with a theoretical understanding of the concept of function, according to which a system always performs only *one* function. A function is thus 'the characteristic of a system that combines a specific input into the system with a specific output'.[33] This *single* function is then formulated in a correspondingly vague or abstract way—as 'adjudication', for example. However, this does not satisfy the interests of many scholars, who wish to construct a rich and substantive picture of the legal, social, and political relevance that courts have for social order.

To make more precise and farther-reaching statements, many authors therefore admit a plurality of functions. It may then be possible to identify as functions of the judicial system such things as conflict resolution, providing a forum for disputes, social control, law-making, and routine administrative work, as well as the legitimation of other actors or even of the polity and its legal system as a whole.[34] We pick up on such understandings of functions and will show that contemporary international courts, similar to state courts, render a whole series of contributions when they 'decide in accordance with international law'.

Before we describe this in greater detail, we should say that in our view, positing a judicial function does not necessarily require that this function be legally assigned to the court. Within the framework of a post-black-letter jurisprudence, it would not be appropriate to be guided exclusively by legal

Handbuch des Staatsrechts der Bundesrepublik Deutschland, vol 5 (3rd edn, CF Müller 2007) 726–30. Art 14(1) International Covenant on Civil and Political Rights (ICCPR): All persons shall be equal before the courts and tribunals. In the determination of any criminal charge against him, or of his rights and obligations in a suit of law, everyone shall be entitled to a fair and public hearing by a competent, independent and impartial tribunal established by law [...]. Similarly Art 6(1) ECHR.

[32] See Christoph Möllers, *Gewaltengliederung: Legitimation und Dogmatik im nationalen und internationalen Rechtsvergleich* (Mohr Siebeck 2005) 94–134; for a comparative analysis see Giuseppe de Vergottini, *Diritto costituzionale comparato* (5th edn, CEDAM 1999) 619–734.

[33] Michael Esfeld, 'Funktion' in Petra Kolmer and Armin G Wildfeuer (eds), *Neues Handbuch philosophischer Grundbegriffe*, vol 1 (Alber 2011) 842.

[34] Böckenförde, *Verfassungsfragen der Richterwahl* 87–99; Klaus F Röhl, *Rechtssoziologie: Ein Lehrbuch* (Carl Heymanns 1987) 520–1; similarly for international courts Dinah Shelton, 'Form, Function, and the Powers of International Courts' (2008–2009) 9 Chicago J Intl L 537, 542.

mandates. A jurisprudence that does not limit itself to doctrinal constructions, but also seeks to grasp the law in its social and political contexts, must go beyond legally assigned functions.[35] Judicial decisions can even have functions that judges do not see themselves. A comparison with market transactions may clarify and support this point. Making a purchase has many social functions, including, among other things, meeting basic supply needs, social integration, and the efficient allocation of resources. Those functions typically do not form part of the incentives of market participants, and yet they are legally relevant. Scholarly perspectives need to distance themselves from the self-understanding of actors and elucidate those dimensions of their actions that they themselves might not see.

As this study will go on to demonstrate, the activity of international courts can be broken down into four primary functions: (a) dispute settlement in individual cases; (b) the stabilization of normative expectations; (c) law-making; and (d) the control and legitimation of public authority. To be sure, other conceptualizations, as well as further differentiations, are possible. For example, one could draw a distinction between functions of the first, second, and possibly even third order—on the basis, for instance, of whether and in what way a certain function is legally posited as a task, whether it lies within the horizon of the actors' consciousness, or how direct the connection is between judicial activity and the specific social consequence.

Some authors argue that dispute settlement is the *primary* function, while all others are merely *secondary*. Luhmann, for example, believes that making and stabilizing law happens, as it were, 'at arm's length'.[36] Alain Pellet writes in a similar vein that the additional functions of the stabilization of normative expectations and law-making are important, but he regards them as implicit or derived functions.[37] Indeed, judicial institutions may well consider themselves committed first and foremost to a specific functional activity. A scholarly examination should, however, detach itself from the self-perception of the actors and also illuminate obscured dimensions of their actions. The multifunctional analysis therefore makes it possible not least to better understand and elucidate differences between international courts. International criminal jurisdiction, for example, can hardly

[35] Ever since Rudolf von Jhering, *Der Zweck im Recht*, vol 1 and 2 (4th edn, Breitkopf und Haertel 1904), English translation of vol 1 *Law as a Means to an End* (Isaak Husik tr, Boston Book Company 1913), this is beyond question. Still, our argument goes beyond Jhering. While Jhering aims only at purpose in the sense of 'subjective motives', such motives are secondary in our analysis.

[36] Luhmann, *Law as a Social System* 280.

[37] Alain Pellet in Andreas Zimmermann and others (eds), *The Statute of the International Court of Justice: A Commentary* (2nd edn, OUP 2012) Art 38 para 56.

be grasped under a primary function of dispute settlement, as proposed by Luhmann and Pellet. The concept of what constitutes a dispute would have to be expanded—in a way that holds little plausibility—to encompass, for example, the relationship between the accused war criminal Duško Tadić and the members of the UN Security Council or the former Prosecutor Carla del Ponte. This constellation can hardly be interpreted as a dispute in need of settlement.

a) Dispute settlement

The traditional understanding that places the function of dispute settlement squarely in the centre rests on the hope that the authority of a court's pronouncement will settle a dispute that, on an international level, bears the special danger of a military conflict, with all its attendant horrors. Although it is our central concern to overcome this one-dimensional view, resolving a dispute certainly remains an important contribution. International courts are and should remain a part of the mechanisms for 'pacific' settlement of disputes, as the title of Chapter VI of the UN Charter puts it euphemistically.[38]

To the extent that international courts have spoken explicitly about their functions, they have often stressed this particular one. The International Court of Justice (ICJ) has repeatedly invoked the statement of the Permanent Court of International Justice (PCIJ) according to which judicial dispute settlement was simply an alternative to direct interstate negotiations. It stated that the aim of the Court must be to facilitate direct and amicable agreement on that path.[39] Elsewhere it affirmed: 'The function of this Court is to resolve international legal disputes between States.'[40] Similarly, an arbitral tribunal declared that it had not been charged by the parties with the 'mission' of assuring the coherence and development of arbitral adjudication but only sought to settle the existing dispute between the parties, without taking into account potential consequences for future disputes.[41]

[38] On the euphemistic nature see Georges Abi-Saab, 'Cours général de droit international public' (1987) 207 Recueil des cours 9, 129–39.

[39] *North Sea Continental Shelf (Germany v Denmark and Netherlands)* (Judgment) [1969] ICJ Rep 3, para 87, with reference to the order of the PCIJ, *Free Zones of Upper Savoy and District of Gex (France v Switzerland)* PCIJ Rep Series A No 22, 3(13); see also *Passage through the Great Belt (Finland v Denmark)* (Request for the Indication of Provisional Measures: Order) [1991] ICJ Rep 12, para 35.

[40] *LaGrand (Germany v USA)* (Request for the Indication of Provisional Measures: Order) [1999] ICJ Rep 9, para 25.

[41] *Romak (Romak SA v Uzbekistan)* PCA Case No AA 280 (UNCITRAL Award) (26 November 2009) para 171. 'Ultimately, the Arbitral Tribunal has not been entrusted, by the Parties or otherwise, with a mission to ensure the coherence or development of "arbitral jurisprudence". The Arbitral Tribunal's mission is more mundane, but no less important: to resolve the present dispute between the Parties in a reasoned and persuasive manner, irrespective of the unintended consequences that this Arbitral Tribunal's analysis might have on future disputes in general.'

However, if one examines a decision only in the light of a single function, there is a danger of misjudging its full relevance and of criticizing it on the basis of inadequate criteria. The function of dispute settlement should not be made into an absolute. To begin with, a dispute can continue even after a decision has been rendered. If that happens, does it mean that the court has necessarily failed in its task? In the light of additional functions a nuanced picture emerges, and at times even a positive verdict about decisions that were not particularly successful in the function of dispute settlement. One well-known example provides a vivid illustration.

b) Stabilization of normative expectations

The *Nicaragua* decision of the ICJ did not resolve the conflict between Nicaragua and the United States. The Court did not live up to its function of settling disputes between states.[42] In this regard the process even had a negative effect, since it motivated the US to withdraw its unilateral recognition of the ICJ's jurisdiction.[43] But this observation should not be the end of a functional analysis. If one looks at the decision within the function of *stabilizing normative expectations*, the second central function of international courts in our interpretation, it can be judged more positively. The Court affirmed cardinal norms of international law—especially the prohibition of the use of force—in the face of contrary practices by one of the two superpowers at the time. If a court identifies a breach of law, this fundamentally confirms the validity and strengthens the normativity of the law.[44] It would be strange to place this outside of the functions of the ICJ.

The stabilization of normative expectations is among the characteristic contributions of a court when it declares what the law means in a concrete case, who is in the right, and who is in the wrong. Conceiving adjudication from this function is in line with an understanding that is widespread in legal theory. Not just abstract rules, but also concrete adjudication stabilizes the *normative* expectations on which any social order rests.[45] Normative expectations are those which are maintained when disappointed, in contrast to *cognitive* expectations, which adjust in the case of disappointment.[46] Adjudication as an affirmation of the validity of law can also be grasped as

[42] *Militarv and Paramilitary Activities in and against Nicaragua (Nicaragua v USA)* (Merits) [1986] ICJ Rep 14.

[43] US Statement (1985) 24 Intl L Materials 1742–5.

[44] Correspondingly, on the justification of a breach of the law as an exception, *Nicaragua* para 186.

[45] Jürgen Habermas, *Between Facts and Norms: Contributions to a Discourse Theory of Law and Democracy* (William Rehg tr, Polity Press 1997) 427; Luhmann, *Law as a Social System* 162–5.

[46] On the reluctance to learn, Bernhard Schlink, 'Der Preis der Gerechtigkeit' in Horst Dreier (ed), *Rechts- und staatstheoretische Schlüsselbegriffe: Legitimität—Repräsentation—Freiheit: Symposium für Hasso Hofmann zum 70. Geburtstag* (Duncker & Humblot 2005) 9.

a symbolic act or as an act of 'maintaining the system'.[47] At times the task of stabilizing normative expectations is explicit. Article 3, Section 2 of Annex 2 to the Agreement establishing the WTO declares: 'The dispute settlement system of the WTO is a central element in providing security and predictability to the multilateral trading system.' Political science even sees this as *the* central function of international courts; that is, solidifying obligations, upholding the law against future breaches, and in this way overcoming problems of collective action.[48]

Of course, the two functions of dispute settlement and the affirmation of the validity of the law often go hand in hand. The validity of the law and the legal certainty created by judicial decisions are crucial for successful dispute settlement. But these functions can diverge, or at least lead to a divergent assessment. For example, it can serve the purpose of dispute settlement to decide in a minimalist fashion and to keep the determination of the law vague, which does not promote certainty; nor does it provide much support to the normative expectations of the wider legal community. Combining these two roles into a single function is therefore not conducive to a deeper understanding.

Affirming the validity of the law does not depend on whether the unlawful condition is actually corrected or the offender is in fact sanctioned. This theoretical insight accords with the international legal doctrine of 'satisfaction', which can lie solely in the judicial declaration of 'being in the right'.[49] Decisions of international law, in particular, often leave previous state measures untouched. At the same time, it is certainly useful to the maintenance of normative expectation if a judgment is linked to consequences; that is, if it leads to enforcement of the law or sanctions the offender.[50] This latter aspect is particularly evident in international criminal law, which quite clearly does not fit under the function of dispute settlement. Here it is more plausible to look at the aspect of law enforcement,[51] which we see as falling

[47] On 'regime maintenance' see Shany, 'No Longer a Weak Department of Power?' 81–2.

[48] Clifford J Carrubba, 'Courts and Compliance in International Regulatory Regimes' (2005) 67 The Journal of Politics 669; Laurence R Helfer and Anne-Marie Slaughter, 'Why States Create International Tribunals: A Response to Professors Posner and Yoo' (2005) 93 California L Rev 899, 931–6.

[49] Christina Hoss, 'Satisfaction' in Rüdiger Wolfrum (ed), *Max Planck Encyclopedia of Public International Law* <http://opil.ouplaw.com/home/EPIL> accessed 27 January 2014, paras 23–8. A nice example of symbolic satisfaction is also the firing of a salute in front of the flag of the injured state; on this see para 17.

[50] To be sure, one can identify the enforcement function and the sanctioning function as further autonomous functions, and further add a compliance function; see for example Shelton, 'Form, Function, and the Powers'. For our purpose, a further breakdown here does not add anything.

[51] Thus also William W Burke-White, 'A Community of Courts: Toward a System of International Criminal Law Enforcement' (2002–2003) 24 Michigan J Intl L 1; on the goals of international criminal jurisdiction see Robert Cryer and others, *An Introduction to International Criminal Law and Procedure*

within the function of stabilizing normative expectations. This view is not contradicted by the fact that international courts do not dispose of their own mechanisms of coercion.[52]

c) Law-making

Law-making can be identified as another important function of judicial adjudication.[53] This function must be grasped in an especially circumspect fashion, which is why a separate section is devoted to it.[54] Here it should be merely asserted in advance that judicial law-making must not be equated with legislation. In addition, a distinction must be drawn between law-making for a dispute and the prospective shaping of the legal order. The latter appears problematic against the backdrop of the traditional notion of the separation of powers, though it can hardly be denied as a phenomenon and function of contemporary international jurisdiction.[55] For example, the reasons underlying the ICJ's Nicaragua decision regularly serve to support arguments that construe the international prohibition on using force broadly and the right of self-defence narrowly. Moreover, the decision established the ban as customary law and shaped the accountability of actions by non-state actors.[56] It strengthened the normativity of international law and valiantly developed the law to further international peace.

Even more so than the ICJ, courts within specific sectors are active in law-making. Examples abound in jurisdictional, procedural, and substantive law, often with a far deeper impact on the domestic legal orders than decisions by the ICJ. From the field of investment arbitration one can recall the tribunals that derive their jurisdiction from the most-favoured-nation clause or qualify regulation as expropriation.[57] The Appellate Body of the WTO has bound the panels to its previous decisions, and has established the obligation to hear affected parties in administrative proceedings from the

(2nd edn, CUP 2010) 22–39; see Immi Tallgren, 'The Sensibility and Sense of International Criminal Law' (2002) 13 Eur J Intl L 561.

[52] On international courts' public authority see in detail chapter 3 section A.

[53] Emphatically Abi-Saab, 'Cours général de droit international public' 129.

[54] See chapter 3 section A I.

[55] Alan E Boyle and Christine M Chinkin, *The Making of International Law* (OUP 2007) 268; in detail the contributions in Armin von Bogdandy and Ingo Venzke (eds), *International Judicial Lawmaking: On Public Authority and Democratic Legitimation in Global Governance* (Springer 2012).

[56] *Nicaragua* paras 187–201. See Cristina Hoss, Santiago Villalpando, and Sandesh Sivakumaran, '*Nicaragua*: 25 Years Later' (2012) 25 Leiden J Intl L 131, 132–3; Marcelo Cohen, 'The Principle of Non-Intervention 25 Years after the *Nicaragua* Judgment' (2012) 25 Leiden J Intl L 157; Albrecht Randelzhofer and Oliver Dörr, in Bruno Simma and others (eds), *The Charter of the United Nations: A Commentary*, vol 1 (3rd edn, OUP 2012) Article 2(4) paras 64–6.

[57] Stephan W Schill, 'System-Building in Investment Treaty Arbitration and Lawmaking' in von Bogdandy and Venzke (eds), *International Judicial Lawmaking* 133.

chapeau of Article XX of GATT.[58] The ECtHR has, among other things, introduced pilot judgments, a procedure that had previously failed via the political route,[59] and established a regime of preventive detention.[60] The Inter-American Court of Human Rights has not only declared amnesty laws to be unlawful, but has even proclaimed them void.[61] The UN's criminal tribunals have worked out an entire procedural regime[62] and boldly continue to develop substantive criminal law, for example, with respect to the criminalization of reprisal in interstate conflicts.[63]

At times a court explicitly acknowledges this law-making function: 'It is clear that the Court cannot legislate [...]. This is so even if, in stating and applying the law, the Court necessarily has to specify its scope and sometimes note its general trend.'[64] The self-description of the ICJ states: 'In short, a judgment of the Court does not simply decide a particular dispute but inevitably also contributes to the development of international law. Fully aware of this, the Court takes account of these two objectives in the substance and wording of its judgments.'[65] Other institutions attest a similar understanding. The arbitral Tribunal in *Saipem v Bangladesh* articulated that it was obligated to contribute to the harmonious development of investment protection law, and in so doing

[58] *United States: Import Prohibition of Certain Shrimp and Shrimp Products – Appellate Body Report* (6 November 1998) WT/DS58/AB/R, paras 180–3; see also Michael Ioannidis, 'A Procedural Approach to the Legitimacy of International Adjudication: Developing Standards of Participation in WTO Law' (2011) 12 German L J 1175, 1195–9.

[59] *Broniowski v Poland* ECHR 2004-V; on this see Markus Fyrnys, 'Expanding Competences by Judicial Law-Making: The Pilot Judgment Procedure of the European Court of Human Rights' (2011) 12 German L J 1231; Wojciech Sadurski, 'Partnering with Strasbourg: Constitutionalism of the European Court of Human Rights, the Accession of Central and East European States and the Idea of Pilot Judgments' (2009) 9 Human Rights L Rev 397.

[60] *M v Germany* ECHR 2009; on this then *EGMR Sicherungsverwahrung* (2011) 128 BVerfGE 326 (Federal Constitutional Court of Germany).

[61] Christina Binder, 'The Prohibition of Amnesties by the Inter-American Court of Human Rights' (2011) 15 German L J 1203.

[62] Mia Swart, 'Judicial Lawmaking at the *ad hoc* Tribunals: The Creative Use of the Sources of International Law and "Adventurous Interpretation"' (2010) 70 Zeitschrift für ausländisches öffentliches Recht und Völkerrecht 459.

[63] *Prosecutor v Kupreškić et al* (Judgment) IT-95-16-T (14 January 2000) para 527; on this see Milan Kuhli and Klaus Günther, 'Judicial Lawmaking, Discourse Theory, and the ICTY on Belligerent Reprisals' (2011) 12 German L J 1261.

[64] *Legality of the Threat or Use of Nuclear Weapons* (Advisory Opinion) [1996] ICJ Rep 226, para 18. See also *Dispute Concerning Delimitation of the Maritime Boundary between Bangladesh and Myanmar in the Bay of Bengal (Bangladesh v Myanmar)* (Judgment of 14 March 2012, Declaration Wolfrum) ITLOS Reports 2012, 136.

[65] *The International Court of Justice* (5th edn, 2004) 76 <www.icj-cij.org/information/en/ibleubook.pdf> accessed 23 September 2013.

to do justice to the legitimate expectations of the community of states and of investors.[66]

d) Control and legitimation

Alongside dispute settlement in individual cases and the creation and stabilization of normative expectations, we see the *control and legitimation of public authority* as the fourth central function of international adjudication. First and foremost, this function concerns the exercise of power by state institutions. At issue is the review of national acts against the yardstick of international law. While the traditional doctrine sees the control aspect as incidental to the resolution of a dispute, we maintain that it is of fundamental importance to a complete understanding, especially in the area of human rights and within the regimes of international economic law. Moreover, it is only in light of this fourth function that the effects of international adjudication on different levels of governance become visible—something which is of key interest in debates about the constitutionalization of international law.[67] The traditional horizontal conception of international courts cannot capture any of this.

Many national constitutions—in particular those of post-authoritarian states—open themselves up to international human rights law to ward off a possible relapse. However, it is not only the regime of international human rights protections, but also the law of global trade that contains (shaped by judicial decisions) extensive guidelines for national legislative, administrative, and judicial action.

It is in the light of this function that one can best understand the growing importance of the principle of proportionality in international adjudication.[68] This principle strongly expands the reach of courts, since it allows

[66] *Saipem SpA v People's Republic of Bangladesh* (Decision on Jurisdiction and Recommendation on Provisional Measures) ICSID Case No ARB/05/07 (21 March 2007) para 67. See also *International Thunderbird Gaming v Mexico* (Sep Op Wälde) (26 January 2006) para 16 (NAFTA/UNCITRAL): 'While individual arbitral awards by themselves do not as yet constitute a binding precedent, a consistent line of reasoning developing a principle and a particular interpretation of specific treaty obligations should be respected; if an authoritative jurisprudence evolves, it will acquire the character of customary international law and must be respected.' See also paras 129–30. Moreover, *MCI Power Group LC and New Turbine Inc v Republic of Ecuador* (Decision on Annulment) ICSID Case No ARB/03/6 (19 October 2009) para 24 declares: 'The responsibility for ensuring consistency in the jurisprudence and for building a coherent body of law rests primarily with the investment tribunals.' All decisions available under <italaw.com> accessed 10 January 2012.

[67] On this in detail see chapter 3 section B 2.

[68] On the general development see Emily Crawford, 'Proportionality' in Wolfrum (ed), *Max Planck Encyclopedia of Public International Law*; Enzo Cannizzaro, *Il principio della proporzionalità nell'ordinamento internazionale* (Giuffrè 2000) 429–83; Anne-Charlotte Martineau, 'La technique du balancement par l'Organe d'appel de l'OMC (études de la justification dans les discours juridiques)' (2007) 123 Revue du droit public et de la science politique en France et à l'étranger 991.

them to decide questions that are, in traditional understandings of the separation of powers, reserved for bureaucratic and political institutions. The principle of proportionality allows courts to exert control—capable of situational calibration—over other authorities. It constitutes a crucial instrument in their growth of power.

The control function of international courts contributes to legitimizing the institutions under its jurisdiction, and in particular to the legitimation of the *national* institutions. One should recall once more the judicial development and application of standards for national administrative processes[69] or, most prominently, the work of human rights courts. This is well researched with respect to post-authoritarian systems.[70] Moreover, human rights adjudication can even secure and promote the conditions for democratic processes.[71] Finally, international criminal jurisdiction may well be understood through the function of making a contribution to the processing of the past and thus to the reconciliation of broken societies in a new system, which in turn legitimizes the latter.[72]

International courts can control and legitimize not only national institutions, but also public authority on the international level.[73] At the moment, however, this function is only weakly developed. An early example is the European Nuclear Energy Tribunal within the framework of the Organisation for Economic Co-operation and Development (OECD), which was established precisely in order to control the European Nuclear Energy Agency's strong powers.[74] This task was however soon redirected toward the European Atomic Energy Community, on the one hand, and

[69] Thus for example the *US—Shrimp* decision within the framework of the WTO, *US—Shrimp* paras 180–3; Ioannidis, 'A Procedural Approach'. See also *The 'Juno Trader' Case (Saint Vincent and the Grenadines v Guinea-Bissau)* (Judgment of 18 December 2004) ITLOS Reports 2004, 17, 38 para 77. See further Sabino Cassese, 'Global Standards for National Administrative Procedure' (2004–2005) 68 L and Contemporary Problems 109.

[70] Mahulena Hofmann, *Von der Transformation zur Kooperationsoffenheit? Die Öffnung der Rechtsordnungen ausgewählter Staaten Mittel- und Osteuropas für das Völker- und Europarecht* (Springer 2009) 2–7, 474–6; Pía Carazo Ortíz, 'El Sistema Interamericano de Derechos Humanos: democracia y derechos humanos como factores integradores en Latinoamérica' in Armin von Bogdandy, César Landa Arroyo, and Mariela Morales Antoniazzi (eds), *¿Integración suramericana a través del Derecho? Un análisis interdisciplinario y multifocal* (Centro de Estudios Políticos y Constitucionales 2009) 231.

[71] An analogous interpretation of national constitutional jurisdiction pervades both Habermas, *Between Facts and Norms*, and John H Ely, *Democracy and Distrust: A Theory of Judicial Review* (Harvard UP 1980).

[72] Daniel Joyce, 'The Historical Function of International Criminal Trials: Re-Thinking International Criminal Law' (2004) 73 Nordic J Intl L 461.

[73] Derek W Bowett, 'The Court's Role in Relation to International Organizations' in Vaughan Lowe and Malgosia Fitzmaurice (eds), *Fifty Years of the International Court of Justice: Essays in Honour of Sir Robert Jennings* (CUP 1996) 181.

[74] Convention on the Establishment of Security Controls in the Field of Nuclear Energy.

the International Atomic Energy Agency, on the other, so that the Tribunal never came to exercise its control function.

Broadly discussed, though not yet realized, is this role of the ICJ vis-à-vis the UN Security Council.[75] But the discussion did bear fruit in the *Tadić* decision of the International Criminal Tribunal for the former Yugoslavia (ICTY). The defendant, Tadić, attacked the resolution of the Security Council that served as the legal basis for the Tribunal by asserting that the Security Council lacked the requisite competence. While the Trial Chamber had rejected a review of the legality of Security Council resolutions in the light of the political question doctrine, the Appeals Chamber dismissed that reasoning as obsolete and reviewed the resolution. In the end, to no great surprise, it affirmed the legality of its own existence.[76]

This constellation, wherein a court created by the Security Council as a subordinate organ reviews actions of its creator, may seem strange at first glance. However, it is found in the history of public law, where it has had good results: the judicial control of public authority has developed on the national level in many cases as an appendix to administration.[77] In this light, developments such as the establishment of the World Bank's Inspection Panel or the internal administrative courts of international organizations certainly have potential.[78] These institutions are, in turn, partly subject to oversight by the ICJ.[79] In fact, the ICJ's advisory jurisdiction owes its existence precisely to the idea of a horizontal control of the exercise of authority.[80]

The control function has additional potential, as revealed by a look at national constitutional jurisprudence. International courts can contribute to the legitimation of the legal system in general, and perhaps even exercise a function of social integration. This opens up another dimension of

[75] Erika de Wet, *The Chapter VII Powers of the United Nations Security Council* (Hart 2004) 69–129; Maria I Papa, *I rapporti tra la corte internazionale di giustizia e il consiglio di sicurezza* (CEDAM 2006) 287–358; Antonios Tzanakopoulos, *Disobeying the Security Council* (OUP 2011) 94–110.

[76] *Prosecutor v Duško Tadić* (Decision on the Defence Motion for Interlocutory Appeal on Jurisdiction) IT-94-1-AR 72 (2 October 1995) paras 13–48; on the argumentation of the first instance, (Decision on the Defence Motion on Jurisdiction) IT-94-1-T (10 August 1995) paras 23–4; similarly also the International Criminal Tribunal for Rwanda (ICTR), *Prosecutor v Joseph Kanyabashi* (Decision on Jurisdiction) ICTR-96-15-T (18 June 1997) paras 17–29.

[77] Sabino Cassese, 'Die Entfaltung des Verwaltungsstaates in Europa' in Armin von Bogdandy, Sabino Cassese, and Peter M Huber (eds), *Handbuch Ius Publicum Europaeum*, vol 3 (CF Müller 2010) 3, paras 50–1; Michel Fromont, 'Typen staatlichen Verwaltungsrechts in Europa' in von Bogdandy et al (eds), *Handbuch Ius Publicum* 551, para 20.

[78] See chapter 2 section C 1.

[79] *Judgment No 2867 of the Administrative Tribunal of the International Labour Organization upon a Complaint Filed against the International Fund for Agricultural Development* (Advisory Opinion) [2012] ICJ Rep 10.

[80] Robert Y Jennings in Andreas Zimmermann and others (eds), *The Statute of the International Court of Justice* (OUP 2006) General Introduction para 5 with reference to fn 8.

the *Nicaragua* decision. It helped the ICJ to regain the trust of developing countries, which had previously been shaken by the decisions on Namibia, in particular.[81] To that extent, the ICJ—and indirectly even the system of international law—gained legitimacy vis-à-vis a world community that had expanded in the wake of decolonization. The control and legitimation of the exercise of authority, on both the national and international level, thus constitutes a further function of international courts.[82]

2. The exercise of public authority

The multifunctional approach shows a much wider relevance of international courts than the one-dimensional view does. International adjudication shapes social interactions in multifarious ways. This insight leads to the second basic concept of the present study: the exercise of international public authority. In the current international order there is a presumption that when an international court renders legal decisions, it exercises international public authority. This qualification is quite simply fundamental to our subsequent train of thought, for it is only on its basis that international adjudication requires an elaborated justification of its own. Because of the importance of this basic conceptual move, a separate section is devoted to it in chapter 3.[83]

Here it should only be noted, by way of introduction, that the traditional understanding of public authority—which is focused on the disposition over means of coercion—is too narrow in an age of global governance. It needs to be expanded in order to deal with contemporary international phenomena both legally and in terms of legitimacy. After all, many international courts resemble domestic courts even without having means of physical coercion at their disposal.[84] To grasp this, we define public authority as the ability, grounded in law, to restrict the freedom of other actors, or to shape their use of freedom in a similar way.

This broad conception of authority is based on a fundamental consideration. If public law, in accordance with the liberal–democratic tradition, is

[81] *Legal Consequences for States of the Continued Presence of South Africa in Namibia (South West Africa) notwithstanding Security Council Resolution 276 (1970)* (Advisory Opinion) [1971] ICJ Rep 16; *South West Africa Cases (Ethiopia v South Africa; Liberia v South Africa)* (Preliminary Objections) [1962] ICJ Rep 319; *South West Africa Cases (Ethiopia v South Africa; Liberia v South Africa) Second Phase* (Judgment) [1966] ICJ Rep 6. See Edward McWhinney, 'Judicial Settlement of Disputes: Jurisdiction and Judiciability' (1990) 221 Recueil des cours 9, 36–45; Abi-Saab, 'Cours général de droit international public' 255–8.

[82] Sabino Cassese, *I Tribunali di Babele: I giudici alla ricerca di un nuovo ordine globale* (Donzelli 2009).

[83] See chapter 3 section A 2.

[84] In detail Jeffrey K Staton and Will H Moore, 'Judicial Power in Domestic and International Politics' (2011) 65 Intl Organization 553.

understood as a system that protects individual freedom and makes collective self-determination possible, every act with repercussions for these normative principles must come under scrutiny to the extent that these repercussions are significant enough to raise justified doubts about the legitimacy of an act. This brings us to the next point.

3. Democracy

Qualifying international adjudication as an exercise of public authority gives rise to many questions, chief among them that concerning its legitimation. The traditional understanding situates the basis of legitimacy in the consensus of states that sustain the court. We do not question that this consensus forms an important resource of legitimacy, but invoking it is not enough to meet the need for legitimation for many decisions.[85]

The question of legitimation has diverse aspects. For example, the issue could be whether international courts are effective at all.[86] One might also ask what notions of justice they follow, or whether they might be acting as extensions of powerful states.[87] We focus on the question about their democratic legitimation. This kind of examination of judicial activity requires a good deal of preliminary reflection. For many readers the question itself will not make immediate sense and requires careful theoretical instruction; its groundwork will therefore be laid out in a separate section.[88] However, since it can easily arouse concerns of an unduly radical critique of international courts that is overly fixated on sovereignty,[89] it should be emphasized in advance that our approach does not entertain such a fixation.

We will not develop the criteria of democratic legitimation in such a way that any action on the international level which cannot be traced back to the democratic will of a single state will appear deeply problematic. We are not among those authors who use the argument of democracy to delegitimize international adjudication.[90] Such efforts are for the most part based on a

[85] Similarly Ulfstein, 'Institutions and Competences' 148.

[86] See Yuval Shany, 'Assessing the Effectiveness of International Courts: A Goal-Based Approach' (2012) 106 AJIL 225.

[87] On the legitimacy discussion in general see, among others, Jutta Brunnée and Stephen J Toope, *Legitimacy and Legality in International Law* (CUP 2010) 1–19; Jan Klabbers, 'Setting the Scene' in Klabbers, Peters, and Ulfstein, *The Constitutionalization of International Law* 1, 37–44.

[88] See chapter 3 section C.

[89] Most recently for example Richard Bellamy, 'Die demokratische Verfassung' in Gret Haller, Klaus Günther, and Ulfried Neumann (eds), *Menschenrechte und Volkssouveränität in Europa: Gerichte als Vormund der Demokratie?* (Campus Verlag 2011) 103, 109–10; similarly Ran Hirschl, *Towards Juristocracy: The Origins and Consequences of the New Constitutionalism* (Harvard UP 2004); Eric A Posner, *The Perils of Global Legalism* (University of Chicago Press 2009) 227.

[90] Robert Bork, *Coercing Virtue: The Worldwide Rule of Judges* (AEI Press 2003), quoted in Eric A Posner and John Yoo, 'Judicial Independence in International Tribunals' (2005) 93 California L Rev 1, 5: 'Judges

particularistic understanding of democracy that stops at national borders and conceives of states as self-sufficient entities. In the wake of globalization, and given the interconnections of the twenty-first century, such an understanding is less persuasive than ever.

Indeed, the goal of the present study is not a general pushback against international judicial authority, but rather a theoretically guided calibration of how it should be understood and developed further to fulfil its potential. As already indicated in connection with the function of control and legitimation, we understand international courts as institutions that can deal with legitimacy deficits, for example those arising from the extraterritorial effects of national actions. International law offers a unique possibility of giving a voice to individuals who are affected by the actions of a foreign state. An international court that develops and applies such law can thus ameliorate problems of democratic inclusion.[91] There are a number of judicial innovations that can be understood as a reaction to problems of legitimation and can be explicated especially well from the democratic perspective, as chapter 4 will show.

To avoid another possible misunderstanding of our focus on democracy, it is not our intention to bring the noise and heat of quarrelling political disputes as they might unfold in parliament into the dignified hearing chambers and shielded deliberation rooms of international courts, to transform them somehow into political assemblies. We do not interpret judicial activity simply as 'political'[92] or call for political forms of responsibility. Courts that live up to the expectations placed on them differ markedly from parliaments and political bureaucracies. It is all but indispensable to the legitimation of every court that it operates at a distance from political processes and documents this publicly.

However, differences between judicial and political processes do not answer the question about the democratic legitimation of the power of international judges. This is confirmed by a comparative look at domestic law. In Germany, for example, the current state of scholarship asserts

of international courts—the [ICJ], the European Court of Human Rights, and predictably, the new [ICC], among other forums—are continuing to undermine democratic institutions and to enact the agenda of the liberal Left or New Class.'

[91] Anne Peters, 'Rechtsordnungen und Konstitutionalisierung: Zur Neubestimmung der Verhältnisse' (2010) 65 Zeitschrift für öffentliches Recht 3, 49; for a critical view Alexander Somek, 'The Argument from Transnational Effects I: Representing Outsiders through Freedom of Movement' (2010) 16 Eur L J 315.

[92] See Shapiro, *Courts* 63–4; Karen J Alter, *The European Court's Political Power* (OUP 2009) 3–31. With a broad concept of politics, which encompasses every consideration, one can of course interpret also judicial activity as 'political' without questioning the judicial function; see *Citizens United v Federal Election Committee* (2010) 558 US 1, 47 (US SC); *Helvering v Hallock* (1940) 309 US 106, 119 (US SC). Little is gained by this.

that judicial independence not only does not solve the problem of democratic legitimation, but actually exacerbates it.[93] Article 20 Section 2 of the German Basic Law defines the principle of democracy such that 'all state authority is derived from the people' and German courts render their decisions 'In the Name of the People'.[94] This shows just how essential the democratic justification is for the courts. Much the same holds true for many other legal systems.[95]

While many domestic courts around the world invoke their democratic legitimation in the opening words of their decisions, we find in the same place a void when it comes to international courts. This void identifies our key question: in whose name do they decide, and in whose name should they decide? Or, to put it in functional terms: what is the 'larger whole' at which the functions of the courts are directed? For domestic courts, at least, it is clear that their functions are understood with a view toward the nation-state.[96] This too is implied by the opening formula 'In the Name of the People', 'the Republic', or 'the King', representing the nation. Regardless of all the theoretical problems that attach to the concepts of nation, people, or state, they provide a fairly solid framework for functional analyses.

When it comes to international courts, the corresponding vanishing point of the functional perspective is more difficult to grasp. It is therefore not surprising that international decisions do not know a formula of this kind. Indeed, behind this absence stands not only uncertainty, but also a profound disagreement about a fundamental question: should international courts render their decisions in the name of the states that underpin them, in the name of the international community, as institutions of a specific regime, or, perhaps, in the name of the citizens of the world?

[93] Fundamentally Böckenförde, *Verfassungsfragen der Richterwahl* 72; Andreas Voßkuhle and Gernot Sydow, 'Die demokratische Legitimation des Richters' (2002) 57 Juristenzeitung 673, 673; from a comparative law perspective Ulrich R Haltern, *Verfassungsgerichtsbarkeit, Demokratie und Misstrauen: Das Bundesverfassungsgericht in einer Verfassungstheorie zwischen Populismus und Progressivismus* (Duncker & Humblot 1998) 169–272.

[94] In accordance with Art 25(4) German Law on the Federal Constitutional Court (Gesetz über das Bundesverfassungsgericht), Art 311(1) German Code of Civil Procedure (Zivilprozessordnung), Art 268(1) German Code of Criminal Procedure (Strafprozessordnung), Art 117(1) German Code of Administrative Court Procedure (Verwaltungsgerichtsordnung).

[95] For example Art 454 French Code of Civil Procedure (Code de procédure civile): 'Le jugement est rendu au nom du peuple français'; Art 101(1) Constitution of the Republic of Italy (Costituzione della Repubblica Italiana): 'La giustizia è amministrata in nome del popolo', or Art 20 Decree 2067 of 1997 intended for the Constitutional Court of Columbia (Decreto 2067 de 1991): 'Las Sentencias de la Corte Constiucional se pronunciarán "en nombre del pueblo y por mandato de la Constitución".'

[96] However, there is a growing chorus of voices that assign to domestic courts functions that go beyond this; see Eyal Benvenisti and George W Downs, 'National Courts, Domestic Democracy, and the Evolution of International Law' (2009) 20 Eur J Intl L 59; André Nollkaemper, *National Courts and the International Rule of Law* (OUP 2011) 9–10. We return to this in chapter 4 section C.

C. THREE OBJECTIONS, THREE RESPONSES

Given this thrust of our public law theory of international adjudication based on the notions of multifunctionality, public authority, and democratic legitimation, there is good reason to expect a series of inquiries and objections. In what follows we shall use those we anticipate most to lay out our goals and agenda in further detail.

1. A study of positive law or of normative theory?

The first question that might arise concerns the intended audience of the present study and, related to this, the nature of our contribution. Is it directed chiefly at legal practice (and here especially at international courts and their judges) or rather at political theorists? Does it suggest which interpretations in the light of the democratic principle should be preferred within the law or does the law only give evidence of a general theorem? Are we speaking perhaps as policy experts to state representatives who create the statutes of the courts? Or are we addressing the discipline of jurisprudence, and that with an analytical or rather normative effort? To put it more incisively: does our text argue on the basis of established law, or is it aimed at imparting a new normative orientation? Behind the demand for a clear distinction between *de lege lata* and *de lege ferenda* stands the concern about a problematic—indeed, theoretically untenable—amalgamation of legal, moral, political, and ideological arguments. Formulated in terms of legal theory, at issue is the relationship between internal and external perspectives on the law.

Our book is inspired by the tradition of German state theory and constitutional doctrine which, as a sub-discipline of public law scholarship, aims precisely at transcending—though not negating—such distinctions.[97] Its particular characteristic is that it develops theories in interaction with other disciplines, but with a view toward questions of law-making, law application, and the formulation of legal doctrine. It participates in general discourses which are external to the operation of the law, but also aims at feeding those internal operations by making claims about how to construe positive law. Whether such theories can be scientific or academic is a question of definition. Of course, such constructions cannot come with categorical claims to truth, which prove other constructions wrong by exclusion. Although there is some possibility of falsification, the main standards are internal coherence, reasoned engagement with other approaches, accuracy

[97] Important books in this tradition are Georg Jellinek, *Allgemeine Staatslehre* (3rd edn, Häring 1914); Carl Schmitt, *Constitutional Theory* (Jeffrey Seitzer tr/ed, Duke UP 2007); Hermann Heller, *Staatslehre* (Sijthoff 1934); Udo Di Fabio, *Der Verfassungsstaat in der Weltgesellschaft* (Mohr Siebeck 2001); Oliver Lepsius and others, *Das entgrenzte Gericht* (Suhrkamp 2011).

and circumspection in presenting relevant legal material (legal sources and judicial decisions), and the potential for the understanding and the development of the law.

State and constitutional theory is the sub-discipline that makes it possible to address larger contexts and opens up public law in an interdisciplinary fashion, allowing for the contributions of other disciplines to be incorporated into the law-oriented development of the fundamental concepts. Similar approaches are certainly also found in other scholarly traditions.[98] This kind of theoretical examination seems indicated even by the internal standpoint of legal doctrine, since the cognitive paradigm has long since proved untenable.[99] A reasoned application of the law usually contains a law-making element, a doctrinal construction, and an element of normative proposition. At the same time, any act of law-making must justify itself within a broad horizon of legal principles. The internal perspective focused on application should be open to external considerations while preserving its inherent logic.[100] External perspectives on the law can in turn pursue a broad spectrum of orientations, which are arranged along the fields of sociology, economics, political theory, or practical philosophy. While our theory is informed in particular by political theory and practical philosophy, it sees itself as a principled reconstruction of the law of international courts.

As such, our contribution is aimed at both the interpretation and systematization of the law *and* its further development. In other words: the work of fundamental conceptualization is intended to contribute to argumentations *de lege lata* and *de lege ferenda*. In the process, it must be emphasized that fundamental conceptual analyses can only accompany—but not replace—argumentations of legal policy, legal doctrine, and legal application, since every one of these forms of reasoning must do justice to specific rationalities and rules. Theory-building in the way practised here takes place on a level of abstraction that neither allows, for example, definitive statements about the legitimacy or legality of individual decisions, nor advances concrete demands against individual courts. A concrete proposal must be further supported with additional arguments that are doctrinal, political, or empirical in nature.

[98] See, for example, Léon Duguit, *L'État, le droit objectif et la loi positive* (first published 1901, Franck Moderne preface, Dalloz-Sirey 2003); Léon Duguit, *L'État, les gouvernants et les agents* (first published 1903, Dalloz-Sirey 2005); Klabbers, Peters, and Ulfstein, *The Constitutionalization of International Law*; Martin Loughlin, *Foundations of Public Law* (OUP 2010).

[99] For a detailed discussion see chapter 3 section A 1 c.

[100] Klaus Günther, 'Legal Pluralism or Uniform Concept of Law? Globalisation as a Problem of Legal Theory' (2008) 5 No Foundations <www.helsinki.fi/nofo/NoFo5Gunther.pdf> accessed 23 September 2013.

2. An excessively broad concept of what constitutes a court?

A second possible objection is that our study is improperly broad. It seems difficult already within the context of the state to develop a theory that meaningfully covers all institutions of the third branch, given the manifold differences—in Germany, for example—between a small *Amtsgericht* (district court), the highly specialized *Bundesgerichtshof* (Federal Court of Justice), and the *Bundesverfassungsgericht* (Federal Constitutional Court). The differences between international courts are even greater. This holds especially if, as we propose, one regards as courts all international institutions in which, on the basis of international law, independent and impartial individuals decide cases brought to them in an orderly process and following prescribed legal criteria. This concept is so broad that it encompasses international arbitral tribunals that are not even permanently constituted institutions, something the narrower, classical definition of a court would demand.[101] Indeed, we do not deny that the permanence of an institution is relevant to the judicial decision and to the exercise of authority by international courts. But important contemporary arbitral tribunals differ substantially from earlier ad hoc institutions, since they are tightly embedded institutionally.

For example, the WTO Dispute Panels are closely tied to the WTO Secretariat and are subordinated to the standardizing and disciplining control of the Appellate Body.[102] Something similar—though without a real appeals process—applies to the International Centre for Settlement of Investment Disputes (ICSID) arbitral tribunals, which have built a multilateral regime out of bilateral agreements.[103] Of course there are a number of important differences between the courts and arbitral tribunals, especially with respect to the possible influence of the parties on the appointment of the arbitrators or with respect to jurisdiction. But the transitions are fluid. A consistent terminological differentiation between 'court', 'tribunal', 'panel', and 'arbitral tribunal' may be called for when it comes to more specific research interests; for example, judicial independence, or the possibility of political influence. Nothing in this study would change if we chose another, blander term, say 'judicial institution'.[104]

[101] See for example Christian Tomuschat, 'International Courts and Tribunals' in Wolfrum (ed), *Max Planck Encyclopedia of Public International Law*, paras 1–2.

[102] Our concept of courts encompasses institutions such as the Appellate Body and the Panels of the WTO, even if they do not formally render binding decisions; Art IV(3) WTO Agreement, Arts 16, 17 DSU. Similarly, *Project on International Courts and Tribunals* <www.pict-pcti.org> accessed 10 January 2012; Laurence R Helfer and Anne-Marie Slaughter, 'Toward a Theory of Effective Supranational Adjudication' (1997–1998) 107 Yale L J 273, 338.

[103] Stephan W Schill, *The Multilateralization of International Investment Law* (CUP 2009) 15–9, 321–57.

[104] This awkward term encompasses both permanent courts and courts of arbitration; see Robert O Keohane, Andrew Moravcsik, and Anne-Marie Slaughter, 'Legalized Dispute Resolution: Interstate and Transnational' (2000) 54 Intl Organization 457.

Our broad definition further arouses the suspicion of an all too sweeping reach. It could suggest that all international judicial institutions raise the same problems with regard to the democratic principle. But it is evident that the democratic problem of the International Criminal Tribunal for the former Yugoslavia, established by the UN Security Council, cannot be identical to that of an International Criminal Court based on an international treaty. Likewise, there must be distinctions between international criminal courts in general and the ICJ. Specific characteristics exist for ICSID arbitral tribunals, the WTO Appellate Body, or the ECtHR. A permanent and obligatory jurisdiction throws up other problems than one-time subordination to an arbitral tribunal. The differences are not only institutional, but also related to substantive law. The imposition of a prison term, the determination of a maritime border, the development of human rights, or the concretization of the prohibition against economic discrimination all raise different problems. All this indicates that no uniform profile can be developed with respect to the democratic legitimation of international courts; rather, what is needed is an elaborated theoretical framework in which the democratic principle is brought to bear and attuned to the specific features of the court in question.

We do not contest any of these statements. However, are they reason enough to forego overarching studies on international courts? A multitude of books and book chapters—which deal holistically with international courts, including arbitral tribunals—reveal a considerable need for such studies.[105] We believe that while an overarching theorization is possible, it is imperative—and this was already our concluding reflection in response to the first inquiry—to respect the boundaries of the overarching and therefore necessarily abstracting theoretical level of analysis. The reflections in the present study can only be parts and building stones of argumentations that strive for an understanding of a particular court, examine the legality or legitimation of a particular decision, or present proposals on how to take the particular judicial or political development further.

Sound theory does not guarantee good results. For example, a broadening of democratic processes, rather than empowering weaker parties, could further strengthen already powerful actors.[106] It is possible that resource-poor states are unable to adequately supply the new forums, that non-governmental organizations in the end are beholden to the global west, and that well-organized interest groups will have a particularly strong voice.

[105] Romano, Alter, and Shany (eds), *The Oxford Handbook of International Adjudication*; Kingsbury, 'International Courts'; Ulfstein, 'Institutions and Competences'.

[106] This may explain the concern of some developing countries regarding the admission of *amicus curiae* briefs at the WTO; see chapter 4 section B 2.

Our multifunctional perspective on the activity of international courts is aimed precisely at bringing out differences that are blurred by the sweeping concept of dispute settlement—for example, between the ICJ, which draws a maritime border; the Criminal Tribunal for the former Yugoslavia, which imposes prison sentences; and the WTO Appellate Body, which shapes the regime of international trade. Such differences are easily lost within the notion of dispute settlement. Likewise, our concept of public authority reveals the differences between the ICJ as a court that tends to be weak and the ECtHR as a relatively strong court by comparison. The conceptual framework we develop is intended to facilitate a comparison that specifies commonalities as well as differences. Our response to the objection of taking an inappropriately broad and sweeping approach is that this book precisely does *not* develop a straitjacket with which the differences between the diverse institutions disappear. Therein lies an important distinction to the traditional approach, which conceives of all institutions as institutions of dispute settlement whose legitimacy is grounded in the consensus of states. That approach swallows up all relevant differences. By contrast, our theory makes it possible to recognize the diversity of specific problems, while at the same time allowing for a fruitful comparison and the transfer of insights and achievements.

Even though our concept of international courts is broad, we do not include the Court of Justice of the European Union among the international courts. Admittedly, this institution is based on the Treaty on European Union and the Treaty on the Functioning of the European Union, which formally constitute international treaties. Moreover, there are also many authors who continue to include this body in the circle of international courts.[107] The chief reason behind our choice, however, is that the CJEU is legally and institutionally bound into the framework of the European Union. What needs to be highlighted in this respect is that the CJEU is a true third branch, given that there is a European legislator and a European executive which can respond to the decisions of the court. Such a centralized political framework does not exist for any international court. Excluding the CJEU from our analysis in no way prevents us, however, from using lessons learned in the process of democratization of the European Union for developing a conception of the democratic legitimacy of *international* courts. Clearly distinguishing the context of European integration is indeed a necessary step for meaningful comparison.[108]

[107] Henry G Schermers and Niels M Blokker, *International Institutional Law* (5th edn, Nijhoff 2011) 436, 447–50; Doehring, *Völkerrecht* 477; Benvenisti and Downs, *National Courts* 63; Shany, 'No Longer a Weak Department of Power?' 75.

[108] It is not that 'we have seen the future and it is Europe'; see José E Alvarez, 'The New Dispute Settlers: (Half) Truths and Consequences' (2003) 38 Texas Intl L J 405, 429–31.

3. Eurocentrism?

A third objection could be that our study is Eurocentric. Is the very question of the democratic legitimation of international courts a specifically European or western one?[109] We doubt this is the case and see ourselves supported by many exchanges with non-western voices. Is the approach Eurocentric in the sense that it excludes non-democratic states from a 'universal' order?[110] We do not make any such argument.

But even if the origin of our question were specifically European or western, we do not see how this disqualifies our work. It goes without saying that we approach the issue from our particular vantage point. This vantage point is shaped not only geographically (Amsterdam and Heidelberg, mostly) and temporally (2008–2013), but also by a specific tradition of thinking and the context of contemporary debates on the democratic legitimacy of international institutions. Our statements should be understood in light of this vantage point. Needless to say, they do not come with categorical claims to truth, which consider other views as wrong, but are rather academically argued contributions to a global discourse about international institutions. We are hoping for responses from and debates with scholars writing from different backgrounds. In view of the political, ideological, and cultural fragmentation of global society, every claim to be writing from a global or universal point of view strikes us as potentially hegemonic and guilty of hubris.

We are keenly aware that our approach ultimately leads to a set of further questions and inquiries, some of which are of a factual nature and call for empirical research. They should be explored further before concrete policy proposals are made. For example, we need to know more about the effects of extending the possibilities of third-party intervention in judicial processes. Would that just lead to yet increased dominance of already more powerful states, because resource-weak states could not make adequate use of new opportunities of participation? Are non-governmental organizations not after all closely bound up with the interests of the political west? Before moving on from our conceptual inquiries to policy proposals of any kind it

[109] On the question of how authoritarian regimes fit into the picture of a study oriented toward democratic theory see the persuasive article by Andreas von Staden, 'Democratic Legitimacy of Review Beyond the State: The Need for an Appropriate Standard of Review' (2012) 10 Intl J Const L 1023.

[110] This peril of excluding non-democratic states appears with John Rawls, *The Law of Peoples* (Harvard UP 1999); on this see Gerry Simpson, *Great Powers and Outlaw States: Unequal Sovereigns in the International Legal Order* (CUP 2004).

is necessary to take the differences between international courts and their specific social contexts into closer consideration. Uncertainty in this regard does not detract from our efforts. In fact, we submit that the most interesting questions only emerge from the public law theory of international courts as multifunctional actors who exercise public authority and require democratic legitimacy.

2

Basic Conceptions of International Courts

Today, three basic conceptions dominate the understanding of the practice and scholarship of international courts. By introducing these conceptions, we pursue four intertwined objectives. First, they help us to describe our object of study. Notably, in contrast to most narratives, our account is not linear, but shows how much the choice of a conception—or, if reflected and elaborated, of a theory—matters in grasping the object. Second, we further illustrate that international courts typically perform multiple functions. Third, the present chapter illustrates the growing relevance and authority of international courts and thereby contextualizes the seemingly big leap for our democracy-oriented conception of international adjudication. Fourth, and finally, the present chapter critically assesses the established basic understandings, which also points the way toward the democracy-oriented understanding of international courts.

The first section focuses on the *state-oriented* conception, which sees international courts as mere *instruments of dispute settlement* in a state-centric world order (section A). The sovereign states that undergird them constitute the normative vanishing point in the construction of international law. In contrast, the second basic conception views international courts as *organs of the value-based international community* (section B). A multifunctional interpretation of the praxis of international courts is already possible within this *community-oriented* understanding. At issue here is the protection and development of the international community and its values. The third basic conception presents international courts as *institutions of legal regimes* (section C). It places the shaping of global interdependence at its core and thus also suggests a multifunctional analysis.

Each of these basic conceptions has significant potential for understanding the world of international courts, but each also comes with substantial problems. In particular, none of them capture international courts as actors who exercise public authority and who therefore require a modus of legitimation that lives up to basic premises of democracy. We will therefore close this chapter by pointing the way toward the *democracy-oriented* conception of international adjudication (section D).

Our classifications of both international courts and the wealth of scholarship about them, in light of a limited set of basic conceptions, will not convince everyone in every case; there are, indeed, many borderline cases. However, such cases do not undermine the usefulness of this operation for our argument, as it only aims at providing orientation. We further stress that the set of basic conceptions and the order in which we unfold them should not convey a sense of strict chronological sequence. Rather, *all* of the understandings of international courts continue to be influential. They also overlap and can well be present even in the same judicial decision.[1] Ambivalence and tension within a single decision can well be the fruit of a battle between conceptions held by different judges on the bench.

A. COURTS AS INSTRUMENTS OF DISPUTE SETTLEMENT

The state-oriented basic conception sees courts as instruments of dispute settlement within a state-centric world order. Accordingly, one can say that they decide the concrete case before them in the name of the contending states. This ascription of function and legitimatory foundation strongly constrains the courts' sphere of potential activities. In what follows we lay out this conception, outlining, in a first step, its historical and conceptual contours. It has particularly strong ties to the genesis of the international judiciary and is mostly embedded within particularistic notions of the international order (1). The second step demonstrates this understanding in the praxis of the International Court of Justice (2), and the third does so in the case of other institutions especially bound to it, in particular the Permanent Court of Arbitration and the Iran–United States Claims Tribunal (3).

1. International courts in a state-centric world order

The state-oriented conception remains strongly bound to the original idea behind all judicial adjudication: the decision by two contending parties to involve a third party in their quarrel.[2] Legal history shows that judicial institutions entrusted with the task of resolving contentious issues on the basis of generally accepted norms were often the first institutions built within a community. Dispute settlement in this triadic constellation—embedding the immediate parties to a dispute into a process expanded by a third

[1] See, to this effect, Joseph HH Weiler, 'The Geology of International Law—Governance, Democracy and Legitimacy' (2004) 64 Zeitschrift für ausländisches öffentliches Recht und Völkerrecht 547.

[2] Martin Shapiro, *Courts: A Comparative and Political Analysis* (University of Chicago Press 1981) 1–17.

party—is the original germ seed of the judiciary.[3] The crucial element here is to work through clashing positions and interpretations and thereby defuse the potentially escalating dynamic of measure and countermeasure, seeming breach of the law, reprisal, and retaliation. A judicial decision possesses a unique potential of de-escalation. This function must be distinguished from the enforcement of the law, which was often—and in international law in many areas still is—left to the parties themselves.

The first entry of an international court into the collective memory of international jurists is in line with this basic conception.[4] Moreover, it imparts an almost sacral dimension to the function of dispute settlement, which some courts have made intensive use of to this day.[5] In a treaty of 445 BCE, Athens and Sparta agreed not to go to war as long as one party was willing to submit the contentious point to arbitration. In 432 BCE, Sparta accused Athens of a breach of the treaty, whereupon Athens, in keeping with the treaty, proposed settling the dispute through arbitration; however, Sparta, in breach of the treaty, attacked Athens and suffered a resounding defeat. This defeat was attributed to the fact that Sparta had broken its promise and had therefore incurred the wrath of the gods. The new peace was sealed by the Treaty of Nicias (421 BCE), which committed the parties once again to resolve their quarrels through arbitration. But a short time later it was Athens that accused Sparta of violations and refused to submit to a judicial settlement of the dispute. Sparta attacked Athens once again, this time with the law on its side, and was able to defeat Athens, an outcome that was interpreted once again as divine anger at the lawbreaker.[6] Against this background, even Thucydides had to note it was impossible to attack the party that had offered to submit the issue in dispute to arbitration.[7]

In ancient Greece, forms of judicial arbitration to settle disputes were actively used in relations between the Greek cities. Numerous treaties

[3] Shapiro, *Courts* 1.

[4] On the concept of collective memory see Jan Assmann, *Cultural Memory and Early Civilization: Writing Remembrance, and Political Imagination* (CUP 2011) 111–46.

[5] On the sacral dimension in the ICJ see Dinah Shelton, 'Form, Function, and the Powers of International Courts' (2008–2009) 9 Chicago J Intl L 537, 540.

[6] Louis B Sohn, 'International Arbitration in Historical Perspective: Past and Present' in Alfred HA Soons (ed), *International Arbitration: Past and Prospect* (Nijhoff 1990) 9, 10–1; Heinrich Lammasch, 'Die Lehre von der Schiedsgerichtsbarkeit in ihrem ganzen Umfange' in Fritz Stier-Somlo (ed), *Handbuch des Völkerrechts*, vol 5 (Kohlhammer 1914) 24–6.

[7] For a more detailed discussion see James B Scott, *The Hague Peace Conferences of 1899 and 1907* (Garland Baltimore 1909) 198–9. To be sure, this pronouncement did not turn Thucydides into a champion of the formula 'peace through law'. In the Melian Dialogue, he attributes to Athens the famous statement that law is possible only between equals in power, otherwise the strong do what they can and the weak suffer what they must. Thucydides, 'The History of the Grecian War' in William Molesworth (ed), *The English Works of Thomas Hobbes*, vol 2 (first published around 400 BCE, originally vol 5, para 89, tr Thomas Hobbes, John Bohn 1843) 99.

contained compromissory clauses in which the parties committed themselves to entrust conflicts to an arbitration body.[8] However, such commitments concerned only political entities that recognized each other as equals but were not subject to a common authority. This precondition existed among Greek states (and only among them), though not during the period of the Roman Empire and the Middle Ages. To be sure, the emperor and the pope settled disputes between political entities. They did *not* do so as independent third parties in a conflict between equals, but rather in the exercise of their ultimate authority over subjects.[9]

Only the early modern processes of state formation created a European system of sovereign equality, within the framework of which an international judiciary in the modern sense took shape.[10] Judicial institutions developed as part of a continuum—found to this day in Article 33 Section 1 of the UN Charter—of dispute management, bilateral negotiations, and mediation, closely embedded in the political strategies of the states that employ them.

The Jay Treaty of 1794 between the United States of America and the United Kingdom is regarded as a signal event.[11] It shows the close bond between the praxis of arbitration and diplomatic negotiations. Following the successful American Revolution, relations between the United Kingdom and the United States were fraught with conflict. Among other things, the two countries quarrelled over territorial issues, debt payments, and compensation payments for ships, slaves, and other confiscated property.[12] President George Washington, together with John Jay, the first Chief Justice of the United States, convinced the United Kingdom to submit the disputes to arbitration. Its procedure was then largely in accordance with a political negotiation process and was almost entirely devoid of legal forms of argumentation.[13]

[8] Alexandre Mérignhac, *Traité théorique et pratique de l'arbitrage international: le rôle du droit dans le fonctionnement actuel de l'institution et dans ses destinées futures* (Larose 1895) 18–22 with further references. However, examples from Asia were mostly characterized by hierarchies, Scott, *The Hague Peace Conferences* 195.

[9] Scott, *The Hague Peace Conferences* 200–3; Jackson H Ralston, *International Arbitration from Athens to Locarno* (Stanford UP 1929) 174–6.

[10] For a general discussion of this see Julius Goebel, *The Equality of States: A Study in the History of Law* (Columbia UP 1925); Helmut Quaritsch, *Souveränität: Entstehung und Entwicklung des Begriffs in Frankreich und Deutschland vom 13. Jh bis 1806* (Duncker & Humblot 1986).

[11] Manley O Hudson, *International Tribunals: Past and Future* (Carnegie Endowment for International Peace and Brookings Institution 1944) 3–4; Ram P Anand, *International Courts and Contemporary Conflicts* (Asia Publishing House 1974) 20–1.

[12] Percy E Corbett, *Law in Diplomacy* (Princeton UP 1959) 58–60.

[13] Corbett, *Law in Diplomacy* 145.

In this instance, and subsequently, there was no primarily judicial ethos. The members of the arbitration commission saw themselves less as judges subject to rules of legal discourse, and more as representatives of the party that appointed them.[14] For example, in the formative *Alabama* case,[15] the successful management of the conflict was due more to diplomacy than to legal working.[16] It was only toward the end of the nineteenth century that greater weight began to attach to the idea that a judicial resolution of international conflict should be qualitatively different from processes of political negotiations and follow a legal methodology[17] which, in keeping with the specific logic of the law, creates a sphere of autonomy and thereby somewhat loosens the absolute fixation on the state.

Against this background, advocates of a state-centric conception of international law could take the initiative for further judicialization of international relations. Russia's Tsar Nicholas II took an important step toward a permanent international judiciary in August 1898, when he issued an invitation to a conference with the goal of making 'the great idea of universal peace triumph over the elements of trouble and discord'.[18] The general argument and conviction was that the goal of disarmament could be achieved only in a world in which states, in cases of disputes, resorted not to war but to courts. As a result, an international judiciary emerged from the first Hague Peace Conference in 1899. However, the Permanent Court of Arbitration created in Articles 20–29 of the Hague Convention for the Pacific Settlement of International Disputes was little more than a set of rudimentary procedural rules and a list of persons from which arbitrators could be chosen[19]—nevertheless, this Convention is regarded as a milestone.[20]

An important push toward the further development of an international judiciary came again from the American side. In 1902, Theodore Roosevelt

[14] Compare Hersch Lauterpacht, *The Function of Law in the International Community* (Clarendon 1933) 221. This is still found today. Characteristically, the Greek judge ad hoc Roucounas, in *Application of the Interim Accord of 13 September 1995 (former Yugoslav Republic of Macedonia v Greece)* (Judgment) [2011] ICJ Rep 644, para 170, was the only one who, on the question of merit, voted against the decision in which 'his' country lost.

[15] *Alabama Claims of the United States of America against Great Britain* (Award of 14 September 1872 by the Tribunal of Arbitration Established by Article I of the Treaty of Washington of 8 May 1871) UN Rep Intl Arbitral Awards XXIX, 125.

[16] Ralston, *International Arbitration* 198–9.

[17] See Lammasch, 'Die Lehre von der Schiedsgerichtsbarkeit' 33.

[18] Text of Tsar Nicholas II's rescript at <avalon.law.yale.edu/19th_century/hag99-01.asp> accessed 1 October 2013.

[19] According to Art 23 Hague Convention for the Pacific Settlement of International Disputes (1899), 'each Signatory Power shall select four persons at the most, of known competency in questions of international law, of the highest moral reputation, and disposed to accept the duties of Arbitrators'.

[20] David D Caron, 'War and International Adjudication: Reflections on the 1899 Peace Conference' (2000) 94 AJIL 4.

programmatically handed the *Pious Fund* case over to the Permanent Court of Arbitration and encouraged other states to follow suit. It was clear to him that the great idea of an international judiciary could only take shape if the Court was supplied with cases.[21] Roosevelt also initiated the Second Hague Peace Conference.[22] It may seem paradoxical that Theodore Roosevelt, who pursued an imperialist programme more ardently than perhaps any other American president, championed the judicial settlement of international disputes. The paradox is resolved if one considers his view that 'highly political' conflicts were inherently not legal conflicts. An international judiciary conceived in this way by no means challenged the state-centric world order, but rather was intended to stabilize it.[23]

The Second Hague Peace Conference in 1907 was able to go beyond the achievements of 1899, though not with respect to a reform of the Permanent Court of Arbitration in such a way that it would have lived up to its name, too divergent were the ideas about the world order. Many delegates seemed so thoroughly imbued with the belief that states constituted the basis of the international order that the establishment of any kind of autonomy on the international level—and thus especially an independent court—struck them as highly suspect. A number of participants, among them the French jurist and politician Léon Bourgeois, since 1903 a member of the Permanent Court of Arbitration, believed that states were willing to subordinate themselves to a judiciary only if they could control the individual procedures and the appointment of the judges, especially when highly charged political issues were at stake.[24] This was in keeping with the prevailing opinion.[25]

In this perspective the judicial methodology is subordinated to the logic of negotiation, and the Permanent Court of Arbitration therefore seemed adequate and practical. Friedrich von Martens, probably the most sought-after arbitrator at the time, argued, as a Russian delegate to both peace conferences, that arbitral jurisdiction was solely concerned with settling disputes,

[21] Martti Koskenniemi, 'The Ideology of International Adjudication and the 1907 Hague Conference' in Yves Daudet (ed), *Topicality of the 1907 Hague Conference, the Second Peace Conference* (Nijhoff 2008) 127, 135; on the number of cases decided see Hudson, *International Tribunals* 7–8.

[22] Koskenniemi, 'The Ideology of International Adjudication and the 1907 Hague Conference' 136–7.

[23] Thus also the pioneer of the 'realist' school of international relations, Hans Morgenthau, *Die internationale Rechtspflege: Ihr Wesen und ihre Grenzen* (Noske 1929).

[24] Bourgeois changed his mind later, and after World War I he advocated a strong permanent international court. The Council of the League of Nations thereupon appointed Bourgeois to the Committee of Jurists, which was charged with drafting statutes for a court. In 1920, the year the Permanent Court of International Justice came into being, Bourgeois was awarded the Nobel Peace Prize. See Charles H Brower II, 'The Functions and Limits of Arbitration and Judicial Settlement Under Private and Public International Law' (2008) 18 Duke J Intl and Comparative L 259, 293.

[25] See Philipp Zorn, 'Die beiden Haager Friedenskonferenzen von 1899 und 1907' in Fritz Stier-Somlo (ed), *Handbuch des Völkerrechts*, vol 3 (Kohlhammer 1915) IX, 239.

and this did not require a legal justification of the decision.[26] This clearly reveals the traditional perspective, which regards courts merely as instruments of dispute settlement. That being the case, it is not surprising that 1907 left the state of affairs essentially as it had been in 1899.

Not least because of the growing importance of the second basic conception, which sees international courts as organs of the international community, representatives of the states took a major step after World War I. In 1920, within the framework of the League of Nations, they agreed to establish the PCIJ, which many hailed as an epochal achievement.[27] But in the end, the state-centric basic conception permitted only a weak institution. This is clearly revealed by the highly limited jurisdiction of the PCIJ. According to Article 13 of the Covenant of the League of Nations, jurisdiction was *not* obligatory and was, moreover, limited to those issues regarded as suitable for judicial settlement. Moreover, the Covenant of the League of Nations did not articulate a prohibition of war. Similar to the Treaty of Nicias (421 BCE), the parties, according to Article 12 of the Covenant, merely committed themselves 'in no case to resort to war until three months after the award by the arbitrators or the judicial decision'.

The state-oriented basic conception found its most incisive formulation in the *Lotus* decision of the PCIJ.[28] The Court famously stated:

> International law governs relations between independent States. The rules of law binding upon States therefore emanate from their own free will [...]. Restrictions upon the independence of States cannot therefore be presumed.[29]

Adjudication within the organizational framework of the Permanent Court of Arbitration was also dominated by this view. As the sole arbitrator in the *Islas of Palmas* case, Max Huber, a member and president of the PCIJ, articulated emphatically how the role of his institution should be understood within the context of the international order:

> Sovereignty in the relations between States signifies independence. Independence in regard to a portion of the globe is the right to exercise therein, to the exclusion of any other State, the functions of a State. The

[26] Hans Wehberg, 'Friedrich von Martens und die Haager Friedenskonferenzen' (1910) 20 Zeitschrift für internationales Recht 343, 349.

[27] As James Brown Scott put it on the occasion of the establishment of the PCIJ: 'We should [...] fall upon our knees and thank God that the hope of ages is in process of realization.' James B Scott, 'Editorial Comment' (1921) 15 AJIL 51, 55; see Koskenniemi, 'The Ideology of International Adjudication and the 1907 Hague Conference' 127–8.

[28] At the time this was by no means uncontroversial; for more detail see Armin von Bogdandy and Markus Rau, 'The Lotus' in Rüdiger Wolfrum (ed), *Max Planck Encyclopedia of Public International Law* <http://opil.ouplaw.com/home/EPIL> accessed 27 January 2014, paras 16–20.

[29] *The Case of the SS Lotus (France v Turkey)* (Judgment) PCIJ Rep Series A No 10, 18.

> development of the national organization of States during the last few centuries and, as a corollary, the development of international law, have established this principle of the exclusive competence of the State in regard to its own territory in such a way as to make it the point of departure in settling most questions that concern international relations.[30]

These well-known examples are typical of an ethos widely shared by international judges and of a conception of international judicial praxis within a state-centric global setting.[31] The international judiciary thus works within narrow confines on disputes beyond the major conflicts. Alfred Zimmern theorized that the cohesion of a society determines the field over which a jurisdiction can extend in the first place. As soon as an international judiciary expands to encompass political conflicts, he argued, it starts to run into problems.[32] According to this logic, judicial praxis must remain closely connected to the will of sovereign states, otherwise those states could withdraw completely. While that was probably the case in Zimmern's days, today it seems questionable as a general recommendation.

Were one to search for the reasons behind the state-centric basic conception, one might readily find them in the cautious nature of jurists in difficult situations. It is likely, though, that ideas about the fundamental nature of the international system came into play as well. Those include, first of all, classic liberalism in nineteenth-century international law, which projected social contract theories onto the international order and conceived of the state—equal to the individual—as the normative starting point on whose consensus the legitimate order rested.[33] The state-centric basic conception thereby has a dimension grounded in democratic theory.[34]

In general, however, the state-centric conception is tied to the particularistic paradigm of the international order. That paradigm thinks of states, which tend to be in competition, as the real and only reliable pillar of order. A principled difference therefore exists between public order within a state and the international order. Beyond the state, the best one can achieve is

[30] *Island of Palmas Case (Netherlands v USA)* (Award) (4 April 1928) United Nations Rep of Intl Arbitral Awards vol 2, 829, 838. On the impact of Max Huber see the contributions in 'Symposium: The European Tradition in International Law—Max Huber' (2007) 18 Eur J Intl L 69–197.

[31] Benedict Kingsbury, 'Sovereignty and Inequality' (1998) 9 Eur J Intl L 599, 608.

[32] Alfred Zimmern, *The League of Nations and the Rule of Law 1918–1935* (Macmillan 1936) 12; courts would otherwise turn into an 'array of wigs and gowns vociferating in emptiness'.

[33] Gerry J Simpson, 'Imagined Consent: Democratic Liberalism in International Legal Theory' (1994) 15 Australian YB Intl L 103, 112–5.

[34] See, for example, Ingeborg Maus, *Über Volkssouveränität: Elemente einer Demokratietheorie* (Suhrkamp 2011) 400–3. While we share the view that the democratic principle poses a problem for an international judiciary, we do not consider most proposals for dealing with this problem to be persuasive.

containment of disorder. Approaches under this paradigm are accordingly characterized by scepticism toward attempts at strengthening the international order and efforts to make international institutions more autonomous.[35]

2. The cautious International Court of Justice

In a direct line of continuity with the PCIJ is the ICJ. It operates in an especially difficult environment, which is one reason why it continues to be strongly tied to the first basic conception. It held an almost unique position until 1990, for prior to the fall of the Berlin Wall other international judicial institutions remained largely inactive or were restricted to the European context. That unique position, as well as its universal projection, prompted many to refer to the ICJ (and its predecessor) as the *World Court*,[36] a legitimacy-asserting label that the Court has also used for itself.[37] Over the past 20 years, it has largely lost that unique status. Attempts to position it at the head of the international judiciary[38] have failed so far and offer little promise of success at this time. Today it appears as a rather weak institution compared to other international courts, and one that is incorporated only incompletely into the general dynamic, possibly because it is shaped so deeply by the state-oriented conception.[39] Nevertheless—and perhaps for that very reason—many authors continue to regard it as *the* archetypal international court, as already revealed by the arrangement of conventional accounts.[40]

[35] Morgenthau, *Die internationale Rechtspflege*; Eric A Posner and John C Yoo, 'Judicial Independence in International Tribunals' (2005) 93 California L Rev 1. For a more detailed discussion see Armin von Bogdandy and Sergio Dellavalle, 'Ad hostes docere—Zu den Ursprüngen und zur Präsenz partikularistisch-holistischen Denkens' in Andreas Fischer-Lescano and others (eds), *Frieden in Freiheit: Festschrift für Michael Bothe zum 70. Geburtstag* (Nomos 2008) 847.

[36] See the four volumes by the Max Planck Institute for Comparative Public Law and International Law, by way of example Rudolf Bernhardt, Helmut Steinberger, and Jochen Abr Frowein (eds), *World Court Digest* vol 1 (Springer 1993); Terry D Gill (ed), *Rosenne's The World Court: What It Is and How It Works* (6th edn, Nijhoff 2003); Georges Abi-Saab, 'The International Court as a World Court' in Vaughan Lowe and Malgosia Fitzmaurice (eds), *Fifty Years of the International Court of Justice: Essays in Honour of Sir Robert Jennings* (CUP 1996) 3.

[37] Repeatedly at the Court's internet site; for example, the first sentence under the heading *Jurisdiction*: 'The International Court of Justice acts as a world court' <www.icj-cij.org/jurisdiction> accessed 1 October 2013.

[38] In particular ICJ president Stephen M Schwebel on 26 October 1999 before the UN General Assembly, *Statements by the President* <www.icj-cij.org> accessed 10 October 2012. Karen Oellers-Frahm has proposed a referral procedure, 'Multiplication of International Courts and Tribunals and Conflicting Jurisdiction—Problems and Possible Solutions' (2001) 5 Max Planck YB UN L 67, 99–101.

[39] Comparative assessment by Armin von Bogdandy and Ingo Venzke, 'Beyond Dispute: International Judicial Institutions as Lawmakers' (2011) 12 German L J 979.

[40] As representative for many see Ian Brownlie, *Principles of Public International Law* (7th edn, OUP 2008) 701–25.

Numerous circumstances suggest that the PCIJ's state-oriented basic understanding lived on in the ICJ. The most significant innovations in international law after World War II barely concerned the judiciary. Even more so than the Covenant of the League of Nations, the Charter of the United Nations accepts the elevated status of powerful states. This recognition takes precedence over the judicial protection of the rights of all subjects of international law. Although Article 2 Section 3 of the UN Charter lays down the precept of the peaceful settlement of disputes and Article 92 designates the ICJ as the 'principal judicial organ of the United Nations', the role of the Court is mentioned rather incidentally in Article 33 as one instrument for international dispute settlement among many. The primary responsibility for the preservation of global peace rests with the Security Council, not the ICJ.[41]

There certainly were voices pushing for a strong judiciary,[42] but the system agreed upon by the negotiators in San Francisco did not follow them. Although all members of the UN are automatically signatory parties to the Statute of the ICJ, that circumstance does not establish the Court's jurisdiction.[43] The latter requires an additional act of submission through a *compromis*, unilateral declaration, compromissory clause, or ad hoc agreement.[44] Although to date no fewer than 67 states have submitted unilaterally to the jurisdiction of the Court,[45] in many cases they have done so with a number of important provisos. When Germany unilaterally submitted to the jurisdiction of the ICJ on 5 May 2008, it excluded a series of constellations relevant to national security and also affirmed its right to change or withdraw its submission.[46]

Like its predecessor and the Permanent Court of Arbitration, the ICJ has its seat in the Peace Palace in The Hague, a complex built with funds from Andrew Carnegie and still administered by the Carnegie Endowment

[41] See Art 24(1) UN Charter.

[42] See, for example, UNCIO, *Documents of the United Nations Conference on International Organization (UNCIO) San Francisco* (12 June 1945) UNCIO Doc 913, IV/I/74(1). Helmut Steinberger, 'The International Court of Justice' in Hermann Mosler and Rudolf Bernhardt (eds), *Judicial Settlement of International Disputes* (Springer 1974) 193, 194–5.

[43] Arts 92, 93(1) UN Charter; Art 36(2) ICJ Statute.

[44] Christian Tomuschat in Andreas Zimmermann and others (eds), *The Statute of the International Court of Justice: A Commentary* (2nd edn, OUP 2012) Article 36 paras 34–142.

[45] To date, 70 states have issued declarations according to Art 36(2) ICJ Statute <www.icj-cij.org/jurisdiction/index.php?p1=5&p2=1&p3=3> accessed 1 October 2013.

[46] Declaration according to Art 36(2) ICJ Statute, Publication of the German Parliament 16/9218 (5 May 2008) (Bundestagsdrucksache); Christophe Eick, 'Die Anerkennung der obligatorischen Gerichtsbarkeit des Internationalen Gerichtshofs durch Deutschland' (2008) 68 Zeitschrift für ausländisches öffentliches Recht und Völkerrecht 763; see the more extensive contributions in Andreas Zimmermann (ed), *Deutschland und die internationale Gerichtsbarkeit* (Duncker & Humblot 2004).

for International Peace.[47] The symbolism of the location and of the building highlights the central function that is ascribed to the courts housed there: dispute settlement as a way of preserving peace.[48] Article 38 of the ICJ Statute underscores that it is the task of the Court 'to decide in accordance with international law such disputes as are submitted to it'. The statute does not mention other tasks that are entirely conceivable. In the sense of Article 3 Section 2 of the DSU (Dispute Settlement Understanding) of the WTO, an additional statement could be: 'The ICJ is a central element in providing security and predictability to the system of international law.'

The ICJ is composed of 15 members who are elected in a secret ballot by the General Assembly and the Security Council for a term of nine years, whereby the bench of judges is supposed to represent the 'principal legal systems of the world'.[49] The judges work full-time,[50] and like the Registry and the administration of the Court,[51] they are paid from the budget of the UN.[52] For the biannual of 2010–11, the budget of the ICJ was no less than 46,605,800 US dollars.[53] If a party to a dispute does not have a judge of its nationality on the bench, it can appoint an ad hoc judge.[54] In addition, it is usual practice that each of the five permanent members of the Security Council provides one judge. The power balance of 1945 is clearly reflected on the bench.

Finally, it should be mentioned that the ICJ, in addition to its task of settling disputes between states, can exercise the function of providing expert opinions on behalf of the General Assembly, the Security Council, other organs of the United Nations, or special organizations.[55] By the end of 2011, the Court had rendered 109 decisions in disputes and issued 25 expert opinions.[56] In the first 15 years after its establishment, it decided 33 cases.

[47] Arthur Eyffinger, *The Peace Palace: Residence for Justice, Domicile of Learning* (2nd edn, Carnegie Foundation 1988) 113–28.

[48] Eyffinger, *The Peace Palace* 51.

[49] Arts 3, 4, 9, 10, and 13 ICJ Statute. See Lyndel V Prott, *The Latent Power of Culture and the International Judge* (Professional Books 1979).

[50] Art 16 ICJ Statute and ICJ Rules of Court.

[51] The Registry is intensively involved in the preparations. Anecdotal evidence creates the impression that the Registrar is more influential than some judges.

[52] Art 33 ICJ Statute.

[53] 'Report of the International Court of Justice: 1 August 2010-31 July 2011' (1 August 2011) UN Doc A/64/4 145–7.

[54] Art 31(2), (3) ICJ Statute; critically Iain Scobbie, 'Une hérésie en matière judiciaire? The Role of the Judge ad hoc in the International Court' (2005) 4 L and Practice of Intl Courts and Tribunals 421. The far younger ITLOS also permits judges ad hoc; Art 17 ITLOS Statute.

[55] Art 96 UN Charter.

[56] Ruth Mackenzie and others, *The Manual on International Courts and Tribunals* (2nd edn, OUP 2010) 5; *Judgments, Advisory Opinions and Orders by Chronological Order* <www.icj-cij.org> accessed 10 October 2012.

Thereafter the number declined markedly until the end of the Cold War (a total of 26 decisions), but after that there were more than ever before.[57] In what follows we will sketch out, by way of example, a number of ICJ decisions that are characterized especially vividly by the state-centric conception.

The Court began its work in 1947 with the *Corfu Channel* case between the United Kingdom and Albania. The Security Council had also taken on the issue and called upon both parties to submit the matter without delay to the ICJ.[58] In its complaint, the United Kingdom invoked that resolution by the Security Council as the reason for the Court's jurisdiction.[59] However, the Court based itself on the concrete consent of Albania (*forum prorogatum*) and *not* on an assignment of the dispute and justification of jurisdiction by the Security Council.[60] Such a justification of jurisdiction is today possible for the International Criminal Court under the Rome Statute, but not for the ICJ—at least, not explicitly.[61] In fact, the separate opinion by seven judges explicitly rejected the United Kingdom's argument.[62]

The principle of consensual jurisdiction runs like a thread through large parts of the ICJ's decisions.[63] In the *Anglo-Iranian Oil Company* case of 1952, the Court actually denied its jurisdiction with the argument that it was 'unlikely' that Iran had intended to submit itself to the Court in cases like the present one, even though Iran's unilateral declaration under Article 36 Section 2 of the ICJ Statute could have plausibly established its jurisdiction.[64] Such deference to the will of the disputing parties seems plausible only from the perspective of the state-oriented conception.

Bilateralism is the prevailing perspective.[65] Accordingly, the Court conceives of the possibilities of third parties to intervene in legal proceedings pursuant to Article 62 of the ICJ Statute in very narrow terms—quite different, for example, from what is done in the context of the WTO, where

[57] Cesare PR Romano, 'International Justice and Developing Countries: A Quantitative Analysis' (2002) 1 L and Practice of Intl Courts and Tribunals 367, 380.

[58] Other than in the Statute of the League of Nations, the possibility to give such a recommendation has been explicitly enshrined in Art 36 UN Charter. See UNSC Res 22 (9 April 1947) UN Doc S/RES/22.

[59] *Corfu Channel (UK v Albania)* (Preliminary Objection) [1948] ICJ Rep 15, 17.

[60] *Corfu Channel* 27–8.

[61] See Arts 13(b), 16 Rome Statute; *Corfu Channel* 27–8.

[62] *Corfu Channel*, Sep Op Basdevant, Alvarez, Winiarski, Zoricic, De Visscher, Badawi Pasha, Krylov, 31–2.

[63] Tomuschat, Article 36 para 19.

[64] *Anglo-Iranian Oil Co (UK v Iran)* (Preliminary Objection) [1952] ICJ Rep 93, 105.

[65] For a thorough discussion Bruno Simma, 'From Bilateralism to Community Interest' (1994) 250 Recueil des cours 221.

practice has significantly lowered the requirements of what constitutes 'substantial interest'.[66] Bilateralism is also vividly on display in a characteristic series of disputes over maritime borders. The Court treated those disputes as purely bilateral matters between the contending parties, even though it was hard to overlook that the decisions would shape principles regarding the drawing of borders and thus have an effect that radiated far beyond the concrete cases.[67] In the case between Tunisia and Libya, the Court delimited the boundaries of the continental shelf between the two states and rejected Malta's application to intervene on the grounds that Malta had failed to invoke a legal interest that might have been affected by the decision of the Court. A mere interest in the determination of applicable law was deemed insufficient, since this applied to virtually every state.[68] For the Court, Malta's interests were adequately protected by Article 59 of the ICJ Statute, which limits the reach of the decision to the parties in question. In a dissenting opinion, Judge Jennings aptly criticized this as an 'enervating bilateralism' of the Court, especially since Article 59 of the ICJ Statute did not prevent a development of the law on maritime delimitation through adjudication.[69]

The same logic underpins the Court's position that it cannot decide in cases in which its reasoning implies assessments about the legality of acts by third parties.[70] The *East Timor* case vividly illuminates what that means. In 1975, Indonesia annexed East Timor, until then Portuguese colonial territory, and laid claim to the area as a new province of Indonesia. The UN General Assembly condemned this use of force and affirmed the right of the Timorese people to self-determination.[71] But Australia implicitly recognized Indonesia's claim of sovereignty over East Timor, and eventually, in 1989, it signed a co-operation treaty with Indonesia that extended to the allocation of resources in the region. At this point, Portugal sued Australia

[66] *European Communities: Regime for the Importation, Sale and Distribution of Bananas—Appellate Body Report* (9 September 1997) WT/DS27/AB/R, paras 132–5; see Katrin Arend in Rüdiger Wolfrum, Peter-Tobias Stoll, and Karen Kaiser (eds), *WTO: Institutions and Dispute Settlement* (Nijhoff 2006) Article 10 para 4.

[67] *Continental Shelf (Libyan Arab Jarmahiriya v Malta)* (Application by Italy for Permission to Intervene) [1984] ICJ Rep 3, Diss Op Jennings, para 34.

[68] *Continental Shelf (Tunisia v Libyan Arab Jamahiriya)* (Application by Malta for Permission to Intervene) [1981] ICJ Rep 3, para 13.

[69] *Continental Shelf*, Diss Op Jennings, para 32; similarly *Accordance with International Law of the Unilateral Declaration of Independence in Respect of Kosovo* (Advisory Opinion) [2010] ICJ Rep 403, Declaration Simma, para 2 '[...] the Court's approach reflects an old, tired view of international law [...].'

[70] *Certain Phosphate Lands in Nauru (Nauru v Australia)* (Judgment) [1992] ICJ Rep 240, para 55; *East Timor (Portugal v Australia)* (Judgment) [1995] ICJ Rep 90, para 34.

[71] UNGA Res 3485 (12 December 1975) UN Doc A/RES/3485; see also UNGA Res 31/53 (1 December 1976) UN Doc A/RES/31/53 and UNGA Res 32/34 (28 November 1977) UN Doc A/RES/32/34.

before the ICJ: Australia, it charged, was violating the people's right to self-determination, both its right to freely decide its form of government and its right to control the natural resources in the maritime zones off its shores. Portugal and Australia had recognized the jurisdiction of the Court in accordance with Article 36 Section 2 of the ICJ Statute, though Indonesia had not.

The Court approached the *East Timor* case entirely in light of the state-oriented conception.[72] Every decision, the Court maintained, inevitably contained a statement about the legality of the actions taken by Indonesia. The Court declared that it could not exercise its jurisdiction if the actions of a third party formed the very subject matter of the Court's assessment.[73] This did not change even when the plaintiff asserted that obligations *erga omnes (in casu* the right to self-determination) were violated.[74] The Court was not willing to interpret the 'well-established principle of international law embodied in the Court's Statute, namely, that the Court can only exercise jurisdiction over a State with its consent'[75] in the light of Portugal's request to uphold peremptory legal norms as a member of the international community.

The state-oriented conception insists on strictly respecting the basis of the Court's jurisdiction in the consensus of states that are parties to a dispute, and to deny jurisdiction if there is doubt. To be sure, other basic conceptions also do not strike at the foundation of jurisdiction outlined in terms of positive law, but they would use the available room for interpretation differently. For example, in the *East Timor* case at least two judges held that the Court should have rendered a decision on the legality of Australia's action.[76] Judge Weeramantry, in particular, saw the Court as an organ of the international community and expressed his regret that the majority did not find a better solution for dealing with multilateral conflicts in a closely interconnected world. He also showed how the Court could have recognized the

[72] Christine M Chinkin, 'The East Timor Case (Portugal v Australia)' (1996) 45 ICLQ 712. On what follows see also Catriona Drew, 'The East Timor Story: International Law on Trial' (2001) 12 Eur J Intl L 651; Andreas Zimmermann, 'Die Zuständigkeit des Internationalen Gerichtshofes zur Entscheidung über Ansprüche gegen am Verfahren nicht beteiligte Staaten: Anmerkungen aus Anlaß der Entscheidung des IGH im Streitfall zwischen Portugal und Australien betreffend Ost-Timor' (1995) 55 Zeitschrift für ausländisches öffentliches Recht und Völkerrecht 1051.

[73] *East Timor*, para 27.

[74] *East Timor*, para 29. *Armed Activities on the Territory of the Congo (New Application: 2002) (Congo v Rwanda)* (Judgment) [2006] ICJ Rep 6, paras 64–5; see Matthias Ruffert, 'Special Jurisdiction of the ICJ in the Case of Infringement of Fundamental Rules of the International Legal Order?' in Christian Tomuschat and Jean-Marc Thouvenin (eds), *The Fundamental Rules of the International Legal Order, Jus Cogens and Obligations Erga Omnes* (Nijhoff 2006) 295.

[75] *East Timor*, para 34.

[76] *East Timor*, Diss Op Weeramantry, 150–5; Diss Op Skubiszewski, paras 40–112.

rights of the East Timorese people.[77] But the clear voting ratio shows that the state-centric conception prevailed among the judges of the ICJ.

The position of the Court in dealing with submissions from non-governmental organizations (NGOs) intended as *amicus curiae* briefs is further indicative of its posture. What emerges once again is a self-understanding on the part of the Court that is targeted at dealing with cases under the state-centric conception.[78] In the very first case the Registrar rejected any participation in the proceedings, either in written or oral form.[79] In interstate proceedings, submissions by NGOs could be at most part of the documents presented by the contending parties.[80] On the question of how to deal with *amici curiae,* the judges seem at odds over whether the Court should open itself up further, as the dispute settlement organs of the WTO have done, for example. Gilbert Guillaume, the former president of the ICJ, declared tersely that states and intergovernmental institutions had to be protected against 'the powerful pressure groups which besiege them today with the support of the mass media', and for that reason the ICJ must not open itself up to *amici curiae.*[81]

The state-oriented conception is plainly evident also in the treatment of questions of substantive law. Here it also advises restraint if there is uncertainty about the will of the states. Although other decisions would be possible using teleological or principle-guided arguments, when in doubt the Court usually decides that states are not legally bound.[82] In the *Nuclear Tests* case, the Court found that unilateral declarations by states must be narrowly interpreted when legal obligations are at issue.[83] Even though the Court does not explicitly invoke the general principle of *in dubio mitius*, a series of decisions express noticeable restraint.[84]

Restraint is evident even when the Court becomes active not in a dispute, but in an advisory capacity. In its advisory opinion on *Reservations to the*

[77] *East Timor,* Diss Op Weeramantry, especially 172–3, 213–6.

[78] See chapter 4 section B 2.

[79] See Anna-Karin Lindblom, *Non Governmental Organisations in International Law* (CUP 2005) 303–4.

[80] As in the case *Gabčíkovo-Nagymaros Project (Hungary v Slovakia)* (Judgment) [1997] ICJ Rep 7, through a submission by Hungary.

[81] *Legality of the Threat or Use of Nuclear Weapons* (Advisory Opinion) [1996] ICJ Rep 226, Sep Op Guillaume, para 2.

[82] Such a case is *Arrest Warrant of 11 April 2000 (Congo v Belgium)* (Judgment) [2002] ICJ Rep 3.

[83] *Nuclear Tests Case (Australia v France)* (Judgment) [1974] ICJ Rep 253, para 44, stipulates for a case in which a state voluntarily assumes legal obligations that those obligations should be interpreted narrowly.

[84] For a detailed discussion see Luigi Crema, 'Disappearance and New Sightings of Restrictive Interpretation(s)' (2010) 21 Eur J Intl L 681.

Convention on the Prevention and Punishment of the Crime against Genocide, the Court had been asked for its opinion on the effect of improper reservations. The argumentation of the Court reveals an understanding of international law that is contractual and inspired by private law even when it comes to providing protection against genocide. To be sure, the Court affirmed the existence of principles that are 'binding on States, even without any conventional obligation'.[85] An inadmissible reservation to the Genocide Convention did still not result in any obligation: no intent, no obligation.[86] On this point, the ECtHR, with its community-oriented conception, would come to a contrary decision.[87] In its advisory opinion on the legality of the use of nuclear weapons, as well, the ICJ left the crucial question open in view of the absence of a consensus among states.[88]

The state-oriented conception of international law, which regards the autonomy of states as the overarching principle, remains highly influential. What is not forbidden is allowed, and a Court is not supposed to solidify the normativity of international law. Accordingly, in the *Kosovo* advisory opinion, the Court gave a narrow interpretation of the question submitted by the UN General Assembly—whether the unilateral declaration of independence by the provisional government in Kosovo was compatible with international law—by limiting it to the act of declaration. In that respect it saw no prohibition. With this it avoided providing guidance on a whole series of fundamental questions placed before it: for example, a possible right to secession, the consequences of systematic human rights violations, or the consequences of a declaration of independence.[89] According to the declaration of Bruno Simma, this reveals an 'anachronistic, extremely consensualist vision of international law' as found in the *Lotus* principle.[90]

[85] *Reservations to the Convention on Genocide* (Advisory Opinion) [1951] ICJ Rep 15, 23.

[86] *Reservations to the Convention on Genocide* 27; Diss Op Guerrero, McNair, Read, Hsu Mo, 31; see Ryan Goodman, 'Human Rights Treaties, Invalid Reservations, and State Consent' (2002) 96 AJIL 531.

[87] See section B 3.

[88] In the conventional interpretation this was a case of *non liquet*. Daniel Bodansky, 'Non Liquet and the Incompleteness of International Law' in Laurence Boisson de Chazournes and Philippe Sands (eds), *International Law, the International Court of Justice and Nuclear Weapons* (CUP 1999) 153.

[89] *Kosovo*, especially para 82; Robert Howse and Ruti Teitel, 'Delphic Dictum: How Has the ICJ Contributed to the Global Rule of Law by its Ruling on Kosovo?' (2010) 11 German L J 841.

[90] *Kosovo*, Declaration Simma, paras 2–3, 8; for a more detailed discussion see Armin von Bogdandy and Marc Jacob, 'The Judge as Law-Maker: Thoughts on Bruno Simma's Declaration in the Kosovo Opinion' in Ulrich Fastenrath and others (eds), *From Bilateralism to Community Interest: Essays in Honour of Judge Bruno Simma* (OUP 2011) 809.

3. The Permanent Court of Arbitration and the Iran–United States Claims Tribunal

We will probe further into the state-oriented conception by looking at the praxis of two institutions that have an even stronger bilateral orientation than the ICJ: the Permanent Court of Arbitration (PCA) and the Iran–United States Claims Tribunal. At the same time, though, the discussion of the Permanent Court of Arbitration reveals how traditional institutions find new orientations on old foundations within changing contexts. A look at the Iran–United States Claims Tribunal further illustrates how decisions by an institution conceived in bilateral terms can shape the general evolution of the law.

The Permanent Court of Arbitration, which is the oldest of the international judicial institutions currently in existence, was established at the Hague Peace Conferences in 1899 and 1907 by the Hague Convention on the Pacific Settlement of International Disputes, and took up residence in the Peace Palace in The Hague in 1913. Its Secretariat, the International Bureau, offers support for arbitral processes, functions as a clerk and archivist, and maintains the list of the currently 285 potential arbitrators that may be selected by the contracting powers.[91] In a dispute, the parties form a panel of an uneven number of arbitrators. Each party selects one third of the arbitrators, and the other third is chosen by the arbitrators themselves or by an agreed appointing authority.

The delegates to the two peace conferences in The Hague saw the task of the Permanent Court of Arbitration in settling concrete disputes and agreed on rather rudimentary rules of procedure. They placed the elaboration of the procedure and the appointment of the arbitrators into the hands of the contending parties. Many delegates firmly believed this was necessary for states to hand disputes over to the Court.[92] In the first years of its existence the PCA was certainly used, on the basis of the Hague Convention, and by 1914 it had decided 14 cases.[93] In addition, it assisted international commissions of inquiry in intra-state disputes.[94]

[91] Art 44 Hague Convention on the Pacific Settlement of International Disputes (1907) and Art 23 Hague Convention on the Pacific Settlement of International Disputes (1899).

[92] See chapter 2 section A 1.

[93] Overview in Nisuke Ando, 'Permanent Court of Arbitration' in Wolfrum (ed) *Max Planck Encyclopedia of Public International Law*, para 22.

[94] *Incident in the North Sea (The Dogger Bank Case) (Great Britain v Russia)* International Commissions of Inquiry Report (ICI Rep) (26 February 1905); *Capture of the 'Tavignano' and Cannon Shots Fired at the 'Canouna' and the 'Galois' (France v Italy)* ICI Rep (23 July 1912); *The Steamship 'Tiger' (Germany v Spain)* ICI Rep (8 November 1918); *Loss of the Dutch Steamer 'Tubantia' (Germany v Netherlands)* ICI Rep (27 February 1922); later *'Red Crusader' Incident (Great Britain v Denmark)* ICI Rep (23 March 1962).

Following the establishment of the PCIJ, the PCA was relatively dormant for many decades, but recently it has increasingly offered a forum for arbitral proceedings that take place on a contractual basis different from the Hague Convention. As a rule it assumes a supportive, mostly administrative role. In so doing it has expanded its sphere of activity, especially in the area of investment and commercial arbitration. In addition, it makes possible proceedings not only between states but also with international organizations or private individuals as the parties to a dispute. The PCA has thus changed quite a bit and adjusted to new demands. Currently there are more proceedings taking place under its aegis than ever before.[95]

The performance of effective, flexible, and usually fairly quick dispute settlement makes arbitral tribunals within the framework of the PCA an attractive institution for states as well as private actors. As Tjaco van den Hout, PCA Secretary-General from 1999 to 2008, put it: while it may have been an idealistic project in 1907 to prevail upon states to submit their disputes to the Permanent Court of Arbitration, today they accept the offers of the PCA more often than ever before, and use it above all to advance negotiation processes.[96] Examples include the decision in the *Iron Rhine* case between Belgium and the Netherlands about the application of a border treaty dating back to 1839, or the arbitral decision between the private operators of the Channel Tunnel on the one side and the British and French authorities on the other.[97]

Two observations are particularly relevant to our concerns. First, disputes involving private actors are proliferating vigorously.[98] This already points beyond a state-centric world order. Second, there is hardly a case that does *not* affect the general development of the law beyond the concrete context of a dispute. In other words, the mono-functional analysis of concrete dispute settlement in specific cases falls short.

Another institution among arbitral tribunals, which—more so than almost any other institution—serves concrete case management with the overarching goal of securing peace between states is the Iran–United States Claims Tribunal (IUSCT), created in 1981. During its first years it was housed in the premises of the PCA and received administrative support from it until it moved to its own building in The Hague. The IUSCT

[95] See <www.pca-cpa.org> accessed 10 October 2012.

[96] Tjaco van den Hout, 'Resolution of International Disputes: The Role of the Permanent Court of Arbitration: Reflections on the Centenary of the 1907 Convention for the Pacific Settlement of International Disputes' (2008) 21 Leiden J Intl L 643, 643–4.

[97] *Iron Rhine Arbitration (Belgium v Netherlands)* (Award) (24 May 2005); *Eurotunnel (Channel Tunnel Group Ltd and France-Manche SA v Secretary of State for Transport of the United Kingdom and Minister for Transport of the French Republic)* (Partial Award of 30 January 2007).

[98] As of 23 February 2012 <www.pca-cpa.org/showpage.asp?pag_id=1029>.

is a quite productive institution, though it works on only a single, bilateral situation of the past. The Tribunal has dealt mostly with compensation claims by American investors against Iran, but also with disputes between the two states. By the end of 2010 the Tribunal had worked through a total of 3,936 cases, of which about 3,000 were brought to an amicable resolution. It awarded American parties a total of 2,166,998,515 US dollars, and the few cases still open concern large sums demanded by Iran.[99] Of the nine arbitrators of the Tribunal, the US and Iran each select three, and they select the final three.

An overarching purpose of the IUSCT was and is to contribute to the normalization of relations between Iran and the US. In keeping with this purpose, the adjudication is balanced and conciliatory and only rarely determines clear winners.[100] The lack of legal considerations has certainly been criticized.[101] Still, over the course of time, the Tribunal, in the abundance of its adjudication, has made a contribution to the development of the law—both with a view to substantive law, among other things in the determination of citizenship under international law and in the area of expropriations, and in the handling of procedural rules.[102] Its adjudication takes a position also on general questions of international law.[103] Even an arbitral tribunal that has a purely bilateral orientation and focuses on circumstances completed before its establishment has thus made a contribution to 'a larger legal community'. The mono-functional state-oriented conception of international courts blocks that out.

B. COURTS AS ORGANS OF THE VALUE-BASED INTERNATIONAL COMMUNITY

The second basic conception sees international courts as *organs of the international community* whose values and interests they are supposed to protect and develop. In this view, one could say that they render their decisions

[99] Of those, 3,844 were complaints by private investors and 92 were disputes between states. See Iran–United States Claims Tribunal, *Quarterly Communiqué* (11 January 2011).

[100] Ted L Stein, 'Jurisprudence and Jurists' Prudence: The Iranian-Forum Clause Decisions of the Iran–U.S. Claims Tribunal' (1984) 78 AJIL 1, 34, 44.

[101] Graphically expressed by Stein, 'Jurisprudence and Jurists' Prudence' 48: 'a tribunal that opts out of the task of normative elaboration makes it more difficult for later tribunals to rely on law as a source of legitimation. The law remains embryonic, untextured, calcified.'

[102] The jurisprudence has been analyzed in detail in George H Aldrich, *The Jurisprudence of the Iran–United States Claims Tribunal* (Clarendon 1996); see also Christopher Pinto, 'Iran–United States Claims Tribunal' in Wolfrum (ed), *Max Planck Encyclopedia of Public International Law*.

[103] See *Iran v United States (Case No B1)* (2004–2009) 38 IUSCT Rep 77, paras 84–8, 113–5.

less in the name of the disputing parties and more in the name of this community.[104] Whereas the first basic conception looks at courts and tribunals only for their function of dispute settlement, a multifunctional examination is now possible. International courts are supposed to settle disputes, but at the same time they promote a number of other community interests. As organs of the community they control its members. They also promote global interests and articulate universal values. Their legitimacy derives from these functions, and not just from state consent.

The first step in the following discussion once again draws historical outlines and situates this conception within the universalist paradigm of the international order (1). The second step identifies traces of this conception within the praxis of the ICJ (2). The third step does the same for other institutions that are especially committed to it, in particular the European Court for Human Rights, international criminal courts, and the International Tribunal for the Law of the Sea (3).

At the outset it should be noted that in some doctrines the concept of an *organ* might presuppose a corporate body with legal personality.[105] Thus, if international courts are understood as *organs* of the international community, it would be necessary to assert simultaneously that the international community constitutes a corporate body and a subject of international law. That is indeed occasionally advocated,[106] but more commonly international courts are attributed to specific international organizations, even where there is no legal relationship that sets them up as organs.[107] The term *organ* is mostly used here in a non-technical way.

[104] On decisions rendered 'In the Name of the Community of International Law' see Joined Cases C-402/05 P and 415/05 P *Kadi and Al Barakaat International Foundation v Council and Commission* [2008] ECR I–06351, Opinion of AG Maduro, para 34.

[105] Ernst-Wolfgang Böckenförde, 'Organ, Organisation, Juristische Person: Kritische Überlegungen zu Grundbegriffen und Konstruktionsbasis des staatlichen Organisationsrechts' in Christian-Friedrich Menger (ed), *Fortschritte des Verwaltungsrechts: Festschrift für Hans J Wolff zum 75. Geburtstag* (CH Beck 1973) 269.

[106] Mehrdad Payandeh, *Internationales Gemeinschaftsrecht* (Springer 2010) speaks, on the one hand, of organs of the international community (at 131) and, on the other hand, arrives at the conclusion that the international community is a subject under international law (446); on the prevailing understanding see Hermann Mosler, 'The International Society as a Legal Community' (1973) 140 Recueil des cours 1, 28–32, 189–91.

[107] Rainer Hofmann, 'Die Rechtskontrolle von Organen der Staatengemeinschaft' (2007) 42 Berichte der Deutschen Gesellschaft für Völkerrecht 1; August Reinisch, 'Verfahrensrechtliche Aspekte der Rechtskontrolle von Organen der Staatengemeinschaft' (2007) 42 Berichte der Deutschen Gesellschaft für Völkerrecht 43; Thomas Pfeiffer, 'Die Rechtskontrolle von Organen der Staatengemeinschaft: Internationale Organisationen und ihre Rechtsgeschäfte mit Privaten' (2007) 42 Berichte der Deutschen Gesellschaft für Völkerrecht 93. Here, organs are ascribed to specific international organizations and not to the international community as such.

1. International courts as beacons of humanity

In the community-oriented conception, international courts are supposed to consolidate and develop the international community of law and values.[108] Of course they are mostly concerned with disputes between states, but these states are now considered as members of the international community, and adjudication has to take into consideration not only their bilateral relationships, but also the values and interests of that community. According to this view, courts fail in their task if they act only as instruments for settling conflicts between sovereign states.

Although the point of departure of this second basic conception does not reach back into Greek antiquity, it has venerable roots (especially in the notions of the *ius gentium*), which are close to natural law.[109] The individual, state-organized communities are embedded within a larger, in the final analysis universal, context of order from which they derive their legitimacy. This idea of the universal validity of a general law appears for the first time in late antiquity, when Stoicism developed the radically new idea that the entire world is governed by one basic law: by the *logos* that applies to all humans and to which the *nomoi* of the various social entities are subordinated.[110] Many elements of Stoic philosophy were integrated into Christian doctrine and thereby attained political relevance. At first, Christian scholars tried to implement this idea by means of a 'universal monarchy',[111] but after this project had proved impossible, Christian political philosophy responded to the political diversity by developing a *ius inter gentes*—that is, an international law that regulated the interactions between peoples on the basis of shared principles.[112] Hugo Grotius then disconnected international law from the direct reference to the Christian God and grounded it in the nature of humans as social beings.[113] Following

[108] Andreas L Paulus, *Die internationale Gemeinschaft im Völkerrecht: Eine Untersuchung zur Entwicklung des Völkerrechts in Zeiten der Globalisierung* (CH Beck 2001) 225–431; Simma, 'From Bilateralism to Community Interest' 256–84.

[109] In detail Armin von Bogdandy and Sergio Dellavalle, 'Universalism Renewed: Habermas' Theory of International Order in Light of Competing Paradigms' (2009) 10 German L J 5, 10–3.

[110] Hans von Arnim, *Stoicorum veterum fragmenta* 4 vols (vols 1–3 first published 1903–1905, vol 4 1924 by Maximilian Adler, GS Saur 2004).

[111] Dante Alighieri, *De Monarchia* (first published 1310–1314, Sumptibus Guiliemi Braumüller 1874); English: Dante, *Monarchy* (Prue Shaw tr, CUP 1996).

[112] Francisco Suarez, 'De legibus, ac Deo legislatore' in James B Scott (ed), *Selections from three Works: The Photographic Reproduction of the Selections from the Original Editions*, vol 1 (first published 1612, Clarendon 1944); English: 'A Treatise on Laws and God the Lawgiver' in James B Scott (ed), *Selections from Three Works: The Translation*, vol 2 (Gwladys L Williams, Ammi Brown, and John Waldron trs, Clarendon 1944) 3.

[113] Hugo Grotius, *De iure belli ac pacis: Libri tres, in quibus ius naturae & gentium, item iuris publici praecipua explicantur* (first published 1646, Hein & Co 1995); English: *De iure belli ac pacis libri tres: The Translation*, vol 2 (James B Scott ed, Francis W Kelsey tr, Oceana 1964).

Grotius, international law advanced to become the law of humanity that lays down the basic rules of universal sociality.

Today, universalist conceptions of international law are carried by different currents of thinking. For example, the paradigmatic legal principle of *ius cogens* is closely linked with Alfred Verdross, possibly the most important representative of Catholic natural law in the international law of the twentieth century.[114] In relation to an international judiciary, a particularly influential advocate was Hersch Lauterpacht. More recently, this universalist thinking has been developed by Antônio Cançado Trindade and Christian Tomuschat.[115] In this context the doctrine of the constitutionalization of international law currently offers the most important platform.[116]

The conception owes its political impact in particular to the peace movements. The conception of international courts as organs of the community gains its political momentum from the horrors of modern wars, which brought together committed individuals in the pursuit of a peaceful order.[117] The year 1815, in which the leaders of the restoration launched the era of strict interstate international law with the Congress of Vienna, was also the birth year of the peace movement, which in part seeks to overcome this law, but at least aims to strengthen its peace function.[118]

The British Peace Society was especially successful and achieved the introduction of compromissory clauses into some of the United Kingdom's international treaties.[119] On the European continent, the Italian jurist and politician Pasquale Stanislao Mancini advocated mechanisms of arbitral

[114] Alfred Verdross, 'Forbidden Treaties in International Law' (1937) 31 AJIL 571; Alfred Verdross, 'Jus Dispositivum and Jus Cogens' (1966) 60 AJIL 55; on his influence on the formation of the legal concept of *ius cogens* Bruno Simma, 'Der Beitrag von Alfred Verdross zur Entwicklung der Völkerrechtswissenschaft' in Herbert Miehsler, Erhard Mock, and Bruno Simma (eds), *Ius Humanitatis: Festschrift zum 90. Geburtstag von Alfred Verdross* (Duncker & Humblot 1980) 23, 43–51.

[115] Antônio A Cançado Trindade, 'International Law for Humankind: Towards a New *Jus Gentium* (I)' (2005) 316 Recueil des cours 9; Antônio A Cançado Trindade, 'International Law for Humankind: Towards a New *Jus Gentium* (II)' (2005) 317 Recueil des cours 9; Christian Tomuschat, 'International Law: Ensuring the Survival of Mankind on the Eve of a New Century: General Course on Public International Law' (1999) 281 Recueil des cours 9.

[116] Anne Peters, 'Rechtsordnungen und Konstitutionalisierung: Zur Neubestimmung der Verhältnisse' (2010) 65 Zeitschrift für öffentliches Recht 3.

[117] Lammasch, 'Die Lehre von der Schiedsgerichtsbarkeit' 36–7; Werner Kaltefleiter and Robert L Pfaltzgraff (eds), *The Peace Movements in Europe and the United States* (Croom Helm 1985). On the change in the conduct of war see David A Bell, *The First Total War: Napoleon and the Birth of Warfare as We Know It* (Houghton Mifflin Harcourt 2007); however, see Roger Chickering, 'Total War: The Use and Abuse of a Concept' in Manfred F Boemeke, Roger Chickering, and Stig Förster (eds), *Anticipating Total War: The German and American Experiences, 1871–1914* (CUP 1999) 13.

[118] On the origins see Wilhelmus H van der Linden, *The International Peace Movement 1815–1874* (Tilleul 1987) 31–4, 37–8; Alfred H Fried, *Handbuch der Friedensbewegung* (Verlag der Österreichischen Friedensgesellschaft 1905) 229–31.

[119] Lammasch, 'Die Lehre von der Schiedsgerichtsbarkeit' 38–9.

dispute settlement in trade treaties, consular treaties, and deportation treaties.[120] The relevant Italian praxis exerted influence on other states. By 1914, more than 100 international treaties had been signed that envisaged, in case of a dispute, the establishment of an arbitration tribunal, no doubt with the dominant function of working on concrete disputes. To this extent, the specific demands under this conception were initially in line with the state-centric conception. As so often, in this instance an important historical development was the result of the practical congruence of the demands made by different conceptions. However, the point of reference is different: the understanding of international courts as organs of the community already relates this early arbitral praxis less to the interests of the parties and more to its contribution to securing peace within the community.

In Germany, the Austrian writer and peace activist Bertha von Suttner had a considerable impact with her novel *Die Waffen nieder!* ('Lay Down Your Arms!').[121] She established the Austrian Peace Society and, together with Alfred H Fried, the German Peace Society.[122] Fried shaped the German Pacifist movement in a lasting way, and from 1899 he published the influential journal *Friedens-Warte* ('The Peace Watch'), which established an important connection between the theory and the practice of international law.[123] Crucial impulses for the further development of the international judiciary emerged out of the circle around Fried and the *Friedens-Warte*.[124] Efforts on the national plane led to more international contacts, both on the level of legal scholarship and on that of the peace movements. A group of eminent scholars of international law met in Ghent as early as 1873 to establish the Institut de Droit International. It included, alongside Johann Caspar Bluntschli, a professor of international law from Heidelberg, Pasquale Stanislao Mancini—who, as the first president, also tried to push forward the development of arbitration. In that regard, it was opportune that an

[120] Sohn, 'International Arbitration in Historical Perspective' 12, with reference to Pasquale P Mancini, 'Motion de M Mancini et son acceptation par le parlement italien' (1874) 6 Revue de droit international et de législation comparée 172, 175.

[121] Bertha von Suttner, *Lay Down Your Arms: The Autobiography of Martha von Tilling* (T Holmes tr, 2nd edn, Longmans, Green and Co 1908). Also see Wolfgang Benz (ed), *Pazifismus in Deutschland: Dokumente zur Friedensbewegung 1890–1939* (Fischer Taschenbuch 1988) 7.

[122] Dieter Riesenberger, *Geschichte der Friedensbewegung in Deutschland: Von den Anfängen bis 1933* (Vandenhoeck & Ruprecht 1985) 58.

[123] See Daniel Porsch, 'Die Friedens-Warte zwischen Friedensbewegung und Wissenschaft' (1999) 73 Die Friedens-Warte 39.

[124] On the difficult position of the peace movement under the Weimar Republic and its collapse with the beginnings of National Socialism see Richard Barkeley, *Die deutsche Friedensbewegung 1870–1933* (Hammerich & Lesser 1948).

international tribunal had issued the first significant and widely noted arbitral award in the *Alabama* case.[125]

The International Law Association, likewise founded in 1873, also concerned itself primarily with arbitration, and, at its very first meeting, it passed a resolution to the effect that arbitration was 'the means that is fundamentally just, reasonable, and even obligatory for nations to resolve international differences'.[126] Both institutions followed an ethos that was freighted with civilizational pathos but, in the end, was largely legalistic.[127] Here, it is evident how the peace movement challenged the paradigm of a state-centred global order. According to this movement, the actions that states can engage in are constrained by a universal community of values (using past terminology: precisely in the sense of the 'conscience of the civilized world'). International law and its courts are meant to place limits on states' exercise of power.

Civil society activists had been meeting at international peace conferences almost every year since 1848.[128] The year 1889 also saw the creation of the Inter-Parliamentary Conference, where parliamentarians from various states committed themselves to the goal of peaceful dispute settlement.[129] In 1895, the members passed a draft for the organization of an international court of arbitration, which was used as the basis for discussion at the first Hague Peace Conference in 1899.[130] The development of an international judiciary at the beginning of the twentieth century cannot be understood without the peace movement and its impetus toward a universal order that went far beyond bilateral dispute settlement.[131] Within the peace movement one can even find ideas about overcoming the state-centric order in favour of a world state.

For the advocates of an international judiciary to champion a strong international community the results of the Hague Peace Conferences

125 In the second year of its work, the Institute passed the draft of a procedure for international arbitration. 'Projet de règlement pour la procédure arbitrale internationale' (Session de La Haye 1875) <www.idi-iil.org/idiF/resolutionsF/1875_haye_01_fr.pdf> accessed 1 October 2013. See Martti Koskenniemi, *The Gentle Civilizer of Nations: The Rise and Fall of Modern International Law 1870–1960* (CUP 2002) 39–41.

126 Quoted in Claudia Denfeld, *Hans Wehberg (1885–1962): Die Organisation der Staatengemeinschaft* (Nomos 2008) 115: 'le moyen essentiellement juste, raisonnable, et même obligatoire, pour les nations, de terminer les différends internationaux'.

127 Art 1 Statute of the *Institut de Droit international* specifies as the goal: 'de favoriser le progrès du droit international, en s'efforçant de devenir l'organe de la conscience juridique du monde civilisé'. In more detail Koskenniemi, *The Gentle Civilizer of Nations* 41.

128 Fried, *Handbuch der Friedensbewegung* 234–6; Riesenberger, *Geschichte der Friedensbewegung* 24–36.

129 Siehe Fredrik Sterzel, *The Inter-Parliamentary Union* (PA Norstedt & Söner 1968) 11–28.

130 Fried, *Handbuch der Friedensbewegung* 265; Anand, *International Courts and Contemporary Conflicts* 27.

131 See Lammasch, 'Die Lehre von der Schiedsgerichtsbarkeit' 36.

were disappointing.[132] The verdict of James Brown Scott, an expert on and admirer of the theory of international law that was held by Spanish late Scholasticism, was as apt as it was scathing and gave expression to a widely held belief: 'The Permanent Court is not permanent because it is not composed of permanent judges; it is not accessible because it has to be constituted for each case; it is not a court because it is not composed of judges.'[133]

Still, the Hague Peace Conferences gave the peace movement a boost and an influx of supporters. In the first volume of his opus *Das Werk vom Haag* ('The Work of The Hague'), Walther Schücking offered his interpretation of what had transpired.[134] He preceded it with an epigram from Hegel, which speaks to his view of things: 'Theoretical work achieves more in the world than practical work. Once the realm of ideas is revolutionized, reality cannot hold out.' Hans Wehberg agreed in the second volume, arguing with the classic liberal theory of international relations: given the international (economic) interconnections, it was not in the interest of a state to wage war. Moreover, public opinion was always against it. To keep a state from using the pretext that its rights had been violated as an excuse for war, it was thought imperative to secure the system of substantive international law with a permanent court that settled disputes impartially. Decisions by courts of arbitration were unsuitable for this purpose, since they offered no guidance.[135] In short, for Wehberg the slogan for world peace was: 'More growth of international law through international decisions!'[136] The law-making function of international courts is clearly articulated and justified.

The PCIJ was lauded as an institution that could substantially advance the hopes of humankind.[137] A reflection of the community-oriented understanding can be found, for example, in the Statute of the Court with regard to the sources of law. While Elihu Root, at the Hague Peace Conferences, had pushed for a strong court as the communal organ of the international

[132] See chapter 2 section A I.

[133] Quoted in Anand, *International Courts and Contemporary Conflicts* 33.

[134] Walther Schücking, *The International Union of the Hague Conferences* (Charles G Fenwick tr, Clarendon 1918) I. Schücking's succinct conception of order can be found in his concise 'Die Organisation der Welt' in Wilhelm van Calker (ed), *Staatsrechtliche Abhandlungen: Festgabe für Paul Laband zum 50. Jahrestage der Doktor-Promotion*, vol I (JCB Mohr 1908) 533. See also Frank Bodendiek, *Walther Schückings Konzeption der internationalen Ordnung: Dogmatische Strukturen und ideengeschichtliche Bedeutung* (Duncker & Humblot 2001).

[135] Hans Wehberg, *The Problem of an International Court of Justice* (Charles G Fenwick tr, Clarendon 1918) 8–9.

[136] Wehberg, *The Problem of an International Court of Justice* 11.

[137] See Nicolas Politis, *La justice internationale* (Librairie Hachette 1924) 182: 'l'avènement d'une ère nouvelle dans la civilisation mondiale'. Similarly the remarkable statement by James Brown Scott, 'Editorial Comment' 55.

legal order, the Court had to remain clearly bound to positive international law in his eyes. If gaps became evident in the international legal order, the only choice was to refrain from rendering a decision (*non liquet*).[138] To Baron Descamps of Belgium that was patently unacceptable, and many agreed with him that a case of *non liquet* in most instance was tantamount to a denial of justice. To be sure, Descamps, too, did not speak explicitly about the Court's law-making authority. For him, the issue was simply the application of general legal principles to a concrete case, which could always be resolved judicially.[139] Through adjudication, the Court had the function of developing the law further. Article 38 Section 3 of the PCIJ Statute, according to which general principles constitute a source of law, is seen as an expression of that position.[140] The state-oriented conception may then be the reason why the Court made scant use of this source of law.[141] But its potential is clearly evident in the way in which the ECtHR uses the notion of a 'common European standard' to construct general principles.[142]

Even if the PCIJ administered justice for the most part within the framework of the state-oriented conception, it offered new material for discussion in international law. During the course of nearly two decades, from 1922 to the invasion of the Netherlands in 1940, it decided no fewer than 32 cases, wrote 27 advisory opinions, and issued more than 200 orders.[143] In the process, the Court built up within the defeated states legitimation for the League of Nations' system of peace—no small achievement. Important experts on international law on both sides of the Atlantic projected their hopes onto the young PCIJ and complemented its work with doctrinal, theoretical, and political writings.

Alongside James Brown Scott, Manley O Hudson created a widely noted blueprint for a stronger system of international peace built around a strong judiciary. The recommendations in his programmatic essay 'The Permanent Court of International Justice—An Indispensable First Step' (1923)[144] were conceptually spelled out and theoretically underpinned in his monograph *Progress in International Organization* (1932). Hudson argued that

[138] '[The] Court must not have the power to legislate', quoted in Allain Pellet in Zimmermann and others (eds), *The Statute of the ICJ* Article 38 para 27.

[139] Pellet, Article 38 paras 28–9.

[140] Pellet, Article 38 para 29; on the difficulties of that legal source see Martti Koskenniemi, 'General Principles: Reflexions on Constructivist Thinking in International Law' in Martti Koskenniemi (ed), *Sources of International Law* (Ashgate 2000) 359.

[141] Pellet, Article 38 para 253; Koskenniemi, 'General Principles' 367.

[142] On this see chapter 2 section B 3 a.

[143] Anand, *International Courts and Contemporary Conflicts* 63.

[144] Manley O Hudson, 'The Permanent Court of International Justice—An Indispensable First Step' (1923) 108 Annals of the American Academy of Political and Social Science 188.

no legal system could depend solely on legislation by political organs for its development. Within international law, international courts had to contribute to legal developments through their steady application of the law.[145]

The community-oriented understanding was shaped especially by Hersch Lauterpacht. In 1934, Lauterpacht could already look back upon a remarkable stock of case-law to highlight the legislative side of judicial praxis. Judicial law-making was a necessary characteristic of every legally constituted society, and also on an international level.[146] There are two prominent currents that run through his view on international law. First, he saw as *the* central problem of world order that states, as the interpreters and appliers of the law, are judges on their own matters.[147] Second, he was decidedly opposed to value relativism.[148] Morality stood behind the positive system of law and made it possible to fill in gaps and guide the law in the direction of an enlightened individualism. In this perspective, international law formed a system in which every dispute was amenable to a persuasive resolution.[149] Both currents meet up in the central place that Lauterpacht attributes to the international judiciary. As a centralized authority of interpretation, it was supposed to develop the law further in light of morality. To him, it was not a major problem that an international legislative body did not exist:[150] the judge becomes the enlightened ruler.[151] This thinking was not limited to the legal culture of common law.[152] Nicolas Politis saw the necessity of the development of an independent corpus of law by the Court in service to international justice in much the same way.[153]

While a number of international jurists did see an international judiciary as an organ of the international community, they did not necessarily see it as an element in a development toward political and administrative

[145] Manley O Hudson, *Progress in International Organization* (Fred B Rothman & Co 1981) 80.

[146] Hersch Lauterpacht, *The Development of International Law by the Permanent Court of International Justice* (Longmans, Green and Co 1934) 45–68; see also his *The Development of International Law by the International Court* (Stevens & Sons 1958).

[147] Lauterpacht, *The Development of International Law by the International Court* 52–60; Hersch Lauterpacht, 'De l'interprétation des traités: Rapport et projet de résolutions' (1950) 43 Annuaire de l'institut de droit international, vol 1, 366; Koskenniemi, *The Gentle Civilizer of Nations* 405.

[148] Hersch Lauterpacht, 'Kelsen's Pure Science of Law' in Elihu Lauterpacht (ed), *International Law: Being the Collected Papers of Hersch Lauterpacht*, vol 2.1 (CUP 1975) 404, 428.

[149] Lauterpacht, *The Function of Law in the International Community* 60–9.

[150] Lauterpacht, *The Function of Law in the International Community* 254–5.

[151] See Koskenniemi, *The Gentle Civilizer of Nations* 404: 'In fact, Lauterpacht's utopia is a world ruled by lawyers.'

[152] See Wehberg, *The Problem of an International Court of Justice* 11.

[153] Politis, *La justice internationale* 178–84. See further Ole Spiermann, *International Legal Argument in the Permanent Court of International Justice: The Rise of the International Judiciary* (CUP 2005) 394; Steinberger, 'The International Court of Justice' 214.

institutions beyond the state, let alone in the light of a universal federation or some other form of a world government. By contrast, others certainly interpreted the development of an international judiciary as the first step toward a stronger supra-state order, which would eventually also encompass a legislative body.[154] The latter notion was especially widespread in Germany, where the peace movement and international scholarship liked to invoke Immanuel Kant.[155] In a variety of writings, but especially in his famous treatise 'Perpetual Peace', Kant had affirmed the force of law in international relations. He argued that it was a commandment of reason that states, by analogy to individuals, freed themselves from the state of nature by entering into a contract and submitting to a universally valid legal order.[156] International law, Kant wrote, should be grounded in the federation of independent states,[157] though he appropriately left it open how such a federation should be institutionalized. Precisely for that reason, his treatise on peace allowed many to use it as authority.[158]

A short time later, Hans Kelsen further developed Kant's peace project with his unique incisiveness and powers of construction. To him there was no alternative to the securing of peace through international law with a comprehensive, compulsory jurisdiction.[159] According to Kelsen, the evolution of the law takes place in a continuous process of the centralization of legal authority and the institutional differentiation of law-making (legislation) and law application. He purports that the application of the law is centralized first. The judiciary precedes the legislature.[160] For a lasting international peace, states would have to subordinate themselves to a permanent international court.[161] Kelsen espoused this argument in the view of World

[154] See only Hudson, *Progress in International Organization* 72–88.

[155] On the peace movement, without reference to Kant but entirely in his style, see Fried, *Handbuch der Friedensbewegung* 20–3. However, Lammasch calls reference to Kant's project 'mere decoration'; Lammasch, 'Die Lehre von der Schiedsgerichtsbarkeit' 37.

[156] Immanuel Kant, *Perpetual Peace: A Philosophical Proposal* (Jessie H Buckland tr, first published 1795/1796, Sweet & Maxwell 1927) 24, 29.

[157] Kant, *Perpetual Peace* 29–31.

[158] Bodendiek, *Walther Schückings Konzeption der internationalen Ordnung* 117, 179–82 with further references. See also the symposium 'The European Tradition in International Law: Walther Schücking' (2011) 22 Eur J Intl L 723; especially Frank Bodendiek, 'Walther Schücking and the Idea of "International Organization"' 22 Eur J Intl L 741, 751–4; Mónica García-Salmones, 'Walther Schücking and the Pacifist Tradition of International Law' 22 Eur J Intl L 755, 778–9; Jost Delbrück, 'Law's Frontier—Walther Schücking and the Quest for the Lex Ferenda' 22 Eur J Intl L 801, 802–6.

[159] Jochen Bernstorff, *The Public International Law Theory of Hans Kelsen: Believing in Universal Law* (Thomas Dunlap tr, CUP 2010) 191; Danilo Zolo, 'Hans Kelsen: International Peace through International Law' (1998) 9 Eur J Intl L 306.

[160] Hans Kelsen, *Law and Peace in International Relations: The Oliver Wendell Holmes Lectures, 1940–41* (Harvard UP 1942) 145–8.

[161] Kelsen, *Law and Peace* 150.

War II, looking back at the shameful fall of the League of Nations and looking ahead at the shaping of the post-war world. The crucial mistake in the construction of the League of Nations, he argued, had been setting up the Council and not the PCIJ as the central organ. In the Council every decision had to be unanimous, which meant that no member could be bound against its will. By contrast, international courts make their decisions by majority votes. Kelsen focused especially on this element. Thus, the road to a system of international peace could lead only through a comprehensive, obligatory judiciary.[162]

The conception of international courts as organs of the international community, as advocated by activists of the peace movement and by prominent scholars, overcomes the mono-functional understanding of the courts as mere instruments of dispute settlement. The contending parties are joined by the international community as the normative point of reference. In what follows, we will show the traces of this understanding in the praxis of the ICJ. The development of both basic conceptions allows one to grasp the tensions and fluctuations in the Court, while at the same time making clear what is gained by a multifunctional analysis of international courts.

2. The daring ICJ

We noted earlier that institutions and their decisions could well be shaped by more than one basic conception. This is the case for the ICJ, whose decisions are not bound only to the state-oriented conception.[163] Its predecessor, the Permanent Court of International Justice, occasionally saw itself explicitly if not as an institution of an international community, certainly as an organ of the international legal system.[164] In its first judgment on the *Corfu Channel* case, already cited as evidence for the first basic conception, the ICJ saw its task precisely as that of securing respect for international law. To that end, it stated that the British navy had violated Albania's sovereignty.[165] If, following the first basic conception, it had focused solely on the successful dispute settlement in a state-centric world order, such appreciation would not have been meaningful. As early as the first few years after its establishment, one can find further statements that can be fully understood

[162] Hans Kelsen, 'International Peace—By Court or Government?' (1941) 46 American J of Sociology 571.

[163] Paulus, *Die internationale Gemeinschaft* 305–6.

[164] For example in his prominent dictum: 'From the standpoint of International Law and of the Court which is its organ, municipal laws are merely facts.' *Case Concerning Certain German Interests in Polish Upper Silesia (Germany v Poland)* (Judgment) PCIJ Rep Series A No 7, 19.

[165] 'To ensure respect for international law, of which it is the organ, the Court must declare that the action of the British Navy constituted a violation of Albanian sovereignty.' *Corfu Channel* 35.

only in the complementary light of the community-oriented conception.[166] For instance, in the advisory opinion on *Reservations to the Convention on the Prevention and Punishment of the Crime against Genocide* the ICJ assessed the possibility of reservations when signing a treaty not according to established international law, which would have demanded the consent of *all* signatories, but according to a more flexible standard.[167] It also emphasized that the Convention served universal values. Still, the Court could not bring itself to truly follow this basic understanding. As already discussed, it found, quite in contrast to the later decisions by the ECtHR, that reservations incompatible with the Convention could not establish a binding obligation.[168]

The second conception is even more clearly visible in a decision against the United Kingdom concerning Norway's baseline for the fisheries zone.[169] The Court made its decision on a fairly sparse legal basis using general principles. In the eyes of Hersch Lauterpacht, that is precisely why it was one of the most important decisions.[170] These cases of the early years show a remarkable independent positioning by the Court.[171] The next important piece of evidence for the community-oriented conception did not occur until 1970, when the ICJ created the concept of obligations toward the 'international community as a whole'.[172] This can be understood against the backdrop of the deep crisis in which the Court had found itself in the 1960s. The reasons behind this crisis lay mostly outside of the Court's areas of influence. It goes without saying that the climate during the bloc confrontation at the height of the Cold War was not favourable for an international judiciary. Only a few states recognized its jurisdiction according to Article 36 Section 2 of the ICJ Statute, and some even revoked their recognition.[173]

But the crisis was also self-caused, especially because of the Court's controversial decisions in cases involving South Africa. It had initially affirmed

[166] Shabtai Rosenne, *The Law and Practice of the International Court 1920–2005*, vol 1 (4th edn, Nijhoff 2006) 19; see Steinberger, 'The International Court of Justice' 213–4.

[167] *Reservations to the Convention of Genocide* 21–2.

[168] *Reservations to the Convention of Genocide* 23–7. See also the contrary later practice of the ECtHR, *Loizidou v Turkey* (1995) Series A No 310, paras 65–89.

[169] *Fisheries (UK v Norway)* (Judgment) [1951] ICJ Rep 116.

[170] Hersch Lauterpacht, 'Freedom of the Seas. Implications of the Norwegian Fisheries Case' *The Times* (London, 8 January 1952): 'daring piece of judicial legislation'; quoted in Rosenne, *The Law and Practice* 20.

[171] Georges Abi-Saab, 'Cours général de droit international public' (1987) 207 Recueil des cours 9, 258–61.

[172] *Barcelona Traction, Light and Power Company Limited (Belgium v Spain) (New Application: 1962) Second Phase* (Judgment) [1970] ICJ Rep 3, para 33.

[173] See Claud HM Waldock, 'Decline of the Optional Clause' (1955–1956) 32 British YB Intl L 244; Leo Gross, 'International Court of Justice: Consideration of Requirements for Enhancing Its Role in the International Legal Order' (1971) 65 AJIL 253, 262–3.

its jurisdiction on the question of whether South Africa had violated its authority as a mandate power by introducing the apartheid regime in South West Africa, but shortly thereafter it answered in the negative.[174] Ethiopia and Liberia, as former members of the League of Nations—to the time of which the mandate obligations dated—had brought the suit against South Africa, but the Court of Justice declared that international law knew no right by one member of the community 'to take legal action in vindication of a public interest'.[175] Representatives of African states perceived in the Court's decision the strong influence of the west in seeking to protect a racist regime. Many young states felt confirmed in their reservations about the institution.[176]

In this situation, the UN Secretary-General, at the behest of the General Assembly, asked all members about their assessment of the ICJ.[177] The result was sobering. The comment by the delegate from Ghana was characteristic: the Court would be in a better position 'if international law were more progressive and did not reflect outmoded conservative thought reminiscent of imperialism'.[178] To put it pointedly, many believed that the Court was too much under the guidance of the great powers and too closely associated with European-shaped international law.[179] Under these circumstances, the community-oriented conception seemed to important voices to be a way out of the crisis. As early as 1964, C Wilfried Jenks had asserted in his *The Prospects of International Adjudication*:

> The development of the principal judicial organ of the United Nations into the supreme court of mankind represents a vision for the future rather than a programme of immediately practicable action, but 'where there is no vision the people perish'; all which we cherish most in our existing heritage of law and freedom is due to the visionaries of long ago.[180]

No doubt inspired by such reflections, the Court created the legal institution of the obligations of states toward 'the international community as a

[174] *South West Africa Cases (Ethiopia v South Africa; Liberia v South Africa)* (Preliminary Objections) [1962] ICJ Rep 319; *South West Africa Cases (Ethiopia v South Africa; Liberia v South Africa) Second Phase* (Judgment) [1966] ICJ Rep 6; see Abi-Saab, 'Cours général de droit international public' 253–8.

[175] *South West Africa Cases: Second Phase*, para 88. See Simma, 'From Bilateralism to Community Interest' 295 ('This is traditional bilateralism at its clearest!').

[176] Edward McWhinney, 'Judicial Settlement of Disputes: Jurisdiction and Justiciability' (1990) 221 Recueil des cours 9, 37–40; *South West Africa Cases: Second Phase*, para 49. See the apt criticism in *South West Africa Cases: Second Phase*, Diss Op Jessup, 325.

[177] Steinberger, 'The International Court of Justice' 225–35.

[178] Quoted in Steinberger, 'The International Court of Justice' 226–7.

[179] On the ICJ as guardian of the *ancien régime* Armin von Bogdandy, 'Constitutionalism in International Law: Comment on a Proposal from Germany' (2006) 47 Harvard Intl L J 223, 226.

[180] C Wilfried Jenks, *The Prospects of International Adjudication* (Stevens & Sons 1964) 777.

whole'.[181] Such *erga omnes* obligations included, in addition to the prohibition against violence, respect for fundamental human rights and the prohibition against genocide.[182] In the later *Namibia* advisory opinion, the Court then argued that 'interpretation cannot remain unaffected by the subsequent development of law [. . .]. Moreover, an international instrument has to be interpreted and applied within the framework of the entire legal system prevailing at the time of the interpretation'.[183] The ICJ was cautiously accepting a more dynamic understanding of the law. Increasingly, one finds traces of the idea of a communal legal order in its reasoning.[184]

Hermann Mosler picked up these traces in his lectures at the Hague Academy and presented international law as the legal order of a community in which all subjects were simultaneously members. Accordingly, international law is not merely a network of bilateral relationships between independent states. In his view, mechanisms of dispute settlement are the decisive factors in whether or not international society represents a community under the rule of law.[185] A legal process 'depoliticizes' a dispute and subjects it to an orderly procedure, in which independent judges decide according to objective criteria.[186] In this process, courts are clearly in service to peace, but precisely this requires that they develop the law further in their adjudication and strengthen legal normativity.[187] Against the background of the crisis in the 1960s, Mosler, with new tailwind, fashioned the praxis of the Court according to the community-oriented understanding.

The community-oriented conception appears most often when the issue at stake revolves around the jurisdiction of the Court.[188] Remarkable was especially the decision about the permissibility of Nicaragua's complaint against the United States in the *Case Concerning Military and Paramilitary Activities in and against Nicaragua*.[189] On 9 April 1984, Nicaragua requested that the ICJ open legal proceedings. However, the United States had got wind of Nicaragua's plan and, shortly before Nicaragua filed its complaints,

[181] *Barcelona Traction*, para 33.

[182] *Barcelona Traction*, para 34.

[183] *Legal Consequences for States of the Continued Presence of South Africa in Namibia (South West Africa) notwithstanding Security Council Resolution 276 (1970)* (Advisory Opinion) [1971] ICJ Rep 16, para 53. See also *Aegean Sea Continental Shelf (Greece v Turkey)* (Judgment) [1978] ICJ Rep 3, paras 75–80.

[184] See also the tension within the judgment *Gabčíkovo-Nagymaros*, para 112.

[185] Mosler, 'The International Society as a Legal Community' 11–2.

[186] Mosler, 'The International Society as a Legal Community' 300.

[187] Mosler, 'The International Society as a Legal Community' 305–6.

[188] Art 36(6) ICJ Statute. See for example *Right of Passage over Indian Territory (Portugal v India)* (Preliminary Objections) [1957] ICJ Rep 125.

[189] Abi-Saab sees the *Nicaragua* case as a turning point to a new era. Abi-Saab, 'Cours général de droit international public' 272–4.

Washington submitted a declaration that henceforth all disputes with Central American states should be excluded. This new declaration did not prevent the Court from affirming its jurisdiction. The USA remained obliged to recognize the Court's jurisdiction on the basis of the 1949 declaration because the principle of good faith does not allow such ad hoc change.[190] Also with a view toward Nicaragua, the Court found that that country's will to submit itself to the ICJ's jurisdiction was sufficiently grounded, even though the instrument of ratification for Nicaragua's unilateral declaration of 1929 had never been received by the UN Secretary-General of the League of Nations.[191] Neither this somewhat shaky circumstance nor the revocation of the declaration of submission by the United States dissuaded the Court from affirming its jurisdiction.[192] Moreover, the ICJ declared, the fact that the case had political implications or raised important questions of security policy did not shake its jurisdiction.[193] This dispute was undoubtedly 'highly political in nature', but that did not in any way alter the need to answer legal questions.[194] In answering these questions, the Court supported the customary law validity of the prohibition of the use of force in a broad interpretation and gave the right of self-defence a narrow interpretation.[195] The decision crucially shaped the practical and jurisprudential discourse on this issue. The Court generated and stabilized international normativity and subjected the exercise of state power to judicial review.

In the *Oil Platforms* case the Court then advanced—in downright spectacular fashion—the prohibition of the use of force, even though it had to conclude, in the end, that it had no jurisdiction. But it would not miss the opportunity to contribute to the development of international law and to consolidate its *Nicaragua* case-law.[196] The *Oil Platforms* reasoning and its

[190] *Military and Paramilitary Activities in and against Nicaragua (Nicaragua v USA)* (Jurisdiction of the Court and Admissibility of the Application) [1984] ICJ Rep 392, para 59; with reference to *Nuclear Tests Case (New Zealand v France)* (Judgment) [1974] ICJ Rep 457, para 46; *Nuclear Tests Case (Australia v France)* (Judgment) [1974] ICJ Rep 253, para 43.

[191] *Nicaragua*, paras 36–9.

[192] In more detail as to the circumstances and consequences of the decision Lori F Damrosch, 'The Impact of the *Nicaragua* Case on the Court and Its Role: Harmful, Helpful, or In Between?' (2012) 25 Leiden J Intl L 135.

[193] *Nicaragua*, para 96 '[...] the Court has never shied away from a case brought before it merely because it had political implications or because it involved serious elements of the use of force.' This was apparent not least from the ICJ's judgment *Corfu Channel*.

[194] *Nicaragua*, para 98. See *United States Diplomatic and Consular Staff in Tehran (USA v Iran)* (Judgment) [1980] ICJ Rep 3, paras 35–8.

[195] *Case Concerning Military and Paramilitary Activities in and against Nicaragua (Nicaragua v USA)* (Merits) [1986] ICJ Rep 14, paras 187–201. See Cristina Hoss, Santiago Villalpando, and Sandesh Sivakumaran, '*Nicaragua*: 25 Years Later' (2012) 25 Leiden J Intl L 131, 132–3; Marcelo Cohen, 'The Principle of Non-Intervention 25 Years after the *Nicaragua* Judgement' (2012) 25 Leiden J Intl L 157.

[196] *Oil Platforms (Iran v USA)* (Judgment) [2003] ICJ Rep 161, paras 43–78.

individual opinions clearly reveal divergent conceptions of the international order and the role of the Court. While some considered it necessary for the ICJ, as a community organ, to contribute to generating and stabilizing normative expectations and securing fundamental community interests,[197] others emphasized that the lack of consensus among the contending parties simply did not allow for this.[198]

Further evidence for the community-focused understanding is nested in the Court's advisory opinions.[199] For example, a clear contribution to the development of substantive law came from the *Wall* opinion, in which the Court expressed itself on the right of self-determination and the relationship between the law of occupation and human rights.[200] It affirmed the doctrine of the *erga omnes* obligations from the *Barcelona Traction* case, repeated—with reference to *East Timor*—that the right to self-determination was effective toward all members of the international community, and reasserted—invoking its *Nuclear Weapons* opinion—that there were many rules of the laws of war that are so fundamental for the protection of human beings that they had to be seen as *elementary considerations of humanity.*[201] With a view toward such fundamental components of the communal order, every state has the duty not to recognize and not to support situations resulting from a violation of the fundamental rules. Instead, any state is obliged to counteract them, whereby the Court left the question open as to whether this might be done also by countermeasures that were otherwise illegal.[202] The advisory opinion shows, in its close interlinkage with earlier decisions, with scholarly debate, and with the work of the International Law Commission on State Responsibility, how the Court can contribute to the development of international law in the light of fundamental principles. But it by no means always does so, and that is the point. Rather, it wavers, and this wavering can be interpreted, from a hermeneutic perspective, as a wavering between the two basic conceptions.

Similar to the *Oil Platforms* case, the divergent basic conceptions are on clear display in the *Arrest Warrant* case. Does a Belgian arrest warrant that seeks to hold the Congolese foreign minister responsible for alleged international crimes violate his immunity? Belgium argued that the immunity grounded in customary international law did not extend to prosecutions of

[197] *Oil Platforms (Iran v USA)* (Judgment) Sep Op Simma, para 5.

[198] *Oil Platforms (Iran v USA)* (Preliminary Objection) [1996] ICJ Rep 803, Diss Op Schwebel, 874; *Oil Platforms* (Judgment) Sep Op Buergenthal, paras 20–32, and Sep Op Owada, paras 12–3.

[199] But not consistently, as the *Kosovo* advisory opinion discussed above shows.

[200] *Legal Consequences of the Construction of a Wall in the Occupied Palestinian Territory* (Advisory Opinion) [2004] ICJ Rep 136, paras 86–160.

[201] All of that in three paragraphs: *Wall*, paras 155–7.

[202] *Wall*, para 159.

war crimes and crimes against humanity. While the decision stated apodictically that customary international law knew of no exception to the protection of immunity when it comes to international crimes, it did question the doctrine of universal jurisdiction.[203] The Court's decision is both minimalist and open. The separate and dissenting opinions then show how strongly the judges' understandings about the international system and the role of the Court diverge.[204] While Judges Higgins, Kooijmans, and Buergenthal pointed to the interests of the international community and noted that there certainly was a trend toward affirming a universal jurisdiction for international crimes, Judge Guillaume emphatically rejected the argument that national organs should become agents of an 'ill-defined "international community"'.[205] The judgment attempts to find a mediating position between fundamentally diverging notions of the international system and an international judiciary.

Advocates of a strong international judiciary can point to quite a bit in the praxis of the Court that concurs with this understanding. As early as 1990, Edward McWhinney recognized a new 'community policy-making [and] legislative role that the Court majority increasingly sees for itself'.[206] Bardo Fassbender stated that Article 9 of the Statute of the ICJ, according to which the judges should assure a 'representation of the main forms of civilization and of the principal legal systems of the world', was carried by the idea of a 'representation of the existing international community'.[207] ICJ Judge Antônio Augusto Cançado Trindade, in his *General Course* at the Hague Academy of International Law, looked upon the ICJ as the guarantor of elementary values and an organ for the progressive development of the law in the interest of humanity.[208] The universalist paradigm is well alive within the ICJ. It appears in the notions of obligations *erga omnes* and of the *ius cogens*, and—if not in the majority—in emphatic form in separating and dissenting opinions.[209]

[203] *Arrest Warrant*, para 58.

[204] Thus also Matthias Goldmann, 'Arrest Warrant Case (Democratic Republic of the Congo v Belgium)' in Wolfrum (ed), *Max Planck Encylopedia of Public International Law*, paras 23–4.

[205] *Arrest Warrant*, Joint Sep Op Higgins, Kooijimans, and Buergenthal, paras 51, 75, and Sep Op Guillaume, para 15.

[206] McWhinney, 'Judicial Settlement of Disputes' 191.

[207] Fassbender in Zimmermann and others (eds), *The Statute of the International Court of Justice* Article 9 para 52.

[208] Cançado Trindade, 'International Law for Humankind (II)' 21–3.

[209] *Gabčíkovo-Nagymaros*, Sep Op Weeramantry, 117–8; *Jurisdictional Immunities of the State (Germany v Italy)* (Judgment) [2012] ICJ Rep 99, Diss Op Cançado Trindade, paras 117–316.

3. The European Court of Human Rights

Whereas the conception of courts as organs of an international community appears only sparsely in judgments of the ICJ, it leads the practice of the ECtHR.[210] The ECtHR is part of the reorganization of the European system undertaken after World War II. It is based on the aim of preventing human rights violations and ensuring democratic politics.[211] At the Hague Europe Congress in 1948, civil society activists raised the demand for a European court that was supranational, that is endowed with strong powers. The second basic conception was strongly present from the very outset. According to Winston Churchill, the president of the Congress, such a court would render the 'judgment of the civilized world'.[212]

The further development can be vividly depicted with the help of the first two basic conceptions. Irrespective of the early importance of the community-oriented conception, initially the state-oriented basic conception was dominant. Within the framework of the Council of Europe set up in 1949, discussions over a court of human rights continued, but the governments resisted a strong judiciary that provided individuals with the possibility of filing a complaint. Instead, with the European Convention on Human Rights they created a mechanism that granted governments considerable influence. Many saw the Convention in the important, but tightly circumscribed, role of alerting the Convention states in cases of serious human rights violations. A court, so the expectation went, would not play a major role.[213]

States could initiate proceedings against other Convention states before the European Commission for Human Rights, which was established in 1954 with its seat in Strasbourg.[214] Natural persons, provided the Convention states had issued a declaration to that effect, could approach the Commission with a petition if they felt violated in their Convention rights and had exhausted domestic remedies.[215] It was then incumbent upon the

210 The term *international community* can be understood as a global phenomenon, *the* international community, but also as a more regional phenomenon, as in the case of the European and Interamerican Courts of Human Rights.

211 Ed Bates, *The Evolution of the European Convention on Human Rights: From Its Inception to the Creation of a Permanent Court of Human Rights* (OUP 2010) 45–9. See also Andrew Moravcsik, 'The Origins of Human Rights Regimes: Democratic Delegation in Postwar Europe' (2000) 54 Intl Organization 217, 220–43.

212 In A Robertson (ed), *Collected Edition of the 'Travaux Préparatoires' of the European Convention on Human Rights*, vol 1 (Nijhoff 1975) 34. Similarly Pierre-Henry Teitgen, 'Presentation of the Report of the Committee on Legal and Administrative Questions' in Robertson, *Collected Edition* 264, 292.

213 Bates, *The Evolution of the ECHR* 8–10.

214 Art 24 Convention for the Protection of Human Rights and Fundamental Freedoms (ECHR) in its original version, 213 UNTS 221, in force since 3 September 1953.

215 Arts 25–27 ECHR original version.

Commission to determine the facts in an adversarial process, to launch an investigation if necessary, and to bring the dispute to an amicable resolution while respecting the Convention rights.[216] If that could not be achieved, the Commission, on the basis of Article 31 of the European Convention on Human Rights in its original version, wrote a report about the facts of the case along with an assessment of the legal situation, which it presented to the Committee of Ministers and the states involved.[217] The Commission could also launch proceedings before the Court, to the extent that the states involved had recognized its jurisdiction. Only the Commission and the states could appear as parties before the Court, not the complainant herself. In addition, if the Court's jurisdiction was recognized, interstate proceedings could also be initiated.[218] Then, as today, the Committee of Ministers watched over the implementation of the Court's decisions.[219]

Access to the Court led through the eye of the needle that was the Commission.[220] Many Convention states, including Germany, initially submitted to the European Court of Human Rights for only a limited time. The jurisdiction was so weak that the Belgian judge Henri Rolin asked, in a 1965 essay that drew broad interest: 'Has the European Court of Human Rights a Future?'[221] Like many, Rolin was sceptical, precisely because the ECtHR was embedded in a system that showed strong traces of a state-oriented understanding of the international system. However, that was to change fundamentally.[222]

Under Rolin's presidency, the Court decided that a state had violated the Convention for the first time in 1968.[223] In the seminal *Belgian Languages* case,[224] a slim majority of the Court ruled against Belgium that one aspect of the highly political Belgian language regime constituted impermissible unequal treatment (violation of Article 14 ECHR in conjunction with Article 2 First Protocol). Already in the judgment on preliminary objections, Belgium had failed in its argument that the language laws were outside of the

[216] Art 28 ECHR original version.

[217] Art 31(2) ECHR original version.

[218] Art 48 ECHR original version.

[219] Art 54 ECHR original version.

[220] See Mikael Rask Madsen, '"Legal Diplomacy"—Law, Policy and the Genesis of Postwar European Human Rights' in Stefan-Ludwig Hoffmann and Daniel Moyn (eds), *Human Rights in the Twentieth Century* (CUP 2011) 62.

[221] Henri Rolin, 'Has the European Court of Human Rights a Future?' (1965) 11 Harvard L J 442.

[222] On this transformation Mikael Rask Madsen, 'The Protracted Institutionalization of the Strasbourg Court: From Legal Diplomacy to Integrationist Jurisprudence' in Jonas Christoffersen and Mikael Rask Madsen (eds), *The European Court of Human Rights between Law and Politics* (OUP 2011) 43.

[223] *Neumeister v Austria* (1968) Series A No 8.

[224] *Case 'Relating to Certain Aspects of the Laws on the Use of Languages in Education in Belgium'* (1968) Series A No 6.

Convention's field of application, since it was highly political and part of its *domaine réservé*.[225] The Court unanimously rejected this position: as soon as a case concerned the application of the Convention, the Court's jurisdiction was established. There was no *domaine réservé*.[226] In a truly forward-looking manner, the Court further emphasized that the rights of the Convention had to be interpreted in such a way as to allow them to develop their full effect.[227] On the whole, the Court positioned itself as an organ of a community with considerable autonomy toward the Convention states.[228]

In the face of this development, the United Kingdom, which was especially committed to the state-oriented understanding, contemplated withdrawing from the Court's jurisdiction, especially since it had lost a number of cases. Apparently, the UK authorities had misjudged the Court's potential.[229] The case *Golder v United Kingdom* revolved around the rights of prisoners. Golder intended to bring a civil case against a guard for libel, and to that end he wanted to seek the advice of a lawyer. His request was turned down, and Golder appealed to the European Commission of Human Rights. Following the logic of the *Lotus* principle, the United Kingdom argued that the Convention should be narrowly interpreted as a treaty between states that limited the free exercise of their sovereignty.[230] The Court, however, found that the right to a fair trial (Article 6 ECHR) entailed the right of access to the Court. Moreover, the refusal constituted an unjustified interference in Golder's right to correspondence (Article 8 ECHR). The reasoning is especially revealing in its remarks on the method of interpretation. The ECtHR's interpretation of the Convention was guided by the preamble and the principle of the rule of law. The Convention, so the Court maintained, had to be interpreted by taking into consideration its goal and purpose, so that in concrete situations of conflict real utility could be derived from the codified rights. Moreover, the interpretation needs to take all relevant rules of international law applicable between the parties into consideration, which, according to Article 38 Section 1 lit c of the ICJ Statute, encompassed general legal principles. The ability to bring a civil case before

[225] *Case 'Relating to Certain Aspects of the Laws on the Use of Languages in Education in Belgium'* (1967) Series A No 5.

[226] *Use of Languages in Education in Belgium* (1967).

[227] *Use of Languages in Education in Belgium* (1968) 28.

[228] Bates, *The Evolution of the ECHR* 225–38; WP Gormley, 'The Development of International Law through Cases from the European Court of Human Rights: Linguistics and Detention Disputes' (1967–1968) 2 Ottawa L Rev 382, 393–405.

[229] On the original expectations see Anthony Lester, 'UK Acceptance of the Strasbourg Jurisdiction: What Really Went On in Whitehall in 1965' (1998) PL 237.

[230] *Golder v UK* (1973) Series B No 16, para 15: 'Limitations of this kind on the free exercise of sovereignty are not to be presumed.'

a judge was such a recognized legal principle, as was the prohibition against the denial of justice. According to the Court, Article 6 of the ECHR must be read in this light.[231]

A short time later, in *Tyrer v United Kingdom*, the Court came up with the path-breaking formulation that the Convention was a *living* instrument and had to be interpreted in the light of the present day.[232] This argument further strengthened its autonomy against the Convention states. The case involved a birching that was inflicted on Tyrer, a 15-year-old pupil on the Isle of Man. The Court judged this to be degrading punishment in violation of Article 3 of the ECHR.

In *Sunday Times v United Kingdom*, the ECtHR found that the temporary order by a British court restricting the publication of a report about a drug scandal constituted impermissible interference in the freedom of opinion and of the press according to Article 10 of the ECHR. A central theme was the intensity of judicial review. Against the United Kingdom, which demanded a scope of discretion,[233] the Court found that the possibility of limiting rights generally had to be narrowly construed.[234] With the review of proportionality, the Court strengthened its position further and subjected the state's exercise of public authority to increasingly tight control, even if this was kept flexible by the doctrine of the *margin of appreciation*.[235]

Notwithstanding this increasingly self-confident dispensing of justice as a community organ, more and more Convention states accepted the Court's jurisdiction. At that time, as Jochen Abr. Frowein put it aptly, a sleeping beauty was awakening.[236] In the end, even the United Kingdom has not withdrawn from it—so far.[237]

[231] *Golder v UK* (1975) Series A No 18, paras 26–36.

[232] *Tyrer v UK* (1978) Series A No 26, para 31; on this see Rudolf Bernhardt, 'Evolutive Treaty Interpretation, Especially of the European Convention on Human Rights' (1999) 42 German YB Intl L 11, 17–20.

[233] *Sunday Times v UK (No 1)* (1977) Series B No 28 (1982) paras 153–9.

[234] *Sunday Times v UK (No 1)* (1979) Series A No 30, paras 62–7.

[235] Some observers believe that the Court uses it especially to protect powerful states. On this see Yuval Shany, 'Toward a General Margin of Appreciation Doctrine in International Law?' (2006) 17 Eur J Intl L 907, 912. Eyal Benvenisti, 'Margin of Appreciation, Consensus, and Universal Standards' (1999) 31 NYU J Intl L and Politics 843, 845–6.

[236] Jochen Abr Frowein, 'European Integration through Fundamental Rights' (1984–1985) 18 U Michigan J L Reform 5, 8.

[237] On the most recent plans within the current governing majority in Britain see Alice Donald, Jane Gordon, and Philip Leach, *The UK and the European Court of Human Rights: Equality and Human Rights Commission Research Report 83* (Equality and Human Rights Commission Report Series Spring 2012) 174–7 <www.equalityhumanrights.com/uploaded_files/research/83._european_court_of_human_rights.pdf> accessed 10 October 2012.

It was important to the strengthening of the community-oriented conception that a number of states assigned the rights of the Convention the function of basic legal rights within their domestic legal order—as did France, the Netherlands, Austria, Switzerland, and the United Kingdom.[238] After the fall of the Berlin Wall, many of the states in transition also assigned the ECHR and its Court an important role in the domestic protection of basic rights.[239] Against this legitimizing background, the Court took courageous steps in the light of the community-oriented conception. The judgment in *Loizidou v Turkey*, which concerned the rights of a Cypriote woman to the property she had left behind when she fled her home in response to Turkey's occupation of northern Cyprus, was path-breaking. The Court recognized a violation of the right of ownership according to Article 1 of the First Protocol and stated that Turkey should pay damages.[240] There are two statements about its decision on jurisdiction which are especially pioneering: the Court decided that Turkey's Convention obligations also extended beyond its national borders to territories over which it exercised effective control[241] and that substantive or territorial limitations, as Turkey had formulated in its reservation, were not permissible, since they would seriously weaken the functioning of the Commission and the Court and impair the effectiveness of 'the Convention as a constitutional instrument of European public order (ordre public)'.[242] Yet the impermissibility of the reservations did not mean that the treaty did not apply to Turkey. Instead, in a bold step, the Court declared that Turkey was fully bound to the Convention. In this way, it positioned itself decidedly as a community organ and made significant contributions to the substantive development of the law, much different from the ICJ's actions on a comparable question in the advisory opinion on the Genocide Convention.[243]

[238] Christoph Grabenwarter and Katharina Pabel, *Europäische Menschenrechtskonvention: Ein Studienbuch* (5th edn, CH Beck 2012) 15–8; detailed contributions in Hellen Keller and Alec Stone Sweet (eds), *A Europe of Rights: The Impact of the ECHR on National Legal Systems* (OUP 2008).

[239] A detailed discussion can be found in Mahulena Hofmann, *Von der Transformation zur Kooperationsoffenheit? Die Öffnung der Rechtsordnungen ausgewählter Staaten Mittel- und Osteuropas für das Völker- und Europarecht* (Springer 2009).

[240] *Loizidou v Turkey* ECHR 1996-VI; *Loizidou v Turkey* (Article 50) ECHR 1998-IV.

[241] *Loizidou v Turkey* (1995) para 62.

[242] *Loizidou v Turkey* (1995) para 75; see earlier *Belilos v Switzerland* (1988) Series A No 132, paras 50–60. More detail in Hans-Konrad Ress, 'Die Zulässigkeit territorialer Beschränkungen bei der Anerkennung der Zuständigkeit des Europäischen Gerichtshofs für Menschenrechte: Anmerkungen zum Urteil des Europäischen Gerichtshofs für Menschenrechte im Fall *Loizidou* gegen die Türkei vom 23. März 1995' (1996) 56 Zeitschrift für ausländisches öffentliches Recht und Völkerrecht 427, 427–38; Susan Marks, 'Reservations Unhinged: The *Belilos* Case before the European Court of Human Rights' (1990) 39 ICLQ 300.

[243] See *Reservations to the Convention of Genocide.*

In aggregate, the system of the European Convention on Human Rights has developed in favour of a community-oriented and against the state-oriented conception, being supported by new protocols and legislative measures by the Convention states. Of particular importance in this process is the growing role of the individual. Initially, the control system granted individuals only a tightly circumscribed role. The reports of the Commission after Article 31 of the ECHR (original version) were not even conveyed to the individual complainants. From the early 1980s onward, however, a practice established that the legal counsel of the individuals in question could act before the Court in the same way as the representatives of the Convention states. The centre of the control system shifted increasingly to the Court. A milestone was reached when the Eleventh Protocol took effect in 1998. The Protocol disbanded the Commission and established the Court as a permanent institution that the individual could appeal to directly.[244] As the number of cases demonstrates, this triggered an enormous, perhaps even explosive dynamic. By 1997, the Court had decided from its inception a total of 837 cases. In 2001 alone it decided 888, and since 2006 it has decided more than 1,000 cases a year. The number of new individual complaints has risen steadily, reaching 64,500 new complaints in 2011 in a single year, with a total of 161,500 pending appeals.[245] This volume of cases is hardly manageable.[246]

The Court is using the crisis to develop itself further in the sense of the second conception. Since many individual complaints result from the same problems, the Court proposed, in a position paper in 2003, to address these fundamental causes by means of so-called pilot judgments.[247] In this

[244] For an assessment see Alec Stone Sweet, 'Sur la constitutionnalisation de la convention européenne des droits de l'homme: cinquante ans après son installation, la cour européenne des droits de l'homme conçue comme une cour constitutionnelle' (2009) 20 Revue trimestrielle des droits de l'homme 923.

[245] ECtHR, *50 Years of Activity: The European Court of Human Rights: Some Facts and Figures* (April 2010) <www.echr.coe.int/NR/rdonlyres/ACD46A0F-615A-48B9-89D6-8480AFCC29FD/0/FactsAndFigures_EN.pdf> accessed 3 August 2012; ECtHR, *The European Court of Human Rights in Facts and Figures* (January 2012) <www.echr.coe.int/NR/rdonlyres/C99DDB86-EB23-4E12-BCDA-D19B63A935AD/0/FAITS_CHIFFRES_EN_JAN2012_VERSION_WEB.pdf> accessed 3 August 2012.

[246] This surely has to do also with geographical expansion. Hungary, the Czech Republic, Slovakia, and Bulgaria joined in 1992, Poland in 1993, Romania and Slovenia in 1994, Lithuania in 1995, Albania, Andorra, and Estonia in 1996, Croatia, 'Macedonia', Latvia, Ukraine, and Moldova in 1997, and Russia in 1998. Since 1999, when Protocol 11 came into force, Armenia, Azerbaijan, Bosnia, and Herzegovina joined in 2002, Serbia (and Montenegro) in 2004, Monaco in 2005, and Montenegro in 2006. The ECHR now extends to a total of 47 states. For more detail see Christian Tomuschat, 'The European Court of Human Rights Overwhelmed by Applications: Problems and Possible Solutions' in Rüdiger Wolfrum and Ulrike Deutsch (eds), *The European Court of Human Rights Overwhelmed by Applications: Problems and Possible Solutions* (Springer 2009) 1, 10–13.

[247] Drafting Group on the Reinforcement of the Human Rights Protection Mechanism, *Position Paper of the European Court of Human Rights on Proposals for Reform of the European Convention on Human Rights and other Measures as Set Out in the Report of the Steering Committee for Human Rights of 4 April 2004 (CCDH(2003)006 final)*, 12 September 2003, Document CDDH-GDR (2003) 024, paras 1–15. See also

way, it would identify systematic deficits and demand changes to national laws. Cases resulting from the same causes would be suspended in order to address the problem with general measures. However, within the framework of the general reform efforts related to the Fourteenth Protocol, the government representatives could not agree on setting up a procedure for pilot judgments. Nevertheless, the Committee of Ministers drafted a resolution in which it invited the Court to identify in relevant cases what it considered the underlying systematic problem, so as to contribute in this way to finding appropriate solutions.[248] At the same time, it recommended to the Convention states that they take general measures to implement these judgments.[249] Even though the Convention states were thus unable to agree on the introduction of a formal pilot procedure, they prepared precisely that path for the Court within the Committee of Ministers.

The ECtHR understood this as a summons to substantially push the further development of ECHR law. The path-breaking case *Broniowski v Poland* concerned compensation for property which the complainant, like 80,000 other affected individuals, had been forced to abandon between 1944 and 1953 in the eastern province of pre-war Poland. In this first pilot judgment, the Court obligated Poland to effectively secure the property rights of the complainant and all individuals in the same position through appropriate legislation and administrative praxis.[250] To that end it based itself explicitly on the resolution and the recommendation of the Committee of Ministers.[251]

The pilot judgment doctrine is a daring piece of law-making, as it shifts the structure of competence within the system of European human rights protections in several dimensions.[252] According to Article 46 Section 1 of the ECHR, the Convention states are, in principle, at liberty to determine how to implement the judgments of the Court, especially since judgments by the ECtHR are declaratory. The discretion at the national level, which the Court certainly mentioned in *Broniowski*,[253] is now strongly constrained by the pilot judgments, since they contain concrete guidelines. It can nevertheless be justified with the community-oriented view of international courts,

Markus Fyrnys, 'Expanding Competences by Judicial Lawmaking: The Pilot Judgment Procedure of the European Court of Human Rights' (2011) 12 German L J 1231, 1239–41.

248 Committee of Ministers, *Judgments Revealing an Underlying Systemic Problem* (12 May 2004) Res 3 (2004).

249 Committee of Ministers, *Improvement of Domestic Remedies* (12 May 2004) Rec 6 (2004).

250 *Broniowski v Poland* ECHR 2004-V, Operative Part, para 4.

251 *Broniowski v Poland*, paras 190, 193 ('threat to the future effectiveness of the Convention machinery').

252 In detail Fyrnys, 'Expanding Competences by Judicial Lawmaking' 1244–51.

253 *Broniowski v Poland*, paras 192–3.

whereas this kind of law-making without a change to the treaty could only meet with rejection under the state-oriented conception.[254]

The community-oriented conception further shows up when the Court justifies an innovative decision with a *European consensus* on the matter. In important cases, the Court expands a Convention right by arguing that the action of the complainant was worthy of protection according to a clear international trend.[255] With that, the ECHR becomes a transmission belt that forces the dominant understanding of a right within the community of Convention states upon all of them.

The example of the ECtHR clearly shows that the understanding of international courts as a mere instrument of case-specific dispute settlement is inadequate as a general paradigm. Its current praxis can be explained much better under the community-oriented conception. The ECtHR's pronounced role as an institution of a pan-European system for protecting basic rights stands in marked contrast to the ICJ. This different orientation is favoured by a number of circumstances, namely the compulsory jurisdiction, the individual right of action, the support from national constitutional law, and the clear focus on an area in which judicial protagonism is largely accepted. The core issue is *not* to settle a bilateral dispute, but to protect individual rights.

Thus, the ECtHR has laid a thick layer of legal normativity over the domestic constitutions. Similar to the adjudication of state constitutional courts, it creates, stabilizes, and develops normative expectations. Early on, the Court explicitly recognized this dimension, which extends beyond the individual case. In its decision on the interstate complaint that Ireland brought against the United Kingdom in response to the fight against terrorism in the Northern Ireland conflict, especially with regard to the methods of interrogation that were used, the Court stated that its judgments served not only to decide the cases brought before it, but contributed more generally to protecting the Convention rights, clarifying them, and developing them further.[256] Later it elaborated that it usually followed its former decisions as precedents, since that served legal security and the orderly development of what it itself calls case-law.[257] Finally, there is no question that

[254] Vladimiro Zagrebelsky, 'Questions autour de Broniowski' in Lucius Caflisch and others (eds), *Liber Amicorum Luzius Wildhaber: Human Rights—Strasbourg Views* (NP Engel 2007) 521.

[255] *Christine Goodwin v UK* ECHR 2002-VI, paras 84–92; see also *Hirst v UK (No 2)* ECHR 2005-IX, paras 78–82; *Konstantin Markin v Russia* ECHR 2012, paras 99–100, 126.

[256] *Ireland v UK* (1978) Series A No 25, para 154 ('The Court's judgments in fact serve not only to decide those cases brought before the Court but, more generally, to elucidate, safeguard and develop the rules instituted by the Convention, thereby contributing to the observance by the States of the engagements undertaken by them as Contracting Parties').

[257] *Cossey v UK* (1990) Series A No 184, para 35.

the Court controls and legitimizes the exercise of public authority on the national level. All this inevitably leads to further inquiries on the democratic legitimacy of international adjudication, which we take up in the following chapters.[258]

4. International criminal courts

The state-oriented basic conception seems even more implausible for international criminal courts than it does for the ECtHR. Among all international courts, they are bound to the idea of the community with a special intensity. To be sure, there are scholars that see them as instruments of powerful states.[259] We do not deny that there is indeed some evidence to that effect. However, the present study does not investigate this aspect, since it does not ask about causes and motives, but about the reasons used in the decision-making praxis.

The concept of international crimes against humanity, the *delicta iuris gentium*, reaches back a long way. Acts of piracy are considered a classic example.[260] The law regards pirates as enemies of humanity, *hostis humani generis*, and every power was permitted to render judgment upon them.[261] The project of an international criminal court also has a venerable tradition.[262] As early as 1872, Gustave Moynier, president of the International Committee of the Red Cross, drafted a statute. Article 227 of the Versailles Treaty envisaged charging the German Emperor before an international tribunal with 'a supreme offence against international morality and the sanctity of treaties'; that is, an offence not only against bilateral but also community

[258] See already *EGMR-Entscheidungen* (2004) 111 BVerfGE 307, 315–31 (Federal Constitutional Court of Germany), English: <http://www.bverfg.de/en/decisions/rs20041014_2bvr148104en.html> accessed 3 February 2014; *EGMR Sicherungsverwahrung* (2011) 128 BVerfGE 326, 366–72 (Federal Constitutional Court of Germany); Albrecht Weber, 'Grundrechtsschutz in Europa—Kooperation oder Kooperationsverweigerung? Anmerkungen zum Verhältnis zwischen EGMR und BVerfG' in Metin Akryük and others (eds), *Staat und Recht in europäischer Perspektive: Festschrift Heinz Schäffer* (Manzsche Verlags- und Universitätsbuchhandlung 2006) 911; Jan Bergmann, 'Das Bundesverfassungsgericht in Europa' (2004) 31 Europäische Grundrechte-Zeitschrift 620–3; Jean-Paul Costa, 'On the Legitimacy of the European Court of Human Rights' Judgments' (2011) 7 Eur Const L Rev 173; Donald, Gordon, and Leach, *The UK and the ECtHR* 162–4.

[259] Kenneth Anderson, 'The Rise of International Criminal Law: Intended and Unintended Consequences' (2009) 20 Eur J Intl L 331, 334. Classically Judith N Shklar, *Legalism* (Harvard UP 1964).

[260] Brigitte Stern, 'A propos de la competence universelle…' in Emile Yakpo and Tahar Boumedra (eds), *Liber Amicorum Judge Mohammed Bedjaoui* (Kluwer Law International 1999), 735–6.

[261] It is no accident that this position formed in relation to piracy, since those acts concern the high seas, which do not belong to any state territory. Taking action against pirates thus does not touch on the territorial sovereignty of other states. Santiago Villalpando, 'The Legal Dimension of the International Community: How Community Interests Are Protected in International Law' (2010) 21 Eur J Intl L 387, 406.

[262] William Schabas, *An Introduction to the International Criminal Court* (3rd edn, CUP 2007) 1–21.

interests.[263] Within the framework of the League of Nations, proposals for an international criminal court multiplied: the PCIJ was to be joined by a 'High Court of International Justice' to pass judgment on crimes against the international order and against universal international law.[264] These efforts bore fruit for the first time after World War II, with criminal convictions of some of the Axis powers' chief war criminals for crimes against peace, war crimes, and crimes against humanity.[265] However, international criminal courts, provided for in Article 6 of the Genocide Convention, were not to become permanent.

The current international criminal judiciary began in the early 1990s as a reaction to serious crimes that occurred during the breakup of Yugoslavia.[266] In 1993, the UN Security Council established the ad hoc International Criminal Tribunal for the former Yugoslavia (ICTY).[267] Its purpose is to prosecute those responsible for international crimes in that conflict and thereby contribute to restoring peace, end on-going crimes, and prevent future ones. With a seat in The Hague, 16 permanent judges, and a pool of 27 trial judges (Article 13(1)(d) ICTY Statute), it is the first international tribunal since World War II to prosecute war crimes, genocide, and crimes against humanity. A tribunal like this is not cheap: for 2010–2012, the UN General Assembly has approved a budget of 301,895,900 US dollars.[268]

But the Assembly did get something for its money. Trials against 161 individuals were conducted. In the course of these proceedings, the ICTY has consolidated the normativity of humanitarian international law. Moreover, its rich case-law has developed both procedural and substantive international criminal law.[269] Matters which stand out are the development of the

[263] See Quincy Wright, 'Proposal for an International Criminal Court' (1952) 46 AJIL 60.

[264] For an overview of the efforts within the framework of the League of Nations and then the United Nations see UNGA, 'Historical Survey of the Question of International Criminal Jurisdiction: Memorandum Submitted by the Secretary-General' (1949) UN Doc A/CN.4/7/Rev.1, 2–3.

[265] Art 6 IMT Charter; Johannes Fuchs and Flavia Lattanzi, 'International Military Tribunals' in Wolfrum (ed), *Max Planck Encyclopedia of Public International Law*; ILC, 'Report of the International Law Commission to the General Assembly' (July 1950) UN Doc A/1316, 374–8; Robert Cryer and others, *An Introduction to International Criminal Law and Procedure* (2nd edn, CUP 2010) 109–200.

[266] See 'Interim Report of the Commission of Experts Established pursuant to Security Council Resolution 780' (10 February 1993) UN Doc S/25274, Annex; see also UNSC Res 771 (13 August 1992) UN Doc S/RES/771; UNSC Res 780 (6 October 1992) UN Doc S/RES/780.

[267] UNSC Res 827 (25 May 1993) UN Doc S/RES/827.

[268] <www.icty.org/> accessed 3 August 2012.

[269] On law-making in the practice of the ICTY see Milan Kuhli and Klaus Günther, 'Judicial Lawmaking, Discourse Theory, and the ICTY on Belligerent Reprisals' (2011) 12 German L J 1261; Allison M Danner, 'When Courts Make Law: How the International Criminal Tribunals Recast the Laws of War' (2006) 59 Vanderbilt L Rev 1; Fausto Pocar, 'Criminal Proceedings before the International Criminal Tribunals for the former Yugoslavia and Rwanda' (2006) 5 L and Practice of Intl Courts and Tribunals 89, 95–102; Christopher Greenwood, 'The Development of International Humanitarian Law by the International Criminal Tribunal for the former Yugoslavia' (1998) 2 Max Planck YB UN L 97; Mia Swart, 'Ad hoc

criminal offence of persecution,[270] the applicability of international criminal law in internal conflicts,[271] and the doctrine of the *joint criminal enterprise*.[272] Of particular importance has been the Appeals Chamber, which has accorded to its decision the function of precedent.[273] Today, there is hardly an area of international criminal law in which one can argue without invoking the case-law of the ICTY. Moreover, the Tribunal has exerted influence on general international law—for example in the Furundžija case, where it qualified the prohibition of torture as *ius cogens* and declared that the protection of human dignity is such a central principle that it pervades the entire corpus of international law.[274] The Tribunal could not be any further from the conception of international order that the PCIJ articulated so strikingly in its *Lotus* decision. Instead, in its first judgment, the Appeals Chamber noted concisely: 'A State-sovereignty approach has been gradually supplanted by a human-being-oriented approach. Gradually the maxim of Roman law *hominum causa omne jus constitutum est* (all law is created for the benefit of human beings) has gained a firm foothold in the international community as well.'[275]

The weakening of the state-oriented basic conception is also due to the International Criminal Tribunal for Rwanda (ICTR). Within a mere 100 days in 1994, 800,000 individuals died in Rwanda in massacres perpetrated mostly by Hutu militias. In response, the UN Security Council set up the ad hoc Tribunal for Rwanda, with its seat in Arusha, Tanzania. The ICTR is very similar to the slightly older ICTY and shares with it the appellate instance in The Hague.[276] By 2012 the ICTR had found 45 defendants guilty and had

Rules for ad hoc Tribunals? The Rule-Making Power of the Judges of the ICTY and ICTR' (2002) 18 South African J on Human Rights 570.

[270] *Prosecutor v Mladen Naletilić, Vinko Martinović* (Judgment) IT-98-34 (3 May 2006) para 574.

[271] *Prosecutor v Duško Tadić* (Decision on the Defence Motion for Interlocutory Appeal on Jurisdiction) IT-94-1-AR 72 (2 October 1995) para 83.

[272] *Prosecutor v Milomir Stakić* (Judgment) IT-97-24-A (22 March 2006) paras 58–104, 380; see Allison M Danner and Jenny S Martinez, 'Guilty Associations: Joint Criminal Enterprise, Command Responsibility, and the Development of International Criminal Law' (2005) 93 California L Rev 75; Nicola Piacente, 'Importance of the Joint Criminal Enterprise Doctrine for the ICTY Prosecutorial Policy' (2004) 2 J Intl Crim Justice 446.

[273] *Prosecutor v Zlatko Aleksovski* (Judgment) IT-95-14/1-A (24 March 2000) para 113.

[274] *Prosecutor v Anto Furundžija* (Judgment) IT-95-17/1-T (10 December 1998) paras 143–57. On the legal implications of qualifying the prohibition against torture as *ius cogens* see Erika de Wet, 'The Prohibition of Torture as an International Norm of *jus cogens* and Its Implications for National and Customary Law' (2004) 15 Eur J Intl L 97. See Jochen von Bernstorff and Ingo Venzke, 'Ethos, Ethics, and Morality in International Relations' in Wolfrum (ed), *Max Planck Encyclopedia of Public International Law* <http://opil.ouplaw.com/home/EPIL> accessed 27 January 2014.

[275] *Prosecutor v Duško Tadić*, para 97.

[276] UNSC Res 955 (8 November 1994) UN Doc S/RES/955. Differences, also in the substantive law jurisdiction, are of no further relevance here.

acquitted ten.[277] It focuses on major criminals and those who were in leading positions. Other defendants have to answer in so-called *Gacaca* courts in Rwanda, as well as in ordinary Rwandan and foreign criminal courts. For the two years 2010 and 2011, the UN General Assembly passed a budget of 245,295,800 US dollars for the ICTR and provided 693 staff positions.[278] Among the areas of criminal law to which the ICTR has especially contributed are the offences of incitement to violence (hate speech), genocide, and crimes against humanity, especially with a view to sexual violence.[279]

Without the ad hoc criminal tribunals, the Rome Statute of the International Criminal Court (ICC) would hardly have been passed in Rome in 1998 and come into effect in 2002.[280] We owe this Court especially to the engagement of civil society.[281] Many consider its creation the emblem of a new era in the safeguarding of fundamental values of the international community[282] and the symbol of a constitutionalization of international law.[283] According to Antonio Cassese, an influential author and former president of the ICTY, international crimes, being serious violations of universal values, are a matter for the global community; '[h]ence only international courts, expression of the whole international community, can appropriately pronounce on such crimes'.[284]

Very much in this spirit, the Preamble of the Rome Statute invokes the conscience of humanity. The Court was to punish and prevent 'the most serious crimes of concern to the international community as a whole'. As of 2013, 114 states had ratified the Rome Statute. By that date, the Court had dealt with 15 cases in seven different conflict situations, but only one conviction had taken place.[285] Jurisdiction over events on their own territory

[277] <www.unictr.org/> accessed 3 August 2012.

[278] <www.unictr.org/> accessed 3 August 2012.

[279] On hate speech *Prosecutor v Ferdinand Nahimana, Jean-Bosco Barayagwiza, Hassan Ngeze* (Judgement) ICTR-99-52-A (28 November 2007) paras 691–715, 983–8. With the influential *Akayesu* judgment, the ICTR is also the first international court to interpret Arts 2 and 3 of the Genocide Convention. It declared, among other things, that rape and other forms of sexual violence can be regarded as genocide and as crimes against humanity. *Prosecutor v Jean-Paul Akayesu* (Judgment) ICTR-96-4-T (2 September 1998) paras 685–92, 731–4.

[280] Art 126(1) Rome Statute. See Schabas, *An Introduction to the International Criminal Court* 13.

[281] Zoe Pearson, 'Non-Governmental Organizations and the International Criminal Court: Changing Landscapes of International Law' (2006) 39 Cornell Intl L J 243, 250–84.

[282] See for example Luigi Condorelli, 'La cour pénale internationale: Un pas de géant (pourvu qu'il soit accompli...)' (1999) 103 Revue générale de droit international public 7.

[283] Schabas, *An Introduction to the International Criminal Court* 57; Luis Moreno-Ocampo, 'Preface' in José Doria, Hans-Peter Gasser, and M Cherif Bassiouni (eds), *The Legal Regime of the International Criminal Court: Essays in Honour of Professor Igor Blishenko* (Nijhoff 2009) xv.

[284] Antonio Cassese, 'The Rationale for International Criminal Justice' in Antonio Cassese (ed), *The Oxford Companion to International Criminal Justice* (OUP 2009) 123, 127.

[285] <www.icc-cpi.int> accessed 3 August 2012; *Prosecutor v Lubanbga Dyilo* (Judgment of 14 May 2012).

has been transferred to it by three treaty parties (Uganda, the Democratic Republic of Congo, and the Central African Republic).[286] The UN Security Council has charged it with prosecuting serious crimes in Sudan and Libya.[287] In March 2010, the Prosecutor of the Court, on his own initiative, began investigations in Kenya, and in October 2011 in Ivory Coast.[288] Therein are reflected the three pathways to the exercise of jurisdiction as laid down in Article 13 of the Rome Statute: referral by a state party, referral by the UN Security Council, or own initiative.

In the negotiations leading up to the Statute, the role of the UN Security Council and the scope of the Court's jurisdiction were particularly contested.[289] In particular, the permanent members of the Security Council sought to secure their influence. As a result, the Security Council can not only refer conflict situations for investigation to the Prosecutor. It can also defer investigations if it believes they would endanger the peace.[290] However, it is not able to permanently block a trial. The idea of a judicial community organ beyond the control of the great powers has, in principle, carried the day. To be sure, reality may lag behind.[291]

In clear contrast to the ad hoc criminal tribunals, the principle of complementarity pervades the jurisdiction of the Court. Accordingly, a trial is only permissible if a state that has jurisdiction over the individual in question is unwilling or unable to genuinely prosecute.[292] One can interpret this as an expression of the realization that an international judiciary, especially when it intervenes deeply in individual rights, poses a great problem of legitimation. One central concern of the present study is to flesh out this realization.

The multifunctionality of the international criminal courts and tribunals is just as evident as that of the ECtHR. Their contribution to the development of the law and to the control and legitimation of national power is obvious. Added to this is the possible horizontal control of international public authority, for example of the UN Security Council by the ICTY or

[286] <www.icc-cpi.int> accessed 3 August 2012.

[287] UNSC Res 1593 (31 March 2005) UN Doc SC/RES/1593; UNSC Res 1970 (26 February 2011) UN Doc S/RES/1970.

[288] <www.icc-cpi.int> accessed 3 August 2012.

[289] Caroline Fehl, 'Explaining the International Criminal Court: A Practice Test for Rationalist and Constructivist Approaches' in Steven C Roach (ed), *Governance, Order, and the International Criminal Court: Between Realpolitik and a Cosmopolitan Court* (OUP 2009) 75, 89–91.

[290] Art 16 Rome Statute; Art 39 UN Charter; Jakob Pichon, *Internationaler Strafgerichtshof und Sicherheitsrat der Vereinten Nationen: Zur Rolle des Sicherheitsrates bei der Verfolgung völkerrechtlicher Verbrechen durch den IStGH* (Springer 2011) 32–49, 257–73.

[291] Kirsten Ainley, 'The International Criminal Court on Trial' (2011) 24 Cambridge Rev Intl Affairs 309.

[292] Art 17(1)(b) Rome Statute.

of the ICC Prosecutor through the Pre-Trial Chamber. Moreover, the legal process, the taking of the evidence, and finally the verdict may make a significant—if contested—contribution to the processing of the past and possibly to the reconciliation of broken societies.[293] One can see this as part of the legitimizing function. By publicly working through the injustices of past regimes, the courts can legitimize and stabilize the new order.[294] In sum, the predominant interpretation and self-portrayal of the international criminal judiciary is anchored in the community-oriented conception, which is focused especially on the protection and realization of universal values. Its actions are mostly understood and justified with a view toward that goal. The international criminal courts thus appear as *organs* of the international community.

5. The International Tribunal for the Law of the Sea

The conception of international courts as organs of the international community helps further to understand the International Tribunal for the Law of the Sea (ITLOS). At the same time, though, this institution shows how the focus on community values is today becoming too narrow. The law of the sea, so rich in tradition, is surely not a new area of international law, though it has had a judiciary of its own only since 1994. The ITLOS Statute is part of the UN Convention on the Law of the Sea (UNCLOS), which was opened for ratification in 1982 but went into effect only in 1994. With its seat in Hamburg, 21 judges, and a budget of 20,398,600 euros for the two years 2011–2012, ITLOS is in charge primarily of interstate disputes about the application of UNCLOS.[295] However, to its chagrin, the Tribunal is not alone in this function. The currently 162 States Parties can choose between the ITLOS, the ICJ, and arbitration as the forum for a conflict.[296] Even if disputing parties have not recognized the jurisdiction of either the ITLOS or the ICJ, and do not do so ad hoc, they are still obligated to submit to arbitration.[297]

UNCLOS conceives of the seabed beyond the borders of national jurisdiction as the 'common heritage of mankind', which is to be explored and exploited for the benefit of all of humanity.[298] This territory is administered

[293] Daniel Joyce, 'The Historical Function of International Criminal Trials: Re-Thinking International Criminal Law' (2004) 73 Nordic J Intl L 461.

[294] In more detail Richard A Wilson, *Writing History in International Criminal Trials* (CUP 2011); critically Timothy W Waters, 'A Kind of Judgment: Searching for Judicial Narratives after Death' (2010) 42 George Washington Intl L Rev 279, 285–94.

[295] Art 293(1) UNCLOS.

[296] Art 287(1) UNCLOS.

[297] Art 287(3) UNCLOS; the arbitral procedure then follows Annex VII UNCLOS.

[298] Preamble, Arts 125, 136, 311(6) UNCLOS.

by the International Seabed Authority,[299] which is overseen by the Seabed Disputes Chamber of the Tribunal. Among other things, this chamber can draft advisory opinions, and recently it answered fundamental questions on the obligations and responsibilities of states whose companies operate on the territory of the seabed.[300] The Chamber saw its function clearly as part of the administrative mechanism for the use of the seabed, continued to develop fundamental legal principles, and concretized the guidelines for action.[301] In the process, it focused especially on the overarching purpose of the legal regime, to orient the use of the seabed toward the common good.[302] Here the community-oriented conception shines through.

However, the use of the seabed revolves also around economic interests, as do the great majority of the disputes before the Tribunal. They mostly concern the prompt release of vessels,[303] and thus the ITLOS plays a role in securing international shipping, which is indispensable to the global economy. In the case that foreign vessels are seized, for example on the charge of illegal economic activity, there is a possibility of procuring their immediate release upon the posting of a bond. This process can be closely reviewed by the ITLOS.[304] This type of international review conforms to the function of the vertical control of sovereignty.[305] It is noteworthy that, in the tradition of diplomatic protection, it is the flag state that should take up the case and represent it before the ITLOS. However, ship owners increasingly appear directly before the Tribunal, at the behest of the flag states, without a state representative of the petitioning state being present.[306] These elements point beyond the second basic conception to courts as regime institutions.

299 <www.isa.org.jm> accessed 3 August 2012.

300 *Responsibilities and Obligations of States Sponsoring Persons and Entities with Respect to Activities in the Area* (Advisory Opinion) ITLOS Reports 2011, 10.

301 On the function and self-understanding of the tribunal *Responsibilities and Obligations of States Sponsoring Persons and Entities with Respect to Activities in the Area*, para 29.

302 *Responsibilities and Obligations of States Sponsoring Persons and Entities with Respect to Activities in the Area*, paras 76, 151, 159, 222, 230.

303 Art 292 UNCLOS. As of 13 July 2012, the Tribunal has decided 16 cases, ten of which concerned the release of vessels and crews. Two other disputes are currently ongoing <www.itlos.org> accessed 3 August 2012.

304 Arts 73, 292 UNCLOS.

305 *The 'Juno Trader' Case (Saint Vincent and Grenadines v Guinea-Bissau)* (Judgment of 18 December 2004) ITLOS Reports 2004, 17, paras 76–7; *The 'Volga' Case (Russian Federation v Australia)* (Judgment) ITLOS Reports 2002, 10, paras 90–3; see Chester Brown, '"Reasonableness" in the Law of the Sea: The Prompt Release of the Volga' (2003) 16 Leiden J Intl L 621.

306 David Heywood Anderson, 'Prompt Release of Vessels and Crews' in Wolfrum (ed), *Max Planck Encyclopedia of Public International Law*, para 5. Art 292(2) UNCLOS provides that action can be taken in the name of the flag state.

Finally, the ITLOS is the first international judicial institution which explicitly envisages that provisional measures are binding,[307] even if states have not submitted to the jurisdiction of the Tribunal.[308] As an illustrative example one can highlight the dispute between Malaysia and Singapore about *Land Reclamation by Singapore in and around the Straits of Johor*.[309] The Tribunal ordered the creation of an independent expert commission, which would render a finding about the consequences of Singapore's land reclamation project within a year. Singapore was prohibited to pursue any further measures that might violate the rights of Malaysia or do serious harm to the maritime environment.[310] In keeping with the community-oriented conception, the UN Convention also made it possible to protect, with provisional measures not only the positions of the parties, but also the maritime environment as a common good (Article 290 UNCLOS).

We have introduced the Tribunal for the Law of the Sea in the second, community-oriented conception, since its sphere of action is closely linked with the Convention on the Law of the Sea, which, as the 'constitution for the seas',[311] serves the 'common heritage of mankind' and the protection of the maritime environment. The expectations placed in the Tribunal, its multifarious tasks, and its actual practice prove that the state-centric understanding is too narrow. At the same time, though, one can see the inadequacy of the interpretation of the Tribunal merely as an organ of the value-based international community. The majority of cases concern the immediate release of vessels and their crew, which means that the Tribunal secures global maritime trade. From the perspective of the international community this is of interest, but it is still some way from the implementation of universal values like human rights. The Seabed Disputes Chamber, which serves the exploitation of the 'common heritage of mankind', interacts with the International Seabed Authority in regulating economic activity. In conclusion, then, the community-oriented conception of international courts may well grasp the multifunctionality of international adjudication, but it, too, falls short in capturing the role of international courts for the world economy. In addition, the international community as a basis of legitimacy that complements states' consent remains largely nebulous.

[307] Art 290 UNCLOS, Art 25 ITLOS Statute.

[308] Arts 287, 290(5) UNCLOS.

[309] *Land Reclamation by Singapore in and around the Straits of Johor (Malaysia v Singapore)* (Provisional Measures, Order of 8 October 2003).

[310] *Malaysia v Singapore*, para 106. See Donald R Rothwell, 'The Contribution of ITLOS to Oceans Governance through Marine Environmental Dispute Resolution' in Tafsir M Ndiaye and Rüdiger Wolfrum (eds), *Law of the Sea, Environmental Law and Settlement of Disputes: Liber Amicorum Judge Thomas A Mensah* (Nijhoff 2007) 1007, 1019–21.

[311] Alexander Proelß, *Meeresschutz im Völker- und Europarecht: Das Beispiel des Nordostatlantiks* (Duncker & Humblot 2004) 74.

C. COURTS AS INSTITUTIONS OF LEGAL REGIMES

The first two basic conceptions of international courts can provide useful guidance through the thicket of divergent statements about the meaning and purpose of international adjudication. Still, they are not able to completely grasp the dynamic of the international judiciary over the past two decades. Many contemporary judicial institutions extend beyond co-ordination between states and the safeguarding of basic community values. They can often be understood better in terms of the goal of developing a specific international regime that organizes and promotes the interdependence of states. In that sense, one could say they render their decisions in the name of their regime. This section's first step presents this third, regime-oriented basic conception (1). The second step then exemplifies it by looking at dispute settlement under the WTO (2) and the third step refers to the International Centre for Settlement of Investment Disputes (ICSID) (3). Finally, we discuss the regime-oriented basic conception in light of the theory of global governance. In the process, we will demonstrate a new quality of the international judiciary, as well as uncovering the weakness of the third basic conception, which calls for the articulation of a new, democracy-oriented approach to international courts (section D).

1. International adjudication for an interconnected world

The regime-oriented conception can be evinced especially in newer institutions. However, traces are found in the decisions of other courts, and not only in recent times. For a long time there has been international law that could be interpreted as organizing what was called *interdependence* and is now referred to as *globalization*.[312] Arbitral tribunals within the framework of the administrative unions of the nineteenth and early twentieth centuries (Universal Postal Union, Association for Railway Freight Traffic, World Sugar Association, International Telegraph Union) come to mind.[313] They can be understood as institutions for risk distribution and standardization within the framework of border-crossing co-operation. They formed part of the management of emerging interdependence in the industrial age. Their competence was entirely focused on the functioning of the specific legal regime.[314]

[312] See eg Robert Keohane and Joseph Nye, *Power and Interdependence: World Politics in Transition* (Little Brown and Company 1977).

[313] On this Hudson, *Progress in International Organization* 9–15; in more detail Sebastian Kneisel, *Schiedsgerichtsbarkeit in internationalen Verwaltungsunionen (1874–1914)* (Nomos 2009) 13–45.

[314] See Kneisel, *Schiedsgerichtsbarkeit in internationalen Verwaltungsunionen* 97.

In addition, this third basic conception explains, better than the other two, the internal judiciary of international organizations, which has also been taking shape since the beginning of the twentieth century. To be sure, for a long time international organizations remained weak institutions. Using the diction of international relations, they were more arenas for states than independent actors of their own.[315] Still, international organizations, mostly created on the model of domestic ministries, became operative as bureaucracies.[316] As a result they developed a civil servant law, which can be considered the virtual backbone of a bureaucracy. The international administrative tribunals should thus be understood not merely as institutions of dispute resolution between officials and their organization but also in light of the proficiency of the particular organization for the purpose of an effective international configuration of interdependence.[317]

Although parts of international law had long been focused, with highly specific treaty regimes, on shaping the interdependence of states, those parts did not coagulate into a basic conception. The paradigmatic *Lotus* decision reveals this in its emphasis on 'co-existing independent communities'.[318] Even if the radical nature of this statement was always controversial, international law in the twentieth century was based on an understanding of the state as a broad congruence between a people integrated into a nation economically, culturally, and historically, and its organizing public structure. The nation-state, made visible by borders, colourful shapes on maps, symbols, buildings, and iconic individuals, formed—like a kind of cheese dome—an overarching entity within which humans found their place and meaning.[319] It was the highest realization of the people connected in solidarity, the source of the law, and the precondition for and framework of the national economy. For a long time, the community-oriented conception also rested on the premise of the self-sufficient state, though it embedded it within a larger context of a universal order. The interest of the community

315 Ingo Venzke, 'International Bureaucracies from a Political Science Perspective—Agency, Authority and International Institutional Law' (2008) 9 German L J 1401, 1403–4.

316 On the development see David Kennedy, 'The Move to Institutions' (1986–1987) 8 Cardozo L Rev 841, 856–63; Jochen von Bernstorff, 'Procedures of Decision-Making and the Role of Law in International Organizations' in Armin von Bogdandy and others (eds), *The Exercise of Public Authority by International Institutions: Advancing International Institutional Law* (Springer 2010) 775, 780–1.

317 Internal administrative tribunals exist in, among other places, the UN, the International Labour Organization (ILO), the World Bank, the International Monetary Fund, and the OECD. In detail Henry G Schermers and Niels M Blokker, *International Institutional Law* (5th edn, Nijhoff 2011) 462–7.

318 *The Case of the SS Lotus*, para 44.

319 Friedrich Meinecke, *Weltbürgertum und Nationalstaat: Studien zur Genesis des deutschen Nationalstaates* (6th edn, Oldenbourg 1922) 1–11. The dual meaning of the state as, first, the political organization of a society and, second, as the label for the entirety of the social was first formulated by Georg WF Hegel, *Outlines of the Philosophy of Right* (TM Knox tr, OUP 2008) 228–34.

was limited to a few *international* concerns, to the co-ordinated coexistence of states, and especially to the safeguarding of the peace. Even the increasingly important topic of human rights did not by itself question the premise of the self-sufficient state.[320]

The bedrock of international law was *not* a law of interdependence, but of coexistence and co-ordination, as Wolfgang Friedmann has put it so succinctly.[321] Developments that went further began only in the second half of the last century, and at first chiefly between western states.[322] A few forward-looking authors saw in the increasing co-operation a potential new paradigm of international law as such.[323] This co-operation grew to the same degree that interdependence substantially deepened and geographically expanded in the 1990s. The term *globalization* has often been used to describe this process.[324] The starting point is the observation of a massive increase in the interactions between social spheres (for example the economy, culture, science, environment) across state borders. The multifarious developments summed up as *globalization* can be explained not merely as an almost natural process of technological progress but also as the fruit of political and, not least, judicial decisions that dismantle borders of the most diverse kind. This development undermines the premises of the state-oriented conception that we sketched out above, and goes far beyond securing universal values of the international community.

Since the middle of the 1990s, the role of public institutions as it relates to globalization has frequently been referred to as 'global governance'.[325] What

[320] This is already expressed by the title of a pioneering study on the history of modern international law, which emphasizes *nations*: Koskenniemi, *The Gentle Civilizer of Nations*.

[321] Wolfgang Friedmann, *The Changing Structure of International Law* (Stevens & Sons 1964) 60.

[322] Gerd Junne, 'Theorien über Konflikte und Kooperation zwischen kapitalistischen Industrieländern' in Volker Rittberger (ed), *Theorien der Internationalen Beziehungen* (Westdeutscher Verlag 1990) 353, 361; Joseph HH Weiler, 'The Geology of International Law—Governance, Democracy and Legitimacy' (2004) 64 Zeitschrift für ausländisches öffentliches Recht und Völkerrecht 547, 549.

[323] On the first approaches see Friedmann, *The Changing Structure of International Law* 61–3; Michel Virally, *L'organisation mondiale* (Librairie Armand Colin 1970) 32; René-Jean Dupuy, 'Communauté internationale et disparités de développement' (1979) 165 Recueil des cours IV, 21; and on this Pierre-Marie Dupuy, 'A Transatlantic Friendship: René-Jean Dupuy and Wolfgang Friedmann' (2011) 22 Eur J Intl L 401; Abi-Saab, 'Cours général de droit international public' 324–7.

[324] Enquete-Kommission 'Globalisierung der Weltwirtschaft—Herausforderungen und Antworten', Schlussbericht, Publication of the German Parliament 14/9200 (12 June 2002) (Bundestagsdrucksache) 49–59. From the literature: Maria Ferrarese, *Le istituzioni della globalizzazione: Diritto e diritti nella società transnazionale* (Il Mulino 2000) 11–5; Stephan Hobe, 'Die Zukunft des Völkerrechts im Zeitalter der Globalisierung: Perspektiven der Völkerrechtsentwicklung im 21. Jahrhundert' (1999) 37 Archiv des Völkerrechts 253, 254–8.

[325] In more detail James N Rosenau, 'Governance in the Twenty-First Century' (1995) 1 Global Governance 13; Martin Hewson and Timothy J Sinclair, 'The Emergence of Global Governance Theory' in Martin Hewson and Timothy Sinclair (eds), *Approaches to Global Governance Theory* (State University of New York Press 1999) 3; Renate Mayntz, 'Governance Theory als fortentwickelte Steuerungstheorie?' in Gunnar Folke Schuppert (ed), *Governance-Forschung* (2nd edn, Nomos 2006)

is controversial is whether governance largely mirrors globalization, promotes it, or shapes and nourishes it in a way that is beneficial to the common good.[326] What appears largely certain, however, is that governance makes specific contributions to social processes in a globalized world. Those contributions go beyond interstate co-ordination, the securing of peace, and the protection of fundamental values. However, with the exception of the European Union, this takes place not through public institutions of an overarching political and legal system and without reproducing the division of power familiar from domestic constitutions. Instead, governance unfolds within specific regimes. On closer view, there can be seen highly disparate developments whose commonality often lies merely in the fact that they do *not* follow the traditional logic.[327]

Globalization must be accompanied by law. Sometimes the law is provided by bureaucratic and sometimes by judicial institutions. With a view toward the latter, it is remarkable that in the perspective of global administrative law, relevant activities by international courts are actually conceived of as *administration*, to the extent that they go beyond sporadic dispute resolution.[328] Although we do not follow this conceptual line, we do share the understanding that international courts need to be newly assessed in times of global governance. Precisely because of the lack of a fully fledged public structure with legislative, executive, and judicial institutions on the international level, it makes perfect sense to consider all the possible functions of judicial bodies. Like all complex social interactions, globalized social processes require more than merely dispute resolution. To begin with, legal normativity must be established, which calls for the creation and stabilization of normative expectations. The often vague stipulations of international treaties are not sufficient for this. Instead, they must be brought to life in concrete cases. Moreover, global governance cannot function without institutions, which in turn must be legitimized and controlled.

11; Arthur Benz, 'Governance—Modebegriff oder nützliches sozialwissenschaftliches Konzept?' in Arthur Benz (ed), *Governance—Regieren in komplexen Regelsystemen* (VS Verlag für Sozialwissenschaften 2004) 11.

[326] On the possible views see Ferrarese, *Le istituzioni della globalizzazione* 57–63.

[327] For a detailed discussion on this see the contributions in von Bogdandy and others (eds), *The Exercise of Public Authority by International Institutions*; with a classification Schermers and Blokker, *International Institutional Law* 50–9; on the investment protection regime see José E Alvarez, 'The Public International Law Regime Governing International Investment' (2009) 344 Recueil des cours 193.

[328] Richard B Stewart and Michelle R Sanchez Badin, 'The World Trade Organization and Global Administrative Law' in Christian Joerges and Ernst-Ulrich Petersmann (eds), *Constitutionalism, Multilevel Trade Governance and International Economic Law* (Hart 2011) 457, 472–3; Benedict Kingsbury, Nico Krisch, and Richard B Stewart, 'The Emergence of Global Administrative Law' (2005) 68 L and Contemporary Problems 15, 17.

The beginnings of a regime-oriented understanding are already found in the early adjudication of the ICJ, which strengthened the UN. In its advisory opinion on *Reparation for Injuries*, the Court in 1949 accorded the UN international legal personality and thus paved the way for the organization to make a claim against the member state Israel. It thus took the crucial step to international legal subjectivity of international organizations—self-evident today but back then by no means secure.[329] At the same time, the Court formulated the doctrine of implied powers, according to which 'the Organization must be deemed to have those powers which, though not expressly provided in the UN Charter, are conferred upon it by necessary implication as being essential to the performance of its duties'.[330] The Court argued in the vein of functionalism, which would inspire the doctrine and theory of international organizations over the following decades.

The Court expanded this line in the *Certain Expenses* advisory opinion. The question was whether the expenses for two peacekeeping missions could be considered 'expenses of the organization' in the sense of Article 17 Section 2 UN Charter. In substance, however, the issue was whether those missions were at all compatible with the UN Charter. The ICJ responded that treaties in general, and the Charter in particular, had to be interpreted in such a way that their provisions can become effective.[331] Moreover, in this regard one also had to consider the praxis of the organization—another important building block to strengthen a regime.[332] Finally, the Court found that 'when the Organization takes action which warrants the assertion that it was appropriate for the fulfilment of one of the stated purposes of the United Nations, the presumption is that such action is not *ultra vires*'.[333] This, too, serves the effectiveness of international institutions.

In addition, the aforementioned internal administrative tribunals are indispensable for the effective functioning of international organizations', though to that end it must satisfy the standards of the rule of law. It is precisely in this sense that the ICJ has recently been pushing its further development. It reviewed a decision by the International Labour Organization Administrative Tribunal (ILOAT), which ordered the International Fund for Agricultural

[329] *Reparation for Injuries Suffered in the Service of the United Nations* (Advisory Opinion) [1949] ICJ Rep 174, 178–9.

[330] *Reparation for Injuries* 182. See also the criticism in the dissenting opinion of Hackworth, *Reparation for Injuries* 198.

[331] *Certain Expenses of the United Nations (Article 17, paragraph 2, of the Charter)* (Advisory Opinion) [1962] ICJ Rep 151, 157, 159.

[332] *Certain Expenses of the United Nations* 157, 165.

[333] *Certain Expenses of the United Nations* 168.

Development (IFAD) to reinstate an employment relationship.[334] The IFAD maintained before the ICJ that the ILOAT had exceeded its jurisdiction and had committed procedural errors.[335] Yet, the ICJ confirmed the decision of the ILOAT. At the same time, it accorded considerable weight to the fact that only the IFAD, not the complaining employee, could request an advisory opinion and present its position before the ICJ as a party. It maintained that this unequal access to the Court constituted a fundamental problem, and that it was questionable whether a system created in 1946 satisfied the standards of today.[336] Thus, the ICJ is pushing for a reform of the internal administrative tribunals of international institutions, and indirectly for the functional efficiency of international regimes.[337] In these cases, then, the regime-oriented conception certainly shines through in the adjudication of the ICJ. At the same time, as described above, it acts primarily as an instrument of dispute settlement within a state-centric conception.

Other institutions fit much better with the regime-oriented conception, such as the Inspection Panel, with its function of control and legitimation vis-à-vis the World Bank. It was set up in 1993 and operates with three members and the support of a secretariat of its own at the headquarters of the World Bank in Washington. It owes its creation to the sometimes sharp criticism of investment projects that had been promoted by the World Bank. In terms of substantive law, the World Bank responded to this with a series of internally obligatory guidelines. Institutionally it responded with the Inspection Panel, which is characterized by a number of remarkable features. What needs to be emphasized especially is that individuals can lodge a complaint, even if only as an affected group. This channels protest into a judicial procedure before an institution of the World Bank, with the well-known effect of absorbing it.[338] In addition, it allows the board to control the bureaucracy of the World Bank, which has become rather independent.[339] What is more, by opening up the complaints procedures—in

[334] *Judgment No 2867 of the Administrative Tribunal of the International Labour Organization* (Advisory Opinion) [2012] ICJ Rep 10; see also *Application for Review of Judgment No 158 of the United Nations Administrative Tribunal* (Advisory Opinion) [1973] ICJ Rep 166.

[335] *Judgment No 2867*, para 1.

[336] *Judgment No 2867*, para 44. In the concrete case, the Court charged the president of the agricultural fund to convey to it the position of the affected employees. It found in this regard that the situation was fraught with difficulties. In the final analysis, these were not serious enough for the Court to reject the request for an advisory opinion; see paras 3, 46–7.

[337] In 2009, the UN General Assembly introduced the *United Nation Dispute Tribunal* as an internal administrative tribunal with the possibility of appeal.

[338] On this see Niklas Luhmann, *Legitimation durch Verfahren* (2nd edn, Suhrkamp 1989) 100.

[339] On their remarkable independence see Philipp Dann, *The Law of Development Cooperation: A Comparative Analysis of the World Bank, the EU and Germany* (CUP 2013) 39.

conjunction with typical characteristics of a judicial procedure—it has a legitimating effect. Even if the Panel itself cannot make the final decision, but reports to the Executive Committee, its determinations are crucial to the further process. This is due not least to the public nature of the procedure and the report.[340]

In the regime-oriented conception, as in the community-oriented understanding, all functions of a judiciary are addressed. Still, there are substantial differences, since the regime-oriented conception conceives of the international system in a much more fragmented and dynamic way, and by including the domestic regulatory level. In what follows we present two regimes that illustrate this new dimension vividly: the dispute settlement of the WTO and investment arbitration, especially within the framework of the ICSID.

2. The dispute settlement body of the WTO

Like no other multilateral treaty with a global ambition, the General Agreement on Tariffs and Trade (GATT) has embodied the idea of economic interdependence for decades. Together with the OECD, it formed the legal foundation for the economic interconnectedness of the western world after World War II. In the process, the judiciary had and has a crucial role, whereby it has also become evident that successful juridification on the international level must by no means copy established domestic patterns, but that unusual arrangements can also be expedient.[341]

Characteristically enough, both the GATT of 1947 and the WTO Agreement of 1994 lack any reference to the big international themes of peace and human rights; that is, the core themes of the UN-inspired order of international law. Instead, the issue is the functionality of the specific regime to secure international trade. The GATT as a multilateral treaty was originally focused on lowering tariffs. Later agreements have expanded the reach of the regime: one should recall the 1994 Agreements on Trade in Services (GATS), on Trade-Related Aspects of Intellectual Property Rights (TRIPS), on Sanitary and Phytosanitary Measures (SPS), on Technical Barriers to Trade (TBT), and on Subsidies and Countervailing Measures. Especially in the 1990s, the relevant scientific community saw in this the embryo of a law for the global market.[342]

[340] Dann, *The Law of Development Cooperation* 186–7.

[341] On the classification of the GATT and WTO dispute settlement as judicial procedures see chapter 1 section C 2.

[342] Josef Drexl, 'Unmittelbare Anwendbarkeit des WTO-Rechts in der globalen Privatrechtsordnung' in Bernhard Großfeld and others (eds), *Festschrift für Wolfgang Fikentscher* (Mohr Siebeck 1998) 822, 825; the leading work is that of Ernst-Ulrich Petersmann, *Constitutional Functions and Constitutional*

Originally, the GATT was supposed to be part of the International Trade Organization (ITO).[343] But the agreement failed in the US Congress and never went into effect. As a result, the GATT was applied provisionally for decades. It contained only rudimentary guidelines for dispute settlement. After all, it was supposed to become part of the more comprehensive ITO. Only Article XXII of the GATT stipulated that a party to the treaty whose benefit from the agreement was being nullified or impaired by the actions of others could consult with the other side and, should this fail to have any success, submit the matter to all parties to the treaty for examination. As a collective, the latter then had the option of authorizing the aggrieved party to suspend trade concessions in the relationship with the violating party. This mechanism was initially far removed from a judicial mode of dispute management. The daily institutional routine of the GATT was shaped by the same diplomats who had negotiated the agreement. They represented the contending parties and staffed the Secretariat. On their own initiative, they developed, as a way of supporting dispute settlement, the panel process, in which the parties to the agreement charged a panel of three to five independent arbitrators to draft a report. These panels then formulated their recommendations to all parties of the treaty—not only the contending parties—after they had examined the written submissions of the parties and increasingly also oral presentations, and deliberated them *in camera*. The reports as such were recommendations without binding legal force. Throughout, the GATT was a law by and for diplomats.[344]

But interdependence cannot function with diplomacy alone, since diplomatic approaches can hardly generate and stabilize the kind of differentiated normative expectations demanded by transnational economic activity. It therefore comes as no surprise that the GATT developed over the years characteristics of an international organization with a judicial apparatus, which elaborated its legal regime. The mechanism fell increasingly under the influence of lawyers, who brought a juristic–legalistic ethos with them. The change in personnel transformed the mode of operation and brought the reasoning of the *panel* reports closer to judicial decisions.[345] An

Problems of International Economic Law (UP Fribourg Switzerland 1991) especially 210–21; early on Heinz Hauser, 'Domestic Policy Foundation and Domestic Policy Function of International Trade Rules' (1986) 41 Aussenwirtschaft 171; Jan Tumlir, 'International Economic Order and Democratic Constitutionalism' (1983) 34 ORDO 71.

343 On the mechanism of dispute settlement by the ITO see Arts 66, 92–7 of the Havana Charter.

344 Robert E Hudec, *Enforcing International Trade Law: The Evolution of the Modern GATT Legal System* (Butterworth 1993) 7; Robert E Hudec, 'The GATT Legal System: A Diplomat's Jurisprudence' (1970) 4 Journal of World Trade 615; on the change toward a rule-oriented approach see John H Jackson, 'The Case of the World Trade Organization' (2008) 84 Intl Affairs 437.

345 Joseph HH Weiler, 'The Rule of Lawyers and the Ethos of Diplomats: Reflections on the Internal and External Legitimacy of WTO Dispute Settlement' (2001) 35 Journal of World Trade 191, 198–9.

important step in this was the creation of a legal division within the GATT Secretariat in the early 1980s. Henceforth the Secretariat regularly drafted *panel* reports, paid attention to coherence in case-law, and overall promoted the formation of an independent judicial dispute settlement.[346]

The regime orientation became especially apparent at the beginning of the 1990s, when trade interests increasingly conflicted with other international interests. In the reports on the *Tuna Dolphin* cases, the panels found that trade-impeding measures for the protection of dolphins could not be justified on the basis of the general exceptions of the GATT. The law of economic interdependence thus prohibited environmental protection beyond a state's own territory, a decision that evoked considerable criticism.[347] Under the GATT 1947 this criticism could still be countered by noting that the reports found no consensus and were thus not binding.[348] This would no longer be possible under the WTO, which made necessary a recalibration of regime interest and other public concerns.

In 1995, the WTO brought a fundamental institutional development and a further push toward juridification. It set a new dynamic in motion, which for many critics symbolized the triumphal march of globalization in a neo-liberal cast.[349] What is clear is that it must be seen against the backdrop that Francis Fukuyama described—as memorably as it was premature—as the 'End of History', the final breakthrough of a market-centred democratic liberalism.[350] Substantive innovations of the WTO Agreement extended the law of global trade into many new areas. Most of all, however, the judicial mechanism was placed on a new foundation with the Dispute Settlement Understanding (DSU) which forms part of that Agreement.[351] The two essential achievements were the establishment of an appellate instance, the Appellate Body, and the quasi-automatic acceptance of the

What is revealing is that the average length of the reports rose from seven pages (1948–1969) to 15 pages (1970–1979), and after 1985 eventually to 48 pages.

[346] Ernst-Ulrich Petersmann, *The GATT/WTO Dispute Settlement System: International Law, International Organizations and Dispute Settlement* (Kluwer Law 1997) 85.

[347] For example, *United States—Restrictions on Imports of Tuna* (1991) GATT BISD 39S/155, not accepted. For more detail see Ingo Venzke, 'Making General Exceptions: The Spell of Precedents in Developing Article XX GATT into Standards for Domestic Regulatory Policy' (2011) 12 German L J 1111, 1119–21.

[348] Still, these safety mechanisms could not prevent reports on the *Tuna-Dolphin* cases that were not accepted having real repercussions on the legal discourse. See Venzke, 'Making General Exceptions' 1121–9.

[349] Ulrich Brand and others, *Global Governance: Alternativen zur neoliberalen Globalisierung?* (Westfälisches Dampfboot 2000) 104; Lori Wallach and Michelle Sforza, *Whose Trade Organization?* (Public Citizen 1999) especially 3, 217.

[350] Francis Fukuyama, *The End of History and the Last Man* (The Free Press 1992) 39–51.

[351] See only Ernst-Ulrich Petersmann, 'The Transformation of the World Trading System through the 1994 Agreement Establishing the World Trade Organization' (1995) 6 Eur J Intl L 161.

reports by the dispute settlement body, introducing compulsory jurisdiction in all but in name.

While reports under the GATT 1947 required the consensus of the contracting parties to acquire binding force, now, by contrast, consensus is needed in the Dispute Settlement Body, an organ of state representatives, to *prevent* bindingness (Article 16(4) DSU).[352] In substance, this led to the decision-making competence of the reporting organs, which work judicially. This step was accompanied by the newly introduced possibility of appealing a panel decision to a higher instance. Those involved in the negotiations assumed that only a small number of cases would be brought before the Appellate Body. They likely also did not suspect what kind of dynamism a judicial system with an appellate instance could develop. At once, however, the Appellate Body became the heart of the new WTO legal regime.[353]

Perhaps the most important contribution of the Appellate Body, from the perspective of the regime-orientated basic conception of international courts, was that it embedded the specific orientation of the regime into a broader legal context, thereby correcting a worrisome blindness toward other concerns. It was a wise move to staff the Appellate Body in 1995 not primarily with trade experts but with prominent jurists, most of whom were qualified international lawyers of general orientation. They positioned world trade law as part of international law. At the very beginning, a report prominently noted that the GATT should not be 'read in clinical isolation from public international law'.[354] At the same time, the members of the Appellate Body paid tribute to the state-oriented conception of international courts when they stressed the ordinary meaning of treaty texts as the preferred interpretation. In this they were probably reacting to discourses about how the WTO Agreement is compatible with state sovereignty, which was an especially critical debate in the United States. But none of this contradicts a multifunctional analysis. As Michelle Sanchez Badin and Richard B Stewart, a doyen of American administrative law and co-creator of the Global Administrative Law approach, sum it up:

[352] In more detail Armin von Bogdandy, 'Law and Politics in the WTO—Strategies to Cope with a Deficient Relationship' (2001) 5 Max Planck YB UN L 609, 618; Robert Howse, 'The Legitimacy of the World Trade Organization' in Jean-Marc Coicaud and Veijo Heiskanen (eds), *The Legitimacy of International Organizations* (United Nations UP 2001) 355, 374.

[353] In detail Peter van den Bossche, 'From Afterthought to Centrepiece: The WTO Appellate Body and Its Rise to Prominence in the World Trading System' in Giorgio Sacerdoti, Alan Yanovich, and Jan Bohanes (eds), *The WTO at Ten: The Contribution of the Dispute Settlement System* (CUP 2006) 289.

[354] *United States: Standards for Reformulated and Conventional Gasoline–Appellate Body Report* (29 April 1996) WT/DS2/AB/R 17.

> The contentious and protracted Ministerial process for legislation and the underdeveloped normative functions of the WTO administrative branches have required the dispute settlement system to take on the principal burden of updating WTO trade disciplines and addressing relevant non-trade norms, including those reflected in other international agreements and international law generally as well as in domestic law. These circumstances have helped push the dispute settlement process from a purely bilateral and reciprocal system of episodic dispute settlement towards a multilateral system with a regulatory character. This evolution is only partial, and a more traditional approach is reflected in many panel and Appellate Body opinions. But the method and jurisprudence of the Appellate Body have often sought to promote an orderly and transparent system of global trade law to structure the practices of members and the expectations of global economic actors.[355]

The still present regime orientation emerges from the fact that the jurisdiction of the dispute resolution body extends merely to WTO law.[356] In addition, the regime orientation is evident in how the dispute resolution organs position themselves and world trade law in relationship to domestic regulatory autonomy. The Appellate Body has repeatedly affirmed that every member state is, in principle, free to choose its domestic level of protection—for example, with a view toward consumers or the environment—at its own discretion. Nevertheless, this discretion must be exercised within parameters shaped by the WTO law of global economic interconnections; that is, by the perspective of the regime. In addition, the Appellate Body has indicated that in its review of whether trade-restricting measures to protect other legal goods or interests are justified, it engages in a process of weighing and balancing.[357] Some observers see in this the step to a complete proportionality test and interpret this as the expression of a new self-understanding, perhaps even constitutionalist ambitions.[358] How goals

[355] Stewart and Sanchez Badin, 'The World Trade Organization and Global Administrative Law' 470. A series of decisions supported this statement, especially the adjudication on Art X(3) GATT, which spells out the requirements regarding a 'uniform, impartial and reasonable' administration, concerning detailed administrative guidelines under Art VI GATS and the Agreement on Technical Barriers to Trade. On the latter see *United States: Measures Affecting the Production and Sale of Clove Cigarettes—Appellate Body Report* (4 April 2012) WT/DS406/AB/R.

[356] Arts 1–3 DSU. A prescription on applicable law is not found, however. In more detail Joost Pauwelyn, 'The Role of Public International Law in the WTO: How Far Can We Go?' (2001) 95 AJIL 535, 561.

[357] *Korea: Measures Affecting Imports of Fresh, Chilled and Frozen Beef–Appellate Body Report* (11 December 2000) WT/DS161/AB/R and WT/DS169/AB/R, para 162; *Brazil: Measures Affecting Imports of Retreated Tyres—Appellate Body Report* (3 December 2007) WT/DS332/AB/R, para 178. The debate is now also virulent in the interpretation of the Agreement on Technical Barriers to Trade, see, for example, *United States: Certain Country of Origin Labelling (COOL) Requirements—Appellate Body Report* (29 June 2012) WT/DS384/AB/R and WT/DS386/AB/R, para 378.

[358] On the discussion see Venzke, 'Making General Exceptions' 1132–7. See also Deborah Cass, *The Constitutionalization of the World Trade Organization* (OUP 2005) especially 197–8.

of world trade are conveyed with other public concerns within the WTO is of critical importance for the future of the institution.[359]

On the whole, however, it can be noted that precisely because of the case-law of the Appellate Body, WTO law has been embedded into general international law and co-ordination with other regimes has been initiated.[360] This achievement can serve as inspiration especially for the international protection of investments, whose regime orientation at times might appear almost pathological.

3. Investment arbitration within the framework of the ICSID

Today's international investment arbitration, especially within the framework of the International Centre for Settlement of Investment Disputes (ICSID), has similarly taken on a role that goes beyond mere dispute settlement. Of course, dispute settlement remains important, not least because investment disputes have led to military measures in the past.[361] But today it is not limited to settling disputes and serving the cause of international peace. Under the aegis of the World Bank, the goal of promoting the economic development of the south through capital exports from the north initially moved to the fore.[362] Many bilateral investment treaties (BITs) reiterate and affirm the primary goal of the ICSID Convention, to promote the economic prosperity of the host state by means of foreign investment.[363] This goal is to be served if foreign investors can assert their rights directly before an international tribunal, without first having to approach the courts of the host country.[364] But even this scenario does not encompass the role of investment protection in its entire breadth today, as it has strengthened into an important element of the global capital markets law.[365] Investment arbitration serves this market by generating and

[359] On this in greater detail Joseph HH Weiler, 'Law, Culture, and Values in the WTO—Gazing into the Crystal Ball' in Daniel Bethlehem and others (eds), *The Oxford Handbook of International Trade Law* (OUP 2009) 749–72.

[360] Van den Bossche, 'From Afterthought to Centrepiece'. With an emphasis on the regime-stabilizing effect of the opening see Bruno Simma and Dirk Pulkowski, 'Of Planets and the Universe: Self-Contained Regimes in International Law' (2006) 17 Eur J Intl L 483, 510–2.

[361] On the Drago Porter Convention of 1907, which intended to prohibit this, Rudolf Dolzer and Christoph Schreuer, *Principles of International Investment Law* (OUP 2008) 12.

[362] Thomas W Wälde, 'The Specific Nature of Investment Arbitration' in Thomas W Wälde and Philippe Kahn (eds), *New Aspects of International Investment Law* (Nijhoff 2007) 43, 72–6.

[363] See, for example, Agreement between the United Mexican States and the Federal Republic of Germany on the Promotion and Reciprocal Protection of Investments (23 February 2001) Preamble, third recital <unctad.org/sections/dite/iia/docs/bits/germany_mexico.pdf> accessed 10 October 2012; Convention on the Settlement of Investment Disputes between States and Nationals of Other States (ICSID Convention) (14 October 1966) Preamble, first recital.

[364] In detail Dolzer and Schreuer, *Principles of International Investment Law* 214.

[365] The investment dispute between a Swedish energy company and Germany can be examined neither from the peace perspective nor the development perspective; see *Vattenfall AB, Vattenfall Europe*

stabilizing normative expectations, reviewing national measures, and knitting the roughly 3,000 bilateral investment treaties into a dynamic and multilateral system.[366]

Arbitration procedures involving expropriation have certainly existed for a long time.[367] The issues at stake were mostly questions of legality and compensation. Nationalizations by newly independent states gave this area of the law a strong boost, for example during the nationalization of the Libyan oil industry in the early 1970s.[368] What has been path-breaking in the process is that investors—that is, private parties—increasingly appear directly before the arbitral tribunals. By contrast, the *ius standi* of other international judicial bodies generally recognizes only states as parties.[369] As a result, in order to assert their rights and interests before the ICJ, for example, private individuals depend on the diplomatic protection of their home state.[370] Within the framework of the WTO, as well, companies must continue to persuade governments to initiate proceedings.

Virtually all questions of international legal protection in cases of expropriation were contentious for a long time. For example, it was unclear whether foreign investors enjoyed the protection of a separate international standard or should be treated like nationals according to national law, what constituted expropriation in the first place, and how due compensation should be calculated. In the UN General Assembly in the 1960s, state delegates tried in vain to arrive at a consensus on these questions. Instead, the project of a 'New International Economic Order' introduced by developing countries in the 1970s divided the Assembly even further. Against this backdrop, the General Counsel of the World Bank at the time, Aron Broches, pushed the programmatic formula 'procedure before substance'. The first step was to establish procedures for dispute settlement, and substantive law

AG, Vattenfall Europe Generation AG v Federal Republic of Germany (Award) ICSID Case No ARB/09/6 (11 March 2011).

[366] In detail Stephan W Schill, *The Multilateralization of International Investment Law* (CUP 2009) 278–361; Stephan W Schill, 'System-Building in Investment Treaty Arbitration and Lawmaking' in Armin von Bogdandy and Ingo Venzke (eds), *International Judicial Lawmaking: On Public Authority and Democratic Legitimation in Global Governance* (Springer 2012) 133.

[367] See, for example, the Lena Goldfields Arbitration of 1930 as a result of the nationalizations in the wake of the Russian Revolution of 1917—see Van Vechten Veeder, 'The *Lena Goldfields* Arbitration: The Historical Roots of Three Ideas' (1998) 47 ICLQ 747; *Case Concerning the Factory at Chorzów (Germany v Poland)* (Judgment) PCIJ Rep Series A No 9.

[368] See the exemplary and fairly influential case with René-Jean Dupuy as the sole arbitrator: *Texaco Overseas Petroleum Company v Government of the Libyan Arab Republic* (Ad Hoc Award of 19 January 1977) (1977) 104 Journal du droit international 350.

[369] This is now also different for human rights courts (see section B 3) and the Inspection Panel of the World Bank, and, for a long time, the internal administrative tribunals (section C 1).

[370] By way of example *Barcelona Traction*, para 28; *ELSI (USA v Italy)* (Judgment) [1989] ICJ Rep 15, para 49.

would follow in the praxis of applying the law.[371] Broches thus clearly had the law-making role of courts in mind. His effort was successful. Procedural rules and the institutional framework were created with the ICSID.[372] States increasingly entered into bilateral investment agreements that laid down standards of protection for foreign investors and under which—and this was highly important—investors often act as parties to the proceedings and are able to file a suit directly against a host state.

In the 24 years between 1966 and 1990, only 26 cases were brought within the framework of the ICSID. Striking developments began only after 1990, in the very period of globalization. The increase over the past two decades has been impressive. Between 1991 and 2011, 343 disputes were initiated within the framework of the ICSID alone, with the largest annual number of cases occurring in 2011.[373] More than 90 per cent of all cases registered under the ICSID thus date to the period after 1990. In addition, between 2001 and 2011, annulment proceedings were initiated against 34 decisions; in all the preceding years there had only been six.[374] This quantitative development went hand-in-hand with a significant qualitative change.

Aron Broches was successful not only institutionally, but also substantively. The essence of substantive investment protection law, developed during the praxis of arbitration, and this process was deeply shaped by the general goal of investment protection. The law-making within the ICSID framework is particularly noteworthy, considering that there is no permanent international organ for the administration of justice and no uniform legal basis, for example in the form of a multilateral treaty. Nevertheless, out of customary international law and around 3,000 BITs, the diverse arbitral tribunals have fashioned an overarching legal corpus that guides and stabilizes normative expectations.[375] Of course, not all decisions are equally significant or fully coherent. A few arbitral tribunals emphasize explicitly that they are charged by the contending parties solely with deciding a concrete case, not with developing a coherent body of case-law.[376] Others disagree and

[371] On this Dolzer and Schreuer, *Principles of International Investment Law* 20.

[372] Established with the Convention on the Settlement of Investment Disputes between States and Nationals of Other States of 1966 (ICSID Convention) and the ICSID Rules of Procedure for Arbitration Proceedings.

[373] See *ICSID Caseload-Statistics*, Issue 2012–1, 7 <icsid.worldbank.org/ICSID/FrontServlet?requestType=ICSIDDocRH&actionVal=CaseLoadStatistics> accessed 10 October 2012. For a statistic beyond the context of the ICSID see UNCTAD, *Latest Developments in Investor-State Dispute Settlement* IIA Issues Note No 1/2012, 1–3 <unctad.org/en/PublicationsLibrary/webdiaeia2012d10_en.pdf> accessed 10 October 2012.

[374] See *ICSID Caseload-Statistics* 15.

[375] Schill, *The Multilateralization of International Investment Law* 278–361.

[376] See, for example, *AES Corporation v Argentina* (Decision on Jurisdiction) ICSID Case No ARB/02/17 (26 April 2005) para 30; *Romak (Romak SA v Uzbekistan)* PCA Case No AA 280 (UNCITRAL Award of 26

consider themselves obligated to contribute to legal security and a harmonious development of the law.[377] All in all, this praxis of judicial decision-making has shaped central areas of investment protection law. Today it is hardly possible to argue, without referring to earlier cases, what the standard of just and fair treatment entails, what represents a protected investment, what constitutes an expropriation, or how compensation is to be calculated.

The standards of investment protection have been developed in the functional logic of the regime. They significantly constrain the room for manoeuvre of the host states, as decisions made in the wake of Argentina's bankruptcy illustrate. In 2001, in the face of a deep economic crisis and an exploding debt burden, Argentina felt compelled to abandon the fixed exchange rate between the peso and the US dollar and to restrict the export of capital. Formally, these measures affected national and foreign investors equally. But the latter, if they belong to a state that has a BIT treaty with Argentina and has joined the ICSID Convention or has agreed with Argentina on utilizing the ICSID Additional Facility, can sue for the relevant protection standards of the respective BIT directly before international arbitral tribunals.[378] A number of suits against Argentina have been brought since then or are pending, with claims totalling an estimated 80 billion US dollars.[379] The arbitral decisions have been on the whole rather restrictive. Argentina thus experienced at first hand how narrow a state's leeway had become in protecting public order if it did not want to run the risk of having to pay significant compensation to foreign investors.[380]

In this example, critics of the current investment protection regime find confirmation of their rejection of the system.[381] They consider the current

November 2009) paras 170–1; *GEA Group Aktiengesellschaft v Ukraine* (Award) ICSID Case No ARB/08/16 (31 March 2011) para 90.

[377] See, for example, *Saipem SpA v People's Republic of Bangladesh* (Decision on Jurisdiction and Recommendation on Provisional Measures) ICSID Case No ARB/05/07 (21 March 2007) para 67; *Noble Energy Inc and Machalapower CIA LTDA v Republic of Ecuador and Consejo Nacional de Electricidad* (Decision on Jurisdiction) ICSID Case No ARB/05/12 (5 March 2008) para 50; *Enron Creditors Recovery Corp v Argentine Republic* (Annulment Decision) ICSID Case No ARB/01/03 (30 July 2010) para 66.

[378] See Art 25 ICSID Convention; Art 2 Rules Governing the Additional Facility for the Administration of Proceedings by the Secretariat of the International Centre for Settlement of Investment Disputes.

[379] On the estimate see William Burke-White and Andreas von Staden, 'Investment Protection in Extraordinary Times: The Interpretation and Application of Non-Precluded Measures Provisions in Bilateral Investment Treaties' (2007) 48 Virginia J Intl L 307, 311.

[380] This statement should not be understood in the sense of an endorsement of all Argentinian measures. An overview of the adjudication is offered by Stephan W Schill, 'International Investment Law and the Host State's Power to Handle Economic Crises: Comment on the ICSID Decision in LG & E v Argentina' (2007) 24 J Intl Arbitration 265; José E Alvarez and Tegan Brink, 'Revisiting the Necessity Defence: Continental Casualty v. Argentina' (2010–2011) YB Intl Investment L and Policy 319.

[381] The criticism is summarized in a *Public Statement on the International Investment Regime*, 31 August 2010, available, along with a list of the signatories, at <www.osgoode.yorku.ca/public_statement/>

national manoeuvring room too narrow and believe they can detect a certain bias—whether structural or connected with the person of the arbitrator—in favour of investors. Contradictions between different arbitral decisions and the non-transparency and confidentiality of the procedures—which, after all, concern public matters—are identified as fundamental problems of justice. In response to this criticism, it has been asserted that the states in question had freely entered into their obligations and benefited from them economically. Investments are cost-intensive, so the argument goes, and investors depend on stable framework conditions.

Today, the positions have hardened, and the criticism of individual decisions has strengthened into a general critique of the current investment protection law along with its institutions.[382] There is movement in this area of the law, and praxis is changing. For example, it is interesting to observe how the so-called Annulment Committees have expanded their narrow jurisdiction in annulment procedures in the face of the growing criticism. The ICSID Convention, in principle, allows for the annulment of arbitral decisions only on the grounds '(a) that the Tribunal was not properly constituted; (b) that the Tribunal has manifestly exceeded its powers; (c) that there was corruption on the part of a member of the Tribunal; (d) that there has been a serious departure from a fundamental rule of procedure; or (e) that the award has failed to state the reasons on which it is based'.[383] Nevertheless, the arbitrators of the 'second instance' have conceived of their role broadly and have annulled decisions because they believed they had falsely applied the factual case of an emergency.[384] One can perceive this expansion of competence as arising from the perception that a crisis of legitimacy exists in a system that has taken its regime orientation too far.[385]

accessed 10 October 2012. See also Gus Van Harten, *Investment Treaty Arbitration and Public Law* (OUP 2007); Susan D Franck, 'The Legitimacy Crisis in Investment Treaty Arbitration: Privatizing International Law through Inconsistent Decisions' (2005) 73 Fordham L Rev 1521; Muthucumaraswamy Sornarajah, 'Toward Normlessness: The Ravage and Retreat of Neo-Liberalism in International Investment Law' (2009–2010) YB Intl Investment L and Policy 595; David Schneiderman, *Constitutionalizing Economic Globalization* (CUP 2008) 25–108.

[382] On this discussion see the contributions in Michael Waibel and others (eds), *The Backlash against Investment Arbitration* (Kluwer Law International 2010).

[383] Art 52 ICSID Convention.

[384] *Sempra Energy International v Argentine Republic* (Annulment Decision) ICSID Case No ARB/02/16 (29 June 2010) paras 186–229; *Enron Creditors*, paras 406–17. See also Christoph Schreuer, 'From ICSID Annulment to Appeal: Half Way Down the Slippery Slope' (2011) 10 L and Practice of Intl Courts and Tribunals 211.

[385] For a better calibration, numerous proposals can be found in Stephan Schill (ed), *International Investment Law and Comparative Public Law* (OUP 2010).

D. TOWARD A DEMOCRACY-ORIENTED THEORY

The regime-oriented conception of international courts stands in the tradition of functionalism.[386] Theories of interdependence and regime theory have offered theoretical underpinnings that, since the 1990s, have been taken further in theories of global governance.[387] Even though much is controversial, we can identify four core points that deepen our understanding of international courts from this perspective. These points also focus our critique, show deficiencies, and provide points of departure for our democracy-oriented public law theory of international adjudication.

First, with the concept of global governance it is much easier to think about the role of many international judicial bodies in managing the interdependence of states. It guides the view toward the specific nature of the various regimes, organizations, and treaty systems. But in this line of thinking, general international law tends to turn into a residual category on the distant horizon of practical operation.[388] It is also much easier to understand and justify that a particular 'regime interest'—liberalized trade, investment protection, and the efficiency of maritime traffic, in our examples—is pursued through adjudication in a specific regime.[389]

Second, under the notion of global governance there is a change in the understanding of who the actors before international courts are and whom international courts address. Of particular importance, especially vis-à-vis the other two basic conceptions, is the modified understanding of statehood in international law. For example, in Anne-Marie Slaughter's influential—but, as we shall see, in the final analysis inadequate—conception of 'a new world order', the state is 'disaggregated'.[390] This applies especially to its preeminent characteristic in traditional international law, namely its sovereignty.[391] Sovereignty loses its classic meaning of 'autonomy' and mutates into the 'capacity to participate in transgovernmental networks of

[386] A basic work is that of David Mitrany, *A Functional Theory of Politics* (LSE 1975); see also Ernst B Haas, *Beyond the Nation-State: Functionalism and International Organization* (Stanford UP 1964).

[387] Keohane and Nye, *Power and Independence*; Hewson and Sinclair, 'The Emergence of Global Governance Theory'.

[388] This is opposed, for example, by the International Law Commission, 'Fragmentation of International Law: Difficulties Arising from the Diversification and Expansion of International Law' (13 April 2006) ILC Doc A/CN.4/L.682, especially 248, 255.

[389] This is emphasized especially strongly by the systems-theory approaches that are in the tradition of functionalism, for example Andreas Fischer-Lescano and Gunther Teubner, *Regime-Kollisionen* (Suhrkamp 2006).

[390] Anne-Marie Slaughter, *A New World Order* (Princeton UP 2004) 12–5, 18, 31–5; Anne-Marie Slaughter, 'International Law in a World of Liberal States' (1995) 6 Eur J Intl L 503, 516–21; Anne-Marie Slaughter, 'International Law and International Relations' (2000) 285 Recueil des cours 9, 41.

[391] Slaughter, *A New World Order* 266–71.

all types'.[392] The concept of networks is important under this conception for grasping the phenomenon of global governance.[393] It describes stable transnational systems of interaction between different institutions of public authority. Civil servants as well as judges regularly meet in those structures. As such its vision is markedly different from traditional international law, which conceives of the state as a unitary actor.

What is more, this understanding makes it much easier to differentiate between various actors within the state. In this way, the domestic judiciary comes into focus in a new way.[394] The same holds true for the shaping role of international institutions, judicial institutions in our case. Governance theory further consistently emphasizes the importance of private or hybrid actors and the role of individuals. This sharpens the perception of the role of private parties in international judicial procedures, whether as plaintiffs (in investment disputes or before human rights courts) or as powerful actors behind the contending parties, for example as an NGO financing a human rights complaint or a company pushing a government to initiate a suit against a state.[395] Anne-Marie Slaughter, in fact, sees the international actions of states less as an expression of autonomous decisions by the top political leadership and more as the manifestation of interests articulated by individuals, groups, or enterprises.[396]

Third, global governance stands for the turn toward structures and processes that can be formal as well as informal in nature. This turn brings into focus a wealth of new phenomena that cannot be grasped with traditional legal concepts. A way thus opens up to address the role of soft law in judicial reasoning and to subject it to legal analysis.[397]

Finally, the concept of global governance highlights that contemporary governance activities are characterized by multiple levels, as the use of the term 'global' instead of 'international' makes clear. At the back of this is the trend toward giving up distinction according to the various levels; that is,

[392] Slaughter, *A New World Order* 34. Early on Antonia Handler Chayes and Abram Chayes, *The New Sovereignty: Compliance with International Regulatory Agreements* (Harvard UP 1995) 27.

[393] For more detail see Matthias Goldmann, 'Der Widerspenstigen Zähmung, oder: Netzwerke dogmatisch gedacht' in Sigrid Boysen and others (eds), *Netzwerke: 47. Assistententagung Öffentliches Recht* (Nomos 2007) 225.

[394] Eyal Benvenisti, 'Reclaiming Democracy: The Strategic Uses of Foreign and International Law by National Courts' (2008) 102 AJIL 241; André Nollkaemper, *National Courts and the International Rule of Law* (OUP 2011).

[395] See, for example, *Japan: Measures Affecting Consumer Photographic Film and Paper—Panel Report* (31 March 1998) WT/DS44/R, behind which stood Kodak on the US side, and Fuji on the Japanese side.

[396] Slaughter, 'International Law in a World of Liberal States' 508; Slaughter, 'International Law and International Relations' 41.

[397] On this see chapter 4 section C 3.

in terms of international, supranational, and national public authority. This is a fruitful basis for conceiving anew the mapping out of international, supranational, and national courts. Anne-Marie Slaughter, for example, believes that we must transition from international adjudication to a 'global community of courts' based on synergies with national courts.[398] A similar thrust lies behind theories of a Global Administrative Law, which rest on the notion that the bodies of international and national laws form a whole and are best treated from this perspective.[399]

As forward-looking and elucidating as this third basic conception of international adjudication may be, just as weighty are some of the problems that especially arise from its functionalist origins and basis.[400] Weaknesses start to show in particular when it comes to questions of legitimacy. Placing emphasis on the effective pursuit of goals corresponds to the functionalist tradition of thinking. There may very well be constellations in which such references are enough to meet the burden of justifying a specific decision. However, in view of the fact that some courts have gained considerable autonomy, and given the breadth of controversial social issues they are by now adjudicating, the reference to goals no longer provides an adequate strategy, if it ever did. To be sure, the pacifying function of international decisions remains relevant, not least to the realization of democratic governance. But the goal of peace misses a good deal of the phenomenon of an international judiciary. As a result, many international courts tailored to specific sectors seek legitimation from implementing specific goals beyond safeguarding peace.[401] Yet, no matter how important a specific goal may be, it cannot alone resolve all demands to justify public authority. Functional arguments offer no solution to the unavoidable competition between different goals. What is more, the specific focus of an international court can easily lead to a strong orientation toward the 'regime interest' at the expense of other principles.[402] Moreover, the question arises as to how regime-specific

[398] Slaughter, *A New World Order* 100.

[399] Path-breaking on the latter are Sabino Cassese, 'Global Administrative Law: An Introduction' (2005) <www.iilj.org/GAL/documents/Cassesepaper.pdf> accessed 10 October 2012; Kingsbury, Krisch, and Stewart, 'The Emergence of Global Administrative Law'.

[400] On the functionalist roots of the concept of governance see Oliver E Williamson, *The Mechanisms of Governance* (OUP 1996); in addition, James N Rosenau, 'Governance, Order, and Change in World Politics' in James N Rosenau and Ernst-Otto Czempiel (eds), *Governance without Government: Order and Change in World Politics* (CUP 1992) 1, 4.

[401] Dolzer and Schreuer, *Principles of International Investment Law* 149; Carmen Thiele, 'Fragmentierung des Völkerrechts als Herausforderung für die Staatengemeinschaft' (2008) 46 Archiv des Völkerrechts 1, 13; Tomer Broude, 'The Rule(s) of Trade and the Rhetos of Development: Reflections on the Functional and Aspirational Legitimacy of the WTO' (2006–2007) 45 Columbia J Transnational L 221.

[402] Critical on this trend of global governance is, for example, Robert Latham, 'Politics in a Floating World: Toward a Critique of Global Governance' in Hewson and Sinclair (eds), *Approaches to Global Governance Theory* 23; Martti Koskenniemi, 'Global Governance and Public International Law' (2004)

institutions could address the broad range of interests and values of the citizens who are ultimately affected by their decisions. How do they link up with citizens?

The answers that Anne-Marie Slaughter has given to these objections provide a good backdrop against which to contrast our ideas. The key difference is this: Slaughter opts for state-centric networks instead of international institutions. We maintain that her approach is not persuasive—neither in terms of legitimation nor of practicality. No road leads past developing the democratic principle for international institutions.

Like many other authors, Slaughter sees a crucial problem of global governance in its inadequate legitimacy as a secretive, technocratic, and exclusive system without democratic accountability.[403] She seeks the solution in a 'more just' global order, in a global order structured by networks; one that is 'inclusive, tolerant, respectful, and decentralized'.[404] No one will want to dispute this aim, with the exception of the point that networks constitute the best form for achieving it.

To democratize global governance, she proposes a number of points on which there is broad consensus in the discussion, and which are also relevant for international courts.[405] First is the explicit recognition of the dual (internal *and* international) function of actors in global networks, among which she also includes judges. This makes it easier to demand responsibility at every level.[406] Second, she calls for greater transparency for the purpose of greater publicness.[407] A third point demands stronger interaction between the parliamentarians of the states involved in global governance.[408] This parliamentarization would not necessarily have to go hand-in-hand with decision-making authority.[409] A fourth element is the mobilization of transnational networks of citizens (NGOs, interest groups, churches, etc).[410] Fifth, an adjustment of the domestic constitutional order is required, such as parliamentary control of the power of domestic organs exercised on the transnational level.[411] To further strengthen the legitimacy of global governance, she recommends additional measures aimed at the

37 Kritische Justiz 241; Michael Barnett and Martha Finnemore, 'The Power of Liberal International Organizations' in Michael Barnett and Raymond Duvall (eds), *Power in Global Governance* (CUP 2005) 161; and the contributions, from varying perspectives, in Alice D Ba and Matthew J Hoffmann (eds), *Contending Perspectives on Global Governance* (Routledge 2005).

403 Slaughter, *A New World Order* 215. On the debate over accountability see also the contributions in David Held and Mathias Koenig-Archibugi (eds), *Global Governance and Public Accountability* (Blackwell 2005).

404 Slaughter, *A New World Order* 29.

405 Slaughter, *A New World Order* 28–9.

406 Slaughter, *A New World Order* 231–5.

407 Slaughter, *A New World Order* 235–7.

408 Slaughter, *A New World Order* 237–9.

409 Slaughter, *A New World Order* 130.

410 Slaughter, *A New World Order* 239–40.

411 Slaughter, *A New World Order* 241–4.

global responsibility of national representatives. Here we find catchwords such as global deliberative equality, positive recognition of diversity, positive comity, a system of checks and balances between the various transnational structures and networks, and, following the example of the European Union, a principle of subsidiarity.[412]

Anne-Marie Slaughter's book presents an impressive summation of the key concepts of the relevant debates. In the final analysis her answer is too attached to the first, state-oriented conception. In considerable tension with the diagnosis of its 'disaggregation', the state as such remains the key institution for Slaughter.[413] The importance she assigns to global networks is explained by the very fact that she sees in them, and not in international institutions, the resolution of what she regards as the central paradox of globalization, which is that '[w]e need more government on a global and a regional scale, but we don't want the centralization of decision-making power and coercive authority so far from the people actually to be governed'.[414] Anne-Marie Slaughter opts here for global networks of governance, as a result of which one can essentially do without international or even supranational authorities. The latter remain 'more the exception than the rule'[415] and should be restricted to a few fields.

It is not convincing that global networks offer a true alternative to international institutions, since the potential of networks is limited. They are useful as a supplement, but they do not form an alternative to legally constituted institutions.[416] Transparency, responsibility, and constitutional standards can hardly be formulated and implemented against them, and so far there has been no proof of their efficacy. In terms of legitimation, moreover, Slaughter cannot get around 're-aggregating' the state again and locating the centre of legitimacy in its midst. It is here that the theory contains a great internal tension. Above all, however, as we will show in the next step, the already existing authority of international institutions—especially of international courts—can no longer be grasped with Slaughter's concept. That leaves only the alternative of either scaling back the international judiciary as such, or searching for its own mechanisms of democratic legitimation. Our study will take the second path.

A few markers for this road to democratic legitimation can be summarized in this chapter's last step. Today, many international courts enjoy

412 Slaughter, *A New World Order* 245–57.

413 Slaughter, *A New World Order* 248.

414 Slaughter, *A New World Order* 8.

415 Slaughter, *A New World Order* 32.

416 Gunnar Folke Schuppert, 'Verwaltungsorganisation und Verwaltungsorganisationsrecht als Steuerungsfaktoren' in Wolfgang Hoffmann-Riem, Eberhard Schmidt-Aßmann, and Andreas Voßkuhle (eds), *Grundlagen des Verwaltungsrechts*, vol 1 (2nd edn, CH Beck 2012) 1067, 1122–30; see also Goldmann, 'Der Widerspenstigen Zähmung'.

notable autonomy in relation to individual states. International courts do not only have the task of settling disputes between states; instead, they serve additional functions, especially those of generating and stabilizing normative expectations, as well as controlling and legitimizing public authority. That is why the traditional, state-oriented conception strikes us as much too narrow, both analytically and normatively. At the same time, we differ on a number of points from the community-oriented understanding, because we are persuaded by many of the insights generated by the research on global governance. Above all, we regard the premises of global order and the unity of the system as problematic in view of largely unplanned and still unco-ordinated diversity. We see order and unity as regulative ideas, not as the foundation and starting point. Accordingly, we are more persuaded by pluralistic rather than unitary approaches. For that reason, we do not consider the existing diversity as problematic, in principle, but seek to interpret it in the light of functional differentiation. From governance scholarship we also adopt the insight that international institutions and processes should be interpreted in their interaction with domestic institutions and processes.

This scholarship does not fully grasp the public character of international courts. Offering a clear view of this key feature, however, strikes us as indispensable in order to provide a convincing assessment of their legitimacy, of possible problems and promising answers. While the first three basic conceptions see international courts *as instruments in the hands of states, organs of the international community*, or as *institutions of specific legal regimes*, we develop international courts as *actors of international public authority*.

3

Key Elements of a Public Law Theory of Adjudication

Chapter 2 provided a sense of how the international judiciary has strengthened over the last two decades. There are many more active courts, those courts are rendering many more decisions, and these decisions are shaping the international order and domestic legal systems far more than ever before. We have provided numerous examples of how courts, by settling disputes, also generate and stabilize normative expectations and control and legitimize other institutions. These contributions are no longer isolated phenomena. Many international courts are even participating in a form of international regulation that is often called global governance. This development cannot be grasped by the first two basic conceptions—the state-oriented and the community-oriented conceptions. It calls for a re-examination of the international judiciary on the basis of democratic theory, something that neither the first two conceptions nor the regime-oriented one offer. The present chapter lays the conceptual groundwork for such a democracy-oriented conception. It will show, first, that international courts exercise public authority, and how they do so (section A). With these tools, step two will lay out the specific legitimatory problem of international adjudication, and will thereby reconstruct widespread, but often vague, critiques of international courts (section B). Step three will develop a democratic concept for international courts that will make it possible to deal constructively with the challenges of legitimacy (section C).

A. THE PUBLIC AUTHORITY OF INTERNATIONAL COURTS

1. The inevitability of judicial law-making

Adjudicating means making law (a), not only for a concrete case, but also for the future (b). Nevertheless, judicial law-making must be distinguished from political legislation (c).

a) Adjudication and law-making

Judicial decisions require democratic justification only when they qualify as an exercise of public authority. But is the correct judicial decision not really based on a cognitive act of *ascertaining* the meaning of the law for the case at hand (*Rechtserkenntnis*)? If that is so, only the prior political act of legislation requires democratic justification, not the act of applying it through the courts. The court's subsequent act of legal interpretation would merely have to demonstrate its correctness. Democratic demands would be out of place.

The understanding that a correct judicial decision is based on an act of legal cognition continues to be important. Many courts describe their decision-making in this way.[1] Thomas von Danwitz, judge of the Court of Justice of the European Union (CJEU), even implored: 'The basic understanding of the judicial decision as an act of cognition, that is, as a decision-making process determined exclusively by the law, must not [...] be cast into doubt, the hunt for the motives behind the reasons must not be opened.'[2] To be sure, the understanding of judicial decision-making as a pure act of deduction, according to which the law in a specific case flows logically from a legal text, is hardly advocated today.[3] Instead, still quite common is an expertocratic understanding according to which legal obligations in a concrete case can be distilled from the overall context of an international legal treaty according to the inherent rules of the legal discourse from the relevant norm text. This ought to be done in view of its place within the totality of international law and in the light of the substantive logic of the case.[4] As Max Weber put it: '[J]urisprudence [...] establishes what is valid according to the rules of juristic thought, which is partly bound

[1] *Legality of the Threat or Use of Nuclear Weapons* (Advisory Opinion) [1996] ICJ Rep 226 ('ascertain'). Here, too, one should take into account the emblematic statements by the ICJ, *Fisheries Jurisdiction (UK v Iceland)* (Merits) [1974] ICJ Rep 3. In greater detail Pierre-Marie Dupuy, 'Le juge et la règle générale' (1989) 93 Revue Générale de Droit International Public 569.

[2] Thomas von Danwitz, 'Funktionsbedingungen der Rechtsprechung des Europäischen Gerichtshofes' (2008) 43 Europarecht 769. On this conception see Judith N Shklar, *Legalism* (Harvard UP 1964) 12–3.

[3] Ulfried Neumann, 'Theorie der juristischen Argumentation' in Winfried Brugger, Ulfried Neumann, and Stephan Kirste (eds), *Rechtsphilosophie im 21. Jahrhundert* (Suhrkamp 2008) 233, 241. On the 'bouche de la loi' Charles Louis de Secondat de Montesquieu, 'De l'esprit des lois' in Edouard Laboulaye (ed), *Œuvres complètes de Montesquieu*, vol 4 (first published 1748, Kraus 1972) 18.

[4] See, for example, Jean-Marc Sorel and Valérie Boré Eveno in Olivier Corten and Pierre Klein (eds), *The Vienna Convention on the Law of Treaties: A Commentary*, vol 1 (OUP 2011) Article 31 paras 804, 806; ILC, 'Third Report on the Law of Treaties' (1964) 2 YB ILC 5, 53. In more detail Andrea Bianchi, 'Textual Interpretation and (International) Law Reading: The Myth of (In)Determinacy and the Genealogy of Meaning' in Pieter H Bekker, Rudolf Dolzer, and Michael Waibel (eds), *Making Transnational Law Work in the Global Economy* (CUP 2010) 34; Ulfried Neumann, *Wahrheit im Recht: Zu Problematik und Legitimität einer fragwürdigen Denkform* (Nomos 2004) 37.

by logically compelling and partly by conventionally given schemata.'[5] For some scholars, the hereby provided rationality of the law stands against the irrationality of politics.[6]

Such a primarily cognitivistic understanding of the judicial decision is challenged with convincing arguments that open the path to our public law theory of adjudication.[7] In the wake of Kant, it is epistemologically no longer possible to claim that decisions in concrete situations can be deduced from abstract concepts.[8] Since the nineteenth century, legal theory has been wrestling with the precise formulation of this insight and its theoretical and practical implications.[9] Even though the debate remains highly contentious on many points, there are a number of shared positions on which our own reflections can build.

Crucial, to begin with, is Hans Kelsen's insight that the categorical distinction between law-making and law-application is untenable, for every act of applying the law is simultaneously one of law-making.[10] While the *validity* of every norm (abstract or concrete) is derived from a norm on a higher level,[11] the *content* of a legal norm is never completely determined by the higher norm.[12] Although Kelsen believed that there was something like a semantic boundary to possible interpretations, which can be ascertained in an act of legal cognition, the concrete meaning of the norm in a case under litigation cannot be deduced but is always created in an act that involves discretion.[13] Nor can the higher norm determine which of the

[5] Max Weber, 'Science as a Vocation' in Peter Lassman and Irvning Velody (eds), *Max Weber's Science as a Vocation* (Michael John tr, Unwin Hyman 1989) 19.

[6] Fritz Ossenbühl, 'Öffentlich-rechtliche Entschädigung in Verfassung, Gesetz und Richterrecht' (1994) 109 Deutsches Verwaltungsblatt 977, 980.

[7] On the continuing influence of the doctrines of sources and interpretation on the understanding of the judicial decision see Ingo Venzke, 'The Role of International Courts as Interpreters and Developers of the Law: Working out the Jurisgenerative Practice of Interpretation' (2012) 34 Loyola of Los Angeles Intl and Comparative L Rev 99.

[8] Immanuel Kant, *Critique of Pure Reason* (Paul Guyer and Allen W Wood trs/eds, first published 1781, CUP 1999) 267–77.

[9] An early discussion in Oskar Bülow, *Gesetz und Richteramt* (Duncker & Humblot 1885). A historical and legal-theoretical reconstruction in Regina Ogorek, *Aufklärung über Justiz*, vol 2 (2nd edn, Vittorio Klostermann 2008).

[10] Hans Kelsen, 'Wesen und Entwicklung der Staatsgerichtsbarkeit' (1929) 5 Veröffentlichungen der Vereinigung der Deutschen Staatsrechtslehrer 30, 31; Hans Kelsen, *Introduction to the Problems of Legal Theory* (Bonnie Litschewski Paulson and Stanley L Paulson trs, Clarendon 1992) 70.

[11] Hans Kelsen, *Hauptprobleme der Staatsrechtslehre entwickelt aus der Lehre vom Rechtssatze* (2nd edn, Mohr Siebeck 1923) XV, XVI; Kelsen, *Introduction to the Problems of Legal Theory* 56. András Jakab, 'Probleme der Stufenbaulehre' (2005) 91 Archiv für Rechts- und Sozialphilosophie 333, 334. To avoid misunderstandings: for Hans Kelsen even the concrete decision lays down a (concrete) norm for the case at hand.

[12] Kelsen, *Introduction to the Problems of Legal Theory* 78.

[13] Kelsen, *Introduction* 80–1.

possible meanings should be chosen. The meaning is settled only in the act of interpretation.[14]

The cognitivist understanding meets even stronger criticism from the *Freirechtsschule* and, especially influential for today's globalized jurisprudence, from American legal realism. The writings of the so-called New Haven School and of Critical Legal Studies go particularly far. Here the positive legal material mutates into a substance that can be used to justify almost every legal decision and outcome.[15] Martti Koskenniemi argues that international interpretations fluctuate inevitably between the poles of apology and utopia, without positive law being able to offer them real support.[16] Abstract and general norms are losing importance also in systems theory, which moves courts to the centre of a dynamically developing legal system. Here, political bodies stand at the periphery. Judicial decisions are guided primarily by judicial precedent while the sources of law recede into the background.[17] Even analytical legal theory in the wake of legal positivism acknowledges the creative dimension of adjudication.[18] Its defence of the deductive model of reasoning rests not on a belief in the defining force of legal concepts, but on the conviction that the premises put forward by a court for its decision must give reasons. In that sense, the deductive mode of argumentation contributes to judicial rationality.[19] What is at stake here is the *justification* of decisions, not the process of *finding* them.[20]

The linguistic turn has further deepened the understanding of the relationship between the textual surface and the meaning. It has substantiated the inevitability of creative interpretation.[21] In the tradition of Wittgenstein and semantic pragmatism, it is understood that the meaning of words lies in

[14] Kelsen, *Introduction* 82.

[15] Michael Reisman, 'Unilateral Action and the Transformations of the World Constitutive Process: The Special Problem of Humanitarian Intervention' (2000) 11 Eur J Intl L 3; David Kennedy, *The Dark Sides of Virtue: Reassessing International Humanitarianism* (Princeton UP 2004) 35. In more detail Jochen von Bernstorff and Ingo Venzke, 'Ethos, Ethics, and Morality in International Relations' in Rüdiger Wolfrum (ed), *Max Planck Encyclopedia of Public International Law* <http://opil.ouplaw.com/home/EPIL> accessed 27 January 2014.

[16] Martti Koskenniemi, *From Apology to Utopia: The Structure of International Legal Argument* (reissue CUP 2005). See also the earlier discussion by David Kennedy, 'Theses about International Law Discourse' (1980) 23 German YB Intl L 353.

[17] Niklas Luhmann, *Law as a Social System* (Klaus A Ziegert tr, Fatima Kastner and others eds, OUP 2004) 313–5.

[18] Hans-Joachim Koch and Helmut Rüßmann, *Juristische Begründungslehre: Eine Einführung in die Grundprobleme der Rechtswissenschaft* (CH Beck 1982) 248–9, with additional references.

[19] Koch and Rüßmann, *Juristische Begründungslehre* 5–6, 69, 221–36.

[20] Neumann, 'Theorie der juristischen Argumentation' 241.

[21] See Richard Rorty (ed), *The Linguistic Turn: Essays in Philosophical Method* (University of Chicago Press 1967). More detailed discussion in Ingo Venzke, *How Interpretation Makes International Law: On Semantic Change and Normative Twists* (OUP 2012) 30.

their usage.[22] Every decision about usage, every interpretation of an expression participates in the process of assigning meaning.[23]

Summing up, the primarily cognitive model is epistemologically untenable. Of course, this insight is annoying for those who advocate a strong international judiciary. This is evident, for example, in the position of Hersch Lauterpacht: he calls for an 'active' role of the judge in advancing the development of the law, but at the same time he maintains that the judge's decision-making freedom should not be stressed too much, especially in international law.[24] The fear seems to be that if judicial creativity became all too obvious, then the project of international law and adjudication would suffer. While this may have been a persuasive position during the interwar period, maybe even until 1990, it does not offer an argument that convincingly counters the challenges we have formulated above. We will continue to argue why Lauterpacht's (and also Kelsen's) argument on the international judiciary no longer holds, but before that we need to note further distinctions and nuances to bring home the main point: that international adjudication amounts to an exercise of public authority.

b) Law-making for the case at hand and for the future

Law-making in a judicial decision has two dimensions. The first pertains to law-making between the parties to a dispute and lies in the interpretation and application of the relevant legal norms with a view to the case in question. This dimension is also described as the creation of the case-specific or decision-making norm.[25] In this respect the decision is comparable to the administrative act, whose law-making power is not felt beyond the issue at hand.[26] That this dimension already involves a creative element is especially apparent when the courts work with the principle of proportionality, or comparable argumentative standards.[27] When a court decides on the

[22] Ludwig Wittgenstein, *Philosophical Investigations* (Anscombe tr, Basil Blackwell 1953) 14–5.

[23] Robert B Brandom, 'Some Pragmatist Themes in Hegel's Idealism: Negotiation and Administration in Hegel's Account of the Structure and Content of Conceptual Norms' (1999) 7 Eur J Philosophy 164, 180. Earlier, Friedrich Müller, 'Richterrecht—rechtstheoretisch formuliert' in Hochschullehrer der Juristischen Fakultät der Universität Heidelberg (eds), *Richterliche Rechtsfortbildung: Erscheinungsformen, Auftrag und Grenzen* (CF Müller 1986) 65, 78.

[24] Hersch Lauterpacht, *The Function of Law in the International Community* (Clarendon 1933) 103–4; Jochen von Bernstorff, *The Public International Law Theory of Hans Kelsen: Believing in Universal Law* (Thomas Dunlap tr, CUP 2010) 217–8; Martti Koskenniemi, *The Gentle Civilizer of Nations: The Rise and Fall of International Law 1870–1960* (CUP 2002) 403–6.

[25] Müller, 'Richterrecht—rechtstheoretisch formuliert' 78–9.

[26] Path-breaking Otto Mayer, *Deutsches Verwaltungsrecht*, vol 1 (3rd edn, Duncker & Humblot 1924) 135. It should be noted, though, that international courts are regularly able only to determine a legal position but cannot, like many domestic courts, repeal a legal act.

[27] Enzo Cannizzaro, *Il principio della proporzionalità nell'ordinamento internazionale* (Giuffrè 2000); Anne-Charlotte Martineau, 'La technique du balancement par l'Organe d'appel de l'OMC (études de

'suitability', 'necessity', or 'appropriateness' of a measure, it clearly performs an act not of cognition, but of assessment.[28] The triumphal march of the principle of proportionality shows that courts have come to embrace their creative role more openly. Above all, however, proportionality reasoning expands the reach of the courts, and their sphere of authority along the way. The principle of proportionality makes it easier for courts to move into territory that was previously assigned solely to the administrative or political realm; that is, to criteria of bureaucratic expediency and political opportunity.

The second dimension of law-making goes beyond the case at hand. A court's decision, the ruling itself as well as its justification, can constitute a key argument in subsequent legal discourses.[29] Courts that publish their decisions along with their reasoning shape later legal discourse, both with their substantials reasons (*ratio decidendi*) and with their statements made in passing (*obiter dictum*). The addressees are all actors in the legal system, including politicians, administrators, judges, counsels, and the wider public.[30] To that end, courts often formulate abstract maxims, place their decisions into publicly accessible collections and data-bases, and present them in press statements suitable for public consumption.[31] In the process, they are by no means interested solely in making an interesting contribution to a general discussion; rather, many decisions seem tailored toward laying down authoritative premises for the future.[32]

We find striking proof of such law-making dynamics in the law of the WTO. At first glance, the Dispute Settlement Understanding (DSU) seems to virtually prohibit judicial law-making. Article 3 Section 2 of the DSU sets out that the '[r]ecommendations and rulings of the Dispute Settlement Body (DSB) cannot add to or diminish the rights and obligations provided in the covered agreements'. This provision is evidently intended to curtail the

la justification dans les discours juridiques)' (2007) 123 Revue du droit public et de la science politique en France et à l'étranger 991.

[28] Path-breaking Bernhard Schlink, *Abwägung im Verfassungsrecht* (Duncker & Humblot 1976) 131–4; Moshe Cohen-Eliya and Iddo Porat, 'Proportionality and the Culture of Justification' (2011) 59 American J Comparative L 463.

[29] Christian Kirchner, 'Zur konsequentialistischen Interpretationsmethode' in Thomas Eger and Hans-Bernd Schäfer (eds), *Internationalisierung des Rechts und seine ökonomische Analyse: Festschrift für Hans-Bernd Schäfer zum 65. Geburtstag* (Gabler Edition Wissenschaft 2008) 37–9.

[30] Emphatically, though for the domestic context, Lawrence Baum, *Judges and their Audiences* (Princeton UP 2006).

[31] That applies to the vast majority of international courts. Search engines and databases both of the ECtHR and the WTO can serve as examples of this. The practice of (investment) arbitration varies at times, but it also reveals a tendency toward greater publicness in its decisions; see Rule 22 ICSID Administrative and Financial Regulations.

[32] See chapter 1 section B 1 c.

law-making dimension of international adjudication, most likely to counter the kind of development that has occurred at the CJEU. Nevertheless, over more than 15 years, the judicial bodies dealing with the treaties of the WTO have developed an impressive set of case-law.[33] A successful legal argument concerning WTO law is not possible without taking those decisions into account. There is hardly any argument that is more important to the panels and the Appellate Body than reference to previous reports. Online services earn money by preparing those reports in a way that is readily usable for lawyerly purposes.

Provisions similar to Article 3 Section 2 of the DSU are found in the statutes of many courts (see only Article 1136(1) NAFTA; Article 53 ICSID Convention). The perhaps paradigmatic example is Article 59 of the ICJ Statute.[34] Many scholars draw wrong conclusions from them. While it is correct that, according to these provisions, a decision is binding only upon the contending parties in the litigated matter and has no further *binding* effect, they are used all too quickly to declare in the same breath that there is no law-making by international judicial decisions.[35] That is incorrect already in purely legal terms, since all legal systems contain norms (even if not necessarily as positive rules) about the relevance of adjudicated cases for later cases.[36] Moreover, in the vast majority of judicial decisions, reference to earlier decisions constitutes an important building block.[37] That holds even for arbitration, which is only weakly institutionalized. An arbitral tribunal summarized this aptly:

> ICSID arbitral tribunals are established ad hoc, from case to case, in the framework of the Washington Convention, and the present Tribunal knows of no provision, either in that Convention or in the BIT, establishing an obligation of *stare decisis*. It is nonetheless a reasonable assumption that international arbitral tribunals, notably those established within the ICSID system, will generally take account of the precedents established by other arbitration organs, especially those set by other international tribunals. The present

[33] See the references at <www.wto.org> accessed 10 December 2012, accessible through the six volumes of the *Max Planck Commentaries on World Trade Law*. By way of example, Rüdiger Wolfrum, Peter-Tobias Stoll, and Karen Kaiser (eds), *WTO—Institutions and Dispute Settlement*, vol 2 (Nijhoff 2006).

[34] See Humphrey Waldock, 'General Course on Public International Law' (1962) 106 Recueil des cours 1, 91; Chester Brown in Andreas Zimmermann and others (eds), *The Statute of the International Court of Justice: A Commentary* (2nd edn, OUP 2012) Article 59 para 9; Alan E Boyle and Christine M Chinkin, *The Making of International Law* (OUP 2007) 266–9.

[35] In more detail Marc Jacob, 'Precedents: Lawmaking Through International Adjudication' (2011) 12 German L J 1005, 1014–8.

[36] Jacob, 'Precedents' 1007.

[37] For a quantitative study on investment protection law see Jeffery P Commission, 'Precedent in Investment Treaty Arbitration—A Citation Analysis of a Developing Jurisprudence' (2007) 24 J Intl Arbitration 129, 148.

> tribunal will follow the same line, especially since both parties, in their written pleadings and oral arguments, have heavily relied on precedent.[38]

Contrary to positions that are often affiliated with the state-oriented conception, such judicial law-making must not be understood as an arrogation of power by politicized courts that violates the competencies assigned to them. The law-making function is often even legally envisaged. Article 11 of the DSU, for example, stipulates that 'an objective assessment' of a case requires an explanation of the reasons behind the decision. A similar provision is found in Article 56 Section 1 of the ICJ Statute, which requires that a judgment 'state the reasons on which it is based'. Those reasons entail further law-making as they serve as reference points in later cases. Such law-making is usually not criticized, but is mostly accepted by state practice. Representatives of states and legal counsel regularly cite earlier decisions in their briefs and do not question their relevance for adjudicating a new case. Even WTO members, Article 3 Section 2 of the DSU notwithstanding, have by no means impeded this development. Instead, they have largely embraced this judicially generated normativity.

The generation of normativity by courts is an inherent part of their practice of adjudication. The law-making dimension would be weakened if courts refrained from providing reasons or from publishing them, but the price for such a move would be very high. It would in fact be too high, for a number of reasons. The treaties themselves only provide weak normative guidance. Abstract norms alone can hardly generate a stabilization of expectations, since their meaning is all too uncertain in individual disputes. International law thus needs the courts to further develop normative expectations. What is more, it would become largely impossible to criticize international judicial decisions which were not published together with the reasoning. It is thus fully convincing that international courts must explain their decisions.[39] In fact, within the framework of the ICSID, an arbitral tribunal's failure to give reasons for its decision is one of the few grounds under which one party can request an annulment.[40]

[38] *El Paso Energy International Co v Argentine Republic* (Decision on Jurisdiction) ICSID Case No ARB/03/15 (27 April 2006) para 39.

[39] Article 56(1) ICJ Statute states: 'The judgment shall state the reasons on which it is based.' On the requirements in detail Art 95(1) ICJ Rules of Court; Art 30 ITLOS Statute; Art 23(2) ICTY Statute; Art 22(2) ICTR Statute.

[40] Art 52 ICSID Convention.

c) Reasons: on the difference between legislation and judicial law-making

However compelling the refutation of the cognitive model may be, it would be misleading to equate law-making in judicial decisions and political law-making in terms of legal sources. The difference between judicial adjudication and political legislation is one of the most important differentiations within the legal system.[41] We do not question it. To the contrary, we find a comparison between judicial and political law-making helpful in order to further grasp the law-making role of international courts.

The fact that a judicial *decision* implies a choice between alternatives[42] has prompted some authors to describe judicial decision-making generally as 'political'.[43] This qualification also emphasizes the multitude of interests and motives that can guide the judge in her decision.[44] Still, the realization of judicial choice and discretion does not prevent the distinction between judicial and political law-making. Rather, that differentiation credits the fact that fundamentally different institutions are at work, operating in fundamentally different legal settings.

With a view to institutional differences, the first thing that emerges is that every legal system frames the role of the judge entirely differently from that of every political decision-maker. Procedurally, political organs can initiate law-making on their own, while courts depend on a suitable case being brought to them.[45] Only the prosecutors of international criminal courts and tribunals can initiate proceedings *proprio motu*. As far as the justification is concerned, an act of law-making by political organs can be based on all reasons not prohibited by the legal order. Indeed, legislation can be openly political, in the sense of serving the ideas of one party. By contrast, an openly political justification is entirely unacceptable for judicial law-making.[46] But the legitimacy of a court also severely suffers if the proffered judicial arguments look like a mere cover for political positions.

[41] Luhmann, *Law as a Social System* 275–80, with an account of the development.

[42] Luhmann, *Law as a Social System* 282; see also Jacques Derrida, 'Force of Law: The "Mystical Foundation of Authority"' (1989–1990) 11 Cardozo L Rev 919.

[43] Martti Koskenniemi, 'The Politics of International Law' (1990) 1 Eur J Intl L 4; see also Hélène Ruiz Fabri, 'Drawing a Line of Equilibrium in a Complex World' in Giorgio Sacerdoti, Alan Yanovich, and Jan Bohanes (eds), *The WTO at Ten: The Contribution of the Dispute Settlement System* (CUP 2006) 125, 135.

[44] Kelsen already noted that the interpreter, because of semantic indeterminacy, had to resort to extra-legal norms of morality, justice, or social practices: *Introduction to the Problems of Legal Theory* 83.

[45] According to Alexis de Tocqueville, this is perhaps the crucial difference: *Democracy in America*, vol 1 (Alfred A Knopf 1980) 99.

[46] On this, using the example of South America, Marcelo Neves, 'La concepción del Estado de derecho y su vigencia práctica en Suramérica, con especial referencia a la fuerza normativa de derecho supranacional' in Armin von Bogdandy, César Landa Arroyo, and Mariela Morales Antoniazzi (eds), *¿Integración suramericana a través del derecho? Un análisis interdisciplinario y multifocal* (Centro de Estudios Políticos y Constitucionales 2009) 51.

Another difference is that law-making by political organs usually results in general and abstract legal propositions, which as such are binding. By contrast, the legally binding part of a judicial decision is limited to the parties to a dispute.[47] The law-making for all legal subjects takes place less through the operative provisions, the concrete ruling in a disputed case, and more through its reasoning. The latter is not a prescriptive text. Unlike common law, in the international legal system courts that render subsequent decisions are not legally bound to the justifying reasons underlying an earlier decision.[48] The specific nature of international judicial law-making can therefore be described with the distinction between prescriptive and justifying texts.[49]

The realization that a court is not fully bound—that it enjoys discretion, in other words—does not mean that 'anything goes'. Its decision should fit coherently into the web of the law, including previous decisions. Showing this 'fit' is a crucial task of judicial reasoning. Its decision must be linked to earlier decisions in such a way that it is accepted in the future.[50]

This expectation that international decisions be embedded in such a way is legally stabilized. To begin with, international courts almost always decide as a collective body. If one judge proposes an interpretation, the other judges will usually demand that it be appropriately linked to the law, including earlier decisions. Moreover, there are external controls and the law-making competence of international courts is not limitless. The Federal Constitutional Court of Germany, for example, has developed criteria for these limits.[51] In addition, there is an expectation that courts present their reasons in a specific style of reasoning, which is roughly spelled

[47] See only Art 59 ICJ Statute, on this compare Brown, Article 59 para 62.

[48] Alain Pellet in Zimmermann and others, *The Statute of the International Court of Justice* Article 38 para 307.

[49] Ralph Christensen and Hans Kudlich, *Gesetzesbindung: Vom vertikalen zum horizontalen Verständnis* (Duncker & Humblot 2008) 213.

[50] Markus Winkler, 'Die normative Kraft des Praktischen: Robert Brandom und die Rechtstheorie' (2009) 64 Juristenzeitung 821, 827; Brandom, 'Some Pragmatist Themes in Hegel's Idealism' 181; see Jasper Liptow, *Regel und Interpretation: Eine Untersuchung zur sozialen Struktur sprachlicher Praxis* (Velbrück Wissenschaft 2004) 220–7; Luhmann, *Law as a Social System* 227–8.

[51] For German courts *Soraya* (1973) 34 BVerfGE 269, English in Jürgen Böhmer and Clauspeter Hill (eds), *60 Years German Basic Law: The German Constitution and its Court: Landmark Decisions of the Federal Constitutional Court of Germany in the Area of Fundamental Rights* (Malaysian Current L J 2010) 416, 420–1; illustratively *Dreiteilungsmethode* (2011) 128 BVerfGE 193, 209–11; for the CJEU *Kloppenburg* (1987) 75 BVerfGE 223, 242–3; *Maastricht* (1993) 89 BVerfGE 155, 187–8, English in (1994) 33 Intl L Materials 388, 422–3; *Lissabon* (2009) 123 BVerfGE 267, 351–3, English: <http://www.bverfg.de/en/decisions/es20090630_2bve000208en.html> accessed 3 February 2014; *Honeywell* (2010) 126 BVerfGE 286, 305–7, English: <http://www.bverfg.de/en/decisions/rs20100706_2bvr266106en.html> accessed 3 February 2014; on the boundary see also *Rauchverbot in Gaststätten* (2008) 121 BVerfGE 317, 385 (Diss Op Masing). From the Anglo-American perspective Adam N Steinman, 'A Constitution for Judicial Lawmaking' (2003–2004) 65 U Pittsburgh L Rev 545.

out in Articles 31–33 of the Vienna Convention on the Law of Treaties (VCLT).[52] These limitations control and contain judicial power. They also legitimize it.

Judicial reasoning is thus of crucial importance to our theory. But are such reasons anything but masks for political motives?[53] Although they might be at times, concerns of a plain legal cover-up fail to do justice to judicial practice as such.[54] The global appreciation of an independent judiciary has a solid theoretical foundation. Pierre Bourdieu has succinctly noted that the specific mode of judicial justification is 'the basis of a real autonomy of thought and practice, the expression of the whole operation of the juridical field'.[55]

Summing up, the law-making effect of a judicial decision, especially its general dimension, depends not merely on its *voluntas* but also on its *ratio*, on the reasons given. But does it make sense, then, to conceive of judicial law-making as an exercise of public authority? This brings us to the key concept of our approach.

2. The exercise of international public authority

a) The concept of authority and the judicial decision

International adjudication would require no elaborate democratic justification if we were not dealing with the exercise of public authority. But what constitutes the authority of courts that triggers the quest for their legitimacy? Iconographically, Justice holds not only a scale, but also a sword. In developed and well-functioning legal systems, if a decision of a domestic court is not adhered to, a coercive apparatus will enforce it almost automatically. This does not apply to decisions by international courts,[56] which is why their decisions do not fall under the received meaning of public authority. It should be clear at this point that our take on *authority* does *not*

[52] For a more detailed account of these external forms of the legal discourse see Venzke, *How Interpretation Makes International Law* 46–57. See also Mark E Villiger, *Commentary on the 1969 Vienna Convention on the Law of Treaties* (Nijhoff 2009) Article 3 para 30; Sorel and Boré Eveno, *The Vienna Convention on the Law of Treaties* Article 31 para 59; Oliver Dörr in Oliver Dörr and Kirsten Schmalenbach (eds), *Vienna Convention on the Law of Treaties: A Commentary* (Springer 2012) Article 31 para 31.

[53] Some critical cases are mentioned by, for example, David Kennedy, *Of War and Law* (Princeton UP 2006) 122.

[54] Ulfried Neumann, 'Zur Interpretation des forensischen Diskurses in der Rechtsphilosophie von Jürgen Habermas' (1996) 27 Rechtstheorie 415.

[55] Pierre Bourdieu, 'The Force of Law: Toward a Sociology of the Juridical Field' (1986–1987) 38 Hastings L J 814, 820.

[56] For the sphere of international criminal law in particular Rod Rastan, 'Testing Cooperation: The International Criminal Court and National Authorities' (2008) 21 Leiden J Intl L 431; however, for a relativization of this distinction between national and international courts see Jeffrey K Staton and Will H Moore, 'Judicial Power in Domestic and International Politics' 2011 (65) Intl Organization 553.

necessarily imply normative *legitimacy*. Unlike other authors, especially in the line of analytical jurisprudence, we do not understand authority as justified and justifying, but as an actor's capacity.[57] With such an understanding we are in line with notions of the French *puissance public* and the German *öffentliche Gewalt*.

The absence of means of physical coercion could shield international courts from legitimatory demands under the received meaning of public authority. Such an understanding has matured in the context in which the state, legitimate means of coercion, sovereign control over territory, politics, policies, and public law all coincided. According to such an understanding, public authority exists only if the acting institution is able to enforce its will, if necessary through coercive measures.[58]

Today, this received understanding of public authority is too narrow. Our proposal is this: public authority ought to be defined more broadly[59] as the capacity, based on legal acts, to impact other actors in their exercise of freedom, be it legally or simply de facto.[60] This expanded notion of authority is based on a principled argument. If public law is conceived in the liberal-democratic tradition as a system for protecting the principles of individual freedom and allowing for collective self-determination, it must encompass every act that impacts upon these principles, provided this impact is significant enough to plausibly raise the question of legitimacy. The crucial question is whether other legal subjects can evade authority only by incurring considerable disadvantages or relevant costs, or when the act is linked to other mechanisms that effectively encourage these legal subjects to respect it.[61] Applying this understanding to international courts, it bears repeating once more that international courts have left behind their traditional role as mere dispute settlers. They have become influential lawmakers and they often control the authority exercised by other institutions.

[57] Joseph Raz, *The Authority of Law* (Clarendon 1979) 28; Myres McDougal and Harold Laswell, 'The Identification and Appraisal of Diverse Systems of Public Order' (1959) 53 AJIL 1, 9; Ingo Venzke, *How Interpretation Makes International Law* 62–4, 221; *Matthias Goldmann, Internationale öffentliche Gewalt* (Springer 2014, forthcoming).

[58] Robert A Dahl, 'The Concept of Power' (1957) 2 Behavioral Science 201, 202–3; Ralf Dahrendorf, *Über den Ursprung der Ungleichheit unter den Menschen* (Mohr Siebeck 1961) 20.

[59] For our concept of 'definition' see Koch and Rüßmann, *Juristische Begründungslehre* 75.

[60] Thus already Armin von Bogdandy, Philipp Dann, and Matthias Goldmann, 'Developing the Publicness of Public International Law: Towards a Legal Framework for Global Governance Activities' (2008) 9 German L J 1375, 1381–2. Rudiments also in Albrecht Randelzhofer in Theodor Maunz and Günter Dürig (eds), *Grundgesetz: Kommentar* (64th edn, CH Beck 2012) Article 24 para 33; Ondolf Rojahn in Ingo von Münch and Philip Kunig (eds), *Grundgesetzkommentar*, vol 2 (5th edn, CH Beck 2000) Article 24 paras 19, 22.

[61] On this in more detail again Venzke, *How Interpretation Makes International Law* 57–64; Goldmann, *Internationale öffentliche Gewalt*.

Since a more powerful international judiciary is performing functions similar to domestic courts (recalling in particular administrative and constitutional adjudication), the extension of the public law approach suggests itself.

Our definition of international public authority brings together many insights of legal scholarship on global governance, as evidenced by the advent of concepts such as law-making by international institutions,[62] of an 'international' or 'global' administrative law,[63] or of international criminal justice.[64] Support comes from the specific governance debate, too. Whereas it was an important assumption in the early debate on global governance that it came *without* authority, ever more scholars now see that the concept holds great promise both to grasp the facticity of the phenomena and to address the normative challenges.[65] Any conception of public authority which continues to include only national authority fails to grasp the extent to which international institutions influence political self-determination and social interactions. It runs the danger of being blind and deaf toward these important phenomena. Moreover, constitutional courts also do not dispose of any means of coercion to enforce their decisions against parliament and government, and yet, there is no other type of court whose authority is more obvious and whose democratic legitimacy is debated with similar intensity.[66]

Our definition of public authority provides a shared basic conception for national, supranational, and international institutions. At the same time, it does not assert that they are equal institutions of authority; on the contrary, it forms the starting point for grasping their specific characteristics as well as their differences. Thus, public authority of the *state* is typically characterized by the fact that it disposes over the means of physical coercion and can resort to social resources, such as a collective identity.[67] *Supranational* institutions typically set themselves apart from international ones in that

[62] José E Alvarez, *International Organizations as Law-Makers* (OUP 2005).

[63] Benedict Kingsbury, Nico Krisch, and Richard Stewart, 'The Emergence of Global Administrative Law' (2005) 2 L and Contemporary Problems 15; Eberhard Schmidt-Aßmann, 'Die Herausforderung der Verwaltungsrechtswissenschaft durch die Internationalisierung der Verwaltungsbeziehungen' (2006) 45 Der Staat 315.

[64] On the problem of legitimation that attaches to law-making processes see Frank Meyer, *Strafrechtsgenese in Internationalen Organisationen: Eine Untersuchung der Strukturen und Legitimationsvoraussetzungen strafrechtlicher Normbildungsprozesse in Mehrebenensystemen* (Nomos 2012) 601–96, 837–99.

[65] For a reconstruction see Henrik Enroth, 'The Concept of Authority Transnationalized' (2013) 4 Transnational L Theory 336.

[66] In political science scholarship, the call to bring research on international and domestic courts closer together too grows louder; see Jeffrey K Staton and Will H Moore, 'Judicial Power in Domestic and International Politics' (2011) 65 Intl Organization 553, 587.

[67] See only *Maastricht* and *Lissabon*.

their acts are regularly directly applicable in the domestic legal orders. These differences will become important when assessing how much legitimacy is required.

International courts exercise international public authority, first of all, in their decision vis-à-vis the state at the losing end of a case. Although such a decision, unlike those of most domestic courts, is not backed by coercive force, today it is often embedded within potent implementation mechanisms. The Committee of Ministers of the Council of Europe oversees the implementation of judgments by the European Court of Human Rights (Article 46(2) ECHR), and the Fourteenth Protocol has added a specific procedure (Article 46(4) ECHR). International criminal convictions lead to prison sentences.[68] The WTO can permit heavy counter-measures (Article 22 DSU). A successful plaintiff can enforce decisions by ICSID arbitral tribunals with the help of the courts of the treaty states like a decision by a domestic court of last instance.[69] If institutions of the losing host country prove unco-operative, the plaintiff can execute the decision against the assets of the host country in another ICSID treaty state.[70] According to Article 94 Section 2 of the UN Charter, the UN Security Council oversees the decisions of the ICJ.[71] In addition, decisions by international courts can be used by domestic courts or private actors to urge national executives to adhere to international law.[72] Today the failure to honour an international judgment entails reputational costs that are relevant even for heavyweight actors like the United States[73]

[68] Gerard A Strijards in Otto Triffterer (ed), *Commentary on the Rome Statute of the International Criminal Court: Observers' Notes, Article by Article* (2nd edn, CH Beck 2008) Article 103 para 16; David Tolbert, 'The International Tribunal for the Former Yugoslavia and the Enforcement of Sentences' (1998) 11 Leiden J Intl L 655.

[69] Art 54(1) ICSID Convention. Regarding this point, see the recent decision against Argentina, *Enron Creditors Recovery Corporation (formerly Enron Corporation) and Ponderosa Assets, LPP v Argentine Republic* (Decision on the Argentine Republic's Request for a Continued Stay of the Enforcement of the Award) ICSID Case No ARB/01/3 (7 October 2008).

[70] In more detail Christoph H Schreuer, *The ICSID Convention: A Commentary* (2nd edn, CUP 2009) Article 54 paras 23–8; there are now law offices that specialize in tracking down commercial property and enforcing the arbitral decisions.

[71] However, so far the UN Security Council has not been successful in this activity; see Karin Oellers-Frahm, 'Souveräne Streitbeilegung? Überlegungen zu Art. 94 Abs. 2 und Art. 27 UN-Charta' in Jochen Abr Frowein and others (eds), *Verhandeln Für den Frieden-Negotiating for Peace: Liber Amicorum Tono Eitel* (Springer 2003) 169.

[72] On the relevance of such 'compliance constituencies' see Karen J Alter and Laurence R Helfer, 'Nature or Nurture? Judicial Lawmaking in the European Court of Justice and the Andean Tribunal of Justice' (2010) 64 Intl Organization 563.

[73] Thus, even from the perspective of rational choice, Andrew T Guzmán, *How International Law Works: A Rational Choice Theory* (OUP 2008); Laurence R Helfer and Anne-Marie Slaughter, 'Toward a Theory of Effective Supranational Adjudication' (1997–1998) 107 Yale L J 273, 278; Yuval Shany, 'Assessing the Effectiveness of International Courts: A Goal-Based Approach' (2012) 106 AJIL 225.

or Russia.[74] In this way, decisions by international courts regularly build up semantic authority. Such force is not an incidental and marginal characteristic of today's international adjudication, but an essential element of global governance.

b) Precedents in international law

In our definition, the concept of the exercise of public authority extends beyond legal bindingness.[75] Thus it allows for qualifying international case-law as an exercise of public authority, irrespective of the fact that international law has no doctrine of *stare decisis*. Subsequent legal argumentation is expected to build upon relevant earlier decisions. Recourse to precedents is by no means at the discretion of later courts, parties, or other participants in the legal discourse, for if they do *not* use the pertinent precedents, they disqualify themselves and harm their cause.[76] In this way, a published judicial decision shapes the legal order by establishing a point of reference for subsequent juridical discourses. That is what is often called international case-law. Of course, a precedent can never completely predetermine a later decision. Yet that does not remove the aspect of authority. Even a law or treaty cannot fully predetermine a judge's action, and yet it requires democratic legitimation.

One objection to this qualification might be that the general and abstract dimension of judicial law-making depends not only on *voluntas,* but also on its *ratio*. A decision needs to be reasoned. Were statements of a court relevant in later constellations only by virtue of their persuasive power, that would argue against our position. After all, public authority implies that it is able to constrain other legal subjects in the exercise of their power also in the absence of substantive agreement.[77]

This differentiation between *voluntas* and *ratio* is also found in Article 38 Section 1 of the ICJ Statute, which precisely does *not* place a judicial decision on a par with international treaty law, international customary law, or general legal principles. German jurisprudence distinguishes in this regard

[74] On the Russian practice of implementing ECtHR decisions see Angelika Nußberger, 'The Reception Process in Russia and Ukraine' in Helen Keller and Alec Stone Sweet (eds), *A Europe of Rights: The Impact of the ECHR on National Legal Systems* (OUP 2008) 603.

[75] This expansion of the notion of authority parallels developments in German law. Fundamentally: *Osho* (1992) 90 BVerwGE 112 (Federal Administrative Court of Germany); on this see Christian Bumke, 'Publikumsinformationen: Erscheinungsformen, Funktionen und verfassungsrechtlicher Rahmen einer Handlungsform des Gewährleistungsstaates' (2004) 37 Die Verwaltung 3.

[76] On these dynamics see Ingo Venzke, 'Understanding the Authority of International Courts and Tribunals: On Delegation and Discursive Construction' (2013) 14 Theoretical Inquiries in L 381.

[77] This is a typical feature of authority; see Herbert L Hart, *The Concept of Law* (2nd edn, Clarendon 1994) 58; Raz, *The Authority of Law* 11–2. See in further detail Venzke, 'Understanding the Authority of International Courts and Tribunals'.

between *legal sources* (*Rechtsquellen*) on the one hand and—following the cognitivist paradigm—sources of legal *cognition* (*Rechtserkenntnisquellen*) (among others, judicial decisions) on the other. As important as this differentiation may be, the categorical distinction between a legal source and a source of legal cognition endangers an adequate understanding of the significance of precedents to international legal discourse. In many legal discourses and decisions, earlier decisions appear as an argument that is not far behind in authority to the reference to a norm laid down in a legal source. Parties to a dispute contend the meanings of earlier decisions for their case as well as the meanings of treaty clauses, and the court uses earlier judicial statements as authoritative premises for its decision. The well-worn formula that international law does not know a doctrine of *stare decisis* tends to obscure the effect of adjudication rather than help elucidate it.[78]

The shaping of the legal system through precedents is not only a fact, but also has legal foundations. Within the framework of the WTO, for example, Article 3 Section 2 of the DSU not only suggests that adjudication cannot add to or diminish rights, but also sustains the creation of a legal corpus based on decisions. It lays down the goal of 'providing security and predictability to the multilateral trading system'. This, as the Appellate Body has elaborated, gives rise to the obligation to respect the interpretations of preceding reports in later cases.[79] Even if the reports have no binding force beyond the decision in a specific dispute, they create legitimate expectations and must therefore be taken into account in future decisions.[80] Approaches as diverse as Habermas' discourse theory and Luhmann's systems theory agree that stabilizing normative expectations is a central function of the law—a function for which earlier decisions are hardly expendable.[81] In this sense, Article 21 Section 2 of the Rome Statute declares: 'The Court may apply principles and rules of law as interpreted in its previous decisions.' This statement is more in line with how the international legal discourse works and clearly goes beyond the far more limited one in Article 38 Section

[78] In detail Jacob, 'Precedents' 1018–20; further Georges Abi-Saab, 'Les sources du droit international: Essai de déconstruction' in Manuel Rama-Montaldo (ed), *El derecho internacional en un mundo en transformación: Liber amicorum en homenaje al Profesor Eduardo Jiménez de Aréchaga*, vol 1 (Fundación de cultura universitaria 1994) 29.

[79] *Japan: Taxes on Alcoholic Beverages—Appellate Body Report* (4 October 1996) WT/DS8/AB/R, WT/DS10/AB/R, WT/DS11/AB/R 13.

[80] *United States: Final Anti-Dumping Measures on Stainless Steel from Mexico—Appellate Body Report* (30 April 2008) WT/DS344/AB/R, para 162; *United States: Continued Existence and Application of Zeroing Methodology—Appellate Body Report* (4 February 2009) WT/DS350/AB/R, paras 362–5. See also *United States: Sunset Reviews of Anti-Dumping Measures on Oil Country Tubular Goods from Argentina—Appellate Body Report* (29 November 2004) WT/DS268/AB/R, para 188.

[81] Luhmann, *Law as a Social System* 163; Jürgen Habermas, *Between Facts and Norms: Contributions to a Discourse Theory of Law and Democracy* (William Rehg tr, Polity Press 1997) 427–8.

1 lit d of the ICJ Statute, which asserts that judicial decisions are only 'subsidiary means for the determination of rules of law'. International judicial praxis gives far more importance to precedents, with good reason.

Precedents are particularly potent if a hierarchy of judicial bodies exists: in the WTO between a panel and the Appellate Body, in international criminal law between the Trials Chamber and the Appeals Chamber, in the ECHR in the legal recourse from the Chamber to the Grand Chamber. The Appeals Chamber of the ICTY gave vivid expression to the effect of earlier decisions:

> The Appeals Chamber recognises that the principles which underpin the general trend in both the common law and civil law systems, whereby the highest courts, whether as a matter of doctrine or of practice, will normally follow their previous decisions and will only depart from them in exceptional circumstances, are the need for consistency, certainty and predictability. This trend is also apparent in international tribunals.[82]

A court will usually decide in line with its earlier decisions, not only within frameworks of a hierarchical system. Reasons for this practice are that it can invoke the authority of previous judgments, that it serves the principle of coherence and the maxim of equality, and that it contributes to the legitimacy of the legal system. According to the ECtHR, a deviation, unless it is persuasively argued, can violate the principle of a *fair trial*.[83]

Even following the decision of another court can produce a legitimizing effect.[84] For example, earlier decisions between various arbitral tribunals of the investment protection regime regularly exert a precedent effect. While some arbitral tribunals do not want to commit themselves and refer to earlier decisions only as 'sources of inspiration',[85] others see an obligation to 'pay due consideration to earlier decisions'. The goal is to 'meet the legitimate expectations of the community of states and investors towards certainty of the rule of law'.[86] Semantic authority emanates even from legally

[82] *Prosecutor v Zlatko Aleksovski* (Judgment) ICTY-95-14/1-A (24 March 2000) paras 92–6.

[83] See *Atanasovski v former Yugoslav Republic of Macedonia* App No 36815/03 (ECtHR, 14 January 2010) para 38.

[84] Bruno Simma, 'Universality of International Law from the Perspective of a Practitioner' (2009) 20 Eur J Intl L 265, 279; Helfer and Slaughter, 'Toward a Theory of Effective Supranational Adjudication' 318–9.

[85] See for example *AES Corporation v Argentine Republic* (Decision on Jurisdiction) ICSID Case No ARB/02/17 (26 April 2005) paras 31–2; *Romak (Romak SA v Uzbekistan)* PCA Case No AA280 (UNCITRAL Award) (26 November 2009) para 170; *Chevron (Chevron Corporation and Texaco Petroleum Company v Ecuador)* PCA Case No 34877 (UNCITRAL Partial Award on the Merits) (30 March 2010) para 164.

[86] *Saipem SpA v People's Republic of Bangladesh* (Decision on Jurisdiction and Recommendation of Provisional Measures) ICSID Case No ARB/05/07 (21 March 2007) para 67; Stephan W Schill, 'System-Building in Investment Treaty Arbitration and Lawmaking' in Armin von Bogdandy and Ingo Venzke (eds), *International Judicial Lawmaking: On Public Authority and Democratic Legitimation in Global Governance* (Springer 2012) 133, 170–4.

non-binding advisory opinions. A state that acts in accordance with the statements of an ICJ advisory opinion can assume that its actions are lawful.[87] This is of particular relevance, since advisory opinions often contain far-reaching statements.[88]

International precedents are hard to set aside, even if they are not convincing. Indeed, the Federal Constitutional Court of Germany has stated the constitutional obligation of all German courts to follow the case-law of supranational courts (CJEU) and international courts (ECtHR),[89] even when case-law appears dubious. Of course, it remains possible that a decision will be generally considered 'wrong' and fall into oblivion. However, that rarely happens, and as long as such a general view does not exist, a precedent is an act of public authority.

Political decision-makers fully realize that. For example, Brazil's representative noted within the framework of the WTO:

> It was well-known that in practice any decision of a panel or the Appellate Body with regard to a specific case would go beyond such a specific case. Although no binding precedents had been created, the findings and conclusions of panels and the Appellate Body adopted by the DSB had created expectations concerning future interpretations of the DSU and the WTO Agreement. Therefore, in light of these systemic implications of decisions and recommendations pertaining to a specific case, Brazil wished to state its position with regard to certain findings of the Appellate Body.[90]

State actors use international courts deliberately to make law. Three former directors of GATT made an observation as vivid as it is critical: WTO members use the dispute settlement process 'as a means of filling out gaps in the WTO system; first, where rules and disciplines have not been put in place, or, second, are the subject of differences of interpretation. In other words, there is excessive resort to litigation as a substitute for negotiation'.[91]

[87] Jochen Abr Frowein and Karin Oellers-Frahm in Zimmermann and others (eds), *The Statute of the International Court of Justice* Article 65 para 54.

[88] See as a striking example *Responsibilities and Obligations of States Sponsoring Persons and Entities with Respect to Activities in the Area* (Advisory Opinion) ITLOS Reports 2011, 10.

[89] *Belehrung ausländischer Beschuldigter über Recht auf konsularischen Beistand* [2006] Federal Constitutional Court of Germany (2007) 60 Neue Juristische Wochenschrift 499, para 63; *Sofortvollzug einer Ausweisung* [2007] Federal Constitutional Court of Germany (2007) 29 Informationsbrief Ausländerrecht 275.

[90] WTO Dispute Settlement Body, *Minutes of Meeting Held in the Centre William Rappard on 6 November 1998* (14 December 1998) WT/DSB/M/50.

[91] Arthur Dunkel, Peter Sutherland, and Renato Ruggiero, *Joint Statement on the Multilateral Trading System* (1 February 2001) <www.wto.org/english/news_e/news01_e/jointstatdavos_jan01_e.htm> accessed 9 August 2012; further Piet Eeckhout, 'The Scales of Trade—Reflections on the Growth and Functions of the WTO Adjudicative Branch' (2010) 13 J Intl Economic L 3.

Judicial decisions distribute the burden of argumentation in subsequent legal communication. That is especially the case if there is an appeals procedure (that is, a supraordinated decision-making body exists), if a court can decide enough cases to build up its own lines of adjudication, or when the judicial bodies are combined into one system. All these things are phenomena that have been established on the international level only over the past 20 years. The situation may be different in the case of only sporadic and unconnected decisions, which used to be the rule, but are the exception today. Of course, there continue to be international courts that do not exercise public authority. They include, for example, the European Nuclear Energy Tribunal within the framework of the OECD, which is responsible for compensation questions in major nuclear accidents. It has never had a case, and—fortunately—is never likely to get one.[92] However, the theory of an international judiciary must be oriented toward the active institutions, not the dormant ones.

We conceptualize the semantic authority of international courts, their ability to establish their own interpretations as points of reference for the legal discourse, as an exercise of public authority. Domestic courts and international courts are quite comparable in this regard. However, the domestic courts are embedded within a political system. No such system exists on the international level.[93] This difference triggers specific problems of justification that only *international* courts confront.

B. SPECIFIC LEGITIMATION PROBLEMS OF INTERNATIONAL ADJUDICATION

1. Centralized judiciary and a decentralized legislative power

a) Institutional asymmetries

According to one of the core maxims of modern constitutional thought, political law-making and judicial adjudication are phenomena of public authority that are distinct, and yet closely interconnected.[94] A major achievement of constitutional theory is that it has conceptually grasped this simultaneity of separation and connection and stabilized it in judicial institutions. The dominant approach operates under the doctrine of the separation of

[92] <http://www.oecd-nea.org/law/european-nuclear-tribunal.html> accessed 4 October 2013.

[93] This finding, though with contrary conclusions, underlies Lauterpacht's theory of international law; *The Function of Law in the International Community* 245–59.

[94] Much like most legal and constitutional theories; see Ernst-Wolfgang Böckenförde, *Recht, Staat, Freiheit: Studien zur Rechtsphilosophie, Staatstheorie und Verfassungsgeschichte* (expanded edn, Suhrkamp 2006) 143–69; Martin Loughlin, *Public Law and Political Theory* (Clarendon 1992) 138.

powers and embeds the legitimacy of every kind of authority within this interplay.[95] This interplay is not reproduced at the international level—a deep problem for the legitimacy of the international judiciary.

The WTO Agreement provides a vivid illustration of this difference. Article III of the WTO Agreement states:

(1) The WTO shall facilitate the implementation, administration and operation, and further the objectives, of this Agreement and of the Multilateral Trade Agreements [...]
(2) The WTO shall provide the forum for negotiations among its Members concerning their multilateral trade relations [...]
(3) The WTO shall administer the Understanding on Rules and Procedures Governing the Settlement of Disputes (hereinafter referred to as the 'Dispute Settlement Understanding' or 'DSU') in Annex 2 to this Agreement.

Section 1 concerns the executive authority, Section 2 the legislative authority, and Section 3 the judicial authority. With respect to law-making, however, the WTO is to provide (merely) a forum for negotiations (Article III Section 2), and with respect to the executive its task is (merely) to facilitate the implementation, administration, and operation of the Agreement (Article III Section 1). Accordingly, the WTO Agreement precisely does *not* serve to institutionalize autonomous political—especially legislative—processes. To be sure, the WTO, like most international organizations, possesses some competencies of political law-making.[96] In principle, though, making new law is reserved for the process of amending and supplementing the Agreement.

The picture changes completely within the sphere of adjudication.[97] Article III Section 3 of the WTO Agreement stipulates that the WTO is to 'administer' the *Dispute Settlement Understanding* (DSU). According to Article 6 Section 1 of the DSU, this kind of judicial process does not depend

[95] John Locke, *The Second Treatise of Government* (first published 1690, The Liberal Arts Press 1952) 82–91; Giuseppe de Vergottini, *Diritto costituzionale comparato* (5th edn, CEDAM 1999) 346–9; Christoph Möllers, *Gewaltengliederung: Legitimation und Dogmatik im nationalen und internationalen Rechtsvergleich* (Mohr Siebeck 2005) 66–134.

[96] In more detail: Isabel Feichtner, *The Law and Politics of WTO Waivers: Stability and Flexibility in Public International Law* (CUP 2012).

[97] On the process of dispute settlement see David Palmeter and Petros C Mavroidis, *Dispute Settlement in the World Trade Organization: Practice and Procedure* (2nd edn, CUP 2004); Frederico Ortino and Ernst-Ulrich Petersmann (eds), *The WTO Dispute Settlement System 1995–2003* (Kluwer Law International 2004); Klara Leitner and Simon Lester, 'WTO Dispute Settlement 1995–2010—A Statistical Analysis' (2011) 14 J Intl Economic L 191.

on the consent of the defendant, and a losing party cannot prevent the report of an arbitral panel from being adopted by the DSB (Article 16(4) and Article 17(14) DSU).[98]

Conceptually, the WTO Agreement pays tribute to the conventional separation of powers, but it sets up an organization that exercises merely one of these powers. This creates a tension, since the traditional theory requires the existence of all three powers. One could try to defuse this tension with reference to the apolitical and deductive nature of judicial dispute settlement; however, as previously demonstrated, that attempt would miss the mark.

The problem of other international courts is comparable. No ICSID arbitral tribunal can change the investment protection treaties, the UNCLOS review conference cannot change the Convention on the Law of the Sea, and the Council of Europe cannot change the ECHR. With respect to the ICJ and the UN General Assembly, it should be noted that the latter is tasked with 'encouraging the progressive development of international law and its codification'.[99] But a large majority rejected an explicit law-making authority at the founding conference in San Francisco.[100] Later attempts to come up with a legislative role under the existing UN Charter by way of interpretation failed.[101] The circumstance that international organizations usually cannot establish binding rules for states reveals not only the forces fixated on state sovereignty, but also the great uncertainty over how democratic law-making is at all possible on the international level.

This absence of legislative competencies in the sense of Article 38 Section 1 of the ICJ Statute does not imply that other acts by international institutions are legally irrelevant. Global governance is characterized precisely by the fact that many international organizations by now dispose over legal instruments by which their political and administrative organs can create normativity.[102] But these acts, often referred to as soft law, are mostly outside of the legal sources of Article 38 of the ICJ Statute and are therefore not systematically connected to judicial decisions.[103] The disconnect calls

[98] See also Arts 8(9), (11), 13, and 17(7) DSU.

[99] Art 13(1)(a) UN Charter.

[100] Carl-August Fleischhauer and Bruno Simma in Bruno Simma (ed), *The Charter of the United Nations: A Commentary*, vol 1 (3rd edn, OUP 2012) Article 13 paras 7–9.

[101] In more detail Hersch Lauterpacht, 'Codification and Development of International Law' (1955) 49 AJIL 16; Bin Cheng, 'United Nations Resolutions on Outer Space: "Instant" International Customary Law?' (1965) 5 Indian J Intl L 23.

[102] Matthias Goldmann, 'Inside Relative Normativity: From Sources to Standard Instruments for the Exercise of International Public Authority' (2008) 9 German L J 1865.

[103] On the importance of such norms for international courts see chapter 4 section C 3 b.

for closer examination because it reveals the specific nature of the problem of international legitimacy.

b) The treaty and the two-level game

An international treaty typically provides the legal foundations of international adjudication. More so than any other source of international law, this legal instrument makes it possible to utilize domestic resources of legitimacy, especially parliamentary consent.[104] In many states, more important treaties require parliamentary involvement,[105] which means that at first glance an international treaty possesses the same democratic legitimacy as an domestic law. But the initial impression is deceiving.

The content of a treaty is spelled out in diplomatic negotiations, to which the parliamentary procedure is usually only a follow-up. The sequence in Articles 9–11 of the VCLT reveals that as well.[106] A public debate that could influence the agreements, an essential element of democratic legitimacy, is practically impossible.[107] Therein lies the difference from domestic law. Although the content of a bill is usually determined by ministerial bureaucracies and the government, that content can be much more readily changed in the legislative process.

Since this possibility does not exist with international treaties, the parliamentary process is often much less elaborate. The Rules of Procedure of the German Bundestag, for example, call for adoption in only two instead of three deliberations (Article 78(1) GO-BT), and the vote is only about a treaty as a whole, not about individual provisions (Article 81(4) GO-BT). National parliaments, with the exception of the US Congress, show a far greater willingness to follow government proposals on international agreements than they do proposals for domestic legislation. All this weakens the democratic thread of legitimacy that runs through the national parliament.[108] Another aspect is the lack of relevant parliamentary

[104] Our argumentation here relates to states with a democratic constitution. A separate examination is required for citizens living under authoritarian regimes; on this see also chapter 1 section C 3.

[105] From a comparative law perspective see Ingolf Pernice in Horst Dreier (ed), *Grundgesetz-Kommentar*, vol 2 (2nd edn, Mohr Siebeck 2006) Article 59 paras 11–2, 28–48.

[106] In more detail Frank Hoffmeister in Dörr and Schmalenbach (eds), *Vienna Convention on the Law of Treaties* Articles 9–11; Maurice Kamto and others in Corten and Klein (eds), *The Vienna Convention on the Law of Treaties: A Commentary* Articles 9–11.

[107] A counter-example is offered by the successful battle against the Anti-Counterfeiting Trade Agreement.

[108] Meinhard Hilf and Matthias Reuß, 'Verfassungsfragen lebensmittelrechtlicher Normierung im europäischen und internationalen Recht' (1997) 24 Zeitschrift für das gesamte Lebensmittelrecht 289, 293, 297.

knowledge.[109] The autonomy of the executive–administrative actors is thus far greater than in the domestic political process.[110] Political science scholarship shows that many governments make strategic use of the multilevel system to consolidate their position of power against parliamentary bodies and secure policies in case of a change of government.[111]

To be sure, there are numerous attempts to strengthen the relevant role of domestic parliaments.[112] Especially in European Union law-making, domestic parliaments have a number of powers for bringing influence to bear on the government's decision-making.[113] Nevertheless, parliamentary influence encounters nearly insurmountable limits that arise from the logic of the international negotiation processes.[114] Added to this is that international agreements are rarely suitable for domestic politicization, since international compromises are regularly 'grey' and therefore offer a poor point of attack. The global interplay of politics constitutes the exposed flank of parliamentarism.[115]

c) *Why case-law needs a legislator*

The democratic potential of parliamentary legitimation can develop less with an international treaty than with a domestic law. Moreover, international legal provisions encounter another problem unknown to domestic statute law. In the contemporary constitutional state, law means *positive law*.[116] The essential characteristic of positivity is the role of politically accountable institutions.[117] The law is passed by the legislature itself, or at least—in cases of common law or other instances of the judicial development of the law—is

[109] John H Jackson, *The World Trade Organization: Constitution and Jurisprudence* (Royal Institute of International Affairs 1998) 33.

[110] Ernst-Wolfgang Böckenförde, *Staat, Nation, Europa: Studien zur Staatslehre, Verfassungstheorie und Rechtsphilosophie* (Suhrkamp 1999) 103; Michael Zürn, *Regieren jenseits des Nationalstaates: Globalisierung und Denationalisierung als Chance* (Suhrkamp 1998) 233–6, 347–61.

[111] Path-breaking: Robert D Putnam, 'Diplomacy and Domestic Politics: The Logic of Two-Level Games' (1988) 42 Intl Organization 427.

[112] In more detail Rüdiger Wolfrum, 'Kontrolle der auswärtigen Gewalt' (1997) 56 Veröffentlichungen der Vereinigung der Deutschen Staatsrechtslehrer 38.

[113] Art 23(2) German Basic Law (Grundgesetz); from a comparative perspective Christoph Grabenwarter, 'National Constitutional Law Relating to the European Union' in Armin von Bogdandy and Jürgen Bast (eds), *Principles of European Constitutional Law* (2nd edn, Hart 2009) 83, 108–16.

[114] Thus on the EU Philipp Dann, 'The Political Institutions' in von Bogdandy and Bast (eds), *Principles of European Constitutional Law* 237, 267–8.

[115] On the lines of development in contemporary parliamentarism see Armin von Bogdandy, 'Parlamentarismus in Europa: eine Verfalls- oder Erfolgsgeschichte?' (2005) 130 Archiv des öffentlichen Rechts 445.

[116] Path-breaking Georg WF Hegel, *Outlines of the Philosophy of Right* (TM Knox tr, OUP 2008) 19–28.

[117] Ernst-Wolfgang Böckenförde, *Staat, Verfassung, Demokratie: Studien zur Verfassungstheorie und zum Verfassungsrecht* (Suhrkamp 1991) 289.

under its responsibility. The legislature can correct the law-making of the courts at any time.[118] Hans Kelsen, for example, sees the nature and value of democracy precisely also in the ability to amend or abolish legal norms through majority decision.[119]

Under all constitutional systems, the regulation of the economy, which forms the subject of the particularly dynamic WTO and ICSID adjudication, is governed by rules that can be enacted by simple parliamentary majority or even by delegated law-making (ordinances). In fact, one can conceive of the possibility of rapid intervention as a constitutional principle in the law-making procedures.[120] Such domestic control is curtailed in case of international adjudication. Although this curtailment can be undone by new treaties, the processes of negotiating international treaties, especially those of global reach, are slow and protracted. This becomes especially problematic when the social sphere in question is undergoing a rapid change, as is often the case with the economy, or when the paradigms of the existing law are no longer persuasive. One should merely recall how strongly the confidence in the market's self-regulating powers has eroded since the early 1990s; that is to say, the years in which large segments of the existing international economic law were created.

International agreements weaken the positivity of domestic law. If an international legal agreement is in force, it is largely removed from parliamentary intervention. With its approval of a treaty, the parliamentary majority that exists at a particular time places its decision largely beyond the reach of any subsequent majority. Scholarship has shown that this may very well be part of a political strategy.[121]

The erosion of the grasp of the democratic legislator is particularly drastic in the case of a judicialized regime of international law, because 'corrective' national measures, such as selective noncompliance, carry greater costs. To be sure, the democratic sovereignty of new majorities is preserved to some extent through the right of withdrawal.[122] Still, this right supports

[118] On common law see Patrick S Atiyah and Robert S Summers, *Form and Substance in Anglo-American Law: A Comparative Study of Legal Reasoning, Legal Theory, and Legal Institutions* (Clarendon 1987) 141.

[119] Hans Kelsen, *Vom Wesen und Wert der Demokratie* (2nd edn, Mohr Siebeck 1929) 8–9.

[120] In detail Hilf and Reuß, 'Verfassungsfragen lebensmittelrechtlicher Normierung' 290; concerning the economic constitution in Germany and the European Union see David J Gerber, *Law and Competition in Twentieth Century Europe: Protecting Prometheus* (Clarendon 1998) 232.

[121] Judith Goldstein and others, 'Introduction: Legalization and World Politics' (2000) 54 Intl Organization 385, 393; Kenneth W Abbott and Duncan Snidal, 'Hard and Soft Law in International Governance' (2000) 54 Intl Organization 421, 439.

[122] Moreover, a withdrawal is effective only for the future; Arts 56, 70(1) VCLT. A rare example is the withdrawal from the ICSID Convention by Bolivia on the grounds of doubts about legitimacy. Republica de Bolivia, Ministerio de Relaciones Exteriores y Cultos, 'Cancilleria officializa la salida de Bolivia del CIADI' (2007) 46 Intl L Materials 973.

the democratic legitimacy in a similarly inadequate way to that in which the right of emigration supports the legitimacy of a state.[123] It can hardly be regarded as adequate, since it usually offers no realistic opportunities of choice.

Law-making by international courts largely evades the reach of national parliamentary bodies.[124] Procedures for amending treaties or alternative mechanisms for modifying the legal basis of a court often require unanimity or a qualified majority that is difficult to attain. The democratic premise that judicial law-making can be politically corrected with democratic majorities is therefore hardly respected with international adjudication.

These observations do not conclude our reflections, but form merely an interim step. They are not aimed at delegitimizing international adjudication. The maxim of the democratic separation of powers cannot simply be transferred onto the exercise of international public authority without further ado.[125] The International Criminal Tribunal for the former Yugoslavia has aptly stated that 'the constitutional structure of the United Nations does not follow the division of powers found in national constitutions'.[126]

Now, one could try to justify a broad use of international judicial authority by arguing that precisely because of the asymmetrical international institutionalization, international courts should engage vigorously in law-making. In the absence of an effective international legislative body, judicial law-making, in this perspective, would thus not be a problem. It would be even more legitimate here than domestically.[127] That this argument does not hold emerges from the following debate with the most important champions of this position: Hans Kelsen and Hersch Lauterpacht.

d) Why Lauterpacht's and Kelsen's theory is outdated

In his 1933 book *The Function of Law in the International Community*, Hersch Lauterpacht undertook an influential examination of the imbalance between international judicial processes and political–legislative ones. To

[123] On this right see Art 13(3) of the Universal Declaration of Human Rights of 1948, Art 12(2) of the International Covenant on Civil and Political Rights of 1966, Art 2(2) of Protocol No 4 to the European Convention on Human Rights.

[124] The guarantee of an efficient legislator is a leitmotif of the development of many constitutions; see Armin von Bogdandy, *Gubernative Rechtsetzung: Eine Neubestimmung der Rechtsetzung und des Regierungssystems unter dem Grundgesetz in der Perspektive gemeineuropäischer Dogmatik* (Mohr Siebeck 2000) 35–8.

[125] That, however, is how Bruno Simma understands the approach presented here; Bruno Simma, 'Foreword' in von Bogdandy and Venzke (eds), *International Judicial Lawmaking* V, IX–XI.

[126] *Prosecutor v Duško Tadić* (Decision on the Defence Motion for Interlocutory Appeal on Jurisdiction) ICTY-94-1-AR 72 (2 October 1995) para 43.

[127] Sabino Cassese and Mattias Kumm have formulated this argument to us. It was carefully articulated also by Robert Howse, 'Moving the WTO Forward—One Case at a Time' (2009) 42 Cornell Intl L J 223.

advance the PCIJ, he pleaded for an obligatory international judiciary as the most important building block for a stable order of peace. In particular, he defended this demand against the objection that there was no international legislature.[128] A closer analysis of his text reveals that his arguments, persuasive in 1933, no longer carry weight in light of the international judiciary at present.

Lauterpacht's approach can be understood in the context of the system of international law at the time, which many voices in the defeated states of World War I considered unjust. To counter this weakness, Lauterpacht developed a series of legal concepts that would allow courts to deal with these injustices. Since he advocated a private law understanding of international law, these legal concepts are the likes of *clausula rebus sic stantibus, abus de droit*, and *intertemporal law*. It is most important to note that the international law he had in mind is limited to coexistence and co-ordination:

> [International law is] confined to the regulation of the external relations of States. It does not and cannot aim at regulating the lives of the members of the international community in the same intensive and pervading manner as municipal law does. It is mainly adjective law.[129]

It was inconceivable to Lauterpacht, for example, that tariffs could become the object of international regulation.[130] Today, they form the least problematic part of WTO law. Further, although he conceives of courts as law-making institutions, he sees that function as largely restricted to concrete disputes. In the absence of a sufficient number of cases, he hardly sees the courts as actors capable of advancing the development of the legal system as a whole.[131] And if they do so nevertheless, the justice of judicial law-making is guaranteed by 'a spirit of legal equality, common sense, and natural justice', as well as 'a spirit of progress'.[132]

The sphere of tasks of many international courts has since grown far beyond that of regulating coexistence and co-ordination. The private law paradigm is equally insufficient, given the many instances of international public authority. When it comes to questions of weighing and balancing interests in economic law, 'a spirit of legal equality, common sense, and natural justice' and 'a spirit of progress' hardly offer usable guidelines. Lauterpacht already saw the politicization that is necessary today:

[128] Lauterpacht, *The Function of Law in the International Community* 245–59, 344.

[129] Lauterpacht, *The Function of Law in the International Community* 249.

[130] Lauterpacht, *The Function of Law in the International Community* 304–5.

[131] Lauterpacht, *The Function of Law in the International Community* 256. Lauterpacht uses the concepts 'development' and 'clarification of the law' synonymously; in more detail see Venzke, 'The Role of International Courts as Interpreters and Developers of the Law'.

[132] Lauterpacht, *The Function of Law in the International Community* 256.

> This book would entirely fail in one of its main objects if it were understood to question the seriousness of the problem created for obligatory arbitration by the absence of an international legislature. At the same time, however, we believe that the difficulty arising from this defect of international organization cannot be solved by the rejection of obligatory arbitration altogether.[133]

Like his student Lauterpacht, Hans Kelsen pleads for developing the international judiciary even if not accompanied by legislative institutions.[134] Kelsen proceeds rather polemically. The argument that an obligatory international judiciary required an 'international legislative body empowered to reform this legal order' was, according to Kelsen, 'incorrect in every respect'.[135]

Alas, even the arguments of one of the pre-eminent legal scholars of the twentieth century[136] are no longer persuasive today. To begin with, it is necessary once more to consider their context. Kelsen was writing at a time when there was no sign of the emergence of international judicial institutions such as investment arbitration under ICSID or the WTO—which substantially re-shape states' room of manoeuvre, for example in the economic system—or of a human rights courts like that of the ECtHR. The judiciary encountered and supported by Kelsen was limited to territorial disputes and the protection of national minorities, above all. In addition, his model stands under the premise that international treaties convincingly settle territorial disputes and that the principle of national self-determination is respected.

What is more, Kelsen operated with a deeply problematic philosophy of history. According to a 'biogenetic law',[137] the international legal system could be expected to pass through the same evolution that the domestic legal systems had already passed through, Kelsen argued. According to this 'law', what first happens in a legal system is a centralization of the judicial power. The centralization of the legislative and executive power takes place only in later stages. This explains why Kelsen classified international law as a 'primitive legal system'[138] and renders plausible his speculation and his approach.

Such a philosophy of history finds little support, and practically, the developments after 1945 have taken different paths. The highly complex

[133] Lauterpacht, *The Function of Law in the International Community* 344.

[134] Hans Kelsen, *Peace Through Law* (University of North Carolina Press 1944).

[135] Hans Kelsen, *Law and Peace in International Relations: The Oliver Wendell Holmes Lectures, 1940–41* (Harvard UP 1942) 161.

[136] Horst Dreier, 'Hans Kelsen (1881–1973): "Jurist des Jahrhunderts?"' in Helmut Heinrichs and others (eds), *Deutsche Juristen jüdischer Herkunft* (CH Beck 1993) 705.

[137] Kelsen, *Law and Peace in International Relations* 148.

[138] Kelsen, *Introduction to the Problems of Legal Theory* 108–9.

contemporary international legal order can no longer be described as 'primitive' compared to national legal systems. In fact, some international legal regimes are even more developed, more complex, and more differentiated than comparable subject matters of domestic law.[139] Another of Kelsen's hypotheses also remains unproven, namely that a decision by an international court is in fact able to settle disputes that could lead to a military conflict. In summary, we can say that Lauterpacht's and Kelsen's justification of international adjudication without international legislation, a position which remains influential, is no longer persuasive today.

2. The potential and dangers of the constitutionalist argument

a) The constitutionalist approach

The narrative of justification fashioned by Lauterpacht and Kelsen has found its most important continuation in international constitutionalism, in which an international judiciary is interpreted as a kind of constitutional court.[140] Under most constitutions, the political change of constitutional law is far more difficult than a change of simple law, due to specific majorities and special procedures.[141] Constitutional law guides the 'normal' political process and provides the central mechanism that stabilizes the separation and interaction of law and politics in contemporary societies.[142] Should international courts exercise a constitutional function, the asymmetry between the judicial and the political realm could be interpreted not as a shortcoming, but rather as a specific potential.[143]

The question about the processes of constitutionalization in international law, at this time no doubt the most important manifestation of juridical universalism,[144] leads to a complex discussion which we cannot sketch

[139] A vivid example is the comparison of development law in the World Bank, the European Union, and the Federal Republic of Germany; see Philipp Dann, *The Law of Development Cooperation: A Comparative Analysis of the World Bank, the EU and Germany* (CUP 2013).

[140] This is adumbrated in Lauterpacht and Kelsen: Lauterpacht, *The Function of Law in the International Community* 336–9; Kelsen, *Law and Peace in International Relations* 159.

[141] Pedro Cruz Villalón, 'Vergleich' in Armin von Bogdandy, Pedro Cruz Villalón, and Peter M Huber (eds), *Handbuch Ius Publicum Europaeum*, vol 1 (CF Müller 2007) 729, 751–2; Bernd Wieser, *Vergleichendes Verfassungsrecht* (Springer 2005) 85–97.

[142] Habermas, *Between Facts and Norms* 238–86; Luhmann, *Law as a Social System* 357–80.

[143] Comprehensively Thomas Kleinlein, *Konstitutionalisierung im Völkerrecht: Konstruktion und Elemente einer idealistischen Völkerrechtslehre* (Springer 2012); Deborah Z Cass, 'The "Constitutionalization" of International Trade Law: Judicial Norm-Generation as the Engine of Constitutional Development in International Trade' (2001) 12 Eur J Intl L 39.

[144] For more detail on this see chapter 2 section B 1.

out here.[145] Our approach is connected to constitutionalism in many ways, but by no means in every respect. With constitutionalist authors we share the conviction that the stock of principles of the democratic constitutional state is important to international law—whether to its doctrinal reconstruction, to its doctrinal, political, or theoretical critique, or as an inspiration for future configurations.[146] However, we are sceptical about ascribing constitutional functions to existing institutions. That strikes us as 'a step too far'.[147] We do not deny that this approach may lead somewhere with a few courts, specifically the supranational Court of Justice of the European Union,[148] the European Court of Human Rights,[149] and the Inter-American Court of Human Rights;[150] however, as we shall show, this attribution is not persuasive especially for the Appellate Body of the WTO,[151] the International Court of Justice,[152] and the ICSID arbitral tribunals.

If international courts could be interpreted as having a constitutional function for the domestic legal orders, it would be possible not only to justify their de-coupling from an effective legislature. Such an understanding would also legitimize a 'creative' and 'expansive' interpretation of the legal foundations. The ECtHR is a good example. Reference to the constitutional nature of the Convention constitutes a key argument for a path-breaking innovation: obligation in spite of (incompatible) reservations.[153] Thereby, the character of

[145] See merely Jan Klabbers, Anne Peters, and Geir Ulfstein, *The Constitutionalization of International Law* (OUP 2009); Jeffrey L Dunoff and Joel S Trachtman (eds), *Ruling the World? Constitutionalism, International Law, and Global Governance* (CUP 2009).

[146] Constitutional principles are of importance especially in two respects. First, they raise questions to which answers must be found on the international level. Second, the multitude of possible understandings offers clues that can be helpful in the development of solutions.

[147] Robert Howse and Kalypso Nicolaïdis, 'Legitimacy and Global Governance: Why Constitutionalizing the WTO Is a Step Too Far' in Roger B Porter and others (eds), *Efficiency, Equity, and Legitimacy: The Multilateral Trading System at the Millennium* (Brookings Institution Press 2001) 227.

[148] Case 294/83 *'Les Verts' v European Parliament* [1986] ECR 1339, para 23; Joined Cases C-402/05 P and 415/05 P *Kadi and Al Barakaat International Foundation v Council and Commission* [2008] ECR I–06351; on the special role of the CJEU see chapter 1 section C 2.

[149] *Loizidou v Turkey* (1995) Series A No 310, para 75; Christian Walter, 'Die Europäische Menschenrechtskonvention als Konstitutionalisierungsprozeß' (1999) 59 Zeitschrift für ausländisches öffentliches Recht und Völkerrecht 961; Luzius Wildhaber, 'A Constitutional Future for the European Court of Human Rights' (2002) 23 Human Rights Law Journal 161.

[150] *Case of Almonacid-Arellano et al v Chile* Inter-American Court of Human Rights Series C No 154 (26 September 2006) paras 115–28; Christina Binder, 'The Prohibition of Amnesties by the Inter-American Court of Human Rights' (2011) 12 German L J 1203.

[151] Ernst-Ulrich Petersmann, 'Constitutional Functions and Constitutional Problems of International Economic Law in the 21st Century' in *Collected Courses of the Xiamen Academy of International Law*, vol 3 (Nijhoff 2011) 155; Robert Uerpmann, 'Internationales Verfassungsrecht' (2001) 56 Juristenzeitung 565, 569.

[152] *Conditions of Admission of a State to Membership in the United Nations (Article 4 of the Charter)* (Advisory Opinion) [1948] ICJ Rep 57, Individual Op Alvarez, 67–8.

[153] *Loizidou v Turkey* (1995) paras 73–98.

constitutional law was not established, but was introduced as an axiom. Something similar occurs in supposedly technical areas, for example in WTO adjudication concerning 'zeroing'.[154]

We will examine the constitutionalist interpretation of international courts by looking back at the debate over the constitutionalization of European integration. Within the European Economic Community (EEC), what was initially considered as constitutionalization was the juridification of interstate relations by means of legal concepts such as basic liberties interpreted in terms of individual rights, direct effect, and primacy of EC law. All of these were instruments in the hands of an active court.[155] Direct effect and primacy are absent from international law, with the partial exception of the Inter-American Court of Human Rights and some hints in the International Criminal Tribunal for the former Yugoslavia.[156] Moreover, an intensive debate revealed that the original understanding of the constitutionalization of community law was indeed insufficient.[157] Today, the constitutional character of the primary law of the European Union is substantiated with far more elaborate arguments.[158] Among other things, those arguments are based on the fact that this primary law establishes institutions with legislative, executive, and judicial authority, creates a citizenry, grants fundamental rights, and regulates the relationship between legal systems by means of primacy and direct effect. Thus far, a functional comparison yields numerous correspondences between the Union's primary law and domestic constitutions, which support the attribution of a constitutional function to the Court of Justice of the European Union. A similar constellation is absent at the level of international law.

[154] Sungjoon Cho, 'Constitutional Adjudication in the World Trade Organization' (2008) Jean Monnet Working Paper <centers.law.nyu.edu/jeanmonnet/> accessed 9 December 2012.

[155] Ernst-Ulrich Petersmann, 'Welthandelsrecht als Freiheits- und Verfassungsordnung' (2005) 65 Zeitschrift für ausländisches öffentliches Recht und Völkerrecht 543; on the European development see Joseph HH Weiler, 'The Transformation of Europe' (1991) 100 Yale L J 2405.

[156] *Case of Barrios Altos* Inter-American Court of Human Rights Series C No 75 (14 March 2001) paras 41–4; *Case of Almonacid-Arellano et al v Chile*, paras 105–14, 119; Binder, 'The Prohibition of Amnesties by the Inter-American Court of Human Rights' 1208–11. The ICTY noted that amnesty laws that contravene the prohibition against torture cannot become effective on the international level. This can also be determined by international courts: *Prosecutor v Anto Furundžija* (Judgment) ICTY-95-17/1-T (10 December 1998) paras 153–5, on this see Antonio Cassese, 'Y a-t-il un conflit insurmontable entre souveraineté des États et justice pénale internationale?' in Antonio Cassese and Mireille Delmas-Marty (eds), *Crimes internationaux et juridictions internationales* (Presses Universitaires de France 2002) 13, 15–6.

[157] In detail Christoph Möllers, 'Pouvoir Constituant—Constitution—Constiutionalisation' in von Bogdandy and Bast (eds), *Principles of European Constitutional Law* 169–204; Isabelle Ley, 'Kant *versus* Locke: Europarechtlicher und völkerrechtlicher Konstitutionalismus im Vergleich' (2009) 69 Zeitschrift für ausländisches öffentliches Recht und Völkerrecht 317, 320–5.

[158] Claudio Franzius, *Europäisches Verfassungsrechtsdenken* (Mohr Siebeck 2010) 29–86.

b) A constitution-supplementing function?

An advocate of constitutionalism could be tempted to defend the constitutional character of international courts by the fact that their standards of review rest on legal acts that the domestic legislature cannot easily change.[159] This is, indeed, the very nature of obligations under international law: *pacta sunt servanda* (Article 26 VCLT).[160] Of course, neither can a party to a treaty invoke domestic law to justify noncompliance (Article 27 VCLT). There are only very narrow possibilities for unilaterally evading treaty obligations (Articles 54–72 VCLT).[161] By focusing on these features, one could interpret all international law and every international court as having a constitutional function.

Such a relabelling of all of international law does not seem convincing.[162] What would be gained by a constitutionalist interpretation of a German–Dutch border treaty? Expanding and diluting a concept as important as that of the constitution should be carefully considered. Accordingly, advocates of constitutionalism for the most part focus on constitutional norms with substantive criteria. Anne Peters thus defines constitutional norms as 'the bulk of the most important norms which regulate political activity and relationships in the global polity'.[163] These are chiefly norms concerning the use of force, the fundamental status of the individual vis-à-vis public authority, and the founding treaties of the most important international organizations.[164] Although this is one possible understanding, it strikes us as reductionist, since it sets aside the function of the democratic politicization of the legal system.[165] The described phenomena that get by without democratic politicization should rather be interpreted as phenomena of juridification or institutionalization, not of constitutionalization.[166]

[159] Cruz Villalón, 'Vergleich' 748–52, also on the British exception.

[160] Path-breaking Alfred Verdross, *Die Verfassung der Völkerrechtsgemeinschaft* (Springer 1926) 12–33.

[161] Vividly *Gabčíkovo-Nagymaros Project (Hungary v Slovakia)* (Judgment) [1997] ICJ Rep 7, paras 92–115; on this see Christina Binder, 'Die Veränderung innerstaatlicher Verhältnisse als Nichterfüllungsgrund von völkerrechtlichen Vertragsverpflichtungen: Welche Rolle spielen demokratiepolitische und menschenrechtliche Erwägungen?' (2009) 47 Archiv des Völkerrechts 187.

[162] Jeffrey L Dunoff and Joel S Trachtman, 'A Functional Approach to International Constitutionalization' in Dunoff and Trachtman (eds), *Ruling the World?* 3, 9–18.

[163] Anne Peters, 'Compensatory Constitutionalism: The Function and Potential of Fundamental International Norms and Structures' (2006) 19 Leiden J Intl L 579, 582; for a clear account on contrary tendencies see Oliver Diggelmann and Tilmann Altwicker, 'Is There Something Like a Constitution of International Law? A Critical Analysis of the Debate on World Constitutionalism' (2008) 68 Zeitschrift für ausländisches öffentliches Recht und Völkerrecht 623.

[164] Alfred Verdross and Bruno Simma, *Universelles Völkerrecht: Theorie und Praxis* (3rd edn, Duncker & Humblot 1984) 59–220; Bardo Fassbender, *UN Security Council Reform and the Right of Veto: A Constitutional Perspective* (Kluwer Law International 1998).

[165] Joseph HH Weiler, 'Law, Culture, and Values in the WTO—Gazing into the Crystal Ball' in Daniel Bethlehem and others (eds), *The Oxford Handbook of International Trade Law* (OUP 2009) 749, 756.

[166] Goldstein and others, 'Introduction: Legalization and World Politics'; Stefan Oeter, 'Chancen und Defizite internationaler Verrechtlichung: Was das Recht jenseits des Nationalstaates leisten kann'

But even if one accepts the constitutionalist interpretation of some international legal norms, that does not immediately turn the corresponding activity of international courts into constitutional adjudication. Ever since *Marbury v Madison*, it has been the characteristic of constitutional courts to exercise judicial review and to declare parliamentary law unconstitutional.[167] No international court possesses the competence to declare parliamentary acts as inapplicable, let alone invalid. Even the supranational Court of Justice of the European Union, according to Article 263 of the Treaty on the Functioning of the European Union (TFEU), has this authority only for law-making acts by the Union, not for those by national legislatures. In keeping with Article 267 of the TFEU, its constitutional judicial role for the Member States rests on co-operation with domestic courts in the process of the preliminary ruling procedure. This leads to a trail that takes us further.

Even though no international court possesses a constitutional function by its statute, it can gradually manoeuvre itself into such a role by pursuing a corresponding line of adjudication. As already mentioned, the Inter-American Court of Human Rights, the European Court of Human Rights, and also the International Criminal Tribunal for the former Yugoslavia have rendered such decisions. But these rulings are only the first step toward a constitutional role. It is domestic law that determines the domestic rank and effects of international norms and decisions, even under so-called monistic systems.[168] Accordingly, the development of a constitutional role by international courts leans on its recognition by the pertinent domestic organs.

This doctrinal argument is supported by theoretical consideration that such a constitutionalist development has a high need for legitimation. That emerges from the fact that the judicial review of a legislative act should be understood as a quite specific and unusual authority. Moreover, the positioning of a political community within globalization—which is precisely what determining the domestic effects of international rulings is about—is an important question. At stake are democracy and the self-conception of the citizens. The question about the constitutional role of international courts should therefore be decided in accordance with the domestic constitution,

in Michael Zürn and Bernhard Zangl (eds), *Verrechtlichung—Baustein für Global Governance?* (Dietz 2004) 46.

[167] *Marbury v Madison* (1803) 5 US (1 Cranch) 137–80 (US SC).

[168] For one example see the debate on Arts 93 and 94 of the Dutch Constitution (Grondwet); Leonard Besselink, 'Niederlande' in von Bogdandy, Cruz Villalón, and Huber (eds), *Handbuch Ius Publicum Europaeum*, vol 1, 327, 363–5; Ramses A Wessel and Wim E van de Griendt, 'Offene Staatlichkeit: Niederlande' in Armin von Bogdandy, Pedro Cruz Villalón and Peter M Huber (eds), *Handbuch Ius Publicum Europaeum*, vol 2 (CF Müller 2008) 177.

whether directly through relevant provisions or indirectly through recognition by the national judiciary.

By now, the constitutional role of the Court of Justice of the European Union has been accepted, in substance, by all the legislatures and the highest courts of all EU Member States.[169] A similar validation does not exist for any international court. Instead, the constitutional role must be separately examined for every domestic system. Such an examination will not be undertaken here. An overview reveals quite clearly that the attribution of a constitutional role is persuasive only for the European Court of Human Rights and the Inter-American Court of Human Rights. Both treaty systems are anchored in many constitutions precisely with the intent of protecting essential constitutional principles, in particular fundamental rights, through an institution outside the domestic order.[170] By contrast, for other international courts there are no such indicators that would support speaking of a constitutional role.

c) Internal constitutionalization of international organizations

The role of international courts presents itself differently when they constrain the public authority of 'their' international organizations.[171] Here, domestic legal systems are not re-shaped and democratic legislatures are not controlled. At stake is solely the control of international bureaucracies by principles of the liberal constitutional tradition, especially respect for human rights and the limits of conferred powers.[172] The notion of *internal* constitutionalization captures this kind of control of international public authority. Courts, both international and national, assume considerable importance in this process. Experience teaches that in the absence of judicial control, such principles of the constitutional tradition do not thicken and are rarely respected by bureaucracies. At the moment, this task falls more onto domestic than international courts.[173] But even if an international

[169] Parliamentary acceptance is found in the confirmation of the case-law through the ratification of the various amendment agreements.

[170] On the European system of human rights protection see the contributions in Keller and Stone Sweet (eds), *A Europe of Rights*; on the Inter-American system see Binder, 'The Prohibition of Amnesties by the Inter-American Court of Human Rights' 1218–29.

[171] On the control of international organizations see International Law Association, *Accountability of International Organisations, Final Conference Report Berlin 2004* <www.ila-hq.org> accessed 28 January 2014; Jochen von Bernstorff, 'Procedures of Decision-Making and the Role of Law in International Organizations' in Armin von Bogdandy and others (eds), *The Exercise of Public Authority by International Institutions: Advancing International Institutional Law* (Springer 2010) 775; Alvarez, *International Organizations as Law-Makers* 65–108; Jan Klabbers, 'Constitutionalism Lite' (2004) 1 Intl Organizations L Rev 31.

[172] Armin von Bogdandy, 'General Principles of International Public Authority: Sketching a Research Field' (2008) 9 German L J 1909.

[173] Classic is the question of legal review by the UN Security Council; on this see Erika de Wet, *The Chapter VII Powers of the United Nations Security Council* (Hart 2004); on the various constellations see August Reinisch (ed), *Challenging Acts of International Organizations before National Courts* (OUP 2010).

institution does become active in this sense—such as the World Bank Inspection Panel—this hardly suggests a constitutional role, but rather an administrative one. Bureaucracies are controlled, not parliaments. With the exception of the two human rights courts we have mentioned, it is therefore not persuasive to apply to international courts theories of justification that were developed for constitutional courts. The missing international legislator thus poses a huge and specific problem of international adjudication. It cannot be done away with by reference to a constitutional function for international courts.

3. Fragmentation as a problem for democracy

A further problem that is specific to the international judiciary is that its strengthening is closely interwoven with processes of fragmentation. The fragmentation of international law threatens to impair democratic generality, and thus a central element of democratic legitimation. The principle of democratic generality requires a thematic openness of the democratic process, one that makes it possible to take all perspectives into account.[174] This requirement rests on an understanding of the individual as a multidimensional human being who cannot be split into functional logics. On this basis, what is needed are mechanisms of decision-making in which competing perspectives can be negotiated and brought into balance.[175] This in turn implies openness about the outcome.

In light of the principle of democratic generality, it is therefore problematic if a specific functional demand—for example, investment protection or securing global trade—is given priority by pushing other issues into the category of 'exceptions'. It is equally problematic if certain concerns are in fact excluded from consideration by a court because of jurisdictional limitations.[176] The juridification of certain sectors and the ways in which the perspectives of functional regimes permeate issues of jurisdiction, admissibility, and applicable law thus impair democratic generality. To be sure, an institutional differentiation of legal fields is also found in domestic law with specialized courts. However, there are typically institutions in which

[174] The understanding of sectoral fragmentation as a problem for democracy goes back to Jürgen Bast, 'Das Demokratiedefizit fragmentierter Internationalisierung' in Hauke Brunkhorst (ed), *Demokratie in der Weltgesellschaft* (Nomos 2009) 185. On the demand of a general public in the democratic process of lawmaking see also Möllers, *Gewaltengliederung* 31.

[175] Andreas L Paulus, 'Subsidiarity, Fragmentation and Democracy: Towards the Demise of General International Law?' in Tomer Broude and Yuval Shany (eds), *The Shifting Allocation of Authority in International Law: Considering Sovereignty, Supremacy and Subsidiarity: Essays in Honour of Professor Ruth Lapidoth* (Hart 2008) 193, 210.

[176] Bast, 'Das Demokratiedefizit fragmentierter Internationalisierung' 188–9.

diverging perspectives can be brought together, above all parliament and the government. By contrast, on the international level there are hardly any comparable institutions for generalizing and mediating the diverse perspectives.[177] A specific functional perspective prevails in every regime.[178] Among the international bodies, perhaps the UN General Assembly could represent an institution for generalizing and mediating diverse perspectives, balancing secure investment, environmental protection, and social justice. To date, it has hardly been able to live up to such a task.

Fragmentation is not a natural process, and not only due to the ponderousness of the United Nations. Powerful actors have opted for sectoral, functionally defined regimes.[179] They can advance specific concerns much better and with less friction in this way.[180] National lobbies frequently have an interest in sectoral international regimes as well.[181] As a result, democratic generality suffers from the functional differentiation on both the national and international levels and fragmentation turns into a problem for the democratic legitimation of international courts' public authority.

C. A CONCEPT OF DEMOCRACY FOR INTERNATIONAL ADJUDICATION

1. Problem and approach

Plausible answers to the legitimatory problems of international adjudication require a viable concept of democracy. To date, such a concept has been lacking. It is by no means clear how the democratic principle can be positioned vis-à-vis international courts or what it should demand from them. Some readers will doubt whether a democracy-oriented conception can say anything meaningful and might suspect that it could rather turn out to be a dead end. We will show the opposite.

There are various paths for such a concept of democracy. One could simply commit to one of the major general theories of democracy and apply it to the specific constellation of international courts.[182] We proceed from a

[177] Bast, 'Das Demokratiedefizit fragmentierter Internationalisierung' 188–9.

[178] Martti Koskenniemi and Päivi Leino, 'Fragmentation of International Law? Postmodern Anxieties' (2002) 15 Leiden J Intl L 553, 556–62.

[179] On this finding see also von Bernstorff, 'Procedures of Decision-Making and the Role of Law in International Organizations'.

[180] Eyal Benvenisti and George W Downs, 'The Empire's New Clothes: Political Economy and the Fragmentation of International Law' (2007–2008) 60 Stanford L Rev 595.

[181] Eyal Benvenisti, 'Exit and Voice in the Age of Globalization' (1999–2000) 98 Michigan L Rev 167.

[182] From the rich debate: Daniele Archibugi, Mathias Koenig-Archibugi, and Rafaele Marchetti (eds), *Global Democracy: Normative and Empirical Perspectives* (CUP 2011); Nico Krisch, *Beyond Constitutionalism: The Pluralist Structure of Postnational Law* (OUP 2010) 274–6; Gráinne de Burca,

stronger foundation, namely one building on positive law.[183] To this end, we develop a conception of democracy for international courts with the help of the four articles of the Treaty on European Union (TEU) in Title II, 'Provisions on democratic principles'. They contain what are, to our knowledge, the first legal provisions that frame the concept of democracy for institutions beyond the state. Of course, interpreting these seminal provisions should make use of theoretical insights. Nevertheless, it makes a big difference whether the starting point of a legal argument is in positive law or merely in a theoretical construct.

To be sure, the path we have chosen is fraught with possible misunderstandings. First of all, it should be emphasized that the European Union, as it operates today, surely does not offer an exemplar of ideal democratic governance.[184] However, in Articles 9–12 of the TEU we find a framing of democracy for institutions beyond the state that is neither utopian nor apologetic, but plausible and viable.[185] Its core elements are citizenship (Article 9), representation (Article 10), transparency, deliberation, participation, responsiveness, and control (Article 11), as well as a reorientation of domestic parliamentarism (Article 12).

But can this conception fit the international judiciary? There are a lot of doubts. To begin with, it is laid down for the very specific European Union.[186] Surely it would be untenable to simply use these provisions to test the legitimacy, let alone the lawfulness, of international judicial decisions. But that is not the issue here. We will use these provisions only as clues that reveal which aspects should be paid attention to in developing the democratic principle in the international realm. We are not projecting the political model of the EU onto international institutions.[187]

The approach may also seem ill-taken because Articles 9–12 of the TEU do not explicitly deal with the Court of Justice of the European Union. However, these articles do not mention any specific institution. They pertain to all institutions as set out in Article 13 of the TEU, including the Court.

'Developing Democracy Beyond the State' (2007–2008) 46 Columbia J Transnational L 221; Peter Niesen (ed), *Transnationale Gerechtigkeit und Demokratie* (Campus 2012).

[183] For a philosophical defence of a legal approach see Biagio de Giovanni, *Alle origini della democrazia de massa: I filosofi e i giuristi* (Editoriale Scientifica 2013) 14–20, 249–58.

[184] Among many Yves Mény, 'Can Europe Be Democratic? Is it Feasible? Is it Necessary? Is the Present Situation Sustainable?' (2011) 34 Fordham Intl L J 1287, 1301–3; Mario Monti and Sylvie Goulard, *La democrazia in Europa: Guardare lontano* (Rizzoli 2012).

[185] On this demand see the classic discussion in Fritz W Scharpf, *Demokratietheorie zwischen Utopie und Anpassung* (Universitätsverlag Konstanz 1970).

[186] On this problem see chapter 1 section C 3.

[187] See José E Alvarez, 'The New Dispute Settlers: (Half) Truths and Consequences' (2003) 38 Texas Intl L J 405.

Such an approach accords with the grand tradition in which 'all authority', including judicial authority, must be democratically justified.

Yet another objection could be that Articles 9–12 of the TEU are aimed specifically at the *supra*national European Union and are therefore useless even as inspiration for *international* institutions. In fact, the supranational public authority of the CJEU *does* differ qualitatively from international courts.[188] Most important in this respect are its close connection to national courts (Article 267 TFEU), its power to impose financial sanction (Article 260 TFEU), as well as its embededness in the overarching system of the European Union. But that does not rule out taking inspiration from the way in which the Treaty on European Union explicitly spells out democratic principles. The shared point of reference is precisely that both the CJEU and international courts exercise public authority. That creates comparability, since every exercise of public authority leads to the question of its democratic credentials. To be sure, a comparison would be misleading if we arrived at the conclusion that an international judiciary can be democratically legitimated only within an institutional framework like the European Union. That is not going to happen.

Given these difficulties and possible misunderstandings, why are we choosing this complicated comparative and legalistic 'detour', instead of building directly on a strong theory of democracy? We are taking this route because these articles of the TEU, unlike *any theory*, are the outcome of democratic politics. These provisions are among the most visible statements of the Treaty of Lisbon, which was ratified by the parliaments of all Member States, and this with large majorities. Given that legal scholarship, more than normative theory, is in the final analysis oriented toward results capable of generating a consensus, these provisions are a great asset.

The consent of the large majority of the Union's citizens carries such significance because hardly any issue in the process of European integration is as difficult as the question of democracy. The Lisbon Treaty, which introduced these provisions into the TEU, is the fruit of a long and complex political process, of exceedingly elaborate procedures, and of intensive public discussions that build on more than 20 years of debate on European democracy.[189] Even if this is obviously limited to the EU, it can be supposed that these provisions could inspire solutions beyond Europe.

[188] For more detail see chapter 1 section C 2.

[189] In detail Frank Schimmelfennig, 'Legitimate Rule in the European Union' (1996) 27 Tübinger Arbeitspapiere zur Internationalen Politik und Friedensforschung 1 <tobias-lib.uni-tuebingen.de/volltexte/2000/150> accessed 11 June 2012; Hartmut Bauer, Peter M Huber, and Karl-Peter Sommermann (eds), *Demokratie in Europa* (Mohr Siebeck 2005); Beate Kohler-Koch and Berthold Rittberger (eds), *Debating the Democratic Legitimacy of the European Union* (Rowman & Littlefield Publishers 2007); Alexis von Komorowski, *Demokratieprinzip und Europäische Union: Staatsverfassungsrechtliche Anforderungen an die demokratische Legitimation der EG-Normsetzung* (Duncker & Humblot 2010) 155.

A comparative look back solidifies the relevance of this European experience for the broader international debate. Until the 1990s, it was frequently asserted that the then EEC, as a supranational authority, required no democratic legitimation of its own,[190] similar to what is today the prevailing opinion among most international jurists when it comes to international institutions. The political call by European federalists for a European democracy was by no means universally shared. That changed only with the internal market programme at the end of the 1980s. The Maastricht Treaty lays down a first, but vague, reference to democracy. It was then the Federal Constitutional Court of Germany which declared that the democratic principle constituted an essential criterion for the constitutional assessment of supranational authority.[191] The Amsterdam Treaty took another major step in Article 6 EU and clearly committed all EU institutions to the principle of democracy—with little indication, however, of what that meant. With Articles 9–12 of the TEU in the Lisbon version, European democracy is beginning to take legal shape. These articles spell out a key vision, and not through an empty compromise solution, but in a further-reaching synthesis. This synthesis was then the object of complex procedures. In many cases it took constitution-changing majorities in the Member State to bring the Lisbon Treaty into force. All of this recommends the synthesis as the starting point of reflections, and we will show that these reflections indeed offer valuable clues on how one might develop the democratic credentials of international courts.

Our approach is supported by the fact that the discussion leading to Articles 9–12 of the TEU can be understood as part of the broader debate on the democratic legitimation of public institutions beyond the state.[192] This debate gained momentum after the fall of the Berlin Wall when, for one, authors argued that democracy had become a general principle of international law[193] and, for another, the age of globalization commenced with full force. In that process, functionalist strategies of legitimation ran into

[190] Albrecht Randelzhofer, 'Zum behaupteten Demokratiedefizit der Europäischen Gemeinschaft' in Peter Hommelhoff and Paul Kirchhof (eds), *Der Staatenverbund der Europäischen Union: Beiträge und Diskussionen des Symposions am 21./22. Januar 1994 in Heidelberg* (CF Müller 1994) 39, 40–1.

[191] *Maastricht*; in more detail Franz C Mayer, *Kompetenzüberschreitung und Letztentscheidung: Das Maastricht-Urteil des Bundesverfassungsgerichts und die Letztentscheidung über Ultra vires-Akte in Mehrebenensystemen* (CH Beck 2000) 98–120.

[192] On the debate see Markus Krajewski, 'International Organizations or Institutions, Democratic Legitimacy' in Wolfrum (ed), *Max Planck Encyclopedia of Public International Law*; Thomas Christiano, 'Democratic Legitimacy and International Institutions' in Samantha Besson and John Tasioulas (eds), *The Philosophy of International Law* (OUP 2010) 119.

[193] Thomas M Franck, 'The Emerging Right to Democratic Governance' (1992) 86 AJIL 46; Nils Petersen, *Demokratie als teleologisches Prinzip: Zur Legitimität von Staatsgewalt im Völkerrecht* (Springer 2009) 138; critically Martti Koskenniemi, 'Legal Cosmopolitanism: Tom Franck's Messianic World' (2003) 35 NYU J Intl L and Politics 471.

growing difficulties. Abstract goals of the common good justify concrete decisions even less than treaty provisions.[194]

There is an important difference here between the earlier and current debates. The proposals of the 1920s, especially those formulated within the framework of the League of Nations,[195] were—much like those of the euro-federalists in the 1960s, 70s, and 80s,[196] not really aimed at dealing with a deficit in legitimacy. Instead, their goal was the development of federal structures. By contrast, contemporary proposals arise more from the perception of an existing problem of legitimacy. The international debate is more or less at the same stage at which European integration found itself at the end of the 1980s.[197] There is a growing realization that for international institutions the democratic question is becoming urgent, but there is great uncertainty about what persuasive answers might look like.

A last note on terminological choice: there is widespread scepticism about the use of the demanding concept of democracy and many authors prefer the 'leaner' concept of accountability,[198] especially with a view toward the international judiciary.[199] However, it has not proved possible to truly break away from the concept of democracy and to establish that of accountability as autonomous.[200] We believe that it is possible to create a convincing concept of international democracy on the basis of Articles 9–12 of the TEU.[201] We therefore forego working with the concept of accountability.

194 Ingo Venzke, 'International Bureaucracies from a Political Science Perspective—Agency, Authority and International Institutional Law' (2008) 9 German L J 1401, 1411–2; Jan Klabbers, *An Introduction to International Institutional Law* (2nd edn, CUP 2009) 32.

195 Hans Wehberg, *Grundprobleme des Völkerbundes* (Hensel & Co-Verlag 1926) 83–4; Georges Scelle, *Une crise de la Société des Nations: La réforme du Conseil et l'entrée de l'Allemagne à Genève* (Les Presses Universitaires de France 1926) 137–63; Claudia Kissling, 'Repräsentativ-parlamentarische Entwürfe globaler Demokratiegestaltung im Laufe der Zeit: Eine rechtspolitische Ideengeschichte' (2005) Forum Historiae Iuris <http://www.forhistiur.de/index_de.htm> accessed 19 September 2012.

196 See, for example, Eberhard Grabitz, *Gemeinschaftsrecht bricht nationales Recht* (Appel 1966) 103–4; Altiero Spinelli, *Una strategia per gli Stati uniti d'Europa* (Il Mulino 1989) 187–95.

197 On its importance see Joseph HH Weiler, *The European Community in Change: Exit, Voice and Loyalty* (Europa-Institut der Universität des Saarlandes 1987) 21–2.

198 Mark Bovens, Deirdre Curtin, and Paul T Hart (eds), *The Real World of EU Accountability: What Deficit?* (OUP 2010); Deirdre Curtin and André Nollkaemper, 'Conceptualizing Accountability in International and European Law' (2005) 36 Netherlands YB Intl L 3; Jens Steffek, 'Accountability und politische Öffentlichkeit im Zeitalter des globalen Regierens' in Niesen (ed), *Transnationale Gerechtigkeit und Demokratie* 279.

199 Canivet and others (eds), *Independence, Accountability, and the Judiciary* (British Institute of International and Comparative Law 2006).

200 This can be seen pointedly in Ruth W Grant and Robert O Keohane, 'Accountability and Abuses of Power in World Politics' (2005) 99 American Political Science Rev 29.

201 This accords with the notion that democratic legitimation cannot be replaced by one of its aspects, such as accountability, deliberative justification, transparency, or rule of law. On this in more detail see Jürgen Neyer, 'Justice, Not Democracy: Legitimacy in the European Union' in Rainer Forst and Rainer

2. Basic elements

a) *The democratic subject*

The first thing a concept of democracy must do is specify the democratic subject. Some authors take a holistic or communitarian approach to this difficult question and see a single collective as the democratic subject, mostly a nation or a people. The formula 'In the Name of the People', under which many domestic courts decide, gives support to such an approach. The opposite approach follows the individualistic paradigm, which starts from the individual citizens as democratic subjects.[202] Since positing a European people or a global nation is hardly persuasive, supra- and international democracy is currently conceivable only along the individualistic paradigm.

Very much in this vein, the Treaty on European Union uses the term 'people' only for the Member States (Article 1(2) TEU, for example). European democracy comes without positing a European people. Article 9 of the TEU rather establishes Union citizenship as the vanishing point of European democracy.[203] The TEU thus opts for an individualistic approach, which reaches back via Kant all the way to Hobbes.[204] This is confirmed by the EU Charter of Fundamental Rights, which enshrines civil and political rights as individual rights. The same can be extracted from the further wording of Article 9 of the TEU, according to which all citizens 'shall receive equal attention from its institutions, bodies, offices and agencies.' To be sure, the formulation 'to receive attention' seems paternalistic and out of tune with the very object of democracy. It could fit coherently in the constitutions of Saudi Arabia or the Vatican. However, interpreted in good faith within its context, this provision enshrines the principle of civil equality as the guiding democratic principle.[205]

Schmalz-Bruns (eds), *Political Legitimacy and Democracy in Transnational Perspective: Arena Report No 2/11* (ARENA 2011) 13; Frank Nullmeier and Tanja Pritzlaff, 'The Great Chain of Legitimacy: Justifying Transnational Democracy' in Forst and Schmalz-Bruns (eds), *Political Legitimacy and Democracy in Transnational Perspective: Arena Report No 2/11* 43.

[202] On these opposing notions see Armin von Bogdandy, 'Globalization and Europe: How to Square Democracy, Globalization, and International Law' (2004) 15 Eur J Intl L 885, 890.

[203] Article 9 TEU states: 'In all its activities, the Union shall observe the principle of the equality of its citizens, who shall receive equal attention from its institutions, bodies, offices and agencies. Every national of a Member State shall be a citizen of the Union. Citizenship of the Union shall be additional to and not replace national citizenship.'

[204] Norberto Bobbio, *Das Zeitalter der Menschenrechte: Ist Toleranz durchsetzbar?* (Wagenbachs Taschenbuch 1998) 50–5.

[205] In more detail see Samantha Besson, 'Das Menschenrecht auf Demokratie—Eine moralische Verteidigung mit einer rechtlichen Nuance' in Gret Haller, Klaus Günther, and Ulfried Neumann (eds), *Menschenrechte und Volkssouveränität in Europa* (Campus Verlag 2011) 61, 72. On the current state of the debate see Matthias Ruffert in Christian Calliess and Matthias Ruffert (eds), *EUV/AEUV Kommentar* (4th edn, CH Beck 2011) Article 9 EUV para 24 with additional references; Christoph Schönberger in Eberhard Grabitz, Meinhard Hilf, and Martin Nettesheim (eds), *Das Recht der Europäischen Union: Kommentar*, vol 1 (CH Beck issue October 2011) Article 9 EUV.

Union citizenship has blossomed over the past 20 years, to confute its famous dismissal as just a 'cynical exercise in public relations'.[206] After avant-garde scholarship prepared the ground,[207] the CJEU proclaimed union citizenship to have a fundamental legal status.[208] The rich case-law is working on the visibility and relevance of the legal concept that forms the vanishing point of the European concept of democracy.[209]

What can we take away from this European development for international courts? To begin with, the concept of democracy of Article 9 of the TEU reinforces conceptions for the international level that do without positing or requesting the formation of a new people or a new nation, but rather rely on a cosmopolitan or transnational citizenship.[210] Even if one regards the idea of a transnational or a cosmopolitan citizenship as theoretically sound and perhaps even normatively appealing, it might still be asked whether the concept is suitable for legal thought and practice—that is, for guiding legal interpretation, law-making, legal doctrine, and legal critique.

Without question, a transnational—let alone a cosmopolitan—citizenship does not exist as a positive concept of international law. It is not enshrined in any treaty. But it would be excessively positivistic to banish a concept from legal thought for that reason alone and leave it entirely to political theory. Again, European integration provides a telling example. As early as the 1960s, long before citizenship found its way into the EU treaties, Hans Peter Ipsen and Gert Nicolaysen coined the influential legal concept of market citizenship (*Marktbürgerschaft*).[211] The doctrinal justification was that it gives a plausible key to interpreting and developing provisions of the

[206] Joseph HH Weiler, 'Citizenship and Human Rights' in Jan A Winter and others (eds), *Reforming the Treaty on European Union* (Kluwer Law International 1996) 57, 68.

[207] See Josephine Shaw, 'Citizenship of the Union: Towards Post-National Membership?' (1995) 6 Collected Courses of the Academy of European Law 237, 297–346; Carlos Closa, 'Citizenship of the Union and Nationality of Member States' (1995) 32 CML Rev 487.

[208] Case C-184/99 *Grzelczyk* [2001] ECR I-6193, para 31.

[209] This is also revealed by Arts 10(2), 14(2) TEU. Jelena von Achenbach, 'Theoretische Aspekte des dualen Konzepts demokratischer Legitimation für die Europäische Union' in Silja Vöneky and others (eds), *Legitimation ethischer Entscheidungen im Recht: Interdisziplinäre Untersuchungen* (Springer 2009) 191.

[210] In our usage, transnational citizenship relates to organizations with a limited membership (OECD, NATO) and cosmopolitan citizenship to institutions with a global reach (UN, WTO, IMF). For similar ideas see Anne Peters, 'Dual Democracy' in Klabbers, Peters, and Ulfstein, *The Constitutionalization of International Law* 263, 297–302; Utz Schliesky, *Souveränität und Legitimität von Herrschaftsgewalt* (Mohr Siebeck 2004) 689–90; Rainer Forst, 'Transnationale Gerechtigkeit und Demokratie: Zur Überwindung von drei Dogmen der politischen Theorie' in Niesen (ed), *Transnationale Gerechtigkeit und Demokratie* 29, 42–6.

[211] Hans Peter Ipsen and Gert Nicolaysen, 'Haager Konferenz für Europarecht und Bericht über die aktuelle Entwicklung des Gemeinschaftsrechts' (1964) 18 Neue Juristische Wochenschrift 339, 340–1; see also the path breaking study by Eberhard Grabitz, *Europäisches Bürgerrecht zwischen Marktbürgerschaft und Staatsbürgerschaft* (Europa Union Verlag GmbH 1970).

treaty and case-law. The bases of this citizenship were individual rights that flow from supranational sources and that can be enforced against domestic and supranational acts that impinged upon them.

Following this path, legal building blocks for a doctrine of a transnational or a cosmopolitan citizenship appear that might be relevant at least for some international courts.[212] One can think of the ECtHR or the Inter-American Court of Human Rights, which watch over human rights in response to complaints by individuals. In addition, international arbitral tribunals that protect private investors come into view, but also interstate disputes can be interpreted from the perspective of affected individuals, for example those of the WTO.[213] And even for the ICJ, a human rights interpretation is possible.[214] Many scholarly approaches lay out constructs of international law that actually place human rights at the centre of international law.[215] Hersch Lauterpacht already saw the international judiciary in this light.[216] Even advocates of a state-oriented understanding of international law cannot deny that contemporary international law has norms that not only realize Kant's *ius cosmopoliticum*,[217] but in fact surpass it.[218] Building blocks of transnational or even cosmopolitan citizenship are all real and not a legal fantasy.

Of course, not every human rights approach champions a transnational or cosmopolitan citizenship.[219] Many approaches are primarily oriented toward protection, in that spheres of individual freedom are defended

[212] In more detail Anne Peters, 'Das subjektive internationale Recht' (2011) 59 Jahrbuch des öffentlichen Rechts der Gegenwart 411.

[213] On the question of individual rights see *United States: Section 301-310 of the Trade Act of 1974—Panel Report* (22 December 1999) WT/DS152/R, para 7.72.

[214] Most recently *Questions Relating to the Obligation to Prosecute or Extradite (Belgium v Senegal)* [2012] ICJ Rep 422. In more detail Bruno Simma, 'Human Rights before the International Court of Justice: Community Interest Coming to Life?' in Holger S Hestermeyer and others (eds), *Coexistence, Cooperation and Solidarity: Liber Amicorum Rüdiger Wolfrum* (Nijhoff 2012) 577, 590–8.

[215] Antônio A Cançado Trindade, 'International Law for Humankind: Towards a New *Jus Gentium* (I)' (2005) 316 Recueil des cours 9, 252–84; Christian Tomuschat, 'International Law: Ensuring the Survival of Mankind on the Eve of a New Century: General Course on Public International Law' (1999) 281 Receuil des cours 9, 161–2.

[216] Hersch Lauterpacht, *International Law and Human Rights* (Stevens & Sons 1950) 56–60.

[217] Immanuel Kant, *Perpetual Peace: A Philosophical Proposal* (Jessie H Buckland tr, first published 1795/1796, Sweet & Maxwell 1927) 33–4. In more detail Jörg P Müller, *Perspektiven der Demokratie: Vom Nationalmythos Wilhelm Tell zur Weltsicht Immanuel Kants* (Stämpfli 2012) 130–48.

[218] However, the international right of hospitality remains, as with Kant, tightly circumscribed; there is, after all, no global right of freedom of movement. The many migrants who drown in the Mediterranean attest this tragically. See Bas Schotel, *On the Right of Exclusion: Law, Ethics and Immigration Policy* (Routledge 2012); Seline Trevisanut, *Immigrazione irregolare via mare: diritto internazionale e diritto dell'Unione europea* (Jovene 2012).

[219] Gret Haller, 'Einführung' in Haller, Günther, and Neumann (eds), *Menschenrechte und Volkssouveränität in Europa* 11; Peters, 'Dual Democracy' 300.

against public authority.[220] Following Habermas' critique of Ipsen's *market citizenship*, this is insufficient for a meaningful concept of citizenship. The *political* dimension is essential.[221] Title V of the Charter of Fundamental Rights of the European Union, which deals with citizens' rights, confirms this understanding. Accordingly, a transnational or cosmopolitan citizenship requires rights to participate in the international political process and not just rights that protect against infringements. But there are elements in positive law even for the political dimension. Numerous human rights have political content, such as freedom of opinion, freedom of assembly, the freedom to vote (Articles 19, 21, 25 ICCPR), and there are good grounds for arguing that every public authority, including that of international institutions, is bound to these human rights.[222] This is the case even with the international courts themselves. There should be no question that freedom of opinion (Article 19 ICCPR) protects the critical engagement with their decisions.

So we move to the last and most difficult issue: is it persuasive to conceive of a citizenship without a legally defined group and without a right to vote? Neither exist beyond the European Union.[223] We see no conceptual necessity to make citizenship dependent on the establishment of a community under positive law or a right to vote for an international parliament.[224] With a view to international forms of democratic politicization, one should take an open approach and aspire more broadly to develop mechanisms of effective political inclusion. We thus conclude that, while transnational or a cosmopolitan citizenship are indeed not positively enshrined at this time in international law, there are grounds that make it possible to interpret provisions of international law in their light.

We are aware that our reflections run the risk of being understood as utopian, or legal constructs devoid of real life, or kitsch without an adequate reality check.[225] However, cosmopolitan thinking is by no means found only in political theory and jurisprudence. It is also present in political

[220] Kant, *Perpetual Peace* 33–4.

[221] Jürgen Habermas, *The Postnational Constellation: Political Essays* (Max Pensky tr/ed, MIT Press 2001) 58, 94.

[222] International Law Association, *Accountability of International Organisations: Final Report* (2004) <www.ila-hq.org> accessed 10 February 2012.

[223] Christoph Schönberger, 'European Citizenship as Federal Citizenship' (2007) 19 Revue européenne de droit public 61.

[224] Amartya Sen, *The Idea of Justice* (Belknap Press 2009) 321–37; Forst, 'Transnationale Gerechtigkeit und Demokratie' 29; Peters, 'Dual Democracy' 300; Thomas Groß, 'Postnationale Demokratie—Gibt es ein Menschenrecht auf transnationale Selbstbestimmung?' (2011) 2 Rechtswissenschaft 125, 135–43.

[225] Martti Koskenniemi, 'International Law in Europe: Between Tradition and Renewal' (2005) 16 Eur J Intl L 113.

science, which adds an empirical dimension. Michael Zürn distinguishes four models of cosmopolitanism as guiding political action in the international arena: cosmopolitan intergovernmentalism; cosmopolitan pluralism; cosmopolitan federalism; and social cosmopolitan democracy.[226] What all models and many political actors share are the normative principles of the centrality of the individual, the principled equality of all humans, and the idea of global solidarity.[227]

On the level of principle, cosmopolitanism seems well established. The problems lie with the institutional implementation, and it is precisely on this point that the models differ. The intergovernmental model of a cosmopolitan order sees the prerequisites of a democratic order as present only in nation-states. Cosmopolitan pluralism conceives of multilevel systems without an institutional anchoring point, reducing international democracy mostly to a deliberative mode of policy formation.[228] Hence, cosmopolitanism by no means demands strong forms of institutionalization. Only cosmopolitan federalism champions forms of supranational institutionalization, following the example of the European Union. The model of a social cosmopolitan democracy aims additionally at global redistribution under the idea of distributive justice. We seek a path between models two and three. We take from Zürn that cosmopolitan orientations are operative and can be encountered in the dispositions of large segments of the world's population. Cosmopolitan approaches are thus theoretically, normatively, and analytically meaningful. They find so much repercussion in positive law that they are suited as a backdrop for legal reconstruction and critique.

On the whole, then, it seems possible and worthwhile to follow the approach underlying Article 9 of the TEU and to address the decision-making power of international courts from the citizenship perspective. It can inspire processes of judicial interpretation and law-making as well as doctrinal reconstruction.[229] When it comes to justifying international judicial decisions, that should take place not only—and perhaps not even primarily—with a view to the states, but with a view toward the *individuals* who

[226] Michael Zürn, 'Vier Modelle einer globalen Ordnung in kosmopolitischer Absicht' (2011) 52 Politische Vierteljahresschrift 78.

[227] Legally, only the last principle poses difficulties, but it, too, is frequently recognized as a principle of international law, Rüdiger Wolfrum, 'Concluding Remarks' in Rüdiger Wolfrum and Chie Kojima (eds), *Solidarity: A Structural Principle of International Law* (Springer 2010) 225, 226.

[228] In this sense Peters, 'Dual Democracy' 297–302; see also Mattias Kumm, 'The Cosmopolitan Turn in Constitutionalism: On the Relationship Between Constitutionalism in and Beyond the State' in Dunoff and Trachtman (eds), *Ruling the World?* 258.

[229] Please note: the transition from theory to dogmatic construction demands a lot of preconditions and can take place only specifically to every legal regime—that is, by taking into account the particular determinations concerning the right to initiate proceedings, judicial competencies, and the substantive programme of review; on this see chapter 1 sections C 1 and 2.

are, in the final analysis, affected by them—individuals who are not merely holders of defensive positions, but also political subjects, citizens.[230]

b) Dual democratic legitimacy

Our orientation toward citizenship by no means sets aside the role of states, which constitute, via their governments, the most important and powerful subjects of international law. Negating this role would contradict not only existing law,[231] but also a proper understanding of a transnational or cosmopolitan citizenship. For this precisely is another core statement of the second title of the Treaty on European Union: democratic legitimation has a *dual structure* in the EU, proceeding from the citizens of the Union *and* the citizens of the nations constituted in the Member States.[232]

Such dual legitimacy is already evident in the citizenship concept of Article 9 of the TEU. It establishes a union citizenship—which is not original, however, but is additional to national citizenship. Article 10 of the TEU elaborates on this dual approach by laying down two strands of democratic representation.[233] The democratic legitimation of the EU cannot be generated on the supranational level alone, but constitutively depends on the democratic operation of domestic institutions. The democratic legitimation of the supranational institutions is a common achievement and a common concern for all institutions, which are connected in what is often referred to as a multilevel system.

This basic feature triggers another important difference between a concept of democracy for institutions beyond the state and many conventional concepts of democracy. The latter often place the idea of the rule of the majority in the centre and conceive of democracy as the struggle of competing parties for this power.[234] In a complex multilevel structure

[230] Sceptics might want to consider that the refusal to take this step from legal subject to citizen repeats the mistake of state law theory in the German Empire, which misunderstood the democratic forces; see Johannes Masing, *Die Mobilisierung des Bürgers für die Durchsetzung des Rechts: Europäische Impulse für eine Revision der Lehre vom subjektiv-öffentlichen Recht* (Duncker & Humblot 1997) 66–7.

[231] Kate Parlett, *The Individual in the International Legal System: Continuity and Change in International Law* (CUP 2011) 372.

[232] On the model of dual legitimation see Stefan Oeter, 'Federalism and Democracy' in von Bogdandy and Bast (eds), *Principles of European Constitutional Law* 55, 66–8, and Dann, 'The Political Institutions'. A counter-model can be found in Stefan Haack, 'Demokratie mit Zukunft?' (2012) 67 Juristenzeitung 753, 756–61.

[233] Article 10(2) TEU states: 'Citizens are directly represented at Union level in the European Parliament. Member States are represented in the European Council by their Heads of State or Government and in the Council by their governments, themselves democratically accountable either to their national Parliaments, or to their citizens.'

[234] Christoph Schönberger, 'Die Europäische Union zwischen "Demokratiedefizit" und Bundesstaatsverbot: Anmerkungen zum Lissabon-Urteil des Bundesverfassungsgerichts' (2009) 48 Der Staat 535, 544–8.

of legitimation, the idea of majority rule cannot form the key characteristic. Thus one will have to conceptualize democracy beyond the state as a consociational democracy rather than a competitive one.[235] In terms of democratic theory, this orientation is further supported by the fact that democracy beyond the state must do justice to great social, political, and cultural diversity.

With regard to the international level, the democratic legitimation of international institutions must be built upon the democratic mechanisms of their members.[236] Early euro-federalists and champions of a global parliamentarism might entertain the hope that supranational parliaments could carry the essential burden of democratic legitimation, like federal parliaments. By now, however, the insight has prevailed that the democratic processes organized in the domestic constitutional orders constitute an achievement whose quality is hardly reproducible beyond the state in the foreseeable future.[237] The legitimation of international public authority should thus pick up on existing domestic pathways of democratic legitimation and *supplement* them with proper mechanisms.[238] For international courts this means an intrinsic dependence on state-generated legitimation, which may well guide their work of interpretation, for example with doctrines like the 'margin of appreciation' or subsidiarity.[239]

c) From self-government to political inclusion

Articles 9–12 of the TEU further indicate what should be understood as the essential objective of international democracy: political *inclusion*. Thereby, they do not define democracy as self-determination—indeed, the idea of self-determination is hardly a feasible objective of supranational and international institutions.[240] Of course, one could, as to the European Union, understand the EU in the sense that it protects Europeans against external American, Chinese, or Russian control or hegemony. This is the original sense of the international legal concept of self-determination. Such an

[235] Concept coined by Arend Lijphart; on these types see Manfred G Schmidt, *Demokratietheorien: Eine Einführung* (4th edn, VS Verlag für Sozialwissenschaften 2008) 306–18.

[236] Peters, 'Dual Democracy' 271–96.

[237] Thus even Jürgen Habermas, 'Does the Constitutionalization of International Law Still Have a Chance?' in Jürgen Habermas, *The Divided West* (Ciaran Cronin tr/ed, Polity Press 2006) 115, 141–2.

[238] Jürgen Habermas, 'Konstitutionalisierung des Völkerrechts und die Legitimationsprobleme einer verfassten Weltgesellschaft' in Winfried Brugger, Ulfried Neumann, and Stephan Kirste (eds), *Rechtsphilosophie im 21. Jahrhundert* (Suhrkamp 2008) 360, 362.

[239] Regarding this point in more detail see chapter 4 section C 3 a.

[240] Differently, however, Möllers, *Gewaltengliederung* 28–39; Habermas, *Between Facts and Norms* 89–90, 315–28.

understanding is not adequate for the contemporary notion of democracy.[241] The idea of self-determination can then be understood either as *individual* self-determination, though this exceeds the average imagination in the face of the real political processes, or as *collective* self-determination. The latter may be persuasive in a nation-state that rests on a strong collective identity of its citizens. But such an understanding is not persuasive at the European or the international level, because precisely this kind of collective—such a 'we'—does not exist there.

A viable democracy concept for supranational and international institutions requires a less emphatic understanding than fully fledged self-determination. Once again, Articles 9–12 of the TEU offer clues. As essential elements they indicate citizenship under the principle of equality, representation, transparency, participation, deliberation, and responsiveness, as well as the relevant control mechanisms.[242] For all these elements, the concept of inclusion offers a vanishing point.[243] Such inclusion can take place in two ways: via mechanisms that incorporate the citizens collectively—this is the established path that builds on elections (3)—and via mechanisms that provide for the inclusion of individual citizens and groups in specific decision-making procedures (4). Courts can be built into this kind of understanding of democracy much more constructively than into models committed to the idea of political self-determination.

3. The role of representative institutions for international courts

The justification of public authority demands democratic representation.[244] Seen in the light of inclusion, general elections stand out for the simple reason that they constitute the participatory form with the lowest hurdle. They are the least socially selective.[245] Democratic representation is indispensable

[241] On the developments see Anne Peters, *Das Gebietsreferendum im Völkerrecht* (Nomos 1995) 387–458; Daniel Thürer and Thomas Burri, 'Self-Determination' in Wolfrum (ed), *Max Planck Encyclopedia of Public International Law*.

[242] See Schmidt, *Demokratietheorien: Eine Einführung* 418–20; Christoph Möllers, 'Expressive versus repräsentative Demokratie' in Regina Kreide and Andreas Niederberger (eds), *Transnationale Verrechtlichung: Nationale Demokratien im Kontext globaler Politik* (Campus Verlag 2008) 160.

[243] Jürgen Habermas, *Zur Verfassung Europas: Ein Essay* (Suhrkamp 2011) 50; see also Amartya Sen, *The Idea of Justice* (Belknap Press 2009) 321–37; Forst, 'Transnationale Gerechtigkeit und Demokratie: Zur Überwindung von drei Dogmen der politischen Theorie' 29; Peters, 'Dual Democracy' 300; Thomas Groß, 'Postnationale Demokratie—Gibt es ein Menschenrecht auf transnationale Selbstbestimmung?' (2011) 2 Rechtswissenschaft 125, 135–43.

[244] In a new approach Beatrice Brunhöber, *Die Erfindung 'demokratischer Repräsentation' in den Federalist Papers* (Mohr Siebeck 2010) 114–88.

[245] Pascale Cancik, 'Wahlrecht und Parlamentsrecht als Gelingensbedingungen repräsentativer Demokratie' (2013) 72 Veröffentlichungen der Vereinigung der Deutschen Staatsrechtslehrer 268, 316–7.

also for democratic supranational public authority. After 20 years of discussion, this is the key statement of Article 10 Section 1 TEU.[246] So what does this insight mean for the democratic legitimation of international courts?

The history of the concept of representation is complex.[247] What seems certain, though, is that courts should *not* be understood as institutions of democratic representation. They should not be understood in this way in spite of the fact that judges are elected to their office and are not re-elected if they lose the confidence of the political realm, that their decisions display political dimensions, and in spite of the fact that they are supposed to take into account societal beliefs and interests.[248] Ever since the Federalist Papers, the notion of democratic representation has been linked inseparably with parliamentary bodies that act under the logic of political accountability.[249]

Even if courts do not constitute institutions of democratic representation, this study must nevertheless address questions of representation. This is called for by the central role that representative institutions play within the domestic context for the legitimation of courts—by establishing them, financing them, staffing them, and by enacting the provisions they are supposed to apply.[250] Their central role in domestic contexts suggests that international courts also somehow require democratic legitimation conveyed by representative institutions. This is confirmed by Article 10 of the TEU, according to which the functioning of the Union *as a whole*, which thus includes also the Court of Justice of the European Union, rests on the notion of democratic representation.

In order to attune the principle of democratic representation to the specific context of international courts, Article 10 of the TEU holds some important innovative statements. Thus, in accordance with the basic notion of dual legitimation, elections give rise to two strands of democratic legitimacy in structurally different representative institutions: for one, the European Parliament, which is directly elected by the citizens of the Union; for another, the Council of Ministers and European Council, whose legitimation rests on elections by the peoples of the Member States. Between the two, there is a

[246] Article 10(1) TEU states: 'The functioning of the Union shall be based on representative democracy.'

[247] Hasso Hofmann, *Repräsentation: Studien zur Wort- und Begriffsgeschichte von der Antike bis ins 19. Jahrhundert* (4th edn, Duncker & Humblot 2003) 1–28.

[248] Emmanuelle Jouannet, 'Actualité des questions d'indépendance et d'impartialité des juridictions internationales: la consolidation d'un tiers pouvoir international?' in Hélène Ruiz Fabri and Jean-Marc Sorel (eds), *Indépendance et impartialité des juges internationaux* (Editions A Pedone 2010) 271, 283–90.

[249] Adalbert Podlech, 'Repräsentation' in Otto Brunner, Werner Conze, and Reinhart Koselleck (eds), *Grundgeschichtliche Grundbegriffe*, vol 5 (Klett-Cotta 2004) 509, 522–31.

[250] Andreas Voßkuhle, *Rechtsschutz gegen den Richter: Zur Integration der Dritten Gewalt in das verfassungsrechtliche Kontrollsystem vor dem Hintergrund des Art. 19 Abs. 4 GG* (CH Beck 1993) 47–50, 63–4; for legal comparison Anja Seibert-Fohr (ed), *Judicial Independence in Transition* (Springer 2012).

clear preponderance of the strand of legitimation that runs via the national parliaments, which emerges especially from Article 48 of the TEU, as well as the strong role of the Council of Ministers and the European Council in the decision-making procedures.

Article 10 Section 2 of the TEU represents major developments of the representation principle.[251] It is a huge step to conceive of a transnational parliament that *does not* represent a people as a democratic and representative assembly of citizens.[252] It seems equally important that Article 10 Section 2 of the TEU likewise qualifies executive bodies such as the European Council and the Council of Ministers as bodies of democratic representation, for under national constitutions, executive bodies have no such role.[253]

If one transfers these reflections to the international level, they initially confirm traditional notions about the democratic legitimation of international courts. Their establishment and legal basis are mostly enshrined in international treaties that draw their democratic legitimation from the domestic procedure of parliamentary ratification.[254] While we do not question the democratic significance of this parliamentary consent, we see limits to its legitimatory power: limits that render it advisable—given the development of many international courts—to open up additional sources of legitimation.[255]

Parliamentary institutions exist not only on the domestic and on the supranational level, but also within international institutions. The question arises as to whether such institutions, building on the rationale of Article 10 of the TEU, can be understood as organs of democratic representation capable of supporting international courts. The concern for a parliamentarization of the international realm has a venerable tradition.[256] Indeed, there are proposals to develop international parliamentary assemblies along the lines of the European Parliament.[257] Jürgen Habermas, for example, argues that the UN General Assembly, re-formed in the light of a global parliamentarism, should be in charge of the development of the political constitution

[251] Art 10(2) TEU. [252] On this in more detail see section C 2 b.

[253] Alexander Hanebeck, *Der demokratische Bundesstaat des Grundgesetzes* (Duncker & Humblot 2004) 199–205, 279–82, 312–3.

[254] Exceptions are the UN Criminal Tribunals for the former Yugoslavia and Rwanda set up through a resolution of the UN Security Council; see UNSC Res 827 (25 May 1993) UN Doc S/RES/827 and UNSC Res 955 (8 November 1994) UN Doc S/RES/955, as well as the Inspection Panel of the World Bank; see chapter 2 section C 1.

[255] In detail see section B 1.

[256] Wehberg, *Grundprobleme des Völkerbundes* 83–4; Kissling, 'Repräsentativ-parlamentarische Entwürfe'.

[257] Richard Falk and Andrew Strauss, 'On the Creation of a Global Peoples Assembly: Legitimacy and the Power of Popular Sovereignty' (2000) 36 Stanford J Intl L 191.

of global society and calibrate the parameters of justice.[258] Should such parliamentary institutions ever come into being, we might expect that they will be established with mechanisms that pass on to international courts the democratic legitimation generated within them. However, these are political projects for the future.

If there are no directly elected international parliamentary assemblies, there are, however, parliamentary institutions that are composed of representatives from domestic parliaments. The Inter-Parliamentary Union (IPU) is a first example, a somehow universal parliament of parliaments.[259] Regional examples are found in the Parliamentary Assembly of the Council of Europe, which has a substantive role in the election of judges to the ECtHR, the parliament of MERCOSUR, the Pan-African Parliament of the African Union, the Inter-Parliamentary Assembly of ASEAN, or the parliamentary assemblies of NATO and the OSCE.[260] How should one rate the democratic relevance of such institutions, which are not directly elected, do not respect the principle of electoral equality, frequently have only narrow competencies, and are mostly unknown to the broader public?

These questions lead into unchartered territory. In light of the history of democratic representation[261] and given the current structure of transnational publics, direct election should not be posited as a necessary criterion for the democratic relevance of such international bodies.[262] Democratic processes as established and organized in domestic constitutional systems are currently difficult, if not impossible, to reproduce on the international level.[263] Article 10 Section 2 of the TEU confirms this understanding, as it posits even executive organs such as the European Council and the Council of Ministers as institutions of democratic representation. If the peoples of Europe consider such bodies as possible institutions of democratic representation, one can hardly deny such qualification to international parliamentary assemblies.

[258] Habermas, 'Konstitutionalisierung des Völkerrechts und die Legitimationsprobleme einer verfassten Weltgesellschaft' 369, 376.

[259] Felix Arndt, 'International Parliamentary Assemblies' in Wolfrum, *Max Planck Encyclopedia of Public International Law*, paras 5–10; Scelle, *Une crise de la Société des Nations* 137–47.

[260] See Markus Krajewski, 'Legitimizing Global Economic Governance through Transnational Parliamentarization: The Parliamentary Dimensions of the WTO and the World Bank' (2010) 136 TranState Working Papers <http://econstor.eu/dspace/handle/10419/41583> accessed 7 April 2014; Isabelle Ley, 'Zur Politisierung des Völkerrechts: Parlamentarische Versammlungen im Außenverhältnis' (2012) 50 Archiv des Völkerrechts 191.

[261] On this see Hofmann, *Repräsentation*.

[262] For a different view Joseph HH Weiler, 'European Democracy and Its Critics: Polity and System' in Joseph HH Weiler, *The Constitution of Europe* (CUP 1999) 264, 266.

[263] Habermas, 'Does the Constitutionalization of International Law Still Have a Chance?' 139–43.

Again, serious misunderstandings can arise as our considerations run the risk of taking an apologetic turn. According to the arguments laid out above, global governance could now seem to satisfy the democratic principle, given the core role of national executives in international institutions. The concerns over the fate of democracy under globalization would thus be without grounds.[264] Such an understanding of democracy would hardly contain any normative projection and would rather constitute a betrayal of the principle.

Conceptually, one can chart a path here between utopia and apology by qualifying the broad notion of representation—as suggested by Article 10 Section 2 of the TEU—with further elements, in particular transparency, deliberation, and participation.[265] By now the importance of these elements has come to be generally recognized, not as a replacement for, but as a supplement to democratic representation.[266] This move is confirmed by Title II of the Treaty on European Union. Its Article 11 states as democratic requirements the promotion of public debates and open, transparent, regular dialogue between institutions and citizens.[267] These criteria can be understood so that institutions legitimated only indirectly through elections can contribute to their democratic legitimation *if* their procedures and practice are inclusive.

Such institutions can become relevant, for example, for the election of judges or the enactment of soft law upon which the courts can draw. More precisely, an international court that uses soft law instruments in its reasoning has to examine the inclusiveness of the relevant decision-making process.[268] This step does not demand anything unusual. In nearly every constitutional state today, a court has to determine whether applicable law

[264] Jean-Marie Guéhenno, *Das Ende der Demokratie* (Deutscher Taschenbuch Verlag 1996).

[265] In detail Schmidt, *Demokratietheorien* 236–53; Peters, 'Dual Democracy' 268–71. An early statement on the need for deliberation: Edmund Burke, 'Speech in the House of Commons against Pitt's Proposal for a Committee to Consider Parliamentary Reform (7 May 1782)' in David Horn and Mary Ransome (eds), *English Historical Documents 1714–1783*, vol 10 (Routledge 1957) 225.

[266] Habermas, 'Konstitutionalisierung des Völkerrechts und die Legitimationsprobleme einer verfassten Weltgesellschaft' 362; Udo Di Fabio, 'Der neue Art. 23 des Grundgesetzes—Positivierung vollzogenen Verfassungswandels oder Verfassungsneuschöpfung?' (1993) 32 Der Staat 191. See also the prominence of deliberation in the Lisbon decision by the Federal Constitutional Court of Germany, *Lissabon* 351–3.

[267] Article 11(1) and (2) TEU states: '(1) The institutions shall, by appropriate means, give citizens and representative associations the opportunity to make known and publicly exchange their views in all areas of Union action. (2) The institutions shall maintain an open, transparent and regular dialogue with representative associations and civil society.'

[268] A similar understanding of democracy is advocated by Amartya Sen, *The Idea of Justice* 87–113. Concretely with a view toward international courts: Robert Howse, 'A New Device for Creating International Legal Normativity: The WTO Technical Barriers to Trade Agreement and "International Standards"' in Christian Joerges and Ernst-Ulrich Petersmann (eds), *Constitutionalism, Multilevel Trade Governance and Social Regulation* (Hart 2006) 383, 393–4.

conforms to respective constitutional principles. Such assessments require a further doctrinal elaboration of international organizations' law-making procedures.[269] Important elements for the democratic quality are precisely the transparency, publicness, and deliberativeness of a process or the participation of NGOs.[270] This leads to the conclusion that an international parliamentary organ does not generate democratic representation by its mere establishment, but depends on the inclusive quality of its work. It must be *acquired by hard work*. Our chapter on the election of judges and on the use of soft law in judicial decisions will elaborate on these considerations.

4. The foundations of court-generated democratic legitimation

While political representation is indispensable, it does not exhaust the democratic idea. Accordingly, Article 11 of the TEU contains further guidelines for more inclusiveness. Transparency, the involvement of affected individuals, and dialogue—the cornerstones of Article 11—are of particular importance for an international judiciary, because they identify strategies by which courts can contribute to their democratic legitimation.[271] It is important to note that these strategies can only *deepen* democratic legitimation, but they cannot *replace* representative institutions.

A first aspect is the transparency of the exercise of public authority. This is so important that EU law ordains already, in Article 1 Section 2 of the TEU, that decisions be made 'as openly as possible'—that is, transparently. The democratic importance of transparency is underscored by Article 11 Sections 1 and 2 of the TEU.[272] As in Article 9 and Article 10 Section 1 of the TEU, the provision is not specific to any institution and therefore encompasses judicial action.

This renders it advisable to conduct judicial procedures, for example, transparently—and this not just for the parties, but also for the wider public that might be affected. But a transparent reasoning, too, offers a strategy through which a court can contribute to its own democratic legitimation. Such a justification allows the scholarly and general public to engage much better with a judicial decision. Under Article 11 of the TEU, a deliberative public that engages with the decisions taken by the European institutions is

[269] On procedural law see von Bernstorff, 'Procedures of Decision-Making and the Role of Law in International Organizations'.

[270] Peters, 'Dual Democracy' 315–8.

[271] Martin Nettesheim in Grabitz, Hilf, and Nettesheim (eds), *Menschenrechte und Volkssouveränität in Europa* Article 11 EUV para 5; in greater detail Joana Mendes, 'Participation and the Role of Law after Lisbon: A Legal View on Article 11 TEU' (2011) 48 CML Rev 1849.

[272] On the importance of transparency see Case C-64/05 P *Sweden v Commission* [2007] ECR I-11389, paras 54, 64.

an objective of the European concept of democracy. Applied to international courts, this means that judicial decisions can strengthen transnational publics. Of particular importance is that courts lay out clearly the principled arguments, the de facto assumptions, and the objectives aimed for. This does not rule out a certain openness regarding the precise doctrinal justification and the application in future constellations; rather, such openness allows subsequent adjudication to be responsive to the discourse, which is in itself an element of international democracy.[273]

Democratic inclusion also calls for political participation beyond elections. With respect to the international judiciary, citizens' initiatives and referenda—much-studied forms of such inclusion—are hardly relevant. More important is the participation by affected and interested parties in the decision-making processes. Scholarship has demonstrated that such participation, especially if it is enriched with deliberative elements, can serve the democratic principle.[274] Article 11 Section 2 of the TEU rests on this understanding. Aspects especially pertinent for strengthening democratic legitimation in judicial procedure are a relevant dialogue of the court with the disputing parties, the involvement of third parties, and the possibility of *amicus curiae* briefs.

But how can one interpret the judicial procedure as generating democratic legitimation without calling into question, on the one hand, the decision-making monopoly of the judges and, on the other, a qualified concept of democracy that goes beyond consultation? A first path connects to the discourse about the case in the courtroom. Here the discourse is not restricted to substantive questions or means of evidence, but extends also to legal questions. In its reasoning, the court should engage with the arguments that the parties submit.

The open discussion of interests and positions invigorates democracy, since it nourishes the democratic public. A judicial decision can participate in this and thus acquire legitimation, provided it is tied into a public discourse.[275] This demands, however, that the court regards such discourses as relevant and shows itself to be responsive to them. Against this backdrop, the participation of NGOs as civil society actors takes on democratic relevance. They can mediate the participation of citizens in the exercise of

[273] In more detail see chapter 4 section C 1 c.

[274] Beate Kohler-Koch, 'The Organization of Interests and Democracy' in Kohler-Koch and Rittberger (eds), *Debating the Democratic Legitimacy of the European Union* 255.

[275] John Rawls, 'The Idea of Public Reason Revisited' (1997) 64 U Chicago L Rev 765; Quoc Loc Hong, 'Constitutional Review in the Mega-Leviathan: A Democratic Foundation for the European Court of Justice' (2010) 16 Eur L J 695.

public authority.[276] There is no reason why this should not also apply to judicial proceedings, of course taking into account their specific characteristics.

Another way by which courts can acquire democratic legitimation is the creation and promotion of broader deliberative processes. This leads back to the objective of our approach—to link the theory of the contemporary international judiciary with the research on global governance in particular and the democratic politicization of international politics in general. It is one of our core insights that the success of many international courts leads to the need for an accompanying international politicization. If international courts succeed in promoting this kind of politicization, they can support their own democratic legitimation.

To be sure, not every form of politicization holds democratic potential. A legally and institutionally unrestrained struggle for power has no such quality. But if the pursuit of interests takes place within legally hedged pathways, which are responsive to democratic requirements, then this holds promise. On the national level, such a production of legitimacy happens above all through parliamentary processes. On the international level, other processes are conceivable in which this kind of legitimacy-generating politicization can take place. One might think of politicization in multilateral, legally framed and hedged institutions into which political actors introduce their interests and convictions. In these spheres the power asymmetries are moderated, which serves the democratic ideal of civil equality.[277]

Finally, one might ponder whether the acceptance that a court actually gains for its decisions should be considered another source of support for its democratic legitimation. Some voices incline in this direction.[278] However, acceptance is a sociological, not a normative category.[279] For the most part it describes the willingness of a legal subject to acknowledge a norm as binding upon one's own behaviour. The opposite is rejection. Acceptance in this sense is indispensable for *every* legal order, whether autocratic or

[276] Needless to say, there are numerous problems; in greater detail see chapter 4 section B 2. On the conceptual level see Jochen von Bernstorff, 'Zivilgesellschaftliche Partizipation in Internationalen Organisationen: Form globaler Demokratie oder Baustein westlicher Expertenherrschaft?' in Brunkhorst (ed), *Demokratie in der Weltgesellschaft* 277; Michael Zürn, 'Internationale Institutionen und nichtstaatliche Akteure in der Global Governance' in Michael Zürn and Matthias Ecker-Ehrhardt (eds), *Gesellschaftliche Politisierung und internationale Institutionen* (Suhrkamp 2014, forthcoming).

[277] In greater detail see chapter 4 section C 3. But see also the concerns of Benvenisti and Downs, 'The Empire's New Clothes'; Nicole Deitelhoff, '(Is) Fair Enough? Legitimation internationalen Regierens durch deliberative Verfahren' in Niesen, *Transnationale Gerechtigkeit und Demokratie* 103, 112–7.

[278] Karin Oellers-Frahm, 'Lawmaking through Advisory Opinions' (2011) 12 German L J 1033, 1054; Binder, 'The Prohibition of Amnesties by the Inter-American Court of Human Rights' 1229; Tullio Treves, 'Aspects of Legitimacy of Decisions of International Courts and Tribunals' in Rüdiger Wolfrum and Volker Röben (eds), *Legitimacy in International Law* (Springer 2008) 169.

[279] Thus also in demarcation to *acceptability*; see Habermas, *Between Facts and Norms* 155.

democratic.[280] A decision by the court of the Vatican can win acceptance even though, given the absolutist form of the Vatican's government,[281] it is surely not democratically legitimated.[282]

Now, one might object that the belief in legitimacy forms a precondition for acceptance, that therefore acceptance has a normative element to it. However, the belief in legitimacy can arise from various sources, and can come, as already shown by Max Weber, without democratic legitimation.[283] Even if democratic law requires acceptance and democratic processes usually promote acceptance, acceptance and democratic legitimation are phenomena that should not be mingled.[284] Within the contemporary theories of democracy and law there are hardly any approaches that regard acceptance as a democratic category. Such reluctance is confirmed by Articles 9–12 of the TEU, which do not use this term either. The absence of the notion of acceptance in the provisions on democratic principles is particularly notable because the 'tacit consent of the citizens' was long considered essential support for the legitimacy of European institutions.[285]

[280] Hart, *The Concept of Law*; Kelsen developed the same idea using the concept of the necessary general effectiveness of the legal system in *Introduction to the Problems of Legal Theory* 28–32. Similarly also the systems theory of Luhmann, *Legitimation durch Verfahren* (2nd edn, Suhrkamp 1989) 34.

[281] Art 1 Fundamental Law of Vatican City State (Legge Fondamentale dello Stato della Città del Vaticano): 'Il Sommo Pontefice, Sovrano dello Stato della Città del Vaticano, ha la pienezza dei poteri legislativo, esecutivo e giudiziario.'

[282] See the judgment against Gabriele Paolo of 6 October 2012; the mild punishment (house arrest) probably has to do also with a desire to win acceptance; Sentenza del Tribunale dello Stato della città del vaticano nel processo penale a carico dell'imputato Gabriele Paolo (Prot N 8/12 Reg Gen Pen) <press.catholica.va> accessed 11 February 2012.

[283] Max Weber, *Economy and Society* (Guenther Roth and Claus Wittich eds, University of California Press 1978) 212.

[284] Ernst Benda, *Akzeptanz als Bedingung demokratischer Legitimität?* (Europa Union Verlag 1988) 1, 23.

[285] Hong, 'Constitutional Review in the Mega-Leviathan' 713–4.

4

Pathways of Democratic Legitimacy

The legitimacy of an international judicial decision can rely on various sources, such as the consensus of the contending parties, the successful resolution of a conflict, the development of a viable legal regime, the juridification of power relations, and the promotion of shared interests. When we focus on democratic legitimacy, we do not deny or belittle the relevance of these other sources. However, the legitimation that flows from them runs the risk of no longer adequately watering the flourishing landscape of international adjudication. That is precisely the reason why we seek to open up the additional source of democratic legitimacy. Since the provision of legitimacy, like the supply of water, should be seen as a system, this newly developed source affects all the others.

To introduce more closely the problem of this chapter, we borrow from the German doctrine on domestic judicial legitimacy.[1] It also shows for the international level both the legitimatory potential of the consensus of states (traditionally the most important source of legitimation of international courts) and its limits. It is indisputable that the ratification of a court's statute by democratic states and the consent to the law that it applies imparts democratic legitimacy. To begin with, a founding statute ratified by parliament[2] justifies the existence of an international court with its mandate of adjudication. It imparts what German doctrine calls the *institutional* legitimation of a court. In addition, as long as the court applies a treaty ratified in parliament, this imparts *substantive* legitimation for its exercise of authority. If international judges are appointed by institutions that are politically

[1] In more detail with a view toward domestic courts see Andreas Voßkuhle and Gernot Sydow, 'Die demokratische Legitimation des Richters' (2002) 57 Juristenzeitung 673, 676–9. Seminal is Ernst-Wolfgang Böckenförde, 'Die Demokratie als Verfassungsprinzip' in Josef Isensee and Paul Kirchhof (eds), *Handbuch des Staatsrechts der Bundesrepublik Deutschland*, vol I (CF Müller 1987) 887. See also Christoph Möllers, 'Legalität, Legitimität und Legitimation des Bundesverfassungsgerichts' in Matthias Jestaedt and others, *Das entgrenzte Gericht: Eine kritische Bilanz nach sechzig Jahren Bundesverfassungsgericht* (Suhrkamp 2011) 298.

[2] Exceptions exist above all with the International Criminal Tribunals for the former Yugoslavia and Rwanda, as well as the Inspection Panel of the World Bank.

accountable,[3] such appointments provide the court *personal* legitimation. International courts are accordingly democratically legitimated vis-à-vis the citizens of a ratifying state in the following ways: *institutionally, substantively*, and *personally*.

But that by no means settles the democratic question. For the issue is not merely that strands of legitimation *exist at all*; rather, they must generate an *adequate* measure of democratic legitimation, and important authors are already questioning whether German parliaments (on the regional and the federal level) impart sufficient democratic legitimation to German courts.[4] The situation is much more difficult still for international courts, where the chains of legitimation are, by necessity, much longer and more convoluted.[5]

One must therefore probe additional mechanisms that could democratically justify international adjudication. This chapter lays out how international law can be developed further in this regard. At the same time, its goal is to render plausible our democracy-oriented public law theory of adjudication. To that end, the present chapter zooms in on the selection of *judges*, the judicial *procedures*, and the framing and reasoning in the judicial *decision*.

If this chapter has the thrust of applying insights of a public law theory, it should be stressed that it will remain at a high level of abstraction, with all the limits that this entails. Before our reflections can feed into concrete policy proposals, they need to be further concretized for every court, especially in light of its specific legal and political setting.[6]

We will proceed in three large steps, which take up many aspects of current debates. Our aim is to interconnect these debates and move them forward through the new perspective afforded by the public law theory of international adjudication. Given the importance of democratic representation, the first section (A) examines the role of deliberative bodies in the selection of judges. Beyond that, courts can generate their own democratic legitimation if they proceed in a transparent, deliberative, and participatory manner and embed themselves into relevant publics (section B). Finally, the democratic principle provides clues as to what judges should say. They can calibrate their review in light of the principle of democracy, refer to the law-making of other institutions, and promote the democratic quality of political processes (section C).

[3] On this see Michael Wood, 'The Selection of Candidates for International Judicial Office: Recent Practice' in Tafsir M Ndiaye and Rüdiger Wolfrum (eds), *Law of the Sea, Environmental Law and Settlement of Dispute: Liber Amicorum Judge Thomas A Mensah* (Nijhoff 2007) 357.

[4] See, for example, Voßkuhle and Sydow, 'Die demokratische Legitimation des Richters'.

[5] On the specific legitimatory problems of international courts see chapter 3 section B.

[6] In more detail see chapter 1 section C 2.

For further democratization in practice, this chapter banks on the good sense of governments and international judges. This may seem naïve.[7] Judges, in particular, can form an 'epistemic community'[8] or an 'invisible college'[9] far removed from the ideas, interests, and values of most citizens.[10] This, of course, is untenable under the principle of democracy. Under no circumstance may the 'community' be closed or the 'college' invisible.[11] In any event, the strategies sketched out in what follows are hopeless without a critical and attentive public, even if they will mostly be implemented by executives and judges.[12] All this calls for sensitivity to problems of legitimation—a sensitivity our study is intended to promote.

A. JUDGES

The democratic principle demands powerful representative institutions.[13] That is why many legal systems accord an important role to parliamentary bodies in filling high judicial offices domestically.[14] That approach will be pursued for international judges. To that end, the first step is to analyze the specific logic of the office in question (1). On this basis, the procedures for the selection of judges will be laid out (2). This leads to the question of whether international deliberative assemblies are able to convey democratic legitimation to international judges if involved in the selection process (3).

Our reflections will lead to the conclusion that more transparency, deliberativeness, and parliamentary participation are called for in the

[7] Classic discussion in Jeremy Bentham, 'Truth versus Ashhurst: Or, Law as It Is, Contrasted with What It Is Said to Be' in John Bowring (ed), *The Works of Jeremy Bentham*, vol 5 (William Tait 1843) 231, 235–7; on this see Gerald J Postema, *Bentham and the Common Law* (Clarendon 1986) 202–4.

[8] Daniel Terris and others, *The International Judge: An Inquiry into the Men and Women Who Decide the World's Cases* (OUP 2007) 64.

[9] Oscar Schachter, 'The Invisible College of International Lawyers' (1977) 72 Northwestern U L Rev 217; on this see David Kennedy, 'The Politics of the Invisible College: International Governance and the Politics of Expertise' (2001) 6 Eur Human Rights L Rev 463.

[10] A classic and influential work is that of Édouard Lambert, *Le gouvernement des juges et la lutte contre la législation sociale aux États-Unis* (Giard 1921).

[11] Path-breaking discussion by Peter Häberle, 'Die offene Gesellschaft der Verfassungsinterpreten' in Peter Häberle, *Verfassung als öffentlicher Prozess: Materialien zu einer Verfassungstheorie der offenen Gesellschaft* (Duncker & Humblot 1978) 155.

[12] A sobering view by Patrizia Nanz and Jens Steffek, 'Zivilgesellschaftliche Partizipation und die Demokratisierung internationalen Regierens' in Peter Niesen and Benjamin Herborth (eds), *Anarchie der kommunikativen Freiheit: Jürgen Habermas und die Theorie der internationalen Politik* (Suhrkamp 2007) 87.

[13] See chapter 3 section C 1.

[14] For a comparative legal view see Anja Seibert-Fohr (ed), *Judicial Independence in Transition* (Springer 2012); on the US see Russell Wheeler, 'Judicial Independence in the United States of America' in Seibert-Fohr (ed), *Judicial Independence in Transition* 521.

appointment of international judges. To pre-empt misunderstandings, it should be emphasized that this approach does not advocate a politicization of the courts. For example, the direct election of judges in many US states reveals such serious problems that it hardly serves as a model.[15] Personnel policy, substantive politics, and election campaigns constitute different fields. Accordingly, many parliaments have created committees for the selection of judges, which are characterized by confidentiality.[16] In what follows, we focus on the question of whether the participation of deliberative international bodies is at all capable of strengthening the democratic legitimation of international judges.

1. What makes a good bench? A democracy-oriented reconstruction

A process can be elucidated only in light of its purpose. When it comes to the process of selecting international judges, there are five core points. They include first of all independence, impartiality, and the legal expertise of the candidates. Another factor—and this should no longer come as a surprise—is their basic understanding of international adjudication and of the tasks of a specific court. Finally, attention must be paid to the *international* representativeness of the bench.

Independence, impartiality, and legal expertise of the judges are not only requirements under the rule of law, but are also democratic necessities.[17] Judges can fulfil the democratic mandate entrusted to them only if they render their decisions independently, impartially, and expertly. That is what the citizens expect from them. Judicial power that does not live up to these standards is illegitimate by all standards. These requirements are inherent in their legal mandate. We consider it a trend favourable to the democracy-oriented understanding that these requirements have by now been largely legally enshrined for international judges, even if more can certainly be done in that regard, too.

[15] Charles G Geyh, 'Judicial Election Reconsidered: A Plea for Radical Moderation' (2012) 35 Harvard J L and Public Policy 623, 631–8.

[16] In more detail Axel Tschentscher, *Demokratische Legitimation der dritten Gewalt* (Mohr Siebeck 2006) 284–6, 315–21. On the domestic level we see parliamentary involvement in elections, for example Art 2(2) Constitution of the United States of America; Art 94(1)2 German Basic Law (Grundgesetz); Art 150 Constitution of Estonia (Eesti Vabariigi põhiseadus); Art 135(1) Constitution of the Republic of Italy (Costituzione della Repubblica Italiana). See also Kate Malleson and Peter H Russell (eds), *Appointing Judges in an Age of Judicial Power: Critical Perspectives from around the World* (University of Toronto Press 2006).

[17] Anja Seibert-Fohr, 'Introduction: The Challenge of Transition' in Seibert-Fohr (ed), *Judicial Independence in Transition* 1, 1–3. To be sure, a greater rule of law does not invariably mean more democracy, Gianluigi Palombella, 'The Rule of Law Beyond the State: Failures, Promises, and Theory' (2009) 7 Intl J Const L 442, 453.

Although independence and impartiality, in particular, might seem self-evident at first glance, for a long time that was by no means the case, especially among arbitrators. Many acted with a diplomatic ethos and the self-understanding of delegates who remained obliged to the parties that appointed them.[18] An important demand by champions of the nineteenth-century peace movement was that arbitrators serve the law and not one particular party. They were not listened to for a long time. At the Hague Peace Conference, the proposal that the members of the Permanent Court of Arbitration should affirm on oath to 'decide to the best of their knowledge and conscience and with complete impartiality and neutrality' failed because many delegates did not actually want individual arbitrators to act impartially.[19] Some, entirely in keeping with the state-oriented understanding, may have believed that an individual, even as a judge, was in any case hardly able to transcend the perspective and interests of *his* state. By contrast, Elihu Root, very much in line with the community-oriented understanding, championed the independence of the judiciary, with the US Supreme Court serving as his example.[20]

Within the framework of the League of Nations it was possible to articulate the requirements profile more in line with that of an independent institution.[21] Article 2 of the Statute of the Permanent Court of International Justice (now Article 2 of the Statute of the International Court of Justice) specified: 'The Court shall be composed of a body of independent judges [...]'.[22] Similar formulations are today found in all court statutes.[23]

Nevertheless, to this day the demand is raised, even by invoking the democratic principle,[24] that judges should be subject to the influence of their respective governments. That is the only way, the argument goes, for the will of the parties to a treaty to be effectively brought to bear.[25] Such a demand squares nicely with the state-oriented understanding of an international judiciary, but is likely to be rejected outside of it. However, it is

[18] See chapter 2 section A 1.

[19] Heinrich Lammasch, 'Die Lehre von der Schiedsgerichtsbarkeit in ihrem ganzen Umfange' in Fritz Stier-Somlo (ed), *Handbuch des Völkerrechts*, vol 5 (Kohlhammer 1914) 1, 136–7.

[20] Ram P Anand, *International Courts and Contemporary Conflicts* (Asia Publishing House 1974) 34.

[21] Manley O Hudson, *International Tribunals: Past and Future* (Carnegie Endowment for International Peace and Brookings Institution 1944) 9–10.

[22] See, for example, Art 2 ITLOS Statute, Art 21 ECHR, Art 36(3) Rome Statute.

[23] Overview in Mariano J Aznar-Gómez in Andreas Zimmermann and others (eds), *The Statute of the International Court of Justice: A Commentary* (2nd edn, OUP 2012) Art 2 para 5; Nienke Grossman, 'Legitimacy and International Adjudicative Bodies' (2009) 41 George Washington Intl L Rev 107, 123–4.

[24] Jack L Goldsmith and Eric A Posner, *The Limits of International Law* (OUP 2005) 212, 223.

[25] Eric A Posner and John C Yoo, 'Judicial Independence in International Tribunals' (2005) 93 California L Rev 1, 28, 55.

difficult for both the regime-oriented and the community-oriented understanding to counter this argument effectively in terms of democratic theory. Only the democracy-oriented conception, which relates international courts to a transnational and potentially cosmopolitan citizenship, can establish a solid counterpoint. This idea is already adumbrated in Hersch Lauterpacht: 'impartiality [...] is in the last resort a personal quality of intellect and conscience. [...] It presupposes on [the judges'] part the consciousness of being citizens of the world.'[26]

Independence and impartiality are important not only in the selection of judges but during their entire mandate, since they are indispensable preconditions for a legitimate judiciary.[27] Recent cases have brought greater attention to this issue.[28] In 2003, Israel wrote to the Registry of the ICJ that the Egyptian judge Nabil Elaraby should be excluded from the legal advisory procedure in the matter of *Legal Consequences of the Construction of a Wall in the Occupied Palestinian Territory* because he had already spoken publicly about central questions. Although the ICJ rejected the request, Judge Thomas Buergenthal, in his dissenting opinion, spelled out the problem.[29] The appeals panel for the Special Court for Sierra Leone arrived at the opposite conclusion: a monograph about the Revolutionary United Front (RUF) by Judge Geoffrey Robertson led to his exclusion from a trial against RUF member Issay Sesay.[30]

Securing the independence, impartiality, and legal expertise of international judges is a project as incomplete as it is imperative.[31] Those qualities do not exhaust the profile of what is required of an international judge. According to Article 9 of the ICJ Statute, in selecting the judges 'the electors shall bear in mind [...] that in the body as a whole the representation of the main forms of civilization and of the principal legal systems of the world should be assured'. Article 36 Section 8 of the Rome Statute of the

[26] Hersch Lauterpacht, *The Function of Law in the International Community* (Clarendon 1933) 247.

[27] Art 40(2) Rome Statute; Art 16(1) ICJ Statute; Art 21(3) ECHR; Art 7(1) ITLOS Statute; in more detail Jiří Malenovský, 'L'indépendance des juges internationaux' (2010) 349 Recueil des cours 9.

[28] Chester Brown, 'The Evolution and Application of Rules Concerning Independence of the "International Judiciary"' (2003) 2 L and Practice of Intl Courts and Tribunals 63; Philippe J Sands and others, 'The Burgh House Principles on the Independence of the International Judiciary' (2005) 4 L and Practice of Intl Courts and Tribunals 247.

[29] *Legal Consequences of the Construction of a Wall in the Occupied Palestinian Territory* (Order) [2004] ICJ Rep 3; *Wall* (Advisory Opinion) Diss Op Buergenthal, 7–11. See Yuval Shany and Sigall Horovitz, 'Judicial Independence in The Hague and Freetown: A Tale of Two Cities' (2008) 21 Leiden J Intl L 113, 115–8, 120–9.

[30] *Prosecutor v Sesay, Kallon and Gbao (RUF Case)* (Decision on Defence Motion Seeking the Disqualification of Justice Robertson from the Appeals Chamber) SCSL-2004-15-AR15 (13 March 2004).

[31] Eyal Benvenisti and George W Downs, 'Prospects for the Increased Independence of International Tribunals' (2011) 12 German L J 1057.

International Criminal Court specifies the latter as an 'equitable geographic representation' and also demands a 'fair representation of female and male judges'. These and similar stipulations in other statutes rest on a complex understanding of legitimation, one that lays out criteria of justice that go well beyond democratic equality. The protection of diversity is a normative principle on par with the democratic principle.

Of particular importance to our concerns is whether a candidate's understanding of the court's tasks constitutes a criterion that should be taken into account in his or her election. According to what we have argued so far, this is an aspect of great significance. A judge who advocates a state-oriented understanding will make different choices in important constellations than a judge who feels committed to the community-oriented understanding. Judges who have a regime-oriented basic understanding will often come up with a different interpretation than those concerned with questions of legitimation. This issue should be addressed in the selection process, as it will influence the court's operation.

The relevant rules allow for this and should therefore be interpreted that way. For example, Article 2 of the ICJ Statute calls for persons of 'high moral character'.[32] What if not the basic understanding of international law should make up the 'moral character' of an international judge—that is, his basic normative orientation? However, attitudes that go beyond the basic understanding of international adjudication can be of such importance to the future development of a court that they should enter into the nomination process. One might think of the positioning of the specific international court in relation to domestic courts, or of the conflict between environmental protection and trade liberalization in the development of global trade law. These are fundamental normative and contentious questions within contemporary societies. In earlier times it might have been possible to believe in a universally binding, supra-positive system that offered orientation on these questions. Lauterpacht's notion of the office of the judge as a 'priesthood in the service of an idea transcending any particular interest'[33] expresses such an understanding. Today such thinking in terms of natural law is no longer persuasive.

[32] Similarly Art 2(1) ITLOS Statute; Art 14(1) ICSID Convention; Art 21(1) ECHR; Art 36(3)(a) Rome Statute. On the role of the virtues of international officials see Jan Klabbers, 'Controlling International Bureaucracies' in *IILJ International Legal Theory Colloquium Spring 2010* <iilj.org/courses/documents/2010Colloquium.Klabberpp.pdf> accessed 19 September 2012.

[33] Lauterpacht, *The Function of Law in the International Community* 232; on the relevant domestic discussion see Ingwer Ebsen, 'Der Beitrag des Bundesverfassungsgerichts zum politischen Grundkonsens' in Gunnar F Schuppert and Christian Bumke (eds), *Bundesverfassungsgericht und gesellschaftlicher Grundkonsens* (Nomos 2000) 83, 86.

2. The nomination and selection process

At this time, the world owes good international judges to executive wisdom, above all. National governments are the most important actors in the selection of judges. For reasons of democratic theory, which underlie Article 10 Section 2 of the TEU, a good deal supports a key role being played by governments. Still, the measures of legitimation conveyed by them are not always satisfactory. The entire process is usually exceedingly intransparent.[34] The selection appears as an executive mystery,[35] which cannot be persuasive under the concept of democracy as developed above. We certainly do not contest that filling the posts of international judges can be an important political instrument of a government and that it is legitimate to opt for a person with a normative vision close to that of the government.[36] Nevertheless, the regular lack of transparency and deliberativeness is subject to critique from the perspective of democratic legitimacy. The principle that holds within a state should also apply to the international level: one should not rely *solely* on the wisdom of governments. Very much in this spirit, we find a growing number of international rules that accommodate the democracy-oriented conception of transparency and deliberativeness.

This trend can best be illustrated by contrasting it with the traditional mode that persists within the framework of the ICSID. As would be expected precisely in an arbitral procedure, the composition of the arbitral tribunals lies largely in the hands of the contending parties. Although the ICSID maintains a list of possible panel members, the parties are not bound to this list.[37] They can appoint any odd number of arbitrators. Should they fail to come to an agreement, the panel will be composed of three members, each party appointing one and the third appointed by common consent. If the panel is not constituted within 90 days, the Chairman of the Administrative Council (the President of the International Bank for Reconstruction and Development[38]) will 'appoint the arbitrator or arbitrators not yet appointed'.[39] Securing independence and impartiality thus has

[34] Ruth Mackenzie and others, *Selecting International Judges: Principle, Process, and Politics* (OUP 2010) 98–9; Edward McWhinney, 'Law, Politics and "Regionalism" in the Nomination and Election of World Court Judges' (1986–1987) 13 Syracuse J Intl L and Commerce 1.

[35] Philippe J Sands, 'The Independence of the International Judiciary: Some Introductory Thoughts' in Steve Charnovitz and others (eds), *Law in the Service of Human Dignity: Essays in Honour of Florentino Feliciano* (CUP 2005) 313, 319.

[36] For a comparative view on this see Graham Gee, 'The Persistent Politics of Judicial Selection' in Seibert-Fohr (ed), *Judicial Independence in Transition* 121.

[37] Arts 3 and 40 ICSID Convention.

[38] Art 5 ICSID Convention.

[39] Art 38 ICSID Convention. See in detail the ICSID Rules of Procedure for Arbitration Proceedings.

been poorly institutionalized.[40] No wonder additional legal guarantees are called for.[41]

Greater autonomy is found within the framework of the WTO, which promotes independence, impartiality, and judicial expertise.[42] Similar to the ICSID regime, the WTO Secretariat maintains a list of potential experts who are available as panel members.[43] WTO members suggest experts for inclusion on the list, but it is the Dispute Settlement Body (DSB), the political decision-making body in the dispute settlement procedures, that makes the final decision. If a complaint is lodged, the WTO Secretariat proposes nominations to the parties to the dispute, which these shall not oppose 'except for compelling reasons' (Article 8 (6) DSU). In principle, nationals of the parties to the dispute cannot serve on the panels.[44] If there is no agreement on the panel, its composition will be decided by the WTO Director-General.[45] Many panel members are ministerial officials, but they are not to receive any instructions in their capacity as panel members.[46]

There is much more autonomy for the Appellate Body, as it is composed of seven permanent members, a setup that also supports their self-understanding as judges. In addition, the DSB utilizes a selection committee[47] that conducts interviews with the candidates, consults with interested delegations, and then submits to the DSB a proposal which, to date, has always been accepted.[48] By previous practice, the US and the EU always provide one member. Hegemonial structures are more than evident.[49]

[40] In more detail Daphna Kapeliuk, 'The Repeat Appointment Factor: Exploring Decision Patterns of Elite Investment Arbitrators' (2010) 96 Cornell L Rev 47.

[41] Indications are found in Art 57 ICSID Convention (Disqualification Request) and Rule 9 ICSID Rules of Procedure for Arbitration Proceedings. Proposals in Audley Sheppard, 'Arbitrator Independence in ICSID Arbitration' in Christina Binder and others (eds), *International Investment Law for the 21st Century: Essays in Honour of Christoph Schreuer* (OUP 2009) 131.

[42] In more detail Meinhard Hilf, 'Das Streitbeilegungssystem der WTO' in Meinhard Hilf and Stefan Oeter (eds), *WTO-Recht: Rechtsordnung des Welthandels* (Nomos 2005) 505.

[43] Art 8(4) DSU. [44] Art 8(3) DSU.

[45] Art 8(6)–(7) DSU. On the role of the WTO Secretariat see Armin von Bogdandy, 'Law and Politics in the WTO—Strategies to Cope with a Deficient Relationship' (2001) 5 Max Planck YB UN L 609, 615.

[46] Art 8(9) DSU. See Joseph HH Weiler, 'The Rule of Lawyers and the Ethos of Diplomats: Reflections on the Internal and External Legitimacy of WTO Dispute Settlement' (2001) 35 J World Trade 191.

[47] WTO Dispute Settlement Body, *Establishment of the Appellate Body—Recommendations of the Preparatory Committee for the WTO* (10 February 1995) WT/DSB/1, para 13. In more detail Victoria Donaldson, 'The Appellate Body: Institutional and Procedural Aspects' in Patrick F Macrory and others (eds), *The World Trade Organization: Legal, Economic and Political Analysis*, vol 1 (Springer 2005) 1277.

[48] On the mechanism of selection see Art 17(2) DSU, Art IX WTO Agreement.

[49] Richard H Steinberg, 'Judicial Lawmaking at the WTO: Discursive, Constitutional, and Political Constraints' (2004) 98 AJIL 247, 264.

The provisions for the permanent international courts offer much greater possibilities for democratic legitimation, but those have been largely dormant and unused. For example, Article 6 of the ICJ Statute recommends that each state, prior to making its nominations, consults 'its highest court of justice, its legal faculties and schools of law, and its national academies and national sections of international academies devoted to the study of law'. Such steps can strengthen transparency, deliberativeness, and participation. Similarly, the Rome Statute of the ICC suggests that States Parties, when nominating judges, use 'the procedure for the nomination of candidates for appointment to the highest judicial offices in the State in question'.[50] In fact, the Rome Statute requires states to submit a statement justifying their nominations.[51] Moreover, the Assembly of States Parties is to establish an Advisory Committee on Nominations to ensure the quality of nominations and enhance the Court's legitimation.[52] In addition, a committee was set up that assists in filling the position of the Prosecutor.[53] Such regulations should be understood in the spirit of the democracy-oriented understanding in the sense that they are aimed at a deliberative process, a process that the actual selection procedures as of now unfortunately do not fully satisfy.[54]

In light of a transnational or outright cosmopolitan concept of democracy, it is particularly interesting when international bodies choose judges. The most important example can be found at the European Court of Human Rights. Its judges are selected for a nine-year term through a majority vote by the Parliamentary Assembly of the Council of Europe from a list of three candidates nominated by each contracting party.[55] Three preliminary steps precede the election. First, states must nominate suitable national candidates (Article 21(1) ECHR), whereby the Parliamentary Assembly recommended as early as 1999 that the candidatures be publicly announced.[56] The UK has been doing this

[50] Art 36(4)(a) Rome Statute; for the election of the justices of the German Federal Constitutional Court see Arts 5–8 Law on the Federal Constitutional Court (Gesetz über das Bundesverfassungsgericht).

[51] Art 36(3) Rome Statute; in more detail Mackenzie and others, *Selecting International Judges* 68.

[52] On the practice see Assembly of States Parties, *Report of the Bureau on the Establishment of an Advisory Committee on Nominations of Judges of the International Criminal Court* (30 November 2011) ICC-ASP/10/36.

[53] Assembly of States Parties, Search Committee for the Position of the Prosecutor of the International Criminal Court, *Terms of Reference* (6 December 2010) ICC-ASP/9/INF.2.

[54] For a critique see already Mackenzie and others, *Selecting International Judges* 98–9; McWhinney, 'Law, Politics and "Regionalism"'.

[55] Art 22 ECHR. In more detail Andrew Drzemczewski, 'Election of Judges to the Strasbourg Court: An Overview' (2010) 15 Eur Human Rights L Rev 377.

[56] Parliamentary Assembly of the Council of Europe, *National Procedures for Nominating Candidates for Election to the European Court of Human Rights* (24 September 1999) Rec 1429 (1999) and *Candidates for the European Court of Human Rights* (27 January 2009) Rec 1646 (2009).

since 1998.[57] It has candidates interviewed by an independent commission, and for the most part follows the proposed nominations of that committee. In Germany, the Federal Justice Ministry for the first time, ahead of the last selection of judges, published notices calling for suitable individuals to express their interest in the judgeship.[58]

Second, since 2010 a seven-member evaluation committee has examined the list of candidates.[59] Its job is to verify that the qualifications demanded of candidates in Article 21 of the ECHR have been met. Should that not be the case, the committee itself, in closed consultation with the contracting party, can propose candidates.[60]

Step three involves a closed, personal hearing of the candidates before the parliamentary subcommittee created in 1999.[61] It subsequently makes a confidential recommendation to the members of the Parliamentary Assembly, which eventually selects the judges. This process has led to positive politicization. For example, a candidate list submitted by Malta was rejected on the grounds that no woman was nominated.[62]

The election of judges to the ECtHR shows how the democratic idea can be taken into account on the international level.[63] The relevant criteria have been elaborated in an open and deliberative political process.[64] Of course, problems continue. A study on the ECtHR noted that in the domestic part of nomination processes, the political loyalty of a candidate often weighed

[57] Henry G Schermers, 'Election of Judges to the European Court of Human Rights' (1998) 23 Eur L Rev 568, 574; Evelyne Lagrange, *La représentation institutionnelle dans l'ordre international: Une contribution à la théorie de la personnalité morale des organisations internationales* (Kluwer 2002) 247.

[58] Jens Meyer-Ladewig, *Europäische Menschenrechtskonvention: Handkommentar* (3rd edn, Nomos 2011) Article 22 para 8; subsequently, the list of candidates is drawn up by the federal government.

[59] Established on the basis of the Committee of Ministers of the Council of Europe, *Establishment of an Advisory Panel of Experts on Candidates for Election as Judge to the European Court of Human Rights* (10 November 2010) CM/Res(2010)2 and *Establishment of the Advisory Panel of Experts on Candidates for Election as Judge to the European Court of Human Rights—Implementation* (8 December 2010) Decision CM/Del/Dec(2010)1101/1.7E.

[60] Committee of Ministers, CM/Res(2010)2, para 5.

[61] Parliamentary Assembly of the Council of Europe, *Election of Judges to the European Court of Human Rights* (24 September 2009) Res 1200 (1999).

[62] The rejection was impermissible, however: *Advisory Opinion on Certain Legal Questions Concerning the Lists of Candidates Submitted with a View to the Election of Judges to the European Court of Human Rights* (ECtHR, 12 February 2008). On the issue of the underrepresentation of women see Art 36(8)(a)(iii) Rome Statute; Art 7(5) Statute of the African Court on Human and People's Rights. See also Nienke Grossman, 'Sex on the Bench: Do Women Judges Matter to the Legitimacy of International Courts' (2011–2012) 12 Chicago J Intl L 647.

[63] Meyer-Ladewig, *Europäische Menschenrechtskonvention* Article 22 para 2.

[64] Armin von Bogdandy and Christoph Krenn, 'On the Democratic Legitimacy of Europe's Judges: A Principled and Comparative Reconstruction of the Selection Procedures' in Michal Bobek (ed), *Selecting Europe's Judges: A Critical Review of the Appointment Procedures to the European Courts* (OUP 2014, forthcoming).

more heavily than his or her suitability, and that the parliamentary interview in the Council of Europe was by no means always aimed at transparency and quality.[65] Still, it can hardly be denied that the ECtHR offers an example for a practicable and fundamentally promising path—one that can inspire the processes for selecting judges also in other courts.[66]

Indeed, the statutes of other courts permit developments in the same direction toward more democracy. The ICJ Statute provides that the 15 judges are appointed with an absolute majority in a secret vote by the UN General Assembly and the Security Council for a nine-year term, with the possibility of re-election.[67] Something similar applies to the 18 judges of the ICC: they are elected by the Assembly of States Parties, though without the possibility of re-election.[68] Candidates for the ITLOS are elected if they receive the most votes at a meeting of the States Parties and a two-thirds majority of them are present and voting.[69] Selection to the International Criminal Tribunals for the former Yugoslavia (ICTY) and Rwanda (ICTR) is done by international bodies: the UN Secretary-General collects proposals from the states, the UN Security Council uses them to draw up a list, and the UN General Assembly elects the 14 (ICTY) and 11 (ICTR) judges.[70] Numerous international legal regulations thus assign competences to international bodies in the election of judges.

3. The democratic potential of international bodies

Are such international bodies able to impart democratic legitimation? The answer depends on the following question: in whose name do international judges decide? Since many domestic courts speak the law in the name of the people, much argues in favour of involving the representative body of

[65] Jutta Limbach and others (eds), *Judicial Independence: Law and Practice of Appointments to the European Court of Human Rights* (Interights 2003) <www.interights.org> accessed 20 September 2012; for a dramatic picture Norbert Paul Engel, 'More Transparency and Governmental Loyalty for Maintaining Professional Quality in the Election of Judges to the European Court of Human Rights' (2012) 32 HRLJ 448.

[66] Once again: there can be no uniform standard for all courts; Anja Seibert-Fohr, 'Judicial Independence—The Normativity of an Evolving Transnational Principle' in Seibert-Fohr (ed), *Judicial Independence in Transition* 1279, 1345–78; Vicki C Jackson, 'Judicial Independence: Structure, Context, Attitude' in Seibert-Fohr (ed), *Judicial Independence in Transition* 19.

[67] Arts 3, 4, 9, 10, 13 ICJ Statute; see also UNGA and UNSC, Election of Five Members of the International Court of Justice: Memorandum by the Secretary-General, (26 July 2005) UN Doc A/60/186-S/2005/446.

[68] Art 36 Rome Statute.

[69] Though with the possibility of re-election; Arts 2, 4, 5 ITLOS Statute.

[70] Art 13 *bis* ICTY Statute; Art 12 ICTR Statute. The Statute of the ICTY was enacted by the UNSC, Resolution 827 of 25 May 1993, UN Doc S/RES/827, and that of the ICTR by UNSC Res 955 (8 November 1994) UN Doc S/RES/955. The difference between permanent judges and judges *ad litem* can be disregarded here.

the democratic sovereign in the selection of the judges, in particular of the highest judges. But what institutions and bodies should pick international judges, as long as the peoples who are subject to their decisions have not formed a new people? Very different answers start to emerge depending on whether one conceives of international courts as instruments of dispute settlement within a state-oriented world order, as organs of a value-based international community, as regime institutions in an interdependent world, or—precisely—as institutions of public authority that must in the final analysis be justified in light of the individuals whose freedom is shaped by their judgments, however indirectly and mediated that may be.

The state-oriented conception traces international adjudication back to the states that, as main subjects of international law, establish international courts. The courts decide in the name of the contending states that have submitted to their jurisdiction. Accordingly, governments as the appointed representatives of the state under international law play a crucial role in the selection of judges.[71] The participation of international bodies in judicial elections is at best harmless, an ornamentation. The community-oriented approach, contrariwise, assigns greater importance to community interests and institutions. It sees international courts as organs of the international community, whose values and interests they are supposed to protect and develop. Accordingly, they render their decisions not so much in the name of the contending states as in the name of that community. Provisions of international law that bind international bodies into the process thus make sense and have legitimatory potential. They can be understood as an institutional reinforcement of the interests of the community against national governments. However, the community-oriented conception is hardly focused specifically on democratic legitimation. The regime-oriented approach is similar to the community-oriented one when it comes to the meaning of the possible participation of international bodies.

What is consistent with all three basic conceptions is the call for a stronger involvement of domestic parliaments, once it is accepted that domestic and foreign policy are no longer strictly separated. Even under the state-oriented understanding, the notion that the appointment of international judges is inherently a matter for governments as part of foreign policy should be in retreat. In particular within the framework of global governance, many decision-making processes are so closely intertwined that it is increasingly implausible under all conceptions to think of 'foreign policy' as the prerogative of the executive and exclude it from parliamentary control. The

[71] See, for example, Art 7(2) VCLT.

international processes that lead to the appointment of judges should be aligned with the more parliamentary-focused procedures for high domestic judges.[72]

But that still leaves open the question about the democratic function of international bodies. It can be answered only with the democracy-oriented basic conception, which sees democratic potential in international forums, especially those with a parliamentary focus. Crucial factors are transparency, participation, and deliberation. As laid out in detail above, a procedure can generate democratic legitimation if it has a transparent, deliberative, and participatory focus.[73] Parliamentary bodies have a special potential in this regard, but other bodies can also draw from this source.

However, the implementation of these abstract guidelines must be careful and circumspect, especially since the three dimensions of democratic legitimation certainly stand in a tense relationship to one another.[74] Transparency can have a negative effect on deliberativeness. Bodies open to the media easily lend themselves to showcase speeches, and participants are often hardly willing to revise positions once they have been publicly staked out, or to make public compromises. It is also questionable whether a public debate is really suited to addressing the job profile of a judge. It is meaningful, however, that such assemblies specify in an open and contentious political process the requirements for being a judge, as has happened in the Parliamentary Assembly of the Council of Europe.[75] The selection process in itself, by contrast, might require a more shielded procedure. As an example one could look at the UN General Assembly when the election of Christopher Greenwood as a judge on the ICJ was on the agenda. On the one hand, there was notable criticism in public

[72] See Art 23c(2) Austrian Federal Constitutional Laws (Österreichische Bundes-verfassungsgesetze); now also in Germany, Art 1(3) Federal Judicial Election Act (Bundeswahlgesetz); in more detail Martina Mayer, *Die Europafunktion der nationalen Parlamente in der Europäischen Union* (Mohr Siebeck 2012) 113–6.

[73] See chapter 3 section C 3.

[74] Thomas Risse, 'Transnational Governance and Legitimacy' in Arthur Benz and Yannis Papadopoulos (eds), *Governance and Democracy: Comparing National, European and International Experiences* (Routledge 2006) 179; Jürgen Habermas, 'Concluding Comments on Empirical Approaches to Deliberative Politics' (2005) 40 Acta Politica 384.

[75] A number of procedural adjustments aim at increasing the depth and objectivity of the factual basis for the Assembly's decision. This includes standardized *curricula vitae* and personal interviews to be conducted by one of the Assembly's sub-committees. They were introduced in Parliamentary Assembly of the Council of Europe, *Procedure for Examining Candidatures for the Election of Judges to the European Court of Human Rights* (22 April 1996) Res 1082 (1996); again debated after first experiences and refined in Parliamentary Assembly of the Council of Europe, *Election of Judges to the European Court of Human Rights* (24 September 1999) Res 1200 (1999). For a good overview of all the reforms initiated by the Assembly see the report prepared by the Assembly's Committee on Legal Affairs and Human Rights, *Procedure for Electing Judges to the European Court of Human Rights* (7 December 2012) AS/Jur/Inf (2012) 02 rev4. For an analysis see von Bogdandy and Krenn, 'How to Select Europe's Judges'.

about his nomination, especially because of his legal opinion on the Iraq war.[76] A public debate in the UN General Assembly could certainly have addressed these doubts about his suitability in a legitimacy-creating discourse about basic conceptions of international law and the role of the ICJ. On the other hand, such a debate could have lost sight of the requirements profile of candidates and could have degenerated into a general political squabble about the Iraq war, losing sight of the selection objective. A body that works less in the public light could be better suited to examining the requirements profile for judges in an expedient way. Such a body can certainly generate democratic legitimation. The latter depends crucially on the manner in which it is established and on the discursive quality of its work. It is even conceivable to generate more transparency without harming the necessary confidentiality.[77]

The potentially clashing concerns of transparency, participation, and deliberation usually lead to a middle path between public debate and secret committee. The targeted inclusion of representatives of a critical public and a duty to provide reasons can satisfy the democratic concerns better than a public squabble. Following the example of the ECtHR, an international selection committee could include the public through a preliminary publication of a justified proposal with the possibility of critique and revision. The above-described procedure, by which the members of the Appellate Body are appointed, has this kind of discursive potential.

In summary, it should be noted that when it comes to the selection of judges one should not bet only on the wisdom of governments. Instead, their key role must be embedded into more transparent procedures that incorporate the national parliaments. In addition, international bodies can make a legitimatory contribution if they specify the general criteria for judges and promote a discursive engagement about the candidates. To be sure, such bodies can only support the legitimacy of candidates, but cannot on their own establish it. A complete shifting of the selection to the international level lacks the social—especially the communicative—preconditions. The selection of judges should be a common responsibility of domestic and international institutions, to be taken seriously in light of democratic principles.

[76] Julian Ku, *Will the ICJ Have a US-Style Nomination Fight? (We Can Only Hope)* (3 November 2008) <opiniojuris.org> accessed 20 September 2012. In like manner, global civil society actors are active in the election of judges and the appointment of the Prosecutor at the ICC. See Coalition for the International Criminal Court, *Delivering on the Promise of a Fair, Effective and Independent Court: Election of ICC and ASP Officials: Judges* <www.iccnow.org> accessed 20 September 2012.

[77] For sensible proposals see Alberto Alemanno, 'Access to Information versus Privacy in the Process of Selection: Is there a reasonable middle ground?' in Michal Bobek (ed), *Selecting Europe's Judges*.

B. THE JUDICIAL PROCESS

The democratic legitimation of public authority takes place not only through election and the chains of legitimation connected to it, but also through its exercise in a transparent, deliberative, and participatory fashion. International courts themselves can strengthen the democratic legitimation of their decisions if they shape their procedures accordingly and embed themselves into relevant publics. In this way, it is possible to develop the judicial process in light of the democratic principle without questioning the court's monopoly over its decision.[78]

This path has particular importance since procedural law is much framed by the courts themselves, which means that they themselves can promote the democratic idea.[79] To be sure, some of the procedural law is laid down in the treaty statutes. International courts can still often enact the rules of procedure on their own.[80] In addition, they often publish directives on the judicial process, even if the statutes do not establish an explicit competency.[81] Although such directives (also called *practice directions* or *guidelines*)[82] are not legally binding, they exert normative force. Every party to a procedure is well advised to adhere to them. Last but not least, courts shape and develop procedural law laid down in their statute through their judgments.[83]

The basic conceptions of international adjudication as laid out above are highly relevant for the interpretation of procedural law. According to the state-oriented conception, the procedure should be aligned with the will of the parties to a dispute.[84] That understanding's private law orientation pushes for a view of judicial procedures in which the court subordinates itself as far as possible to the submissions and motions of the parties.[85] By contrast, under the community-oriented conception, the court is an organ

[78] See chapter 3 section C 4.

[79] In more detail Markus Benzing, *Das Beweisrecht vor internationalen Gerichten und Schiedsgerichten in zwischenstaatlichen Streitigkeiten* (Springer 2010) 31–113; Chester Brown, *A Common Law of International Adjudication* (OUP 2007) 6–9.

[80] Art 30(1) ICJ Statute; Art 16 ITLOS Statute; Art 17(9) DSU; Art 25(d) ECHR; Art 15 ICTY Statute; Art 14 ICTR Statute.

[81] In more detail Shabtai Rosenne, 'The International Court of Justice: New Practice Directions' (2009) 8 L and Practice of Intl Courts and Tribunals 171.

[82] Rule 50 ICC Rules of Procedure and Evidence.

[83] Jean-Marc Sorel, 'International Courts and Tribunals, Procedure' in Rüdiger Wolfrum (ed), *Max Planck Encyclopedia of Public International Law* <http://opil.ouplaw.com/home/EPIL> accessed 17 September 2013, para 1.

[84] Shabtai Rosenne, *The Law and Practice of the International Court 1920–2005*, vol 1 (4th edn, Nijhoff 2006) 9–14.

[85] On the principle of *non ultra petita* see *Guzzardi v Italy* (1980) Series A No 39, Diss Op Fitzmaurice, para 4; *Oil Platforms (Iran v USA)* (Judgment) [2003] ICJ Rep 161, Sep Op Buergenthal, paras 3–10.

of a universal order that overarches the contending parties. It is supposed to pursue also the interests and values of the community, something that suggests greater independence from the parties.[86] In the regime-oriented conception, procedure is aimed at an effective shaping of interdependence and tends to be concerned with legal security and a speedy decision. The democracy-oriented conception does not question the importance of the latter, but it insists that these requirements be pursued in a way that is transparent, deliberative, and open to participation. In light of this, the discussion that follows deals with the publicness and transparency of the procedure (1), the intervention of third parties and *amicus curiae* briefs (2), and the democratic potential of a legal remedy (3).

1. Publicness and transparency

a) Oral proceedings

Starting points for publicness and transparency arise first of all in the oral proceedings, which some court statutes explicitly secure. Article 46 of the ICJ Statute stipulates: 'The hearing in Court shall be public, unless the Court shall decide otherwise, or unless the parties demand that the public be not admitted.'[87] The detailed Rules of Court show an understanding for the importance of discursive constraints.[88] Moreover, since 2004, the procedures of the ICJ have been broadcast live. This step, according to the Court, is a response to the extraordinary interests of the general public.[89]

Article 26 of the ITLOS Statute is closely modelled on the ICJ.[90] Article 40 Section 1 of the ECHR also stipulates: 'Hearings shall be in public unless the Court in exceptional circumstances decides otherwise.'[91] In addition, the documents kept by the Registrar of the Court are usually open to the public. A remarkable praxis was developed by the Inter-American Court of Human Rights (IACtHR), which has its seat in San José, Costa Rica. In exceptional procedures,[92] it conducts public sessions in other treaty states of

[86] Robert Kolb in Zimmermann and others (eds), *The Statute of the International Court of Justice* General Principles of Procedural Law paras 29–32.

[87] Similarly Art 26(2) ITLOS Statute. On the public nature of the proceedings see Sabine von Schorlemer in Zimmermann and others (eds), *The Statute of the International Court of Justice* Article 46 paras 5–6; Rosenne, *The Law and Practice of the International Court 1920–2005*, vol 3, 1283–342.

[88] Arts 54–72 ICJ Rules of Court. In more detail Sorel, 'International Courts and Tribunals, Procedures' para 18.

[89] Rosenne, *The Law and Practice of the International Court 1920–2005*, vol 1, 8. 'Report of the International Court of Justice: 1 August 2003–31 July 2004' (2 September 2004) UN Doc A/59/4, para 266.

[90] Art 74 ITLOS Rules of the Tribunal corresponds to Art 59 ICJ Rules of Court.

[91] See also Rules 33(2), 63(2) ECtHR Rules of Court. Oral proceedings are the rule only before the Grand Chamber.

[92] Arts 12, 13 IACtHR Rules of Procedure.

the American Convention on Human Rights, which brings it closer to the citizens and allows for concrete insights into its work.[93]

In the context of the WTO, as well, the dispute procedure has opened itself to the democratic demands of publicness and transparency, though this is not called for in the DSU.[94] Rather, according to Article 14 Section 1, Article 18 Section 2, and Article 17 Section 10 of the DSU, the proceedings and documents are to be confidential. However, an interpretation of these regulations has prevailed that is innovative and public-friendly. It was inspired by the Sutherland Report, which declared that 'the degree of confidentiality of the current dispute settlement proceedings can be seen as damaging to the WTO as an institution'.[95]

Still, the proceedings often remain behind closed doors, which the WTO justifies with reference to the interests of the contending parties and trade secrets. This applies especially to proceedings before the panels, which, compared to the Appellate Body, are more strongly bound to an ethos of arbitration. Given this practice, the position of the panel in the *Hormone Beef II* case, which dealt with a food safety and moral issue of great public interest, was particularly welcome: it held public hearings and justified this by stating that, among other things, the stipulations about confidentiality referred solely to the internal deliberations of the panels, but not to the exchange of arguments between the parties.[96] Likewise, the parties and the Panel in *Measures Affecting the Importation of Apples from New Zealand*[97] decided to make their expert meetings and further proceedings accessible to the public.[98]

[93] Pablo Saavedra Alessandri and Gabriela Pacheco Arias, 'Las sesiones "itinerantes" de la Corte Interamericana de los Derechos Humanos' in Sergio García Ramírez and Mireya Castañeda Hernández (eds), *Recepción nacional del derecho internacional de los derechos humanos y admisión de la competencia contenciosa de la Corte Interamericana* (Universidad Nacional Autónoma de México 2009) 37; Manuel E Góngora Mera, *Inter-American Judicial Constitutionalism: On the Constitutional Rank of Human Rights Treaties in Latin America through National and Inter-American Adjudication* (Instituto Interamericano de Derechos Humanos 2011) 20.

[94] Lothar Ehring, 'Public Access to Dispute Settlement Hearings in the World Trade Organization' (2008) 11 J Intl Economic L 1021.

[95] Peter Sutherland and others, *The Future of the WTO: Addressing Institutional Challenges in the New Millennium: Report by the Consultative Board to the Director-General Supachai Panitchpakdi* (2004) paras 261–2.

[96] *United States: Continued Suspension of Obligations in the EC-Hormones Dispute—Panel Report* (31 March 2008) WT/DS320/R, para 7.49. See also *WTO Hearings on Banana Dispute Opened to the Public* (29 October 2007) <www.wto.org> accessed 20 September 2012.

[97] *Australia: Measures Affecting the Importation of Apples from New Zealand—Panel Report* (9 August 2010) WT/DS367/R.

[98] *WTO Hearings on Apple Dispute Opened to the Public* (16 June 2009) <www.wto.org> accessed 20 September 2012.

Compared to the panel stage, public proceedings are more common with the Appellate Body,[99] whose members see themselves more as judges, even though this is not called for in the DSU.[100] The Appellate Body noted in 2009:

> In practice, the confidentiality requirement in Article 17.10 has its limits. Notices of Appeal and Appellate Body reports are disclosed to the public. Appellate Body reports contain summaries of the participants' and third participants' written and oral submissions and frequently quote directly from them. Public disclosure of Appellate Body reports is an inherent and necessary feature of our rules-based system of adjudication. Consequently, under the DSU, confidentiality is relative and time-bound.[101]

Proceedings within the framework of the ICSID usually provide the public less access than those in the WTO. However, they find themselves all the more confronted with calls for greater transparency,[102] since investment arbitration proceedings often involve important public interests.[103] In June 2005, the OECD Investment Committee backed demands in this direction. In terms of democratic theory, what is especially notable is how it combined publicness, legitimacy, and effectiveness with the further development of the law:

> There is a general understanding among the Members of the Investment Committee that additional transparency, in particular in relation to the publication of arbitral awards, subject to necessary safeguards for the protection of confidential business and governmental information, is desirable to enhance effectiveness and public acceptance of international investment arbitration, as well as contributing to the further development of a public body of jurisprudence.[104]

However, the implementation of these demands cannot happen only by decision of international institutions, but requires the consent of the parties to a dispute.[105] Rule 32 Section 2 of the ICSID Rules of Procedure for

[99] On the self-understanding of judges see Claus-Dieter Ehlermann, 'Six Years on the Bench of the "World Trade Court": Some Personal Experiences as Member of the Appellate Body of the World Trade Organization' (2002) 36 J World Trade 605.

[100] *United States: Continued Existence and Application of Zeroing Methodology—Appellate Body Report* (4 February 2009) WT/DS350/AB/R, Annex III, para 6.

[101] *US: Continued Zeroing* Annex III, para 4.

[102] Carl-Sebastian Zoellner, 'Third-Party Participation (NGO's and Private Persons) and Transparency in ICSID Proceedings' in Rainer Hofmann and Christian J Tams (eds), *The International Convention for the Settlement of Investment Disputes (ICSID): Taking Stock After 40 Years* (Nomos 2007) 179.

[103] Campbell McLachlan and others, *International Investment Arbitration: Substantive Principles* (OUP 2007) 57.

[104] OECD Investment Committee, *Transparency and Third Party Participation in Investor-State Dispute Settlement Procedure*, Statement (June 2005) 1.

[105] See, for example, *Aguas Argentinas SA, Suez, Sociedad General de Aguas de Barcelona SA and Vivendi Universal SA v Argentine Republic* (Order in Response to a Petition for Transparency and Participation as Amicus Curiae) ICSID Case No ARB/03/19 (19 May 2005) para 6.

Arbitration Proceedings has stipulated since 2006 that the panel may open up the proceedings, unless one of the parties objects.[106] Moreover, at least excerpts of the panel's reasoning must be made public, even if the parties do not consent to this.[107]

For the international criminal courts and tribunals, the public nature of the proceedings is the rule.[108] According to Rule 79 of the ICTY Rules of Procedure and Evidence, for example, the only time this does not apply is if public order, morality, security, or the protection of a witness require a closed court. Should a tribunal decide to exclude the public, it must make its reasons public, a stipulation that underscores the exceptional nature of such a move.[109] On the whole, then, one can discern a general development to greater publicness, a trend that accommodates the democracy-oriented conception.

b) Decision-making by judges

Beyond the oral proceedings, the judicial decision-making process itself—that is, the deliberations of the judges—could follow the principles of publicness and transparency. However, at first glance it seems hardly possible to reconcile this with the stipulations and the praxis of international courts. Article 54 Section 3 of the ICJ Statute declares that '[t]he deliberations of the Court shall take place in private and remain secret'.[110] This is something that many courts are adamant about. Shortly before the announcement of the preliminary measures in the *Nuclear Test* case between Australia and France, the Australian press had reported on the expected decision on the basis of leaked information, something the Court sharply condemned.[111]

While there are good reasons for the internal deliberations of a court to be confidential, there are certainly possibilities for some meaningful

[106] This has proven advantageous; Joachim Delaney and Daniel B Magraw, 'Procedural Transparency' in Peter Muchlinski and others (eds), *The Oxford Handbook of International Investment Law* (OUP 2008) 721, 774.

[107] Rule 48(4) ICSID Rules of Procedure for Arbitration Proceedings. On the transparency in ICSID procedures see also McLachlan and others, *International Investment Arbitration* 57–60.

[108] Robert Cryer and others, *An Introduction to International Criminal Law and Procedure* (2nd edn, CUP 2010) 434.

[109] von Schorlemer, Article 46 para 29. The procedural law of the ICC is very similar; see Arts 67, 68(2) Rome Statute.

[110] This corresponds to Art 54 PCIJ Statute and Arts 77, 78 Hague Convention on the Pacific Settlement of International Disputes (1907); see Bardo Fassbender in Zimmermann and others (eds), *The Statute of the International Court of Justice* Article 54 para 1.

[111] ICJ, 'Secrecy of Deliberations' (1973–1974) 28 Intl Court of Justice YB 127, 128, 'making, circulation or publication of such statements is incompatible with the fundamental principles governing the good administration of justice'; in more detail Fassbender, Article 54 para 16.

openings. The Swiss Federal Court can deliberate in public,[112] and the internal deliberations of some Latin American courts can even be followed via live streaming.[113] Even though in some cases this prompts judges to take a more active interest in a case, observers do not consider this praxis as all that positive at this time.[114] Whether such an innovation might have promise on the international level remains to be examined. There is reason to suspect that more transparent realms of decision-making would displace parts of the decision-making process into new back rooms. But at least there is the possibility that such realms could open up new possibilities and constraints of action with democratic potential that are worth exploring.

As with the selection of judges, there are middle paths between complete secrecy and complete publicness in the decision-making process. We see potential especially in the practice of presenting a draft decision for critique. We know it is not rare for decisions to contain completely surprising findings and interpretations that entail consequences the judges did not anticipate. At times, erratic passages are the result of internal power struggles among the judges during which the legal problem is lost sight of. A timely response by the parties can mitigate the danger of dysfunctional legal developments caused by communicative dead-ends that can occur on the bench. Consequently, in some legal systems judges have a duty of notification, which at least allows the parties to take a position on the relevant factual and legal issues.[115] In some situations this is already demanded by the principle of a fair process.[116]

On the international level, an example can be found in WTO law. Any panel must present to the contending parties those excerpts from a decision report that contain factual determinations and descriptive inferences, to which the parties can then respond.[117] Later the panel also presents to the

112 Art 59 Swiss Federal Supreme Court Act (Schweizer Bundesgerichtsgesetz).

113 See merely Mexico's Supreme Court <www.supremacorte.gob.mx> accessed 21 September 2012 and Brazil's Supreme Court <www.tvgratis.tv/tv-gratis-online-media-player/tv-justica-brasil.html> accessed 21 September 2012.

114 With a view toward Brazil see Virgílio Afonso da Silva, 'Deciding without Deliberating' (2013) 11 Intl J Constit L 557, 580–3; Carolina Alves Vestena, 'Participação ou formalismo? O impacto das audiências públicas no Supremo Tribunal Federal brasileiro' (Rio de Janeiro 2010) <bibliotecadigital.fgv.br> accessed 21 September 2012.

115 See Art 139 German Code of Civil Procedure (Zivilprozssordnung), Art 108(2) German Code of Administrative Court Procedures (Verwaltungsgerichtsordnung), Art 265 German Code of Criminal Procedure (Strafprozessordnung) and Art 103(1) German Basic Law (Grundgesetz); on this see *Überraschungsurteil im Zivilprozeß* [1994] Federal Constitutional Court of Germany (1994) 47 Neue Juristische Wochenschrift 1274; Helmuth Schulze-Fielitz in Horst Dreier (ed), *Grundgesetz-Kommentar*, vol 3 (2nd edn, Mohr Siebeck 2008) Article 103(1) para 43.

116 *Atanasovski v former Yugoslav Republic of Macedonia* App No 36815/03 (ECtHR, 14 January 2010) para 38.

117 Art 15(1) DSU.

parties an interim report containing a descriptive section and the panel's findings and conclusion. The parties can then request another review. At the request of a party, the panel may even hold a further meeting with the parties to address the issues that have been identified.[118] Thus, there are certainly possibilities for combining a protected realm of internal court deliberations with democratic publicness and transparency.

c) Individual opinions

Finally, in addition to oral hearings and the deliberations of the court, the possibility of individual opinions can bear potential for democratic legitimation. Article 57 of the ICJ Statute stipulates: 'If the judgment does not represent in whole or in part the unanimous opinion of the judges, any judge shall be entitled to deliver a separate opinion.'[119] This is the usual practice also in other international courts.[120] The DSU is an exception in this regard, as it permits only anonymous opinions.[121]

To the extent that the path to individual opinions is open without any major obstacles, it is usually utilized. It is rare for a decision by the ICJ to be unanimous and without adjacent individual opinions.[122] This practice is occasionally criticized for undermining the authority of the Court;[123] for the most part, though, it garners praise, and rightly so.[124] This assessment is confirmed by the contrary legal situation of the CJEU, which does not permit individual opinions.[125] Individual opinions are relevant in terms of democratic theory, because decisions gain clarity through them.[126] For one, in the practice of some courts they are presented to the majority before

[118] Art 15(2) DSU. [119] This is affirmed in Art 95(2) ICJ Rules of Court.

[120] Art 30(3) ITLOS Statute, Art 125(2) ITLOS Rules of the Tribunal; Art 48(4) ICSID Convention; Art 45(2) ECHR, Rule 74(2) ECtHR Rules of Court.

[121] Art 14(3) DSU.

[122] Until 4 May 2011, the ICJ issued 111 decisions, 27 advisory opinions, and 144 orders, which were accompanied by 1192 'individual opinions' (322 *declarations*, 472 *separate opinions* and 398 *dissenting opinions*). Rainer Hofmann and Tilmann Laubner in Zimmermann and others (eds), *The Statute of the International Court of Justice* Article 57 para 35.

[123] On the discussion Hofmann and Laubner, Article 57 para 35, with further references.

[124] Hofmann and Laubner, Article 57 para 57; André Oraison, 'Quelques réflexions générales sur les opinions séparées individuelles et dissidentes des juges de la Cour internationale de Justice' (2000) 78 Revue de droit international de sciences diplomatiques et politiques 167.

[125] Art 36 CJEU Statute. In more detail Vlad Perju, 'Reason and Authority in the European Court of Justice' (2009) 49 Virginia J Intl L 307.

[126] Edvard Hambro, 'Dissenting and Individual Opinions in the International Court of Justice' (1956–1957) 17 Zeitschrift für ausländisches öffentliches Recht und Völkerrecht 229, 238–9; Mark E Villiger, 'Das Urteil des Europäischen Gerichtshofs für Menschenrechte: Zustandekommen, Bedeutung und Wirkungen' (2008) 127 Zeitschrift für schweizerisches Recht 453, 465.

a decision is announced, and this allows for improvements. For another, there is less pressure to find vague compromise formulas.

For these reasons, the original intent to prohibit individual opinions in the ICC was not retained.[127] In the negotiations about the ICC, judges of the ICTY and the ICTR persuaded the delegates with the arguments that individual opinions are useful for the development of case-law—that is, for stabilizing and generating normative expectations.[128] Generally, individual opinions often lead to more cogently argued opinions by the majority, which serves the public debate about a decision. In some cases, the losing opinion inspires future judges or legislative efforts.[129] Individual opinions allow the public to engage a decision critically and thus serve the democratic principle.

2. Intervention by third parties and *amicus curiae* briefs

The democratic legitimation of a judicial decision can be further served if the procedure has deliberative and participatory elements, especially through intervention by third parties and the inclusion of *amici curiae*. However, similar to what we saw in the selection of judges, the specifics of institutions and of their procedures must be taken into account. A judicial process, even if the judges have great decision-making latitude, must not be equated with a process of political law-making.[130] A court is not a parliamentary assembly, nor should it be. Among other things, courts work under much greater cognitive self-isolation than political institutions.[131] In a way, that is the essence of formalized law-application discourses.[132]

However, the specific nature of the judicial decision, given its multifunctionality, does not mean that judges may hear only the arguments of the parties and take cognizance only of the written submission of the parties to the conflict. It would be deserving of criticism if international judges

[127] ILC, 'Report of the International Law Commission on the Work of its Forty-Sixth Session' (1 September 1994) UN Doc A/49/355; Art 45 Draft Statute for an International Criminal Court.

[128] *Judge Kirk McDonald Urges that the International Permanent Court 'Must Be Effective'* (14 August 1997) No CC/PIO/236-E <www.icty.org/sid/7478/en> accessed 25 September 2012; Lori F Damrosch in Zimmermann and others (eds), *The Statute of the International Court of Justice* Article 56 paras 42–4.

[129] Hofmann and Laubner, Article 57 paras 55–6.

[130] On the differences see chapter 3 section A 1 c.

[131] Niklas Luhmann, *Law as a Social System* (Klaus A Ziegert tr, Fatima Kastner and others eds, OUP 2004) 293–942.

[132] Milan Kuhli and Klaus Günther, 'Judicial Lawmaking, Discourse Theory, and the ICTY on Belligerent Reprisals' (2011) 12 German L J 1261; seminal Klaus Günther, 'Ein normativer Begriff der Kohärenz: Für eine Theorie der juristischen Argumentation' (1989) 20 Rechtstheorie 163.

drew their knowledge about the case in dispute, the facts, its social and political context, possible consequences of alternative decisions, and the relevant law solely from the submitted documents, since the contending parties shape their account of the factual and legal material with the goal of winning the actual case. The idea of democratic inclusion suggests that the flow of information should be broader. The relevant opening of the procedures before many international courts thus constitutes a trend that meets the democracy-oriented understanding halfway.

According to Article 62 of the ICJ Statute, states can petition the ICJ to intervene in ongoing cases.[133] The preconditions are legal standing and an 'interest of a legal nature' that could be affected by the decision.[134] According to Article 43 of the ICJ Rules of Court, international organizations should be notified and submissions from the secretariats should be permitted if their statute is the issue in dispute. This mechanism was consolidated with the reform of the Rules of Court in 2005.[135]

Under the spell of the state-oriented basic understanding, the ICJ was initially highly reluctant to permit interventions by third parties.[136] Over time, however, it has opened up.[137] Like the ICJ, the ITLOS permits interventions even when the intervening party has not submitted to its jurisdiction, which does justice to the functions of the adjudication that extends beyond a specific case.[138] This expansion of the circle of participants possibly impairs the autonomy of the parties.[139] However, given the law-making role of the adjudication, it seems persuasive that these concerns must take a back seat.[140]

The procedures of the WTO are far more open to participation. Here, member states that are not parties to a dispute have always been able to participate in all stages of the procedure (consultation, panel process, appeal,

[133] Santiago Torres Bernárdez, 'L'intervention dans la procédure de la Cour internationale de Justice' (1995) 256 Recueil des cours 193.

[134] An overview can be found in Christine M Chinkin in Zimmermann and others (eds), *The Statute of the International Court of Justice* Article 62 paras 41–54.

[135] Art 43 ICJ Rules of Court; Abdul G Koroma, 'International Court of Justice, Rules and Practice Directions' in Wolfrum (ed), *Max Planck Encyclopedia of Public International Law* para 2.

[136] See chapter 2 section A 2.

[137] Path-breaking *Sovereignty over Pulau Ligitan and Pulau Sipadan (Indonesia v Malaysia)* (Judgment) [2001] ICJ Rep 575. See Art 81(2)(c) ICJ Rules of Court.

[138] Arts 31, 32 ITLOS Statute.

[139] Chinkin, Article 62 para 102.

[140] *Sovereignty over Pulau Ligitan and Pulau Sipadan*, Sep Op Weeramantry, para 13. See also Rüdiger Wolfrum, 'Intervention in the Proceedings before the International Court of Justice and the International Tribunal for the Law of the Sea' in Volkmar Götz and others (eds), *Liber amicorum Günther Jaenicke—zum 85. Geburtstag* (Springer 1998) 427.

multilateral surveillance of the implementation measures).[141] Every member that can assert a 'substantial interest' in a matter before a panel has the right to be heard by the panel and to make written submission.[142] Judicial decisions have considerably scaled back the requirement of a substantial interest.[143]

However, intervening parties within the framework of the WTO, unlike those before the ICJ and the ITLOS, have no explicit right to participate in all negotiations. The scope of the participation is left to the discretion of the panel. In the *EC–Bananas III* case, developing countries requested that they be allowed to participate in all meetings between the panel and the parties to the dispute and to receive copies of all written submissions. The panel, while noting a trend toward broadening, found that it had previously always occurred only with the consent of the contending parties, a consent that was lacking in this case. Nevertheless, it did authorize the participation, which it justified in terms of the economic repercussions of the EC banana regime.[144] What shines through here is the understanding of international courts as regime institutions in an interdependent world, one in which the relevant legal issues cannot be reduced to the positions of the parties to a dispute.

The possibilities are much narrower in investment arbitration. Its procedural logic, especially confidentiality and the protection of business secrets, leaves much less room for the participation of third parties.[145] And yet, arbitral tribunals occasionally allowed submissions from intervening parties.[146] In 2004, the NAFTA Free Trade Commission likewise noted that the rules of procedure did not, in principle, argue against a participation by third parties.[147] It recommended that an arbitral panel be guided by the consideration of whether a case concerned a public interest.[148] The ICSID Secretariat

[141] Arts 4(11), 10, 17(4) DSU. Ernst-Ulrich Petersmann, 'Alternative Dispute Resolution—Lessons for the WTO?' in Friedl Weiss (ed), *Improving WTO Dispute Settlement Procedures* (Cameron May 2000) 27, 33–5.

[142] Art 10(2) DSU. The first substantive meeting of the Panel is also to be used to hear the position of third parties, see Appendix 3(6) DSU.

[143] Katrin Arend in Rüdiger Wolfrum and others (eds), *WTO: Institutions and Dispute Settlement* (Nijhoff 2006) Article 10 DSU para 4.

[144] *European Communities: Regime for the Importation, Sale and Distribution of Bananas–Panel Report* (22 May 1997) WT/DS27/R, paras 7.4–7.9. However, the practice is by no means uniform and remains within the discretion of the panels.

[145] Accordingly, until 2006 no guidelines on the intervention by third parties were found in the ICSID Convention.

[146] See McLachlan and others, *International Investment Arbitration* 59 with further references.

[147] NAFTA, *Statement of the Free Trade Commission on Non-disputing Party Participation* (7 October 2004) <www.naftaclaims.com> accessed 28 September 2012.

[148] NAFTA, *Statement of the Free Trade Commission*, para 6(d).

followed suit in an *ICSID Discussion Paper* with a similar thrust, which led to a revision of the Rules of Procedure for Arbitration Proceedings.[149]

Another opening is offered by the inclusion of written submissions by interested third parties who cannot intervene formally. Of particular significance are the *amicus curiae briefs* known from US law. *Amici curiae* usually present themselves as experts; that is, they claim not to have a personal interest in a case.[150] While intervening third parties are mostly treaty parties themselves and have legal standing, *amici curiae* are largely private actors, especially NGOs.[151] Their inclusion has given rise to a considerable debate. For one, there are some dangers, especially those raised by an overrepresentation of strong interests and well-organized lobby groups.[152] For another, the involvement of NGOs opens up new legitimatory potential.[153] This potential—in particular, transmission functions between the Court and the relevant publics—clearly outweighs the dangers.

The development points in this direction, as revealed by a look back in history. The procedural law of the ICJ contains no guidelines. In 1950, the Registrar of the ICJ, in one of the very first cases, rejected the petition by an NGO to submit its position orally and in writing.[154] The situation was different from the outset with respect to the function of issuing advisory opinions, however.[155] Moreover, ever since the *Gabčíkovo-Nagymaros* case it has been clear that *amicus curiae* briefs can be submitted in adversarial proceedings through one of the parties to the dispute.[156] Beyond these markers,

[149] ICSID Secretariat, *Possible Improvements of the Framework for ICSID Arbitration* (22 October 2004) paras 11–5. See especially Rule 37 ICSID Rules of Procedure for Arbitration Proceedings.

[150] Philippe J Sands and Ruth Mackenzie, 'International Courts and Tribunals, Amicus Curiae' in Wolfrum (ed), *Max Planck Encyclopedia of Public International Law*, para 2.

[151] It should be noted that before a few courts, like the ECtHR, private parties themselves have a right of action and states are sometimes also referred to as *amici curiae*. See Luisa Vierucci, 'NGOs before International Courts and Tribunals' in Pierre-Marie Dupuy and Luisa Vierucci (eds), *NGOs in International Law: Efficiency in Flexibility?* (Edward Elgar 2008) 155.

[152] See Hervé Ascensio, '*L'amicus curiae* devant les juridictions internationales' (2001) 105 Revue générale de droit international public 897; Ruth Mackenzie, 'The *Amicus Curiae* in International Courts: Towards Common Procedural Approaches?' in Tullio Treves and others (eds), *Civil Society, International Courts and Compliance Bodies* (Asser 2005) 295; Anna-Karin Lindblom, *Non-Governmental Organisations in International Law* (CUP 2005) 300–65.

[153] Jürgen Habermas, *Between Facts and Norms: Contributions to a Discourse Theory of Law and Democracy* (William Rehg tr, Polity Press 1997) 302–8, 382–3; Nanz and Steffek, 'Zivilgesellschaftliche Partizipation und die Demokratisierung internationalen Regierens'.

[154] *Asylum Case (Colombia v Peru)* (Judgment) [1950] ICJ Rep 266. This was easy since the NGO invoked Art 34(2) ICJ Statute. The determination that the NGO was not a public international organization was thus sufficient for the rejection.

[155] See Art 66 ICJ Statute.

[156] Ulrich Beyerlin, 'The Role of NGOs in International Environmental Litigation' (2001) 61 Zeitschrift für ausländisches öffentliches Recht und Völkerrecht 357, 364.

the handling of *amici curiae* within the ICJ is contested and reflects competing basic understandings.[157]

The treaty provisions of the WTO also provide no guidelines on how to deal with *amicus curiae* briefs, but in this case the legal practice has opened up.[158] As early as the *US–Gasoline* case, the first case within the institutional framework of the WTO, NGOs insisted on being allowed to submit their positions. However, the panel simply ignored their concerns. In the path-breaking *US–Shrimp* case the panel also refused to accept *amicus curiae* briefs, but it was overruled by the Appellate Body, which stated the following:

> The thrust of Articles 12 and 13, taken together, is that the DSU accords to a panel established by the DSB, and engaged in a dispute settlement proceeding, ample and extensive authority to undertake and to control the process by which it informs itself both of the relevant facts of the dispute and of the legal norms and principles applicable to such facts.[159]

The Appellate Body considers itself authorized to receive *amicus curiae* briefs and to take them into account.[160] It standardized this in Rule 16 Section 1 of its Working Procedures. However, this met with criticism from the WTO members, who maintained that the Appellate Body had exceeded its competency and had legislated in this matter of procedural law.[161] A few WTO members have tried to change the procedural rules through the political route, but so far to no avail. Members' criticism has arguably influenced the Appellate Body's later practice, however.

By contrast to the WTO, procedures by the ICSID were tightly closed off. Only the parties to a dispute had access. But here, too, there are elements of opening up, which can be attributed not least to the recognition of the multifunctionality of international adjudication, in particular its deep social impact and its law-making.[162] On the possible participation of civil society, the OECD Investment Committee elaborated the following:

[157] See chapter 2 section A 2.

[158] Robert Howse, 'Membership and its Privileges: the WTO, Civil Society, and the *Amicus* Brief Controversy' (2003) 9 Eur L J 496; Petros C Mavroidis, '*Amicus Curiae* Briefs before the WTO: Much Ado about Nothing' in Armin von Bogdandy and others (eds), *European Integration and International Co-ordination: Studies in Transnational Economic Law in Honour of Claus-Dieter Ehlermann* (Kluwer 2002) 317.

[159] *United States: Import Prohibition of Certain Shrimp and Shrimp Products—Appellate Body Report* (12 October 1998) WT/DS58/AB/R, para 106.

[160] With reference to Art 17(9) DSU *United States: Imposition of Countervailing Duties on Certain Hot-Rolled Lead and Bismuth Carbon Steel Products Originating in the United Kingdom—Appellate Body Report* (10 May 2000) WT/DS138/AB/R, para 39.

[161] *European Communities: Measures Affecting Asbestos and Asbestos-Containing Products—Communication from the Appellate Body* (8 November 2000) WT/DS135/9; WTO General Council, *Minutes of Meeting on 22 November 2000* (23 January 2001) WT/GC/M/60.

[162] On the elements of publicness see Delaney and Magraw, 'Procedural Transparency' with further references.

> Members of the Investment Committee generally share the view that, especially insofar as proceedings raise important issues of public interest, it may also be desirable to allow third party participation, subject however to clear and specific guidelines.[163]

The revision of the ICSID Rules of Procedure for Arbitration Proceedings in 2006, which now permit written submissions by third parties according to Rule 37 Section 2, had thus already been anticipated in practice. In *Aguas Argentinas v. Argentine Republic*, the Tribunal decided that the *amici curiae* were pursuing a public interest, namely the water supply and sewage disposal of the residents of Buenos Aires, and it therefore permitted the submission.[164]

Article 36 Section 2 of the ECHR permits 'every person concerned' not only to participate in oral hearings, but also to submit written comments. The ECtHR often uses such comments—even summarizes them in its decision—and engages with them. Here the role of the NGOs, as in the case of other institutions for the protection of human rights,[165] often goes further still. In important cases they take over the preparations for the case, legal representation, or other kinds of support for individual plaintiffs. In addition, the Council of Europe's Commissioner for Human Rights can submit written comments and also participate in oral hearings.[166]

The procedures before international criminal courts and tribunals are similarly open. The Rules of Procedure and Evidence agreed upon by the State Assembly in the Rome Statute leave it to the chambers to decide on how to deal with such submissions.[167] The same applies according to the Rules of Procedure and Evidence of the ICTY and the ICTR.[168] On this basis, NGOs as well as natural persons (such as experts on international law) are given the opportunity to express their position. In sum, one can state that the interventions by third parties and *amicus curiae* briefs open the judicial procedures in a deliberative and participatory manner and can thereby generate democratic legitimation.

[163] OECD Investment Committee, *Transparency and Third-Party Participation* 1.

[164] *Aguas Argentinas SA*, paras 18–23; *Biwater Gauff (Tanzania) Ltd v United Republic of Tanzania* (Procedural Order No 5) ICSID Case No ARB/05/22 (2 February 2007); see Eduardo Savarese, '*Amicus Curiae* Participation in Investor-State Arbitral Proceedings' (2007) 17 Italian YB Intl L 99.

[165] Thus, for example, with a view to the IACtHR Dinah Shelton, 'The Participation of Nongovernmental Organizations in International Proceedings' (1994) 88 AJIL 611, 638–40; Jona Razzaque, 'Changing Role of Friends of the Court in International Courts and Tribunals' (2001) 1 Non-State Actors and Intl L 169, 184–7.

[166] See Art 36(3) ECHR, which was newly introduced with the Protocol No 14.

[167] Rule 103 ICC Rules of Procedure and Evidence; according to Rule 149 ICC Rules of Procedure and Evidence, this applies also to appeals procedures.

[168] In each case Rule 74 ICTY and ICTR Rules of Procedure and Evidence.

3. A legal remedy

We hold that democratic legitimation can be imparted also by the establishment of a legal remedy.[169] This kind of control undoubtedly serves to legitimate the exercise of judicial authority.[170] But wherein lies its specific democratic potential? A court of appeal can correct mistakes and thus strengthen the judges' attachment to the law. Even if we leave cognitivistic understandings of adjudication far behind, the possibility of *wrong* decisions certainly remains.[171] A higher court can also promote the consistency of the adjudication, which serves the goal of equality. The relevant control processes also make an important contribution to the stabilization of normative expectations and encourage the supervised court to formulate its reasoning in a comprehensible way, which in turn promotes transparency.

Above all, however, the relevant procedures allow for responsiveness. Mechanisms of control can respond to the critical reception of a decision by the public.[172] A supervising court can be the addressee but also the sustaining force of a critical public. If there is a possibility of review, it is more meaningful for such a public to come about and develop.

Overall, international courts do not stand in an ordered relationship to one another, let alone within a hierarchy.[173] Although a co-ordinating role for the ICJ is being discussed, at this time it seems a hopeless undertaking.[174] To little surprise, there is no legal remedy against a decision by the ICJ: 'The judgment is final and without appeal' (Article 60 ICJ Statute). A party to the dispute can merely request the interpretation of the judgment should there be a conflict about its meaning.[175] A judgment can be revisited only under

[169] See Karin Oellers-Frahm, 'International Courts and Tribunals, Appeals' in Wolfrum (ed), *Max Planck Encyclopedia of Public International Law*.

[170] In detail Andreas Voßkuhle, *Rechtsschutz gegen den Richter: Zur Integration der Dritten Gewalt in das verfassungsrechtliche Kontrollsystem vor dem Hintergrund des Art. 19 Abs. 4 GG* (CH Beck 1993) 255–311.

[171] In more detail chapter 3 section A; Ingo Venzke, 'The Role of International Courts as Interpreters and Developers of the Law: Working out the Jurisgenerative Practice of Interpretation' (2012) 34 Loyola of Los Angeles Intl and Comparative L Rev 99; see also Ralph Christensen and Hans Kudlich, *Gesetzesbindung: Vom vertikalen zum horizontalen Verständnis* (Duncker & Humblot 2008); Habermas, *Between Facts and Norms* 9–17.

[172] Instructive in this regard is *Lautsi and Others v Italy* App No 30814/06 (ECtHR, 18 March 2011) concerning crucifixes in the classroom, where the Grand Chamber overturned the decision of the first instance in light of a broad public debate; see Franck Lafaille, 'L'identité catholique de l'Italie est-elle soluble dans l'État de droit constitutionnel (national et européen)?' (2010) 126 Revue du droit public et de la science politique en France et à l'étranger 771; Diletta Tega, *I diritti in crisi: Tra Corti nazionali e Corte europea di Strasburgo* (Giuffrè 2012) 120–8, 154.

[173] See Yuval Shany, *Regulating Jurisdictional Relations between National and International Courts* (OUP 2007).

[174] Karin Oellers-Frahm, 'Multiplication of International Courts and Tribunals and Conflicting Jurisdiction—Problems and Possible Solutions' (2001) 5 Max Planck YB UN L 67.

[175] See Andreas Zimmermann and Tobias Thienel in Zimmermann and others (eds), *The Statute of the International Court of Justice* Article 60 paras 28–31.

the narrowest of circumstances, namely if new facts of a decisive nature become known (Article 61 ICJ Statute).

By contrast, in a few sectoral regimes, especially within international criminal law, we find fully developed legal remedies of the kind known from domestic legal systems.[176] In this area, a legal remedy arises from the human right to a fair trial according to Article 14 Section 5 of the ICCPR: 'Everyone convicted of a crime shall have the right to his conviction and sentence being reviewed by a higher tribunal according to law.' At the ECtHR there is likewise a possibility of referring a decision by a chamber to the Grand Chamber.[177] The Grand Chamber 'shall accept the request if the case raises a serious question affecting the interpretation or application of the Convention or the Protocols thereto, or a serious issue of general importance'[178]. Such procedures can trigger discussion and make it possible to arouse the attention of a broad public.

The Appellate Body of the WTO has shown how the creation of a legal remedy contributes to the stabilization of normative expectations and aids in 'providing security and predictability to the multilateral trading system' (Article 3(2) DSU). In the negotiations for the Marrakesh Agreement, many representatives of the parties to the treaty linked their willingness to submit to compulsory jurisdiction to the possibility of reviewing a decision of the first instance.[179] What is at stake is not only the outcome in an individual case, but the development of the legal system. In the *Japan–Alcoholic Beverages* case, the United States, even though it had prevailed, filed an appeal, since it regarded the reasoning of the panel as faulty and did not want to create a bad precedent.[180]

These experiences have inspired proposals for a review procedure in investment arbitration that goes beyond the currently narrow possibilities for the annulment of an award (Article 52 ICSID). The discussion is extremely contentious.[181] From the perspective of the democracy-oriented

[176] Wolfgang Schomburg and Jan C Nemitz, 'International Criminal Courts and Tribunals, Procedure' in Wolfrum (ed), *Max Planck Encyclopedia of Public International Law*, paras 34–6.

[177] Art 43 ECHR, Art 72 ECtHR Rules of Court; by contrast, decisions by individual judges and committees are final, Arts 27(2) and 28(2) ECHR.

[178] Art 43(2) ECHR.

[179] Peter van den Bossche, 'From Afterthought to Centrepiece: The WTO Appellate Body and Its Rise to Prominence in the World Trading System' in Giorgio Sacerdoti and others (eds), *The WTO at Ten: The Contribution of the Dispute Settlement System* (CUP 2006) 289, 294–300. The Appellate Body is limited to reviewing questions of law (Art 17(6) DSU) and is perhaps better referred to as a reviewing rather than an appeals body; Hilf, 'Das Streitbeilegungssystem der WTO' 519.

[180] *Japan: Taxes on Alcoholic Beverages—Panel Report* (11 July 1996) WT/DS8/R, WT/DS10/R, WT/DS11/R; *Appellate Body Report* (4 October 1996) WT/DS8/AB/R, WT/DS10/AB/R, WT/DS11/AB/R.

[181] Giorgio Sacerdoti, 'Appeal and Judicial Review in International Arbitration and Adjudication: The Case of the WTO Appellate Review' in Ernst-Ulrich Petersmann (ed), *International Trade Law and the*

conception, there is much in favour of a full legal remedy. At the same time, one should not conceal the fact that an appeals body triggers an additional legal dynamic; that is, that it can exacerbate the problem of democratic legitimacy. Under the current conditions, this tension poses a great challenge especially in the law of investment protection, but the nature of judicial decisions can counter this danger at least to some extent, as we will now show.

C. THE DECISION

Judges exercise public authority by rendering a decision. The way in which they shape their decisions offers additional points for supporting their democratic legitimacy. We first apply the democratic principle to methods of judicial reasoning and the limits of judicial law-making (1). We then examine the democratic potential of an interaction with other courts (2), after which we examine how judicial decision-making is embedded within political processes. This last step includes a discussion of the density of judicial review, the use of soft law, and the promotion of democratic politicization (3).

1. Reasons and limits

a) Judicial method from a democracy-oriented perspective

Any ruling needs to be linked in a methodologically appropriate way to the relevant legal sources. Such a demand constitutes a classic way of justifying judicial power, also democratically. A court must justify the outcome of its proceeding. But what should such justification look like? Ideas about what is demanded by good justification diverge considerably. On the one hand, a court can limit itself to laying out its jurisdiction, invoking relevant legal sources and precedents, then leading to the decision with few words. It might not lay open assumptions, arguments, and alternatives in greater detail. Above all, what remains excluded are arguments situated at the margin or outside of the so-called formalistic style of argumentation—that is, considerations that are 'subjective' and 'political' in the broadest sense. Such a mode of justification is found in the French style of law, for example.[182] It

GATT/WTO Dispute Settlement System (Kluwer 1997) 245, 260–1; Karl P Sauvant (ed), *Appeals Mechanism in International Investment Disputes* (OUP 2008); José E Alvarez, 'Implications for the Future of International Investment Law' in Sauvant (ed), *Appeals Mechanism* 29.

[182] Michel Troper and Christophe Grzegorczyk, 'Precedent in France' in Neil MacCormick and Robert S Summers (eds), *Interpreting Precedents: A Comparative Study* (Ashgate 1997) 103, 107–14; Daniel Sarmiento, 'The Silent Lamb and the Deaf Wolves' in Matej Avbelj and Jan Komárek (eds), *Constitutional Pluralism in the European Union and Beyond* (Hart 2012) 285, 310.

can be theoretically justified by maintaining that it promotes legal autonomy and verifiability as much as possible and leaves unjustified precisely the discretionary element, which is seen as not accessible to a rational justification.[183] The judge has the democratic mandate for a discretionary decision within legal boundaries, one that requires no further reasoning.

On the other side of the spectrum is a conception of judicial reasoning under which a court is supposed to explain, with substantive arguments, its use of discretion. Ronald Dworkin and Robert Alexy have sought to solidify this conception theoretically. Practical examples can be found in decisions by the German Federal Constitutional Court or the US Supreme Court.[184] Here the circle of admissible arguments is broader than under the 'formalistic' conception. The two conceptions differ not only in the length of the statement of grounds, but precisely in the ideas of what forms of argumentation constitute good judicial reasoning.

These theoretical and cultural divergences explain many differences in practice, even between closely related legal cultures. The formalistic British understanding, for example, tends to regard freehand constructions on the basis of first principles, political arguments, or consequentialist considerations with suspicion, while in the United States, formal arguments that hew closely to authoritative texts readily appear as a mask that conceals the decisive considerations.[185] Since every reasoning always has to be formulated relative to the group it seeks to convince,[186] international courts face a difficult task.[187]

One answer to this challenge could be a minimalist approach as practised by the ICJ in the *Kosovo* advisory opinion.[188] Cass Sunstein has offered a fitting formula: a reasoning should be 'narrow and shallow'.[189] A decision should be as restrained as possible and not say more than is necessary to

[183] In this sense Hans Kelsen, *Introduction to the Problems of Legal Theory* (Bonnie Litschewski Paulson and Stanley L Paulson trs, Clarendon 1992) 82–3.

[184] In more detail Oliver Lepsius, 'Die maßstabsetzende Gewalt' in Matthias Jestaedt and others, *Das entgrenzte Gericht: Eine kritische Bilanz nach sechzig Jahren Bundesverfassungsgericht* (Suhrkamp 2011) 159, 237–59.

[185] Path-breaking is Patrick S Atiyah and Robert S Summers, *Form and Substance in Anglo-American Law: A Comparative Study of Legal Reasoning, Legal Theory, and Legal Institutions* (Clarendon 1987) 5–35.

[186] Chaim Perelman and Lucie Olbrechts-Tyteca, *The New Rhetoric: A Treatise on Argumentation* (University of Notre Dame Press 1969) 19.

[187] Thus, the ECtHR does not derive the fundamental obligation to provide detailed reasons from the principle of a fair process; *Atanasovski v former Yugoslav Republic of Macedonia*, para 38.

[188] *Accordance with International Law of the Unilateral Declaration of Independence in Respect of Kosovo* (Advisory Opinion) [2010] ICJ Rep 403.

[189] Cass R Sunstein, *One Case at a Time: Judicial Minimalism on the Supreme Court* (Harvard UP 1999); an assessment in Christopher J Peters, 'Assessing the New Judicial Minimalism' (2000) 100 Columbia L Rev 1454.

settle the case. At first glance, this recipe seems almost ideal for the ICJ in particular, which has no compulsory jurisdiction and operates within a difficult political context.

However, Sunstein's formula clashes with the interest in legal security and the need for orientation. Especially on the international level, where political law-making usually proceeds only with great difficulty, it is often only judges that can advance the project of contributing to the possible civilization of the world through law.[190] Moreover, the recommendation 'narrow and shallow' usually clashes with the demand that a decision can be criticized on the basis of its reasoning.[191] In terms of democratic theory, it would be at best a Pyrrhic victory.[192]

Finally, 'narrow and shallow' could only persuade if there were no necessity for the court to grapple with precedents. However, since parties to a dispute develop their positions with reference to precedents and struggle over their interpretation, the reasoning should take a position on this struggle. Thus, even in light of the democratic principle, judicial minimalism offers no solution to how international courts should justify their decisions.[193] Much the same holds for principles such as *in dubio mitius,* which states that when in doubt, the less restrictive interpretation should be chosen.[194]

Pointing in the opposite direction are proposals that international courts should lay bare their 'policy reasons'.[195] To be sure, a court can create greater transparency by doing so, address a broader public, and strengthen discursiveness. At the same time, however, one must bear in mind that such forms of argumentation can easily lead to a de-formalization, and de-formalization usually works in favour of the stronger party.[196]

[190] Immanuel Kant, 'Idee zu einer allgemeinen Geschichte in weltbürgerlicher Absicht' in Karl Vorländer (ed), *Kleinere Schriften zur Geschichtsphilosophie, Ethik und Politik* (first published 1784, Felix Meiner 1964) 3, 12–5; Jürgen Habermas, 'Does the Constitutionalization of International Law Still Have a Chance?' in Jürgen Habermas, *The Divided West* (Ciaran Cronin tr/ed, Polity Press 2006) 115, 121–3.

[191] Sunstein himself seems to have doubts by now; Cass R Sunstein, 'Beyond Judicial Minimalism' (2008) 43 Tulsa L Rev 825.

[192] In detail Jörg Riecken, *Verfassungsgerichtsbarkeit und Demokratie* (Duncker & Humblot 2003) 295–301.

[193] In this sense also *Kosovo*, Declaration Simma.

[194] Rejected, for example, in *Dispute Regarding Navigational and Related Rights (Costa Rica v Nicaragua)* (Judgment) [2009] ICJ Rep 213, para 48; *Ethyl Corporation v Government of Canada* (Award on Jurisdiction) (24 June 1998) para 55 (NAFTA/UNCITRAL); in more detail Rudolf Bernhardt, 'Interpretation in International Law' in Rudolf Bernhardt (ed), *Encyclopedia of Public International Law*, vol 2 (Elsevier 1995) 1416, 1421; Luigi Crema, 'Disappearance and New Sightings of Restrictive Interpretation(s)' (2010) 21 Eur J Intl L 681.

[195] Thus for the Appellate Body Douglas A Irwin and Joseph HH Weiler, 'Measures Affecting the Cross-Border Supply of Gambling and Betting Services (DS 285)' (2008) 7 World Trade Rev 71, 89–99.

[196] Martti Koskenniemi, *The Gentle Civilizer of Nations: The Rise of Modern International Law 1870–1960* (CUP 2002) 494–509.

Irrespective of these difficulties and uncertainties, there are some measures that seem advisable under any circumstance. For example, a court, as is customary in common law courts, should lay out its contextual assumptions.[197] This makes it easier to engage decisions critically and could counteract unintended effects.[198] If such assumptions were in fact spelled out, precedents could be used in a more circumspect and controlled way.[199] Letting expected effects flow into the decision within the weighing of possible consequences is also advisable.[200] Frederick Schauer has aptly noted that 'despite this seeming indeterminacy of the future precedential effect of today's decision, awareness of the future effect of today's decision pervades legal and nonlegal argument'.[201]

b) Systematic interpretation as democratic strategy

Systematic interpretation deserves special emphasis, since it might respond to the problems of fragmentation. In recent decades, international courts have strengthened especially in sector-specific regimes. One should therefore contemplate whether the problems of democratic legitimation tied to it could be countered by systematic interpretation. In institutional terms, this could also serve as guidance to the interaction of international courts.

The rules of the interpretation of treaties stipulate that 'any relevant rules of international law applicable in the relations between the parties' should be taken into account (Article 31(3)(c) VCLT).[202] The potential and reach of this rule have been the subject of intense debate ever since the report of the International Law Commission (ILC) on fragmentation. According to Article 31 Section 3 lit c of the VCLT and the 'principle of systematic integration', the crucial point is that the interpretation of a norm

[197] Oliver Lepsius, 'Was kann die deutsche Staatsrechtslehre von der amerikanischen Rechtswissenschaft lernen?' (2007) 7 Die Verwaltung, Beiheft 319, 320–6.

[198] A decision by the ECtHR on the rights of a terror suspect offers a positive example; *Nada v Switzerland* App No 10593/08 (ECtHR, 12 September 2012).

[199] Thus—for German law—Lepsius, 'Was kann die deutsche Staatsrechtslehre von der amerikanischen Rechtswissenschaft lernen?' 335–9; likewise Laurence R Helfer and Anne-Marie Slaughter, 'Toward a Theory of Effective Supranational Adjudication' (1997–1998) 107 Yale L J 273, 320.

[200] In more detail Gertrude Lübbe-Wolff, *Rechtsfolgen und Realfolgen* (Alber 1981); Niels Petersen, 'Braucht die Rechtswissenschaft eine empirische Wende?' (2010) 49 Der Staat 435; critically Ino Augsberg, 'Von einem neuerdings erhobenen empiristischen Ton in der Rechtswissenschaft' (2012) 51 Der Staat 117.

[201] Frederick Schauer, 'Precedent' (1987) 39 Stanford L Rev 571, 574.

[202] See Nele Matz-Lück, 'Harmonization, Systemic Integration, and "Mutual-Supportiveness" as Conflict-Solution Techniques: Different Modes of Interpretation as a Challenge to Negative Effects of Fragmentation?' (2006) 17 Finnish YB Intl L 39; Joost Pauwelyn, *Conflict of Norms in Public International Law: How WTO Law Relates to Other Rules of International Law* (CUP 2003) 244–74; Joost Pauwelyn, 'Bridging Fragmentation and Unity: International Law as a Universe of Inter-Connected Islands' (2004) 25 Michigan J Intl L 903.

should refer to its legal 'environment'; indeed, to the system of international law as a whole:[203]

> They call upon a dispute-settlement body—or a lawyer seeking to find out 'what the law is'—to situate the rules that are being invoked by those concerned in the context of other rules and principles that might have bearing upon a case. In this process the more concrete or immediately available sources are read against each other and against the general law 'in the background'.[204]

The idea that law forms a system is certainly problematic, particularly within international law.[205] Under the state-oriented conception, according to which international law has a strictly bilateral and co-operative structure, for a long time the prevailing opinion was that no such thing as a system of international law could exist. Leading the way was Heinrich Triepel's rejection of a universal international law.[206] In a similar vein, Herbert Hart argued that one could not speak of a system of international law:[207]

> [I]nternational law not only lacks the secondary rules of change and adjudication which provide for legislature and courts, but also a unifying rule of recognition specifying 'sources' of law and providing general criteria for the identification of its rules.[208]

It is much easier to formulate an idea of an overarching system under the community-oriented conception.[209] In the first contribution of the *Zeitschrift für ausländisches Recht und Völkerrecht*, Viktor Bruns established the following premise on page one: 'The law of nations is a legal system for the community of states, a system of legal principles, legal concepts, and legal propositions that are connected to one another in a system.'[210] This assumption is, however, little reasoned in his text and the concept of community remains

[203] ILC, 'Fragmentation of International Law: Difficulties Arising from the Diversification and Expansion of International Law: Report of the Study Group of the International Law Commission, Finalized by Martti Koskenniemi' (13 April 2006) ILC Doc A/CN.4/L.682, para 479.

[204] ILC, 'Fragmentation'.

[205] See Ulrich Fastenrath, *Lücken im Völkerrecht: Zu Rechtscharakter, Quellen, Systemzusammenhang, Methodenlehre und Funktionen des Völkerrechts* (Duncker & Humblot 1991) 149–51. See Benedict Kingsbury, 'Foreword: Is the Proliferation of International Courts and Tribunals a Systemic Problem?' (1999) 31 NYU J Intl L and Politics 679, 691.

[206] Heinrich Triepel, *Völkerrecht und Landesrecht* (Mohr Siebeck 1899) 27–8. On similar understanding by other authors see Koskenniemi, *The Gentle Civilizer of Nations* 362.

[207] Herbert LA Hart, *The Concept of Law* (2nd edn, Clarendon 1994) 92.

[208] Hart, *The Concept of Law* 214.

[209] Similarly Bruno Simma and Dirk Pulkowski, 'Of Planets and the Universe: Self-Contained Regimes in International Law' (2006) 17 Eur J Intl L 483; Klaus Zemanek, 'The Legal Foundations of the International System' (1997) 266 Recueil des cours 9, 62.

[210] Viktor Bruns, 'Völkerrecht als Rechtsordnung' (1929) 1 Zeitschrift für ausländisches öffentliches Recht und Völkerrecht 1; in more detail Eyal Benvenisti, 'The Conception of International Law as a Legal System' (2008) 50 German YB Intl L 393.

as underdetermined as the notion of system. With the further development of the system of international law, this approach has become more plausible. But it remains beset with problems, not least because the developments are fragmented.

Moreover, thinking in terms of systemic unity raises problems under the principle of democracy. In the past, the concept of systemic unity was used to counter efforts at reform by the democratic legislator.[211] And yet the idea of systemic unity is not invariably anti-democratic. In Hans Kelsen it mutated into an epistemological postulate.[212] Along this line, the concept was developed further and simultaneously pruned. Today, the 'system' is not understood as something that is inherent to the positive law, but as an order that is construed and brought to the law.[213] In this sense, the idea of systemic unity continues to play a plausible and fruitful role in legal theory and practice,[214] not least in the discussion over the fragmentation of international law.[215] For example, the very idea of fragmentation, of the differentiation of subsections, rests on the assumption that a 'whole', a system, exists in the first place.

From a legal point of view, the systematic argument is even compelled by law, namely by Article 31 Section 3 lit c of the VCLT. Even if courts rarely invoke this norm explicitly, the idea of systemic unity underpins many judicial arguments.[216] Seminal for the discourse was the legitimacy-asserting statement of the WTO Appellate Body in its very first decision that the GATT must not be read in 'clinical isolation' from international law.[217] One of the most strongly institutionalized parts of international law, international trade law within the framework of the WTO, thus positions itself not as separate from general international law, but as a part of it.[218]

[211] Oliver Lepsius, 'Hat die Europäisierung des Verwaltungsrechts Methode? Oder: Die zwei Phasen der Europäisierung des Verwaltungsrechts' (2010) 10 Die Verwaltung, Beiheft 179, 194–202; Duncan Kennedy, *A Critique of Adjudication: Fin de siècle* (Harvard UP 1997) 215–21.

[212] Kelsen, *Introduction to the Problems of Legal Theory* 55–71; similarly Lauterpacht, *The Function of Law in the International Community* 60–84.

[213] Ralph Christensen and Hans Kudlich, *Theorie richterlichen Begründens* (Duncker & Humblot 2001) 142–6, 158; Stefan Oeter, 'Zur Zukunft der Völkerrechtswissenschaft in Deutschland' (2007) 67 Zeitschrift für ausländisches öffentliches Recht und Völkerrecht 675, 685–6.

[214] Ralph Christensen and Andreas Fischer-Lescano, 'Die Einheit der Rechtsordnung: Zur Funktionsweise der holistischen Semantik' (2006) 4 Zeitschrift für Rechtsphilosophie 8.

[215] Matthew Craven, 'Unity, Diversity and the Fragmentation of International Law' (2003) 14 Finnish YB Intl L 3, 7.

[216] *Legal Consequences for States of the Continued Presence of South Africa in Namibia (South West Africa) notwithstanding Security Council Resolution 276 (1970)* (Advisory Opinion) [1971] ICJ Rep 16, para 53. See also ILC, 'Fragmentation' 310.

[217] *United States: Standards for Reformulated and Conventional Gasoline–Appellate Body Report* (29 April 1996) WT/DS2/AB/R, 17. For a detailed discussion on the background see chapter 2 section C 2.

[218] Differently from the legal system of the European Union, which treats its autonomy as a first principle; Joined Cases C-402/05 P and 415/05 P *Kadi and Al Barakaat International Foundation v Council and Commission* [2008] ECR I–06351, para 316.

Such systematic interpretation is supported by the presumption that the rights and duties of a subject of international law should not clash.[219] The ICJ formulated this presumption as an interpretive rule: 'It is a rule of interpretation that a text emanating from a government must, in principle, be interpreted as producing and intended to produce effects in accordance with existing law and not in violation of it.'[220] All in all, then, the rules of interpretation in the VCLT justify calibrating the law of different regimes. In many cases this can ameliorate the problems of fragmentation.[221]

To be sure, there are serious obstacles to be surmounted. A court might not have the competence to look beyond the law of its regime or the membership in the two legal regimes may not coincide.[222] There is also a danger that a judicial institution that is part of a functionally tailored regime will interpret other norms in the light of its functional orientation.[223] Human rights lawyers are quite concerned that the WTO or investment arbitration panels might set precedents on human rights.

But in many cases the issue is rather one of situating the norm to be interpreted within the context of universal international law (that is binding on all subjects) or of multilateral treaties with a global reach. For the potential to be realized, a reciprocal referencing by international judicial panels is of particular promise. The differing perspectives should be brought together through dialogue in the shared language of international law. The systematic interpretation thus reveals itself as a co-operative undertaking.[224] For such an undertaking, courts must open themselves up, and there are indications that they are doing so.[225] Still, the evidence for a substantial and continuous dialogue remains meagre.[226] For a dialogue to be a dialogue and

[219] Bruno Simma and Theodore Kill, 'Harmonizing Investment Protection and International Human Rights: First Steps Towards a Methodology' in Christina Binder and others (eds), *International Investment Law for the 21st Century* (OUP 2009) 678, 686–91.

[220] *Right of Passage over Indian Territory (Portugal v India)* (Preliminary Objections) [1957] ICJ Rep 125, 141; *Oil Platforms* (Judgment) para 41.

[221] Clarence W Jenks, 'The Conflict of Law-Making Treaties' (1953) 30 British YB Intl L 401, 427–9.

[222] Lorand Bartels, 'Applicable Law in WTO Dispute Settlement Proceedings' (2001) 35 J World Trade 499, 501–12; ILC, 'Fragmentation' para 450; Ulf Linderfalk, 'Who Are "the Parties"? Article 31, Paragraph 3 (c) of the 1969 Vienna Convention and the "Principle of Systemic Integration" Revisited' (2008) 55 Netherlands Intl L Rev 343.

[223] Pauwelyn, *Conflict of Norms in Public International Law* 242–3.

[224] Ruti Teitel and Robert Howse, 'Cross-Judging: Tribunalization in a Fragmented but Interconnected Global Order' (2009) 41 NYU J Intl L and Politics 959, 967.

[225] Bruno Simma, 'Universality of International Law from the Perspective of a Practitioner' (2009) 20 Eur J Intl L 265; Rosalyn Higgins, 'A Babel of Judicial Voices? Rumination from the Bench' (2006) 55 ICLQ 791; Mark E Villiger, 'The Dialogue of Judges' in Christine Hohmann-Dennhardt and others (eds), *Durchsetzung und Verfahren: Festschrift für Renate Jäger* (Engel 2011) 195.

[226] Suzannah Linton and Firew Kebede Tiba, 'The International Judge in an Age of Multiple International Courts and Tribunals' (2009) 9 Chicago J Intl L 407, 419; for a more positive view Jonathan

not just interaction, an idea of a common responsibility for the legitimate operation of international law is needed. Mere comity is not sufficient to achieve an interweaving of sectoral perspectives.[227] In addition, some sectors of international law are not equipped with courts or similar institutions, a circumstance that is often not accidental but has strategic reasons behind it.[228] In particular, the interaction between economic interests and environmental interests is a dialogue between unequals. These problems are grave, but they do not question that the systematic interpretation is, in principle, a promising strategy also under our democracy-oriented conception of international adjudication.

In conclusion, one should recall that systematic interpretation, as is the case with all other methods of interpretation, typically cannot develop the one right result. The need for a justification, as indispensable as it is for legitimizing a decision, does not undo the court's discretion. Discretion certainly remains about who prevails in a case, how the court stabilizes normative expectations, which new expectations it generates, how intensively it controls the exercise of power, and whom it legitimizes and delegitimizes. The established rules of interpretation are quite patient. However, the democratic principle implies a boundary against which this patience breaks.

c) The limits of a decision and its justification

Identifying a boundary for a court's discretion proves extraordinarily difficult.[229] What is clear, at least, is that we are dealing with a question of the separation of powers, though in a new guise, given the institutional set-up of international law.[230] In terms of discourse theory, the delimitation of competency between legislative, law-applying, and law-enforcement bodies is conceptualized as the distribution of possibilities of access to different sorts of reasons, and that approach is followed here. The most important distinction in discourse theory is that between the discourses on justifying and applying norms.[231] This interpretation of the separation of powers assumes that the positive law conveys the results of democratic processes

I Charney, 'Is International Law Threatened by Multiple International Tribunals?' (1998) 271 Recueil des cours 101, 347–56.

[227] On comity Elisa D'Alterio, 'From Judicial Comity to Legal Comity: A Judicial Solution to Global Disorder?' (2011) 9 Intl J Const L 394.

[228] Benedict Kingsbury, 'International Courts: Uneven Judicialization in Global Order' in James Crawford and Martti Koskenniemi (eds), *The Cambridge Companion to International Law* (CUP 2012) 203.

[229] Fuad Zarbiyev, 'Judicial Activism in International Law—A Conceptual Framework for Analysis' (2012) 3 J Intl Dispute Settlement 247, 250–1; Iris Canor, *The Limits of Judicial Discretion in the European Court of Justice* (Nomos 1998) 19–35, 135–68.

[230] See in detail chapter 3 section B 1.

[231] Habermas, *Between Facts and Norms* 192; Günther, 'Ein normativer Begriff der Kohärenz' 167–75.

and is therefore a normative source for the legitimacy of public authority.[232] These processes are the setting for discourses whose participants can resort to the entire spectrum of pragmatic, ethical, and moral reasons.

The courts, as actors who apply the law, draw on the democratic legitimacy generated by the legislative process. According to this discourse–theoretical understanding of the liberal–democratic separation of power, 'the judiciary must be separated from the legislature and prevented from programming itself'.[233] Law-creation in judicial proceedings is bound to the specific rules of discourse on applying norms. Even if a creative element is inherent in every act of interpretation and application, it is indispensable that judicial power refer to the democratic political process and remain dependent on it. These reflections confirm our distinction between judicial and political law-making.[234]

Discourse theory itself further recognizes that a strict separation of political law-making and judicial law-application would likely slow down—indeed restrict—the juridification of complex and dynamic social relationships.[235] As discourse theory does not want to curtail this development which it sees, in principle, as civilizing, it grants the courts an additional sphere of competency, though at the price of great vagueness:

> To the extent that legal programs are in need of further specification by the courts [...] juristic discourses of application must be visibly supplemented by elements taken from discourses of justification. Naturally, these elements of a quasi-legislative opinion- and will-formation require another kind of legitimation than does adjudication proper. The additional burden of legitimation could be partly satisfied by additional obligations for courts to justify opinions before an enlarged critical forum specific to the judiciary.[236]

Application discourses should thus be expanded 'to the extent that legal programs are in need of further specification by the courts'. Courts then have a corresponding mandate. The foundations of international law are especially often in need of such specification and international courts have a mandate to do so, as we have already shown above.[237]

The German Federal Constitutional Court has developed clues as to how that mandate of the courts can be specified, but also limited. It sees the judicial law-making on the supranational and international level restricted by

[232] Habermas, *Between Facts and Norms* 151–7.

[233] Habermas, *Between Facts and Norms* 172.

[234] See chapter 3 section A 1 c.

[235] Thus on the CJEU Canor, *The Limits of Judicial Discretion in the European Court of Justice* 43–88.

[236] Habermas, *Between Facts and Norms* 439–40. See also Tobias Lieber, *Diskursive Vernunft und formelle Gleichheit: Zu Demokratie, Gewaltenteilung und Rechtsanwendung in der Rechtstheorie von Jürgen Habermas* (Mohr Siebeck 2007) 225–34.

[237] See chapter 3 section A 1 b.

the overall 'program' of a treaty.[238] This limit of judicial institutions resembles that of political institutions of a supranational organization, since the latter also possesses competency only within the framework of the goals of a treaty.[239] This confirms our approach of regarding international courts, like international organizations, as actors of global governance. However, this still does not define a clear boundary, since the goals of treaties are mostly formulated in an open manner.

The German Federal Constitutional Court is aware of that openness, and indeed adds indicators of whether a judicial decision exceeds the programme of a treaty. Most importantly, it starts with a presumption for the admissibility of international judicial law-making. The latter is only impermissible 'if it changes clearly recognisable statutory decisions which may even be explicitly documented in the wording (of the Treaties), or creates new provisions without sufficient connection to legislative statements. This is above all not permissible where case-law makes fundamental policy decisions over and above individual cases or as a result of the further development of the law causes structural shifts to occur in the system of the sharing of constitutional power and influence [...]'.[240]

Thus both discourse theory and the German Federal Constitutional Court proceed from the assumption that judicial law-making is by no means impermissible in principle; instead, it is inherent in the democratic mandate of international courts. The democratic orientation of both approaches makes them outstanding exponents of the democracy-focused conception. To be sure, the criteria for the permissibility of judicial law-making are open, something that can hardly be avoided both theoretically and doctrinally. We do not see this as a disadvantage, since this openness allows later courts to react responsively to the public debate surrounding a particular decision. In all likelihood, courts will make better use of democratic *opportunities* of justification if they know that their decisions can be controlled by other courts.

[238] *Honeywell* (2010) 126 BVerfGE 286, para 64 (Federal Constitutional Court of Germany) English: <http://www.bundesverfassungsgericht.de/entscheidungen/rs20100706_2bvr266106en.html> accessed 31 January 2014; *NATO-Strategiekonzept* (2001) 104 BVerfGE 151, para 126, English: <http://www.bverfg.de/en/decisions/es20011122_2bve000699en.html> accessed 3 February 2014. From the literature Matthias Klatt, *Making the Law Explicit: The Normativity of Legal Argumentation* (Hart 2008) 5–7; Konrad F Walter, *Rechtsfortbildung durch den EuGH* (Duncker & Humblot 2009) 41–3.

[239] Jan Klabbers, *An Introduction to International Institutional Law* (2nd edn, CUP 2009) 59–64; Armin von Bogdandy, 'General Principles of International Public Authority: Sketching a Research Field' (2008) 11 German L J 1909, 1933.

[240] *Honeywell*, para 64. On the discussion of the decision see Leslie Manthey and Christopher Unseld, 'Der Mythos vom contra-legem-Verbot: Vom Umgang des EuGH mit einem Verfassungsprinzip' (2011) 64 Die öffentliche Verwaltung 921.

2. Judicial interaction as democratic control

The legal demands on international decisions call for mechanisms that watch over their implementation. Probably the most important mechanism is the principle of collegiality. Nearly all decisions of nearly all international courts are collegial. If the bench is staffed with independent, impartial, and learned individuals, every judge must justify every position within the group.[241] In this sense, the principle of collegiality, the interaction between the judges of a court, serves the democratic principle.[242] The principle of collegiality concretizes the democratic principle not in the sense of the idea of representation, but much more simply thanks to reciprocal control.

External institutions complement this internal mechanism. External control is exercised increasingly by domestic courts. Such control is sometimes interpreted as inherently confrontational and perilous for the international judiciary.[243] Although this threat is real, overall it seems more convincing to highlight the legitimatory potential of such control.[244] Of course, it needs to be exercised in light of the common responsibility of international and domestic courts for the legitimacy and efficiency of international law.

Legally, this control is possible because it is the domestic constitutional law that decides how an international decision affects the internal legal order.[245] Although international courts have occasionally tried to assert direct effect for their decisions, with the exception of the Inter-American Court of Human Rights, they have hardly prevailed.[246] In light of the democratic principle, it is convincing that the internal effect of an international legal decision is determined by the constitutional law of the legal system

[241] On this see chapter 3 section A I c.

[242] Voßkuhle and Sydow, 'Die demokratische Legitimation des Richters' 679.

[243] See Jochen Abr Frowein, 'Die traurigen Missverständnisse: Bundesverfassungsgericht und Europäischer Gerichtshof für Menschenrechte' in Klaus Dicke and others (eds), *Weltinnenrecht: Liber amicorum Jost Delbrück* (Duncker & Humblot 2004) 279, 280–1.

[244] Heiko Sauer, *Jurisdiktionskonflikte in Mehrebenensystemen* (Springer 2008); Andreas Voßkuhle, 'Der europäische Verfassungsgerichtsverbund' (2010) 29 Neue Zeitschrift für Verwaltungsrecht 1, 6–8; Anne Peters, 'Rechtsordnungen und Konstitutionalisierung: Zur Neubestimmung der Verhältnisse' (2010) 65 Zeitschrift für öffentliches Recht 3, 59–61.

[245] Daniel Halberstam, 'Local, Global, and Plural Constitutionalism: Europe Meets the World' in Gráinne de Búrca and Joseph HH Weiler (eds), *The Worlds of European Constitutionalism* (CUP 2012) 150, 164–5.

[246] Cautious approaches in this direction in *Namibia*, para 125; *LaGrand (Germany v USA)* (Judgment) [2001] ICJ Rep 466, para 77; *Prosecutor v Tihomir Blaškić* (Decision on the Objection of the Republic of Croatia to the Issuance of Subpoena Duces Tecum) 1997 IT-95-14-T (18 July 1997) paras 65–9; *Jurisdiction of the Courts of Danzig* PCIJ Series B No 15, para 38. From the legal decisions of the IACtHR, *Case of Gómez-Palomino v Peru* Inter-American Court of Human Rights Series C No 136 (22 November 2005) paras 90–6, 149, 153; *Case of 'The Last Temptation of Christ' (Olmedo-Bustos et al) v Chile* Inter-American Court of Human Rights Series C No 73 (5 February 2001) paras 87–90; in more detail Góngora Mera, *Inter-American Judicial Constitutionalism* 49–54.

receiving it. How much a constitutional system opens itself to the international judiciary is a constitutional decision of the highest importance, and one that can turn out differently from one constitution to the next, due to different constitutional traditions and convictions.[247]

With few exceptions, domestic constitutional law does not accord international judicial decisions direct effect within the internal legal system—at least not in principle, and never across the board. Their implementation requires domestic institutions to become active.[248] Thus, as a rule international courts can only determine a violation of the law; they do not possess the authority to declare that an internationally unlawful act is void or inapplicable.

This apparent weakness of international adjudication turns out to be a support for its legitimacy. It fits well with the democratic principle, since interposed domestic institutions can serve as the 'enlarged critical forum'.[249] It relieves international legal decisions from the burdens of legitimation that they are not always capable of bearing by opening up another mechanism of democratic legitimation.[250] Domestic courts can formulate legitimatory standards.[251]

We are not advocating that domestic courts should elevate themselves into a kind of regular appeals body against international rulings.[252] The internal rejection of an international decision can easily damage the authority of an international court and the still infant process of international juridification. If a domestic court should extraordinarily take such a decision, such a move would require weighty reasons.[253] It must be keenly aware that it damages both the international process of juridification and

[247] On the immediate effect as a weighing of constitutional-legal positions see Niels Petersen, 'Determining the Effect of International Law through the Prism of Legitimacy' (2012) 72 Zeitschrift für ausländisches öffentliches Recht und Völkerrecht 223.

[248] In detail Armin von Bogdandy, 'Pluralism, Direct Effect, and the Ultimate Say: On the Relationship between International and Domestic Constitutional Law' (2008) 6 Intl J Const L 397.

[249] See section C 1 c.

[250] Nico Krisch, *Beyond Constitutionalism: The Pluralist Structure of Postnational Law* (OUP 2010) 255–61.

[251] For example *Solange I* (1974) 37 BVerfGE 271, para 56 (Federal Constitutional Court of Germany), English in *Decisions of the Bundesverfassungsgericht—Federal Constitutional Court—Federal Republic of Germany*, vol 1/I (Nomos 1992) 270; *Frontini Franco* (1973) Sentenza 183/1973 (1974) 9 Europarecht 255, 262 (Constitutional Court of Italy); *Abdelrazik v Minister of Foreign Affairs* (2010) 2009 FC 580, para 51 (Federal Court of Canada); *Ahmed et al v HM Treasury* (2010) 2010 WLR 378, para 61 (UK Supreme Court); Sentencia T-025/2004 (Constitutional Court of Colombia); see also *Case of the 'Mapiripán Massacre' v Colombia* Inter-American Court of Human Rights Series C No 134 (15 September 2005); *Case of the Ituango Massacres v Colombia* Inter-American Court of Human Rights Series C No 148 (1 July 2006); *Kadi*, para 322.

[252] On this see section B 3.

[253] For a critical assessment Case C-93/02 P *Biret International SA v Council* [2003] ECR I-10497, paras 66–7; Sentencia No 1939 (Constitutional Chamber of the Supreme Tribunal of Justice of Venezuela).

the principle of openness to international law, which in many countries is constitutionally enshrined.

3. Embeddedness in political processes

The democratic principle demands that courts—domestic as well as international—be embedded within the overall context of democratic politics. However, that context looks different on the international level than it does within the framework of a state. Nevertheless, some mechanisms are perfectly comparable. For example, the political context can be taken into consideration by international courts when they calibrate their review, a mechanism familiar from domestic courts (a). Another pertinent issue is how international courts rely on soft law instruments, enacted by political institutions (b). A third strategy is to work toward the democratization of administrative processes (c).

a) Democratically calibrated intensity of review

International courts control and thereby legitimate other institutions. This oversight function vis-à-vis the bearers of public authority must be calibrated in light of the democratic principle. The relevant discussion on the domestic courts suggests as much.[254] Although the debate about the right intensity of judicial review (level of scrutiny) has been long established on the international level, it has found a new urgency within the framework of global governance.

The old discussion—conducted mostly under the state-oriented conception—was informed above all by state sovereignty. What was derived from this discussion, in the sense of the *Lotus* decision, is a presumption against obligations in international law.[255] This has direct repercussions on the intensity of judicial review, for example by the principle *in dubio mitius*.[256] Whereas for the classic conception of sovereignty domestic democracy is irrelevant, this changes in more recent contributions. Andreas von Staden has expressed it aptly:

> [A] standard of review would need to be sensitive to questions concerning the democratically appropriate level of decision-making with respect to

[254] In detail the contributions in Jochen Abr Frowein (ed), *Die Kontrolldichte bei der gerichtlichen Überprüfung von Handlungen der Verwaltung* (Springer 1993); Martin Kriele, 'Grundrechte und demokratischer Gestaltungsraum' in Josef Isensee and Paul Kirchhof (eds), *Handbuch des Staatsrechts der Bundesrepublik Deutschland*, vol 9 (CF Müller 2011) 183.

[255] In more detail see chapter 2 section A 1.

[256] *The Case of the SS Lotus (France v Turkey)* PCIJ Rep Series A No 10, 18; at times this is still argued today, see, for example, *European Communities: Measures Concerning Meat and Meat Products (Hormones)—Appellate Body Report* (16 January 1998) WT DS26/AB/R, WT/DS48/AB/R, paras 163–5.

> the specific issues governed by the agreement/norm in question and would counsel at least some deference where another level of decision-making appears democratically more appropriate. In other words, such a standard needs to operationalize what can be thought of as 'normative subsidiarity'.[257]

This argument picks up on reflections that develop sovereignty in the light of a democratically understood principle of subsidiarity.[258] Accordingly, the intensity of review concerns the question about the extent to which a court replaces the decision of the controlled institutions with its own decision.[259] On the one side is a review limited to obvious arbitrariness, on the other the complete replacement of the reviewed decision by a new decision on the part of the court.

Unlike the traditional principle of sovereignty, the democracy-oriented conception does not lay down any general presumption. Instead, the calibration of the intensity depends on the norms to be applied, the context, and the concrete case. Stephan Schill has offered proposals in a public law perspective using investment protection as an example.[260] First he draws a distinction according to the issue under review, in three respects: the establishment of the facts, the interpretation of the law, and the weighting of conflicting goods.[261] He lists the following as the criteria of calibration: the concrete formulation of the law to be applied, the concrete circumstances of the measure, the quality of the issuing organ in light of the democratic principle, the quality of the legal process that preceded the edict, the specific function of the international court (especially in relationship to the domestic judiciary), and the nature of the international obligation (that is, whether it is a negative or positive obligation). Yuval Shany's distinction between *inward-looking* and *outward-looking norms* is likewise pertinent. *Inward-looking norms* are those aimed at social interactions within the state. Here there is a presumption for a lower intensity of review. By contrast, *outward-looking norms* are those that belong to the law of coexistence and

[257] Andreas von Staden, 'Democratic Legitimacy of Review Beyond the State: The Need for an Appropriate Standard of Review' (2012) 10 Intl J Const L 1023, 1026.

[258] In more detail Isabel Feichtner, 'Subsidiarity' in Wolfrum (ed), *Max Planck Encyclopedia of Public International Law*, paras 16–30; see also Andreas Follesdal, 'The Principle of Subsidiarity as a Constitutional Principle in International Law' (2013) 2 Global Constitutionalism 37.

[259] In more detail Georg Nolte, 'Der Wert formeller Kontrolldichtemaßstäbe' in Frowein (ed), *Die Kontrolldichte bei der gerichtlichen Überprüfung von Handlungen der Verwaltung* 278; Eberhard Schmidt-Aßmann in Theodor Maunz and others (eds), *Grundgesetz: Kommentar*, vol 3 (CH Beck 2012) Article 19(4) paras 180–217.

[260] Stephan W Schill, 'Deference in Investment Treaty Arbitration: Re-Conceptualizing the Standard of Review' (2012) 3 J Intl Dispute Settlement 577.

[261] Similarly Jan Bohanes and Nicolas Lockhart, 'Standard of Review in WTO Law' in Daniel Bethlehem and others (eds), *The Oxford Handbook of International Trade Law* (OUP 2009) 378.

international law; here this presumption does not exist.[262] With the help of these kinds of doctrinal building blocks, one can calibrate the intensity of judicial review on the democratic principle.[263]

These proposals are not made in a vacuum; instead, they conceptualize developments in adjudication. Path-breaking is the ECtHR's concept of the margin of appreciation. Although it referred initially only to Articles 8–11 of the ECHR, many see it potentially as a general legal principle.[264] The fundamental *Handyside* decision certainly squares nicely with the democracy-oriented conception when it states:

> By reason of their direct and continuous contact with the vital forces of their countries, State authorities are in principle in a better position than the international judge to give an opinion on the exact content of these requirements as well as on the 'necessity' of a 'restriction' or 'penalty' intended to meet them.

What follows from this is

> a margin of appreciation, [...] given both to the domestic legislator [...] and to the bodies, judicial amongst others, that are called upon to interpret and apply the laws in force.[265]

Accordingly, the Court reviews whether the reasons indicated by the domestic institutions do sustain the concrete intervention and whether the intervention is proportionate to the (legitimate) goal; in short, whether the measure is suitable, necessary, and appropriate. The Court developed the elements of its review of proportionality in later decisions.[266] There is a broad discussion on the precise doctrinal and theoretical formulation of this doctrine which need not be elaborated here,[267] since it is not the doctrinal fine points that matter here but the conceptual foundations. Similar lines of

[262] Yuval Shany, 'Toward a General Margin of Appreciation Doctrine in International Law?' (2006) 16 Eur J Intl L 907, 920.

[263] For more detail see Daniel Halberstam, 'Constitutional Heterarchy: The Centrality of Conflict in the European Union and the United States' in Jeffrey L Dunoff and Joel P Trachtman (eds), *Ruling the World? Constitutionalism, International Law, and Global Governance* (CUP 2009) 326; Miguel P Maduro, 'Courts and Pluralism: Essay on a Theory of Judicial Adjudication in the Context of Legal and Constitutional Pluralism' in Dunoff and Trachtman (eds), *Ruling the World?* 356, 372.

[264] Shany, 'Toward a General Margin of Appreciation Doctrine in International Law?'.

[265] *Handyside v UK* (1976) Series A No 24, para 48.

[266] More recently for example *Lautsi and Others v Italy*, para 68; see Christoph Grabenwarter, 'Grundrechtsvielfalt und Grundrechtskonflikte im europäischen Mehrebenensystem' (2011) 38 Europäische Grundrechte Zeitschrift 229.

[267] Mireille Delmas-Marty, 'Marge nationale d'appréciation et internationalisation du droit: Réflexions sur la validité formelle d'un droit commun pluraliste' (2001) 46 McGill L J 923; Susan Marks, 'The European Convention on Human Rights and Its "Democratic Society"' (1995) 66 British YB Intl L 209, 218–21; Grabenwarter, 'Grundrechtsvielfalt und Grundrechtskonflikte'.

case-law, though with different conceptual approaches, are found in other courts—especially within the framework of the global economic governance, which is particularly tricky in light of democratic theory, given the deep contestedness of economic policy.[268] On the whole it can be noted that a conceptualization of an international judiciary on the basis of democratic theory, which pushes for a corresponding calibration of the intensity of oversight, encounters lines of adjudication that meet the argument halfway. We hope that our theory contributes to its understanding and development.

b) The use of soft law

Another way to strengthen the democratic legitimation of the international judiciary lies in the use of soft law. Our previous reflections on the selection process have yielded that international political bodies can generate democratic legitimacy for international courts if they define and apply the criteria for a good bench under the principles of transparency, participation, and deliberation.[269] We now pick this up and show that it can indeed help the democratic legitimacy of international courts if they resort to soft law developed in a way that heeds those principles.

Under the democracy-oriented conception, the lack of a fully fledged political system at the international level creates a major problem of legitimation.[270] It is against this background that soft law enacted by international institutions can become important when international courts use it to justify their decisions. To avoid misunderstanding, we are not arguing that soft law constitutes an easy answer to the democratic question. We are certainly aware of its democratic problematic because soft law usually circumvents national parliaments and is often justified on purely functional grounds.[271] Nevertheless, soft law has democratic potential for judicial decisions.

The ECtHR offers one important example. It bases its path-breaking pilot decisions on a resolution of the Committee of Ministers which calls upon the Court to identify systemic problems on the national level and to recommend how they may be solved. In other words, the committee invites the Court to tell a respective Convention state how it should change its laws.[272] Similarly, in the case of *Greens and M T v United Kingdom*, the Court relied

[268] See on arbitration Schill, 'Deference in Investment Treaty Arbitration'; on the WTO von Staden, 'Democratic Legitimacy of Review Beyond the State'; and for a more general approach Simon Hentrei, 'Generalising the Principle of Complementarity: Framing International Judicial Authority' (2013) 4 Transnational Legal Theory 419.

[269] See section A 3 and chapter 3 section C.

[270] See chapter 3 section B 2.

[271] Critically therefore Jan Klabbers, 'Undesirability of Soft Law' (1998) 67 Nordic J Intl L 381.

[272] *Broniowski v Poland* ECHR 2004-V, paras 190–1 with references to Committee of Ministers, *Judgments Revealing an Underlying Systemic Problem* (12 May 2004) Res 3 (2004) and Committee of Ministers, *Improvement of Domestic Remedies* (12 May 2004) Rec 6 (2004).

extensively on resolutions by the Committee of Ministers that were concerned with the implementation of an earlier, very similar decision (*Hirst*).[273] The committee had endorsed the earlier decision of the ECtHR, and the ECtHR then turned this endorsement into legal argument, legitimizing its new decision.

The ECtHR also makes use of decisions by other institutions, not only those by the Committee of Ministers. Especially important are opinions by the European Commission for Democracy through Law (better known as the Venice Commission), which was established by the Council of Europe as a body of independent experts to accompany the constitutional transformations in Eastern Europe.[274] Ever since, the Commission has been defining the common European constitutional standards which the ECtHR likes to invoke. For example, a Franco-Basque splinter party contested the decision by France's electoral commission which barred it from receiving support from the Spanish-Basque 'mother' party. In the decision, the ECtHR referred in detail to the work of the Venice Commission on party financing (especially the 'Guidelines on Party Financing')—not only the comparative legal parts, but also the political considerations and proposals.[275] Through such references, the Court develops the Convention rights according to political proposals by other institutions. The ECtHR is thus positioning itself as part of an international system with political institutions of law-making. However, it appears at first glance highly doubtful that such a resolution can convey democratic legitimacy to the Court's ruling. Indeed, in the case of the pilot judgment the representatives of the states were unable to agree precisely on establishing a procedure for pilot decisions by way of a new treaty. We come back to this problem after offering more evidence on the use of soft law by international courts.

Some legal decisions of the WTO serve as further cases in point.[276] One can find references to reports by the Committees on Agreement on Technical Barriers to Trade (TBT Committee) and the Agreement on Sanitary and Phytosanitary Measures (SPS Committee).[277] For example, in

[273] *Greens and MT v UK* ECHR 2010, paras 44–7.

[274] <www.venice.coe.int> accessed 22 November 2012.

[275] *Parti nationaliste basque—Organisation régionale d'Iparralde v France* ECHR 2007-II, paras 29–32. The guidelines of the Venice Commission in turn refer to a recommendation by the Committee of Ministers, *Common Rules against Corruption in the Funding of Political Parties and Electoral Campaigns* (8 April 2003) Rec 4 (2003), which the Court adopts. See also with a view toward the Venice Commission *Sejdić and Finci v Bosnia and Herzegovina* ECHR 2009, paras 17, 21–2, 48–9.

[276] Overview in Gregory Shaffer and Joel P Trachtman, 'Interpretation and Institutional Choice at the WTO' (2011–2012) 52 Virginia J Intl L 103.

[277] In detail Andrew Lang and Joanne Scott, 'The Hidden World of WTO Governance' (2009) 20 Eur J Intl L 575; Matthias L Maier, 'Normentwicklung durch WTO-Gremien am Beispiel von Handel und Gesundheitsschutz: Der SPS-Ausschuss' (2007) 68 TranState Working Papers 1.

the *US–Tuna* case, the Appellate Body decided the question of whether a member must regulate product labelling in accordance with international standards on the basis of a decision by the TBT Committee.[278] The Committee had spelled out in detail the provisions of the agreement. The Appellate Body used this committee decision without elaborating on its legal nature.[279] In so doing, it strengthened international political law-making.[280]

Again, such use is not unproblematic, especially under the democratic principle. On the contrary, it must be asked: what quality must relevant political decisions fulfil for their utilization to be legitimate? The *EC–Sardines* case is instructive. Here the Appellate Body decided that the European Community had to base the regulation of the sale of sardines on a standard from the Codex Alimentarius Commission. This Commission is a creation of the UN's Food and Agriculture Organization (FAO) and the World Health Organization (WHO). Its standards as such are not binding. However, the Appellate Body maintained that European legislation, because these standards are referred to in WTO law, had to display 'a very strong and very close relationship' to these international standards in order to be in conformity with the WTO.[281] One would expect a thorough argument for such elevation of a nonbinding standard. However, the Appellate Body did not discuss at all the genesis of this standard, nor the ground or reach of its validity. This silence is not persuasive for the simple reason that the European Community had already argued that such an interpretation turns international standard-setting bodies into 'world legislators'.[282] Even if that statement is overdrawn, a more precise examination of the issue was needed. The Appellate Body thus wasted an opportunity to spell out criteria for legitimate international standardization, in particular for an inclusive procedure in the Codex Alimentarius Commission.[283] Setting

[278] WTO Committee on Technical Barriers to Trade, 'Decision on Principles for the Development of International Standards, Guides and Recommendations with Relation to Articles 2, 5 and Annex 3 of the Agreement' in *Decisions and Recommendations Adopted by the WTO since 1 January 1995* (9 June 2011) WTO Doc G/TBT/1/Rev. 10, 46–8.

[279] *United States: Measures Concerning the Importation, Marketing and Sale of Tuna and Tuna Products–Appellate Body Report* (16 May 2012) WT/DS381/AB/R, paras 366–70.

[280] On law-making decisions in the WTO in detail Isabel Feichtner, 'The Waiver Power of the WTO: Opening the WTO for Political Debate on the Reconciliation of Competing Interests' (2009) 20 Eur J Intl L 615.

[281] *European Communities: Trade Description of Sardines–Appellate Body Report* (26 September 2002) WT/DS231/AB/R, para 245. Similarly *European Communities: Measures Concerning Meat and Meat Products (Hormones)—Panel Report* (18 August 1997) WT/DS48/R; *Hormones—Appellate Body.*

[282] See *European Communities: Trade Description of Sardines–Panel Report* (29 May 2002) WT/DS231/R, para 7.77.

[283] In detail Robert Howse, 'A New Device for Creating International Legal Normativity: The WTO Technical Barriers to Trade Agreement and "International Standards"' in Christian Joerges and Ernst-Ulrich Petersmann (eds), *Constitutionalism, Multilevel Trade Governance and International Economic Law* (Hart 2011) 383; Ingo Venzke, 'Technical Regulation and International Standards: The

such criteria is certainly compatible with the mandate of the WTO judicial bodies, as revealed by the case of the United States against India.[284]

The reasoning of other international courts also resorts to decisions of international organizations, and not only in relation to questions of interpretation, but also to the determination of facts. To that end, the ICJ makes use of resolutions by the UN Security Council and General Assembly.[285] Moreover, in questions of interpretation, international courts—and especially also the ICJ—use outcomes of the ILC, which is committed to the 'progressive codification' of the law. A good example can be found in the ICJ decision about Germany's immunity for war crimes, which repeatedly invokes the codification projects of the ILC.[286]

International courts evidently try to discharge part of their burden of legitimation by invoking the decisions of international political institutions. However, the democratic content of such decisions is not clear at all. Usually soft law is rather seen as an instrument of technocratic global governance. At this point, our theory walks a middle way between uncritical endorsement and categorical rejection. Following the path trodden with respect to the selection of judges, such decisions by political institutions can display democratic content. Transparency, participation, and deliberativeness must be carefully investigated. The use of international standards in the WTO reveals the problem as well as the possible solution, namely a heightened sensitivity to the quality of the processes by which standards are created. Rudiments of this are found in the *US–Tuna* decision, in which the Appellate Body rejected use of an international standard on the grounds that it was enacted by an exclusive rather than an inclusive institution.[287] With statements like these, international courts can help to further the development of political process beyond the state in light of democratic inclusion, contributing thereby to processes of democratic politicization.

EC-Trade Description of Sardines Case' in Sabino Cassese and others (eds), *Global Administrative Law: The Casebook*, vol 2 (3rd edn, Istituto di ricerche sulla pubblica amministrazione 2012) 7.

284 *India: Quantitative Restrictions on Imports of Agricultural, Textile and Industrial Products—Appellate Body Report* (23 August 1999) WT/DS90/AB/R, paras 8–28. Likewise Robert Howse and Petros C Mavroidis, 'Europe's Evolving Regulatory Strategy for GMO's—The Issue of Consistency with WTO Law: Of Kine and Brine' (2000–2001) 24 Fordham Intl L J 317, 325.

285 On the use of UN Security Council and General Assembly Resolutions by the ICJ see Marko D Öberg, 'The Legal Effects of Resolutions of the UN Security Council and General Assembly in the Jurisprudence of the ICJ' (2005) 16 Eur J Intl L 879.

286 *Jurisdictional Immunities of the State (Germany v Italy)* [2012] ICJ Rep 99, paras 55–6, 58, 89, and 93.

287 *US—Tuna II (Mexico)*, para 399.

c) Strengthening political processes

It can serve the democratic legitimation of judicial decisions if they contribute to the politicization of the international system. At first glance this claim might sound quite nonsensical: after all, the strengthening of international courts is hailed as the rolling back of politics within the international system.[288] However, such a contrast between juridicialization and politicization exists only if international politics is understood in the sense of the realistic tradition of international relations—that is, as the conflict-laden pursuit of one's own interests with all available resources of power. With such an understanding of politics, our thesis in fact makes no sense. An old but by now overcome understanding even posited that the presence of a political dispute excludes the jurisdiction of an international court.[289] It goes without saying that such a politicization cannot react to problems of international democratic legitimation.

Legitimatory potential exists with an understanding of politics that conceives of international politicization as the shared creation of legal normativity by political actors in multilateral procedures.[290] Even if such procedures cannot meet the standards of domestic democratic politics centred on parliamentary institutions, the internationally elaborated solution to a problem affecting the citizens of various states bears democratic potential.[291]

The question of democratic politicization is at the centre of Jürgen Habermas' theoretical writings on international law. His conception points far into the future by demanding the UN General Assembly be turned into a parliamentary assembly.[292] But even without realizing this ambitious project, there exists potential for an international democratic politicization.

Habermas is by no means alone with his demand for politicization. With a clear recognition of the legitimatory limits of judicial law-making, three former directors of the GATT and the WTO have also complained that the judicial process must not be overstretched.[293] The admonition by the

[288] See the contributions in Frowein (ed), *Die Kontrolldichte bei der gerichtlichen Überprüfung von Handlungen der Verwaltung*; Kriele, 'Grundrechte und demokratischer Gestaltungsraum'.

[289] Thus Hans Morgenthau, *Die internationale Rechtspflege: Ihr Wesen und ihre Grenzen* (Noske 1929).

[290] Ingo Venzke, 'International Bureaucracies from a Political Science Perspective—Agency, Authority and International Institutional Law' (2008) 9 German L J 1401, 1425. See chapter 3 section C 4.

[291] Mattias Kumm, 'The Cosmopolitan Turn in Constitutionalism: On the Relationship between Constitutionalism in and beyond the State' in Dunoff and Trachtman (eds), *Ruling the World?* 258, 296–301.

[292] Jürgen Habermas, 'Konstitutionalisierung des Völkerrechts und die Legitimationsprobleme einer verfassten Weltgesellschaft' in Winfried Brugger, Ulfrid Neumann, and Stefan Kirste (eds), *Rechtsphilosophie im 21. Jahrhundert* (Suhrkamp 2008) 360, 371.

[293] Arthur Dunkel and others, *Joint Statement on the Multilateral Trading System* (1 February 2001) <www.wto.org> accessed 21 November 2012.

former directors points to political processes of law-making in international organizations.[294]

Similar potential also opens up vertically in domestic administrative processes. In light of the democratic principle, it may be advisable for international courts to refrain from the substantive interpretation of a contested norm and instead derive from it procedural guidelines that lead to a discursive handling of the conflict by the parties. This approach is well developed for constitutional adjudication. A constitutional court can serve the democratic principle precisely by promoting a fair political process.[295] Accordingly, it can strengthen an international court's democratic legitimacy when it turns the handling of the question—multilaterally hedged—back over to the contending parties.[296] It is in this sense that an innovative interpretation of Article XX of the GATT is democratically relevant. The Appellate Body demands that a regulatory state accord procedural rights to actors from other states affected by its regulations.[297] The ITLOS has similarly created procedural rights of the flag state in the domestic procedures of the coastal state (Article 73 UNCLOS).[298] This approach pushes the parties to a conflict to resolve their dispute within a process under the guidance of international law and in the shadow of renewed judicial oversight. The democratic potential lies in various aspects. A lot of what used to be the object of a unilateral decision by one state affecting citizens of another country is now dealt with co-operatively. Affected citizens on the outside now have a voice, where they had none before. Power imbalances are mitigated through the multilateral framework. The domestic administrative procedure, too, opens up new possibilities for inclusion. Such, at least, is the view from the sunny islands of institutionalized multilateralism within the stormy sea of power politics.

[294] For an analysis of the potentials in various organizations see José E Alvarez, *International Organizations as Law-Makers* (OUP 2005); Armin von Bogdandy and others (eds), *The Exercise of Public Authority by International Institutions: Advancing International Institutional Law* (Springer 2010).

[295] John H Ely, *Democracy and Distrust: A Theory of Judicial Review* (Harvard UP 1980) 100; Habermas, *Between Facts and Norms* 263–4.

[296] See Andrea K Schneider, 'Bargaining in the Shadow of International Law: What the Normalization of Adjudication in International Governance Regimes Means for Dispute Resolution' (2009) 41 NYU J Intl L and Politics 789.

[297] *US–Gasoline* 22; *US–Shrimp*, paras 164, 167; in more detail Armin von Bogdandy, 'Legitimacy of International Economic Governance: Interpretative Approaches to WTO Law and the Prospects of Its Proceduralization' in Stefan Griller (ed), *International Economic Governance and Non-Economic Concerns* (Springer 2003) 103; Michael Ioannidis, *Due Process and Participation Rights in WTO Law* (CUP 2014, forthcoming); Terry Macdonald, *Global Stakeholder Democracy: Power and Representation Beyond Liberal States* (OUP 2008) 105–220.

[298] *The 'Juno Trader' Case (Saint Vincent and Grenadines v Guinea-Bissau)* (Judgment of 18 December 2004) ITLOS Reports 2004, 17, 38, paras 77, 102; on the need for circumspect justification in the development of the law by the ITLOS see Michael Wood, 'The International Tribunal for the Law of the Sea and General International Law' (2007) 22 Intl J Marine and Coastal L 351, 367.

5

In Whose Name?

A. COURTS AS ACTORS OF GLOBAL GOVERNANCE

Today, international courts are important institutions. As actors of global governance, they exercise public authority. They settle disputes and stabilize normative expectations—not only those of the contending parties, but of all subjects under international law. They make international law. Important fields are even predominantly shaped by case-law. Last and not least, international courts control other institutions both on a horizontal and vertical level, and can thereby also legitimize them.

Because of the multilevel character of contemporary politics, international courts are actors of not only *international* but also *global* governance. Even if we do not share the approach of a global law, which tends to merge international and domestic law, it is imperative to take into account the multilevel dimension of many international decisions. International adjudication not only impacts the international relationship between states, but also contexts within states, even if international decisions do not enjoy direct effect. One need only recall judicial decisions on expanding human rights, on taxing importers, and on compensating investors. What is more, many international disputes are triggered by internal political constellations or are instigated by private interests.

Precisely in this multilevel view, international adjudication's contribution to democracy comes clearly to the fore. Even if international courts do not protect all interests equally and sometimes even entrench asymmetries, their overall role in the juridification of international relations is uncontestable.[1] This juridification has a fundamentally pacifying effect on

[1] Martti Koskenniemi, *From Apology to Utopia: The Structure of International Legal Argument* (reissue, CUP 2005) 600–15; Esther Brimmer, 'International Politics Need International Law' in Emmanuelle Jouannet and others (eds), *Regards d'une génération sur le Droit International* (Pedone 2008) 113; Benedict Kingsbury, 'International Courts: Uneven Judicialisation in Global Order' in James Crawford and Martti Koskenniemi (eds), *The Cambridge Companion to International Law* (CUP 2012) 203.

international relations, which in turn by and large serves domestic democracy.[2] Moreover, given today's interdependence and corresponding externalities of domestic decision-making, international law and its courts can serve the democratic principle by opening up new possibilities of inclusion.[3] To that extent, our democracy-oriented conception regards the international judiciary, seen in its totality, as a major achievement. But even these systemic accomplishments do not obviate the question of how a specific decision is democratically legitimated which—for example—protects the private lives of one group at the expense of the freedom of press of another,[4] newly penalizes actions in internal conflicts,[5] or annuls amnesties agreed upon democratically.[6]

Of course, there cannot be one simple answer to that question, given the significant variance in how international courts participate in global governance. Among other things, such variance is due to the specific legal parameters, the widely different political contexts, or the very personalities of the judges who must converge on a decision. The heterogeneity within the international judiciary means that not all judicial bodies display the same problems of legitimation. The International Criminal Tribunal for the former Yugoslavia, established by the UN Security Council, certainly differs from the ICSID arbitral tribunals or the ECtHR in this regard. Imposing a prison sentence, drawing a maritime border, developing human rights, or specifying the prohibition against discrimination in economic law all differ deeply in their relevance to individual and collective self-determination and thus in their specific need for democratic legitimacy.

Accordingly, our public law theory of international adjudication, which spells out the democracy-oriented conception, relates back to positive law. It does not propose rigid guidelines of how to improve the democratic legitimation of international judicial decisions. It rather points out approaches that seem worth pursuing: greater deliberativeness in the selection of judges and the judicial processes, a democratically calibrated intensity of review, transparent and case-specific argumentation, a dialogic interconnection of courts, responsibility of domestic organs in the implementation, and judicial support for the development of relevant political processes. How a court reacts concretely to the democratic problematic in its decision, how 'progressive' or 'conservative' it is, whom precisely it gives access to the

[2] Jenny Martinez, 'Towards an International Judicial System' (2003) 56 Stanford L Rev 429, 461.

[3] See chapter 3 section C 4.

[4] *von Hannover v Germany* ECHR 2004-VI.

[5] *Prosecutor v Kupreškić et al* (Judgment) IT-95-16-T (14 January 2000) paras 521–36.

[6] *Case of Barrios Altos* Inter-American Court of Human Rights Series C No 75 (14 March 2001) paras 41–4; *Case of Almonacid-Arellano et al v Chile* Inter-American Court of Human Rights Series C No 154 (26 September 2006) paras 105–14.

judicial procedures, how it shapes the operative provisions and the reasoning of its decision, what kind of intensity of review it applies; all of these are questions of the judges' judgment. Abstract concepts—whether of positive law or theoretical—cannot replace their judgment. But they can certainly inform and perhaps even guide it.

B. IN WHOSE NAME, THEN?

Such guidance, though at a highly abstract level, is what the introductory formula 'In the Name of the People' proposes for many domestic courts. In whose name do international courts render their decisions? Very different formulas come to mind depending on the basic conception of the international judiciary. When understood as instruments of dispute resolution in a state-oriented global system, international courts decide 'In the Name of the Parties'. When seen as organs of the value-based international community, they decide 'In the Name of the International Community'. When conceived as institutions of specific legal regimes in an interdependent world, they decide 'In the Name of the Regime'. Of course, there are also compromise formulas. Particularly popular is the formula 'the International Community of States'.[7] What is the proposal that emerges from our democracy-oriented understanding further refined in a public law theory of international adjudication?

The international administration of justice is based almost entirely on international agreements and intergovernmental interaction. The active legal subjects are primarily those who qualify legally as *states*. Acknowledging and elaborating this feature, our approach first of all opts for an understanding according to which an international court refers back to the states that carry it. This means that it decides 'In the Name of the States'.

Already the formulation 'the States' indicates a great difference to the first conception, according to which courts decide in the name of the disputing *parties*. The notion of 'States' instead of 'Disputing parties' is intended to reveal that a decision is rendered in the name of *all* states that carry a court, and not just the parties to the case at hand. This designation thus testifies to the paradigm shift from bilateralism to multilateralism. Even with the arbitral tribunals of the ICSID or the PCA there are multilateral foundations that point beyond a narrow bilateral understanding.

The *democratic* dimension of 'In the Name of the States' emerges clearly in the logic of Articles 9–12 of the TEU. The reference to the states shows that domestically generated democratic legitimacy is indispensable for

[7] Thus most recently the President of the ICJ Peter Tomka in his address to the UNGA, Press Release No 2012/3 (1 November 2012) <www.icj-cij.org/presscom/files/8/17148.pdf> accessed 31 January 2014.

international adjudication. What is crucial here, however, is to focus not on the unitary subject of international law (in the sense of a horizontal, private law-inspired understanding of international law), but on the domestic constitutional system that generates democratic legitimation. International courts exercise international public authority, which leans on the legitimatory achievements of the domestic constitutional systems. The reference to the states is thus compatible with a citizen-based understanding of democracy. We have shown how that can inform and guide legal practice.[8]

To more clearly bring the democratic dimension to the point, we propose that international courts decide 'In the Name of the Peoples' instead of 'In the Name of the States'. After all, in the final analysis it is all about peoples, not about the apparatus of power or government, even if the latter represent a people. This formula has a solid legal foundation within the right of self-determination in international law. Given their international obligations, even authoritarian states—with the possible exception of the Vatican—can hardly disagree with this formula. Of course, it has a tendency that goes beyond the narrow understanding of the right of self-determination, which arises from its origins in the French Revolution.[9] It expresses the fundamental focus on citizens in a public law theory of adjudication. After all, *people* means the totality of the citizens.[10]

Still, a critical gap remains. Constantin Frantz, a political thinker of the nineteenth century, articulated it vividly. He championed supra-state federalism, though with a view toward monarchical legitimation. With respect to the administration of justice within the North German Confederation (1866–1871, the forerunner of the German empire created in 1870), he noted the following in the chapter 'Dissolution of the Prussian constitution'—it remains wonderfully fitting:[11]

> The situation is very different for courts, for whom it is crucial to state in whose name they administer the law. The monarchy must insist that it happens in the name of the king.[12] [...] Now the question arises in whose

[8] See chapter 4 section C 3.

[9] 'Les lois, décrets, jugements et actes publics sont intitulés: Au nom du peuple français', Constitution of 24 June 1793, Art 61 in J-H Bénard, *Table générale analytique et raisonnée du receuil général annoté des lois, décrets, ordonnances, etc, depuis Juin 1789 jusqu'au mois d'Aout 1830*, vol 3 (L'administration du journal des notaires et avocats 1840) 136.

[10] In more detail on this chapter 3 section C 2 a.

[11] Constantin Frantz, *Die Schattenseite des Norddeutschen Bundes vom preußischen Standpunkte betrachtet* (Stilke und van Munden 1870) 34–5; on his dazzling work see Manfred Ehmer, *Mitteleuropa: Die Vision des politischen Romantikers Constantin Frantz* (Tredition 2012); Michael Dreyer, 'Constantin Frantz: Der Außenseiter des Antisemitismus' in Werner Bergmann and Ulrich Sieg (eds), *Antisemitische Geschichtsbilder* (Klartext 2009) 39.

[12] Today it would have to say: 'The democratic state must guarantee that this happens in the name of the people.'

> name the new Supreme Commercial Court set up by the Confederation should speak? Probably in the name of the Confederation, from which it carries its own name. But where does that leave the judicial sovereignty of the king and the other princes of the Confederation? Or should the Court possibly speak in the name of the confederated princes and the free cities, which would give rise to the peculiar consequence that the Prince of Lippe would have a say in contested issues lying in Prussia. Or should justice be rendered in every instance in the name of those princes in whose lands the disputed issue lies, in which case the unitary nature of the Court would vanish. Or should it happen in the name of the Presidium of the Confederation, in which case it would go against the Constitution of the Confederation, which does not accord the Presidium any judicial authority. For this the constitution would have to be explicitly amended. But in that case the other Confederation princes would lose their judicial authority, which is now the only thing that can still impart to their position [...] some support and dignity. It would be the beginning of the formal mediatization. What to do? The Confederation has chosen the means of keeping silent about the core of the difficulty, to refrain from any explanation in whose name the new Supreme Commercial Court should administer the law. 'Speaking is silver, silence is golden', is an old saying. But the legislator should speak nevertheless, and it will solve no difficulty with its silence.

Constantin Frantz's troubles mirror today's void at the beginning of international judicial decisions: in whose name do they speak the law? Frantz's questions were answered 50 years later by the Weimar Constitution, under which the people took the place of the various monarchs. This hardly offers much of a prospect for today's international judiciary. Neither positive law nor other phenomena point to a world state or a global federation, forming a global people or nation. There is no reason to assume that the ICJ, ITLOS, the ICC, the panels of the WTO and the ICSID could be brought together under an expanded and democratically representative political umbrella of the United Nations or any other world organization. Much the same applies to the regional courts. The Council of Europe with Russia shows no tendency toward a federal organization of which the ECtHR would form a part. The same can be said about the Organization of the American States, which carries the IACtHR.[13] Even the few international associations guided by the example of the European Union struggle to assert themselves within

[13] On the potential in more detail Flávia Piovesan, 'Fuerza integradora y catalizadora del Sistema Interamericano de Protección de los Derechos Humanos' in Armin von Bogdandy and others (eds), *La Justicia Constitucional y su Internacionalización: ¿Hacia un Ius Constitutionale Commune en América Latina?*, vol 2 (Instituto de Investigaciones Jurídicas 2010) 431.

the reality of politics.[14] An international court that would conceive of itself as administering justice 'In the Name of the People', in the sense of all citizens of the world or the citizens of a regional organization, would totally miss its political and legal foundations. Accordingly, our democracy-oriented understanding does *not* advocate this.[15] There is no prospect that our questions about international adjudication today will be met by legal–political developments similar to those that resolved the issues with which Frantz was quarrelling.

Still, under the democracy-oriented conception, the ultimate point of reference must be the individuals whose freedom is shaped by judicial decisions, however indirectly. As we have shown, the concept of a transnational and a cosmopolitan citizenship has a basis in international law—a basis that can serve legal interpretation and further legal developments.[16] Individuals can be involved in a number of ways: as those affected indirectly or even directly by judicial decisions, as participants in transnational and global publics that engage critically with such decisions, or as members of transnational organizations that operate as actors in the procedures. In addition there are stateless individuals, refugees, and members of authoritarian states that are hardly represented by their government. They, too, are endowed by international law with rights that international courts must take into account, and not only in the dimension of protection.

Of course, a citizenship built on such elements is far weaker than a citizenship built on nationality, or than a supranational citizenship.[17] It is equally evident that international law today treats individuals in such a way that they are not reduced to their nationality. They possess rights and opportunities to participate in the exercise of international public authority. In that sense, it is indeed plausible to think of individuals as subjects of democratic legitimation in international law.

However, this point of reference is too weak legally, institutionally, and sociologically as to take the place of the peoples organized through the states. Such a step is not envisaged for the EU, even though union citizenship

[14] Ricardo Vigil Toledo, 'La contribución del Tribunal de Justicia de la Comunidad Andina al proceso de integración suramericana' in Armin von Bogdandy and others (eds), *¿Integración suramericana a través del Derecho? Un análisis interdisciplinario y multifocal* (Centro de Estudios Políticos y Constitucionales 2009) 397; Adriana Dreyzin de Klor, 'Las iniciativas de integración: el Mercosur jurídico' in von Bogdandy and others, *¿Integración suramericana a través del Derecho?* 441.

[15] It was already shown in chapter 2 section B that judicial decisions 'In the Name of the International Community' are also unable to fill this gap, since this community can be hardly thought of as a democratic subject.

[16] In more detail chapter 4.

[17] See chapter 3 section C 2 a.

offers a far stronger foundation. In agreement with important theoretical reconstructions, Articles 9–12 of the TEU point to a plural understanding.[18] We supplement our formula accordingly. International courts decide 'In the Name of the Peoples and the Citizens'.[19]

The doubling in the formula, *In the Name of the Peoples and the Citizens*, reflects the difficulties of new institutions aiming at larger collectives. These difficulties are well known from the history of public law. Constantin Frantz once again articulated them insightfully:

> One can throw the public law of a state into confusion with one stroke, but one cannot organize it anew with one stroke, least of all impart inner strength to the new order. [...] It is self-evident that political liberty cannot attain secure foundations with such rapid and repeated changes. In the present case there would be even less hope of this, because the Constitution of the Confederation, which is now displacing the Prussian one, is not targeted at political freedom, but at commercial freedom and freedom of movement. In the process, the political rights guaranteed by the Prussian Constitution lose their hold, without a replacement being offered.[20]

In contrast to Frantz, we do not regard our formula, which connects to both peoples and citizens, as the expression of conceptual uncertainty or of a transitional phenomenon. Rather, 'In the Name of the Peoples and Citizens' stands for a plural understanding of democratic legitimation. Even if not yet fully spelled out, it bears the greatest potential for legitimate international adjudication. That is also why we prefer this formula to the plain and catchier 'In the Name of the Citizens'. Such a formula, too, could be read so as to address citizens in their diverse roles: as citizens of the state, as citizens of the union, as citizens of the world.[21] Theoretically it may be possible to advocate such a concise formula, but it would be too far removed from the current legal structures. Moreover, it is by no means certain that in the end it is persuasive even as a mere regulative idea, for it has the tendency to obscure the pluralistic structure that a well-developed democratic legitimation of

[18] Differently, however, the proposal by Stephan Wernicke for the CJEU, 'Au nom de qui? The European Court of Justice between Member States, Civil Society and Union Citizens' (2009) 13 Eur L J 380: 'In the Name of the Citizens of the European Union'. See also the approach of Kalypso Nicolaïdis, 'European Democracy and Its Crisis' (2013) 51 J Common Market Studies 351.

[19] This formula has already been occasionally used. See Flavio Rodeghereo in Council of Europe, Parliamentary Assembly, *Official Report of Debates, 1999 Ordinary Session*, vol 1, 5. Given his party-political background (as a member of the *Lega Nord*), it is likely that Representative Rodeghereo associated a different understanding of democracy with this formula. With a similar thrust to ours, though a slightly different formulation and focus, Jürgen Habermas, *Zur Verfassung Europas: Ein Essay* (Suhrkamp 2011) 85: 'Staaten und Bürger'.

[20] Frantz, *Die Schattenseite des Norddeutschen Bundes* 36.

[21] This issue is central in the thinking of Habermas, *Zur Verfassung Europas* 66–8, 86.

international public authority requires. In addition, the short formula could stoke fears of global centralization of the kind that already troubled Kant.[22] From the perspective of our public law theory of international adjudication, international courts speak the law, even if they don't know it, *in the name of the peoples and the citizens.*

C. OUTLOOK

Our study has led to the conclusion that an international judiciary should be understood, interpreted, and developed with a dual reference to peoples organized by states and to supplementary forms of transnational or cosmopolitan citizenship. We think of this result as a contribution to basic research. Our concern is, first of all, of an analytical nature. We wish to grasp more precisely a widespread sense of unease about the legitimacy of international courts, and in so doing help to better formulate that unease in the first place. If we have advanced the reader's understanding of the problem, we have met an important goal.

Since legal scholarship is often meant to be eventually practical, we also put forth constructive proposals. Analysis and proposition have a shared conceptual foundation in the democracy-oriented basic conception of international adjudication. But problems in the proposals do not automatically call into question the analysis. The democracy-oriented conception we have put forth calls for yet more theoretical, doctrinal, and especially also empirical underpinning and development. Only three particularly important thematic areas shall be mentioned in conclusion that may further develop a public law theory of international adjudication. First, law-making by precedent depends not only on the will of the deciding court, but also on later courts and other actors. Now, in this book's discussions we argued against giving democratic relevance to the mere *acceptance* of decisions. However, democratically relevant *recognition* could result from the subsequent public debate—an important topic of future research. But given that judicial decisions are only rarely discussed among the general public, one would have to clarify simultaneously whether debates within legal scholarship should be regarded as democratically legitimizing.[23]

[22] Immanuel Kant, 'Über den Gemeinspruch: Das mag in der Theorie richtig sein, taugt aber nicht für die Praxis' in Wilhelm Weischedel (ed), *Werkausgabe*, vol 11 (first published 1793, Suhrkamp 1977) 125, 169.

[23] Pathbreaking on the quality of relevant juristic discourses see Peter Häberle, 'Die offene Gesellschaft der Verfassungsinterpreten' in Peter Häberle, *Verfassung als öffentlicher Prozess: Materialien zu einer Verfassungstheorie der offenen Gesellschaft* (Duncker & Humblot 1978) 155; see also Alexander Somek, 'Legal Science as a Source of Law: A Late Reply by Puchta to Kantorowicz' German L J (forthcoming).

In the process, particular attention should be paid to the mechanisms that transform a decision into a key decision, a leading case, with an especially potent influence in shaping the legal order.[24] At first glance, it is the discourse of interpreters that turns a decision into a key decision, a circumstance that could be of particular importance in terms of democracy. However, it has been demonstrated that such debates are often not very open and are also strategically 'orchestrated'.[25] Litigation strategy, too, is an important force behind the development of precedents. All these considerations, in short, lead to a wide field of sociological research of considerable normative relevance.[26]

A second important area of research concerns our assertion that successful international juridification frequently entails a need for international politicization. As a matter of fact, a number of judicial decisions draw on resolutions by international organs and committees. Therein lies great potential. Here, too, the preconditions under which one accords a democratic quality to relevant resolutions must be specified in greater detail.[27] After all, invoking resolutions whose legitimacy is dubious could in fact further exacerbate the democratic problem. We have shown how international courts can shift some of their burden of legitimation onto other institutions by using soft law. And this can also be formulated as a fundamental critique of the present book: when all is said and done, given the problems that beset international political processes, isn't it in the end better to be governed by international courts rather than international bureaucratic apparatuses? This question leads to a third thematic complex.

From a public law theory of international adjudication, international courts need to further develop mechanisms for transparency, participation, and deliberativeness. The potential of these principles must be theoretically consolidated, doctrinally concretized with respect to the specific characteristics of the various courts, and empirically tested. Important questions await a more detailed clarification conceptually and empirically. How can the tension between transparency and deliberativeness be resolved? How can the participation by interested parties be reconciled with the postulate

[24] On the mechanisms internal to courts, even if using the CJEU as an example, see Marc Jacob, *Unfinished Business: Precedent and Case-Based Reasoning in the European Court of Justice* (CUP 2014, forthcoming) 30–58, 144–70.

[25] For an illuminating study see Antoine Vauchez, 'The Transnational Politics of Judicialization: *Van Gend en Loos* and the Making of EU Polity' (2010) 16 Eur L J 1.

[26] Developing this further, Mikael Rask Madsen, 'Sociological Approaches to International Courts' in Karen J Alter and others (eds), *The Oxford Handbook of International Adjudication* (OUP 2014, forthcoming).

[27] For a detailed discussion see Isabelle Ley, *Opposition im Völkerrecht* (Springer 2014).

of political equality? What are the conditions under which the dialogue among jurists can be seen as part of a deliberating public?

Notwithstanding these and other uncertainties, we are convinced of the potential of the democracy-oriented approach. We hope to have shown its internal coherence, its close linkage with the positive legal material, its place in current research, and its potential for the understanding and development of the law. Comparatively, we do not see that the state-oriented, the community-oriented, and the regime-oriented conceptions offer any better answers to the question in whose name international courts render their decisions. The democracy-oriented approach, in spite of all difficulties and in spite of such utopian-sounding concepts as a transnational or cosmopolitan citizenship, offers a viable basis for theorizing and developing the democratic legitimation of international courts today. Our public law theory of international adjudication thus hopes to contribute to both political and scholarly debates across disciplines with the overall aspiration of strengthening the democratic legitimation of international courts' public authority.

Bibliography

Abbott KW and Snidal D, 'Hard and Soft Law in International Governance' (2000) 54 Intl Organization 421

Abi-Saab G, 'Cours général de droit international public'(1987) 207 Recueil des cours 9

Abi-Saab G, 'Les sources du droit international: Essai de déconstruction' in Rama-Montaldo M (ed), *El derecho internacional en un mundo en transformación: Liber amicorum en homenaje al Profesor Eduardo Jiménez de Aréchaga*, vol 1 (Fundación de cultura universitaria 1994) 29

Abi-Saab G, 'The International Court as a World Court' in Lowe V and Fitzmaurice M (eds), *Fifty Years of the International Court of Justice: Essays in Honour of Sir Robert Jennings* (CUP 1996) 3

Achenbach J von, 'Theoretische Aspekte des dualen Konzepts demokratischer Legitimation für die Europäische Union' in Vöneky S, Hagedorn C, Clados M, and Achenbach J von (eds), *Legitimation ethischer Entscheidungen im Recht: Interdisziplinäre Untersuchungen* (Springer 2009) 191

Afonso da Silva V, 'Deciding without Deliberating' (2013) 11 Intl J Constitutional L 557

Ainley K, 'The International Criminal Court on Trial' (2011) 24 Cambridge Rev Intl Affairs 309

Aldrich GH, *The Jurisprudence of the Iran–United States Claims Tribunal* (Clarendon 1996)

Alemanno A, 'Access to Information versus Privacy in the Process of Selection: Is There a Reasonable Middle Ground?' in Bobek M (ed), *Selecting Europe's Judges: A Critical Review of the Appointment Procedures to the European Courts* (OUP 2014, forthcoming)

Alter KJ, 'The Evolving International Judiciary' (2006) Northwestern Public Law Research Paper No 11-50 <http://ssrn.com/abstract=1859507> accessed 17 September 2013

Alter KJ, *The European Court's Political Power* (OUP 2009)

Alter KJ and Helfer LR, 'Nature or Nurture? Judicial Lawmaking in the European Court of Justice and the Andean Tribunal of Justice' (2010) 64 Intl Organization 563

Alter KJ, Romano C, and Shany Y (eds), *The Oxford Handbook of International Adjudication* (OUP 2014)

Alvarez JE, 'Rush to Closure: Lessons of the Tadic Judgment' (1997–1998) 96 Michigan L Rev 2031

Alvarez JE, 'The New Dispute Settlers: (Half) Truths and Consequences' (2003) 38 Texas Intl L J 405

Alvarez JE, *International Organizations as Law-Makers* (OUP 2006)

Alvarez JE, 'Implications for the Future of International Investment Law' in Sauvant KP (ed), *Appeals Mechanism in International Investment Disputes* (OUP 2008) 29

Alvarez JE, 'The Public International Law Regime Governing International Investment' (2009) 344 Recueil des cours 193

Alvarez JE and Brink T, 'Revisiting the Necessity Defence: Continental Casualty v. Argentina' (2010–2011) YB Intl Investment L and Policy 319

Alves Vestena C, 'Participação ou formalismo? O impacto das audiências públicas no Supremo Tribunal Federal brasileiro' (Rio de Janeiro 2010) <bibliotecadigital.fgv.br> accessed 21 September 2012

Anand RP, *International Courts and Contemporary Conflicts* (Asia Publishing House 1974)

Anderson K, 'The Rise of International Criminal Law: Intended and Unintended Consequences' (2009) 20 Eur J Intl L 331

Ando N, 'Permanent Court of Arbitration' in Wolfrum R (ed), *Max Planck Encyclopedia of Public International Law* <http://opil.ouplaw.com/home/EPIL> accessed 27 January 2014

Anoushirvani S, 'The Future of the International Criminal Court: The Long Road to Legitimacy Begins with the Trial of Thomas Lubanga Dyilo' (2010) 22 Pace Intl L Rev 213

Archibugi D, Koenig-Archibugi M, and Marchetti R (eds), *Global Democracy: Normative and Empirical Perspectives* (CUP 2011)

Arend K in Wolfrum R, Stoll P-T, and Kaiser K (eds), *WTO: Institutions and Dispute Settlement* (Nijhoff 2006), Art 10 DSU

Arndt F, 'International Parliamentary Assemblies' in Wolfrum R (ed), *Max Planck Encyclopedia of Public International Law* <http://opil.ouplaw.com/home/EPIL> accessed 27 January 2014

Arnim H von, *Stoicorum veterum fragmenta* 4 vols (vols 1–3 first published 1903–1905, vol 4 1924 by Adler M, GS Saur 2004)

Ascensio H, 'L'*amicus curiae* devant les juridictions internationales' (2001) 105 Revue générale de droit international public 897

Assmann J, *Cultural Memory and Early Civilization: Writing Remembrance, and Political Imagination* (CUP 2011)

Atiyah PS and Summers RS, *Form and Substance in Anglo-American Law: A Comparative Study of Legal Reasoning, Legal Theory, and Legal Institutions* (Clarendon 1987)

Augsberg I, 'Von einem neuerdings erhobenen empiristischen Ton in der Rechtswissenschaft' (2012) 51 Der Staat 117

Aznar-Gómez MJ in Zimmermann A, Tomuschat C, Oellers-Frahm K, and Tams C (eds), *The Statute of the International Court of Justice: A Commentary* (2nd edn, OUP 2012) Art 2

Ba AD and Hoffmann MJ (eds), *Contending Perspectives on Global Governance* (Routledge 2005)

Barkeley R, *Die deutsche Friedensbewegung 1870–1933* (Hammerich & Lesser 1948)

Barnett M and Finnemore M, 'The Power of Liberal International Organizations' in Barnett M and Duvall R (eds), *Power in Global Governance* (CUP 2005) 161

Bartels L, 'Applicable Law in WTO Dispute Settlement Proceedings' (2001) 35 J World Trade 499

Bast J, 'Das Demokratiedefizit fragmentierter Internationalisierung' in Hauke Brunkhorst (ed), *Demokratie in der Weltgesellschaft* (Nomos 2009) 185

Bates E, *The Evolution of the European Convention on Human Rights: From Its Inception to the Creation of a Permanent Court of Human Rights* (OUP 2010)

Bauer H, Huber PM, and Sommermann K-P (eds), *Demokratie in Europa* (Mohr Siebeck 2005)

Baum L, *Judges and their Audiences* (Princeton UP 2006)

Bell DA, *The First Total War: Napoleon and the Birth of Warfare as We Know It* (Houghton Mifflin Harcourt 2007)

Bellamy R, 'Die demokratische Verfassung' in Haller G, Günther K, and Neumann U (eds), *Menschenrechte und Volkssouveränität in Europa: Gerichte als Vormund der Demokratie?* (Campus Verlag 2011) 103

Bénard J-H, *Table générale analytique et raisonnée du receuil général annoté des lois, décrets, ordonnances, etc, depuis Juin 1789 jusqu'au mois d'Aout 1830*, vol 3 (L'administration du journal des notaires et avocats 1840)

Benda E, *Akzeptanz als Bedingung demokratischer Legitimität?* (Europa Union Verlag 1988)

Bentham J, 'Truth versus Ashhurst: Or, Law as It Is, Contrasted with What It Is Said to Be' in Bowring J (ed), *The Works of Jeremy Bentham*, vol 5 (William Tait 1843) 231

Benvenisti E, 'Margin of Appreciation, Consensus, and Universal Standards' (1999) 31 NYU J Intl L and Politics 843

Benvenisti E, 'Exit and Voice in the Age of Globalization' (1999–2000) 98 Michigan L Rev 167

Benvenisti E, 'The Conception of International Law as a Legal System' (2008) 50 German YB Intl L 393

Benvenisti E, 'Reclaiming Democracy: The Strategic Uses of Foreign and International Law by National Courts' (2008) 102 AJIL 241

Benvenisti E and Downs GW, 'The Empire's New Clothes: Political Economy and the Fragmentation of International Law' (2007–2008) 60 Stanford L Rev 595

Benvenisti E and Downs GW, 'National Courts, Domestic Democracy, and the Evolution of International Law' (2009) 20 Eur J Intl L 59

Benvenisti E and Downs GW, 'Prospects for the Increased Independence of International Tribunals' (2011) 12 German L J 1057

Benz A, 'Governance—Modebegriff oder nützliches sozialwissenschaftliches Konzept?' in Benz A (ed), *Governance—Regieren in komplexen Regelsystemen* (VS Verlag für Sozialwissenschaften 2004) 11

Benz W (ed), *Pazifismus in Deutschland: Dokumente zur Friedensbewegung 1890–1939* (Fischer Taschenbuch 1988)

Benzing M, *Das Beweisrecht vor internationalen Gerichten und Schiedsgerichten in zwischenstaatlichen Streitigkeiten* (Springer 2010)

Bergmann J, 'Das Bundesverfassungsgericht in Europa' (2004) 31 Europäische Grundrechte-Zeitschrift 620

Bernhardt R, 'Interpretation in International Law' in Bernhardt R (ed), *Encyclopedia of Public International Law*, vol 2 (Elsevier 1995) 1416

Bernhardt R, 'Evolutive Treaty Interpretation, Especially of the European Convention on Human Rights' (1999) 42 German YB Intl L 11

Bernhardt R, Steinberger H, Frowein J Abr (eds), *World Court Digest* vol 1 (Springer 1993)

Bernstorff J von, 'Zivilgesellschaftliche Partizipation in Internationalen Organisationen: Form globaler Demokratie oder Baustein westlicher Expertenherrschaft?' in Brunkhorst H (ed) *Demokratie in der Weltgesellschaft* (Nomos 2009) 277

Bernstorff J von, 'Procedures of Decision-Making and the Role of Law in International Organizations' in Bogdandy A von, Wolfrum R, Bernstorff J von, and others (eds), *The Exercise of Public Authority by International Institutions: Advancing International Institutional Law* (Springer 2010) 775

Bernstorff J von, *The Public International Law Theory of Hans Kelsen: Believing in Universal Law* (Dunlap T tr, CUP 2010)

Bernstorff J von and Venzke I, 'Ethos, Ethics, and Morality in International Relations' in Wolfrum R (ed), *Max Planck Encyclopedia of Public International Law* <http://opil.ouplaw.com/home/EPIL> accessed 27 January 2014

Besselink L, 'Niederlande' in Bogdandy A von, Cruz Villalón P, and Huber PM (eds), *Handbuch Ius Publicum Europaeum*, vol 1 (CF Müller 2007) 327

Besson S, 'Das Menschenrecht auf Demokratie—Eine moralische Verteidigung mit einer rechtlichen Nuance' in Haller G, Günther K, and Neumann U (eds), *Menschenrechte und Volkssouveränität in Europa* (Campus Verlag 2011) 61

Beyerlin U, 'The Role of NGOs in International Environmental Litigation' (2001) 61 Zeitschrift für ausländisches öffentliches Recht und Völkerrecht 357

Bianchi A, 'Textual Interpretation and (International) Law Reading: The Myth of (In)Determinacy and the Genealogy of Meaning' in Bekker PH, Dolzer R, and Waibel M (eds), *Making Transnational Law Work in the Global Economy* (CUP 2010) 34

Binder C, 'Die Veränderung innerstaatlicher Verhältnisse als Nichterfüllungsgrund von völkerrechtlichen Vertragsverpflichtungen: Welche

Rolle spielen demokratiepolitische und menschenrechtliche Erwägungen?' (2009) 47 Archiv des Völkerrechts 187

Binder C, 'The Prohibition of Amnesties by the Inter-American Court of Human Rights' (2011) 12 German L J 1203

Bobbio N, *Das Zeitalter der Menschenrechte: Ist Toleranz durchsetzbar?* (Wagenbachs Taschenbuch 1998)

Böckenförde E-W, 'Organ, Organisation, Juristische Person: Kritische Überlegungen zu Grundbegriffen und Konstruktionsbasis des staatlichen Organisationsrechts' in Menger C-F (ed), *Fortschritte des Verwaltungsrechts: Festschrift für Hans J Wolff zum 75. Geburtstag* (CH Beck 1973) 269

Böckenförde E-W, *Verfassungsfragen der Richterwahl* (Duncker & Humblot 1974)

Böckenförde E-W, 'Die Demokratie als Verfassungsprinzip' in Isensee J and Kirchhof P (eds), *Handbuch des Staatsrechts der Bundesrepublik Deutschland*, vol 1 (CF Müller 1987) 887

Böckenförde E-W, *Staat, Verfassung, Demokratie: Studien zur Verfassungstheorie und zum Verfassungsrecht* (Suhrkamp 1991)

Böckenförde E-W, *Staat, Nation, Europa: Studien zur Staatslehre, Verfassungstheorie und Rechtsphilosophie* (Suhrkamp 1999)

Böckenförde E-W, *Recht, Staat, Freiheit: Studien zur Rechtsphilosophie, Staatstheorie und Verfassungsgeschichte* (expanded edn, Suhrkamp 2006)

Bodansky D, 'Non Liquet and the Incompleteness of International Law' in Boisson de Chazournes L and Sands P (eds), *International Law, the International Court of Justice and Nuclear Weapons* (CUP 1999) 153

Bodendiek F, *Walther Schückings Konzeption der internationalen Ordnung: Dogmatische Strukturen und ideengeschichtliche Bedeutung* (Duncker & Humblot 2001)

Bodendiek F, 'Walther Schücking and the Idea of "International Organization"' (2011) 22 Eur J Intl L 741

Bogdandy A von, *Gubernative Rechtsetzung: Eine Neubestimmung der Rechtsetzung und des Regierungssystems unter dem Grundgesetz in der Perspektive gemeineuropäischer Dogmatik* (Mohr Siebeck 2000)

Bogdandy A von, 'Law and Politics in the WTO—Strategies to Cope with a Deficient Relationship' (2001) 5 Max Planck YB UN L 609

Bogdandy A von, 'Legitimacy of International Economic Governance: Interpretative Approaches to WTO Law and the Prospects of Its Proceduralization' in Griller S (ed), *International Economic Governance and Non-Economic Concerns* (Springer 2003) 103

Bogdandy A von, 'Globalization and Europe: How to Square Democracy, Globalization, and International Law' (2004) 15 Eur J Intl L 885

Bogdandy A von, 'Parlamentarismus in Europa: eine Verfalls- oder Erfolgsgeschichte?' (2005) 130 Archiv des öffentlichen Rechts 445

Bogdandy A von, 'Constitutionalism in International Law: Comment on a Proposal from Germany' (2006) 47 Harvard Intl L J 223

Bogdandy A von, 'General Principles of International Public Authority: Sketching a Research Field' (2008) 9 German L J 1909

Bogdandy A von, 'Pluralism, Direct Effect, and the Ultimate Say: On the Relationship between International and Domestic Constitutional Law' (2008) 6 Intl J Constitutional L 397

Bogdandy A von, Dann P, and Goldmann M, 'Developing the Publicness of Public International Law: Towards a Legal Framework for Global Governance Activities' (2008) 9 German L J 1375

Bogdandy A von and Dellavalle S, 'Ad hostes docere—Zu den Ursprüngen und zur Präsenz partikularistisch-holistischen Denkens' in Fischer-Lescano A, Gasser H-P, Marauhn T, Ronzitti N (eds), *Frieden in Freiheit: Festschrift für Michael Bothe zum 70. Geburtstag* (Nomos 2008) 847

Bogdandy A von and Dellavalle S, 'Universalism Renewed: Habermas' Theory of International Order in Light of Competing Paradigms' (2009) 10 German L J 5

Bogdandy A von and Jacob M, 'The Judge as Law-Maker: Thoughts on Bruno Simma's Declaration in the Kosovo Opinion' in Fastenrath U, Geiger R, Khan D-E and others (eds), *From Bilateralism to Community Interest: Essays in Honour of Judge Bruno Simma* (OUP 2011) 809

Bogdandy A von and Krenn C, 'On the Democratic Legitimacy of Europe's Judges: A Principled and Comparative Reconstruction of the Selection Procedures' in Bobek M (ed), *Selecting Europe's Judges: A Critical Review of the Appointment Procedures to the European Courts* (OUP 2014, forthcoming)

Bogdandy A von and Rau M, 'The Lotus' in Wolfrum R (ed), *Max Planck Encyclopedia of Public International Law* <http://opil.ouplaw.com/home/EPIL> accessed 27 January 2014

Bogdandy A von and Venzke I, 'Beyond Dispute: International Judicial Institutions as Lawmakers' (2011) 12 German L J 979

Bogdandy A von and Venzke I (eds), *International Judicial Lawmaking: On Public Authority and Democratic Legitimation in Global Governance* (Springer 2012)

Bogdandy A von, Wolfrum R, Bernstorff J von, and others (eds), *The Exercise of Public Authority by International Institutions: Advancing International Institutional Law* (Springer 2010)

Bohanes J and Lockhart N, 'Standard of Review in WTO Law' in Bethlehem D, McRae D, Neufeld R, and van Damme I (eds), *The Oxford Handbook of International Trade Law* (OUP 2009) 378

Bourdieu P, 'The Force of Law: Toward a Sociology of the Juridical Field' (1986–1987) 38 Hastings L J 814

Bovens M, Curtin D, and Hart PT (eds), *The Real World of EU Accountability: What Deficit?* (OUP 2010)

Bowett DW, 'The Court's Role in Relation to International Organizations' in Lowe V and Fitzmaurice M (eds), *Fifty Years of the International Court of Justice: Essays in Honour of Sir Robert Jennings* (CUP 1996) 181

Boyle AE and Chinkin CM, *The Making of International Law* (OUP 2007)

Brand U, Brunnengräber A, Schrader L and others, *Global Governance: Alternativen zur neoliberalen Globalisierung?* (Westfälisches Dampfboot 2000)

Brandom RB, 'Some Pragmatist Themes in Hegel's Idealism: Negotiation and Administration in Hegel's Account of the Structure and Content of Conceptual Norms' (1999) 7 Eur J Philosophy 164

Brimmer E, 'International Politics Need International Law' in Jouannet E, Ruiz Fabri H, and Sorel J-M (eds), *Regards d'une génération sur le Droit International* (Pedone 2008) 113

Broude T, *International Governance in the WTO: Judicial Boundaries and Political Capitulation* (Cameron May 2004)

Broude T, 'The Rule(s) of Trade and the Rhetos of Development: Reflections on the Functional and Aspirational Legitimacy of the WTO' (2006–2007) 45 Columbia J Transnational L 221

Brower CH II, 'The Functions and Limits of Arbitration and Judicial Settlement Under Private and Public International Law' (2008) 18 Duke J Intl and Comparative L 259

Brown C, 'The Evolution and Application of Rules Concerning Independence of the "International Judiciary"' (2003) 2 L and Practice of Intl Courts and Tribunals 63

Brown C, '"Reasonableness" in the Law of the Sea: The Prompt Release of the Volga' (2003) 16 Leiden J Intl L 621

Brown C, *A Common Law of International Adjudication* (OUP 2007)

Brown C in Zimmermann A, Tomuschat C, Oellers-Frahm K, and Tams C (eds), *The Statute of the International Court of Justice: A Commentary* (2nd edn, OUP 2012) Art 59

Brownlie I, *Principles of Public International Law* (7th edn, OUP 2008)

Brunhöber B, *Die Erfindung* 'demokratischer Repräsentation' *in den Federalist Papers* (Mohr Siebeck 2010)

Brunnée J and Toope SJ, *Legitimacy and Legality in International Law* (CUP 2010)

Bruns V, 'Völkerrecht als Rechtsordnung' (1929) 1 Zeitschrift für ausländisches öffentliches Recht und Völkerrecht 1

Bülow O, *Gesetz und Richteramt* (Duncker & Humblot 1885)

Bumke C, 'Publikumsinformationen: Erscheinungsformen, Funktionen und verfassungsrechtlicher Rahmen einer Handlungsform des Gewährleistungsstaates' (2004) 37 Die Verwaltung 3

Burca G de, 'Developing Democracy Beyond the State' (2007–2008) 46 Columbia J Transnational L 221

Burke E, 'Speech in the House of Commons against Pitt's Proposal for a Committee to Consider Parliamentary Reform (7 May 1782)' in Horn D and Ransome M (eds), *English Historical Documents 1714–1783*, vol 10 (Routledge 1957) 225

Burke-White WW, 'A Community of Courts: Toward a System of International Criminal Law Enforcement' (2002–2003) 24 Michigan J Intl L 1

Burke-White WW and Staden A von, 'Investment Protection in Extraordinary Times: The Interpretation and Application of Non-Precluded Measures Provisions in Bilateral Investment Treaties' (2007) 48 Virginia J Intl L 307

Caflisch L, 'Cent ans de règlement pacifique des différends interétatiques' (2001) 288 Recueil des cours 245

Cançado Trindade AA, 'International Law for Humankind: Towards a New Jus Gentium (I)' (2005) 316 Recueil des cours 9

Cançado Trindade AA, 'International Law for Humankind: Towards a New Jus Gentium (II)' (2005) 317 Recueil des cours 9

Cancik P, 'Wahlrecht und Parlamentsrecht als Gelingensbedingungen repräsentativer Demokratie' (2013) 72 Veröffentlichungen der Vereinigung der Deutschen Staatsrechtslehrer 268

Canivet Andenæs MT, Fairgrieve D (eds), *Independence, Accountability, and the Judiciary* (British Institute of International and Comparative Law 2006)

Cannizzaro E, *Il principio della proporzionalità nell'ordinamento internazionale* (Giuffrè 2000)

Canor I, *The Limits of Judicial Discretion in the European Court of Justice* (Nomos 1998)

Carazo Ortíz P, 'El Sistema Interamericano de Derechos Humanos: democracia y derechos humanos como factores integradores en Latinoamérica' in Bogdandy A von, Landa Arroyo C, and Morales Antoniazzi M (eds), *¿Integración suramericana a través del Derecho? Un análisis interdisciplinario y multifocal* (Centro de Estudios Políticos y Constitucionales 2009) 231

Caron DD, 'War and International Adjudication: Reflections on the 1899 Peace Conference' (2000) 94 AJIL 4

Carrubba CJ, 'Courts and Compliance in International Regulatory Regimes' (2005) 67 The Journal of Politics 669

Cass DZ, 'The "Constitutionalization" of International Trade Law: Judicial Norm-Generation as the Engine of Constitutional Development in International Trade' (2001) 12 Eur J Intl L 39

Cass DZ, *The Constitutionalization of the World Trade Organization* (OUP 2005)

Cassese A, 'Y a-t-il un conflit insurmontable entre souveraineté des États et justice pénale internationale?' in Cassese A and Delmas-Marty M (eds), *Crimes internationaux et juridictions internationales* (Presses Universitaires de France 2002) 13

Cassese A, 'The Rationale for International Criminal Justice' in Cassese A (ed), *The Oxford Companion to International Criminal Justice* (OUP 2009) 123

Cassese S, 'Global Standards for National Administrative Procedure' (2004–2005) 68 L and Contemporary Problems 109

Cassese S, 'Global Administrative Law: An Introduction' (2005) <www.iilj.org/GAL/documents/Cassesepaper.pdf> accessed 10 October 2012

Cassese S, *I Tribunali di Babele: I giudici alla ricerca di un nuovo ordine globale* (Donzelli 2009)

Cassese S, 'Die Entfaltung des Verwaltungsstaates in Europa' in Bogdandy A von, Cassese S, and Huber PM (eds), *Handbuch Ius Publicum Europaeum*, vol 3 (CF Müller 2010) 3

Charney JI, 'Is International Law Threatened by Multiple International Tribunals?' (1998) 271 Recueil des cours 101

Cheng B, 'United Nations Resolutions on Outer Space: "Instant" International Customary Law?' (1965) 5 Indian J Intl L 23

Chickering R, 'Total War: The Use and Abuse of a Concept' in Boemeke MF, Chickering R, and Förster S (eds), *Anticipating Total War: The German and American Experiences, 1871–1914* (CUP 1999) 13

Chinkin CM, 'The East Timor Case (Portugal v Australia)' (1996) 45 ICLQ 712

Chinkin CM in Zimmermann A, Tomuschat C, Oellers-Frahm K, and Tams C (eds), *The Statute of the International Court of Justice: A Commentary* (2nd edn, OUP 2012) Art 62

Cho S, 'Constitutional Adjudication in the World Trade Organization' (2008) Jean Monnet Working Paper <centers.law.nyu.edu/jeanmonnet/> accessed 9 December 2012

Christensen R and Fischer-Lescano A, 'Die Einheit der Rechtsordnung: Zur Funktionsweise der holistischen Semantik' (2006) 4 Zeitschrift für Rechtsphilosophie 8

Christensen R and Kudlich H, *Theorie richterlichen Begründens* (Duncker & Humblot 2001)

Christensen R and Kudlich H, *Gesetzesbindung: Vom vertikalen zum horizontalen Verständnis* (Duncker & Humblot 2008)

Christiano T, 'Democratic Legitimacy and International Institutions' in Besson S and Tasioulas J (eds), *The Philosophy of International Law* (OUP 2010) 119

Closa C, 'Citizenship of the Union and Nationality of Member States' (1995) 32 CML Rev 487

Cohen M, 'The Principle of Non-Intervention 25 Years after the Nicaragua Judgment' (2012) 25 Leiden J Intl L 157

Cohen-Eliya M and Porat I, 'Proportionality and the Culture of Justification' (2011) 59 American J Comparative L 463

Commission JP, 'Precedent in Investment Treaty Arbitration—A Citation Analysis of a Developing Jurisprudence' (2007) 24 J Intl Arbitration 129

Condorelli L, 'La cour pénale internationale: Un pas de géant (pourvu qu'il soit accompli . . .)' (1999) 103 Revue générale de droit international public 7

Corbett PE, *Law in Diplomacy* (Princeton UP 1959)

Costa J-P, 'On the Legitimacy of the European Court of Human Rights' Judgments' (2011) 7 Eur Constitutional L Rev 173

Craven M, 'Unity, Diversity and the Fragmentation of International Law' (2003) 14 Finnish YB Intl L 3

Crawford E, 'Proportionality' in Wolfrum R (ed), *Max Planck Encyclopedia of Public International Law* <http://opil.ouplaw.com/home/EPIL> accessed 27 January 2014

Crema L, 'Disappearance and New Sightings of Restrictive Interpretation(s)' (2010) 21 Eur J Intl L 681

Cruz Villalón P, 'Vergleich' in Bogdandy A von, Cruz Villalón P, and Huber PM (eds), *Handbuch Ius Publicum Europaeum*, vol 1 (CF Müller 2007) 729

Cryer R, Friman H, Robinson D, and Wilmshurst E, *An Introduction to International Criminal Law and Procedure* (2nd edn, CUP 2010)

Curtin D and Nollkaemper A, 'Conceptualizing Accountability in International and European Law' (2005) 36 Netherlands YB Intl L 3

Dahl RA, 'The Concept of Power' (1957) 2 Behavioral Science 201

Dahrendorf R, *Über den Ursprung der Ungleichheit unter den Menschen* (Mohr Siebeck 1961)

Daillier P, Pellet A, Forteau M, and Müller D, *Droit International Public* (8th edn, Librairie Générale de Droit et de Jurisprudence 2009)

D'Alterio E, 'From Judicial Comity to Legal Comity: A Judicial Solution to Global Disorder?' (2011) 9 Intl J Constitutional L 394

Damrosch LF, 'The Impact of the *Nicaragua* Case on the Court and Its Role: Harmful, Helpful, or In Between?' (2012) 25 Leiden J Intl L 135

Damrosch LF in Zimmermann A, Tomuschat C, Oellers-Frahm K, and Tams C (eds), *The Statute of the International Court of Justice: A Commentary* (2nd edn, OUP 2012) Art 56

Dann P, 'The Political Institutions' in Bogdandy A von and Bast J (eds) *Principles of European Constitutional Law* (2nd edn, Hart 2009) 237

Dann P, *The Law of Development Cooperation: A Comparative Analysis of the World Bank, the EU and Germany* (CUP 2013)

Danner AM, 'When Courts Make Law: How the International Criminal Tribunals Recast the Laws of War' (2006) 59 Vanderbilt L Rev 1

Danner AM and Martinez JS, 'Guilty Associations: Joint Criminal Enterprise, Command Responsibility, and the Development of International Criminal Law' (2005) 93 California L Rev 75

Dante Alighieri, *De Monarchia* (first published 1310–1314, Sumptibus Guiliemi Braumüller 1874)

Dante Alighieri, *Monarchy* (Shaw P tr, CUP 1996)

Danwitz T von, 'Funktionsbedingungen der Rechtsprechung des Europäischen Gerichtshofes' (2008) 43 Europarecht 769

Degenhart C, 'Gerichtsorganisation' in Isensee J and Kirchhof P (eds), *Handbuch des Staatsrechts der Bundesrepublik Deutschland*, vol 5 (3rd edn, CF Müller 2007) 726

Deitelhoff N, '(Is) Fair Enough? Legitimation internationalen Regierens durch deliberative Verfahren' in Niesen P (ed), *Transnationale Gerechtigkeit und Demokratie* (Campus 2012) 103

Delaney J and Magraw DB, 'Procedural Transparency' in Muchlinski P and others (eds), *The Oxford Handbook of International Investment Law* (OUP 2008) 721

Delbrück J, 'Law's Frontier—Walther Schücking and the Quest for the Lex Ferenda' (2011) 22 Eur J Intl L 801

Delmas-Marty M, 'Marge nationale d'appréciation et internationalisation du droit: Réflexions sur la validité formelle d'un droit commun pluraliste' (2001) 46 McGill L J 923

Denfeld C, *Hans Wehberg (1885–1962): Die Organisation der Staatengemeinschaft* (Nomos 2008)

Derrida J, 'Force of Law: The "Mystical Foundation of Authority"' (1989–1990) 11 Cardozo L Rev 919

Di Fabio U, 'Der neue Art. 23 des Grundgesetzes—Positivierung vollzogenen Verfassungswandels oder Verfassungsneuschöpfung?' (1993) 32 Der Staat 191

Di Fabio U, *Der Verfassungsstaat in der Weltgesellschaft* (Mohr Siebeck 2001)

Diggelmann O and Altwicker T, 'Is There Something Like a Constitution of International Law? A Critical Analysis of the Debate on World Constitutionalism' (2008) 68 Zeitschrift für ausländisches öffentliches Recht und Völkerrecht 623

Doehring K, *Völkerrecht* (2nd edn, CF Müller 2004)

Dolzer R and Schreuer C, *Principles of International Investment Law* (OUP 2008)

Donald A, Gordon J, and Leach P, *The UK and the European Court of Human Rights: Equality and Human Rights Commission Research Report 83* (Equality and Human Rights Commission Report Series Spring 2012) <www.equalityhumanrights.com/uploaded_files/research/83._european_court_of_human_rights.pdf> accessed 10 October 2012

Donaldson V, 'The Appellate Body: Institutional and Procedural Aspects' in Macrory PF, Macrory PFJ, Appleton AE, and Plummer MG (eds), *The World Trade Organization: Legal, Economic and Political Analysis*, vol 1 (Springer 2005) 1277

Dörr O in Dörr O and Schmalenbach K (eds), *Vienna Convention on the Law of Treaties: A Commentary* (Springer 2012) Art 31

Dreier H, 'Hans Kelsen (1881–1973): "Jurist des Jahrhunderts?"' in Heinrichs H, Franzki H, Schmalz K, and Stolleis M (eds), *Deutsche Juristen jüdischer Herkunft* (CH Beck 1993) 705

Drew C, 'The East Timor Story: International Law on Trial' (2001) 12 Eur J Intl L 651

Drexl J, 'Unmittelbare Anwendbarkeit des WTO-Rechts in der globalen Privatrechtsordnung' in Großfeld B, Sack R, Möllers TMJ, and others (eds), *Festschrift für Wolfgang Fikentscher* (Mohr Siebeck 1998) 822

Dreyer M, 'Constantin Frantz: Der Außenseiter des Antisemitismus' in Bergmann W and Sieg U (eds), *Antisemitische Geschichtsbilder* (Klartext 2009) 39

Dreyzin de Klor A, 'Las iniciativas de integración: el Mercosur jurídico' in Bogdandy A von, Landa Arroyo C, Morales Antoniazzi M (eds), *¿Integración suramericana a través del Derecho? Un análisis interdisciplinario y multifocal* (Centro de Estudios Políticos y Constitucionales 2009) 441

Drzemczewski A, 'Election of Judges to the Strasbourg Court: An Overview' (2010) 15 Eur Human Rights L Rev 377

Duguit L, *L'État, le droit objectif et la loi positive* (first published 1901, Moderne F preface, Dalloz-Sirey 2003)

Duguit L, *L'État, les gouvernants et les agents* (first published 1903, Dalloz-Sirey 2005)

Dunoff JL and Trachtman JS (eds), *Ruling the World? Constitutionalism, International Law, and Global Governance* (CUP 2009)

Dunoff JL and Trachtman JS, 'A Functional Approach to International Constitutionalization' in Dunoff JL and Trachtman JS (eds), *Ruling the World? Constitutionalism, International Law, and Global Governance* (CUP 2009) 3

Dupuy P-M, 'Le juge et la règle générale' (1989) 93 Revue Générale de Droit International Public 569

Dupuy P-M, 'A Transatlantic Friendship: René-Jean Dupuy and Wolfgang Friedmann' (2011) 22 Eur J Intl L 401

Dupuy P-M and Kerbrat Y, *Droit International Public* (10th edn, Dalloz 2010)

Dupuy R-J, 'Communauté internationale et disparités de développement' (1979) 165 Recueil des cours, IV

Ebsen I, 'Der Beitrag des Bundesverfassungsgerichts zum politischen Grundkonsens' in Folke Schuppert G and Bumke C (eds), *Bundesverfassungsgericht und gesellschaftlicher Grundkonsens* (Nomos 2000) 83

Eeckhout P, 'The Scales of Trade—Reflections on the Growth and Functions of the WTO Adjudicative Branch' (2010) 13 J Intl Economic L 3

Ehlermann C-D, 'Six Years on the Bench of the "World Trade Court": Some Personal Experiences as Member of the Appellate Body of the World Trade Organization' (2002) 36 J World Trade 605

Ehmer M, *Mitteleuropa: Die Vision des politischen Romantikers Constantin Frantz* (Tredition 2012)

Ehring L, 'Public Access to Dispute Settlement Hearings in the World Trade Organization' (2008) 11 J Intl Economic L 1021

Eick C, 'Die Anerkennung der obligatorischen Gerichtsbarkeit des Internationalen Gerichtshofs durch Deutschland' (2008) 68 Zeitschrift für ausländisches öffentliches Recht und Völkerrecht 763

Ely JH, *Democracy and Distrust: A Theory of Judicial Review* (Harvard UP 1980)

Engel NP, 'More Transparency and Governmental Loyalty for Maintaining Professional Quality in the Election of Judges to the European Court of Human Rights' (2012) 32 HRLJ 448

Enroth H, 'The Concept of Authority Transnationalized' (2013) 4 Transnational L Theory 336

Esfeld M, 'Funktion' in Kolmer P and Wildfeuer AG (eds), *Neues Handbuch philosophischer Grundbegriffe*, vol 1 (Alber 2011) 842

Eyffinger A, *The Peace Palace: Residence for Justice, Domicile of Learning* (2nd edn, Carnegie Foundation 1988)

Falk R and Strauss A, 'On the Creation of a Global Peoples Assembly: Legitimacy and the Power of Popular Sovereignty' (2000) 36 Stanford J Intl L 191

Fassbender B, *UN Security Council Reform and the Right of Veto: A Constitutional Perspective* (Kluwer Law International 1998)

Fassbender B in Zimmermann A, Tomuschat C, Oellers-Frahm K, and Tams C (eds), *The Statute of the International Court of Justice: A Commentary* (2nd edn, OUP 2012) Art 9

Fassbender B in Zimmermann A, Tomuschat C, Oellers-Frahm K, and Tams C (eds), *The Statute of the International Court of Justice: A Commentary* (2nd edn, OUP 2012) Art 54

Fastenrath U, *Lücken im Völkerrecht: Zu Rechtscharakter, Quellen, Systemzusammenhang, Methodenlehre und Funktionen des Völkerrechts* (Duncker & Humblot 1991)

Fehl C, 'Explaining the International Criminal Court: A Practice Test for Rationalist and Constructivist Approaches' in Roach SC (ed), *Governance, Order, and the International Criminal Court: Between Realpolitik and a Cosmopolitan Court* (OUP 2009) 75

Feichtner I, *The Law and Politics of WTO Waivers: Stability and Flexibility in Public International Law* (CUP 2012)

Feichtner I, 'Subsidiarity' in Wolfrum R (ed), *Max Planck Encyclopedia of Public International Law* <http://opil.ouplaw.com/home/EPIL> accessed 27 January 2014

Ferrarese M, *Le istituzioni della globalizzazione: Diritto e diritti nella società transnazionale* (Il Mulino 2000)

Fischer-Lescano A and Teubner G, *Regime-Kollisionen* (Suhrkamp 2006)

Fleischhauer C-A and Simma B, in Simma B (ed), *The Charter of the United Nations: A Commentary*, vol 1 (3rd edn, OUP 2012) Art 13

Folke Schuppert G, 'Verwaltungsorganisation und Verwaltungsorganisationsrecht als Steuerungsfaktoren' in Hoffmann-Riem W, Schmidt-Aßmann E, and Voßkuhle A (eds), *Grundlagen des Verwaltungsrechts*, vol 1 (2nd edn, CH Beck 2012) 1067

Follesdal A, 'The Principle of Subsidiarity as a Constitutional Principle in International Law' (2013) 2 Global Constitutionalism 37

Forst R, 'Transnationale Gerechtigkeit und Demokratie: Zur Überwindung von drei Dogmen der politischen Theorie' in Niesen P (ed), *Transnationale Gerechtigkeit und Demokratie* (Campus 2012) 29

Franck SD, 'The Legitimacy Crisis in Investment Treaty Arbitration: Privatizing International Law through Inconsistent Decisions' (2005) 73 Fordham L Rev 1521

Franck TM, 'The Emerging Right to Democratic Governance' (1992) 86 AJIL 46

Frantz C, *Die Schattenseite des Norddeutschen Bundes vom preußischen Standpunkte betrachtet* (Stilke und van Munden 1870)

Franzius C, *Europäisches Verfassungsrechtsdenken* (Mohr Siebeck 2010)

Fried AH, *Handbuch der Friedensbewegung* (Verlag der Österreichischen Friedensgesellschaft 1905)

Friedmann W, *The Changing Structure of International Law* (Stevens & Sons 1964)

Fromont M, 'Typen staatlichen Verwaltungsrechts in Europa' in Bogdandy A von, Cassese S, and Huber PM (eds), *Handbuch Ius Publicum Europaeum*, vol 3 (CF Müller 2010) 551

Frowein J Abr, 'European Integration through Fundamental Rights' (1984–1985) 18 U Michigan J L Reform 5

Frowein J Abr (ed), *Die Kontrolldichte bei der gerichtlichen Überprüfung von Handlungen der Verwaltung* (Springer 1993)

Frowein J Abr, 'Die traurigen Missverständnisse: Bundesverfassungsgericht und Europäischer Gerichtshof für Menschenrechte' in Dicke K, Hobe S, and Meyn K-U (eds), *Weltinnenrecht: Liber amicorum Jost Delbrück* (Duncker & Humblot 2004) 279

Frowein J Abr and Oellers-Frahm K in Zimmermann A, Tomuschat C, Oellers-Frahm K, and Tams C (eds), *The Statute of the International Court of Justice: A Commentary* (2nd edn, OUP 2012) Art 65

Fuchs J and Lattanzi F, 'International Military Tribunals' in Wolfrum R (ed), *Max Planck Encyclopedia of Public International Law* <http://opil.ouplaw.com/home/EPIL> accessed 27 January 2014

Fukuyama F, *The End of History and the Last Man* (The Free Press 1992)

Fyrnys M, 'Expanding Competences by Judicial Law-Making: The Pilote Judgment Procedure of the European Court of Human Rights' (2011) 12 German L J 1231

García-Salmones M, 'Walther Schücking and the Pacifist Tradition of International Law' (2011) 22 Eur J Intl L 755

Gee G, 'The Persistent Politics of Judicial Selection' in Seibert-Fohr A (ed), *Judicial Independence in Transition* (Springer 2012) 121

Gerber DJ, *Law and Competition in Twentieth Century Europe: Protecting Prometheus* (Clarendon 1998)

Geyh CG, 'Judicial Election Reconsidered: A Plea for Radical Moderation' (2012) 35 Harvard J L and Public Policy 623

Gill TD (ed), *Rosenne's The World Court. What It Is and How It Works* (6th edn, Nijhoff 2003)

Giovanni B de, *Alle origini della democrazia de massa: I filosofi e i giuristi* (Editoriale Scientifica 2013)

Goebel J, *The Equality of States: A Study in the History of Law* (Columbia UP 1925)

Goldmann M, 'Der Widerspenstigen Zähmung, oder: Netzwerke dogmatisch gedacht' in Boysen S, Bühring F, Claudio, Franzius C and others (eds), *Netzwerke: 47. Assistententagung Öffentliches Recht* (Nomos 2007) 225

Goldmann M, 'Inside Relative Normativity: From Sources to Standard Instruments for the Exercise of International Public Authority' (2008) 9 German L J 1865

Goldmann M, 'Arrest Warrant Case (Democratic Republic of the Congo v Belgium)' in Wolfrum R (ed), *Max Planck Encyclopedia of Public International Law* <http://opil.ouplaw.com/home/EPIL> accessed 27 January 2014

Goldmann M, *Internationale öffentliche Gewalt* (Springer 2014, forthcoming)

Goldsmith JL and Posner EA, *The Limits of International Law* (OUP 2005)

Goldstein J, Kahler M, Keohane R O, Slaugher A-M, 'Introduction: Legalization and World Politics' (2000) 54 Intl Organization 385

Góngora Mera ME, *Inter-American Judicial Constitutionalism: On the Constitutional Rank of Human Rights Treaties in Latin America through National and Inter-American Adjudication* (Instituto Interamericano de Derechos Humanos 2011)

Goodman R, 'Human Rights Treaties, Invalid Reservations, and State Consent' (2002) 96 AJIL 531

Gormley WP, 'The Development of International Law through Cases from the European Court of Human Rights: Linguistics and Detention Disputes' (1967–1968) 2 Ottawa L Rev 382

Grabenwarter C, 'National Constitutional Law Relating to the European Union' in Bogdandy A von and Bast J (eds), *Principles of European Constitutional Law* (2nd edn, Hart 2009) 83

Grabenwarter C, 'Grundrechtsvielfalt und Grundrechtskonflikte im europäischen Mehrebenensystem' (2011) 38 Europäische Grundrechte Zeitschrift 229

Grabenwarter C and Pabel K, *Europäische Menschenrechtskonvention: Ein Studienbuch* (5th edn, CH Beck 2012)

Grabitz E, *Gemeinschaftsrecht bricht nationales Recht* (Appel 1966)

Grabitz E, *Europäisches Bürgerrecht zwischen Marktbürgerschaft und Staatsbürgerschaft* (Europa Union Verlag GmbH 1970)

Grant RW and Keohane RO, 'Accountability and Abuses of Power in World Politics' (2005) 99 American Political Science Rev 29

Greenwood C, 'The Development of International Humanitarian Law by the International Criminal Tribunal for the former Yugoslavia' (1998) 2 Max Planck YB UN L 97

Gross L, 'International Court of Justice: Consideration of Requirements for Enhancing Its Role in the International Legal Order' (1971) 65 AJIL 253

Groß T, 'Postnationale Demokratie—Gibt es ein Menschenrecht auf transnationale Selbstbestimmung?' (2011) 2 Rechtswissenschaft 125

Grossman N, 'Legitimacy and International Adjudicative Bodies' (2009) 41 George Washington Intl L Rev 107

Grossman N, 'Sex on the Bench: Do Women Judges Matter to the Legitimacy of International Courts' (2011–2012) 12 Chicago J Intl L 647

Grotius H, *De iure belli ac pacis: Libri tres, in quibus ius naturae & gentium, item iuris publici praecipua explicantur* (first published 1646, Hein & Co 1995)

Grotius H, *De iure belli ac pacis libri tres: The Translation*, vol 2 (Scott JB ed, Kelsey FW tr, Oceana 1964)

Guéhenno J-M, *Das Ende der Demokratie* (Deutscher Taschenbuch Verlag 1996)

Günther K, 'Ein normativer Begriff der Kohärenz: Für eine Theorie der juristischen Argumentation' (1989) 20 Rechtstheorie 163

Günther K, 'Legal Pluralism or Uniform Concept of Law? Globalisation as a Problem of Legal Theory' (2008) 5 No Foundations <www.helsinki.fi/nofo/NoFo5Gunther.pdf> accessed 23 September 2013

Guzmán AT, *How International Law Works: A Rational Choice Theory* (OUP 2008)

Haack S, 'Demokratie mit Zukunft?' (2012) 67 Juristenzeitung 753

Haas EB, *Beyond the Nation-State: Functionalism and International Organization* (Stanford UP 1964)

Häberle P, 'Die offene Gesellschaft der Verfassungsinterpreten' in Häberle P, *Verfassung als öffentlicher Prozess: Materialien zu einer Verfassungstheorie der offenen Gesellschaft* (Duncker & Humblot 1978) 155

Habermas J, *Between Facts and Norms: Contributions to a Discourse Theory of Law and Democracy* (Rehg W tr, Polity Press 1997)

Habermas J, *The Postnational Constellation: Political Essays* (Pensky M tr/ed, MIT Press 2001)

Habermas J, 'Concluding Comments on Empirical Approaches to Deliberative Politics' (2005) 40 Acta Politica 384

Habermas J, 'Does the Constitutionalization of International Law Still Have a Chance?' in Habermas J, *The Divided West* (Cronin C tr/ed, Polity Press 2006) 115

Habermas J, 'Konstitutionalisierung des Völkerrechts und die Legitimationsprobleme einer verfassten Weltgesellschaft' in Brugger W, Neummann U, and Kirste S (eds), *Rechtsphilosophie im 21. Jahrhundert* (Suhrkamp 2008) 360

Habermas J, *Zur Verfassung Europas: Ein Essay* (Suhrkamp 2011)

Halberstam D, 'Constitutional Heterarchy: The Centrality of Conflict in the European Union and the United States' in Dunoff JL and Trachtman JP (eds), *Ruling the World? Constitutionalism, International Law, and Global Governance* (CUP 2009) 326

Halberstam D, 'Local, Global, and Plural Constitutionalism: Europe Meets the World' in de Búrca G and Weiler JHH (eds), *The Worlds of European Constitutionalism* (CUP 2012) 150

Haller G, 'Einführung' in Haller G, Günther K, and Neumann U (eds), *Menschenrechte und Volkssouveränität in Europa* (Campus Verlag 2011) 11

Haltern UR, *Verfassungsgerichtsbarkeit, Demokratie und Misstrauen: Das Bundesverfassungsgericht in einer Verfassungstheorie zwischen Populismus und Progressivismus* (Duncker & Humblot 1998)

Hambro E, 'Dissenting and Individual Opinions in the International Court of Justice' (1956–1957) 17 Zeitschrift für ausländisches öffentliches Recht und Völkerrecht 229

Handler Chayes A and Chayes A, *The New Sovereignty: Compliance with International Regulatory Agreements* (Harvard UP 1995)

Hanebeck A, *Der demokratische Bundesstaat des Grundgesetzes* (Duncker & Humblot 2004)

Hart HLA, *The Concept of Law* (2nd edn, Clarendon 1994)

Hauser H, 'Domestic Policy Foundation and Domestic Policy Function of International Trade Rules' (1986) 41 Aussenwirtschaft 171

Hegel GWF, *Outlines of the Philosophy of Right* (Knox TM tr, OUP 2008)

Held D and Koenig-Archibugi M (eds), *Global Governance and Public Accountability* (Blackwell 2005)

Helfer LR and Slaughter A-M, 'Toward a Theory of Effective Supranational Adjudication' (1997–1998) 107 Yale L J 273

Helfer LR and Slaughter A-M, 'Why States Create International Tribunals: A Response to Professors Posner and Yoo' (2005) 93 California L Rev 899

Heller H, *Staatslehre* (Sijthoff 1934)

Hentrei S, 'Generalising the Principle of Complementarity: Framing International Judicial Authority' (2013) 4 Transnational Legal Theory 419

Heuschling L, 'Frankreich' in Bogdandy A von, Cruz Villalón P, and Huber PM (eds), *Handbuch Ius Publicum Europaeum*, vol 2 (CF Müller 2008) 491

Hewson M and Sinclair TJ, 'The Emergence of Global Governance Theory' in Hewson M and Sinclair TJ (eds), *Approaches to Global Governance Theory* (State University of New York Press 1999) 3

Heywood Anderson D, 'Prompt Release of Vessels and Crews' in Wolfrum R (ed), *Max Planck Encyclopedia of Public International Law* <http://opil.ouplaw.com/home/EPIL> accessed 27 January 2014

Higgins R, 'A Babel of Judicial Voices? Rumination from the Bench' (2006) 55 ICLQ 791

Hilf M, 'Das Streitbeilegungssystem der WTO' in Hilf M and Oeter S (eds), *WTO-Recht: Rechtsordnung des Welthandels* (Nomos 2005) 505

Hilf M and Reuß M, 'Verfassungsfragen lebensmittelrechtlicher Normierung im europäischen und internationalen Recht' (1997) 24 Zeitschrift für das gesamte Lebensmittelrecht 289

Hirschl R, *Towards Juristocracy: The Origins and Consequences of the New Constitutionalism* (Harvard UP 2004)

Hobe S, 'Die Zukunft des Völkerrechts im Zeitalter der Globalisierung: Perspektiven der Völkerrechtsentwicklung im 21. Jahrhundert' (1999) 37 Archiv des Völkerrechts 253

Hoffmeister F in Dörr O and Schmalenbach K (eds), *Vienna Convention on the Law of Treaties: A Commentary* (Springer 2012) Arts 9–11

Hofmann H, *Repräsentation: Studien zur Wort- und Begriffsgeschichte von der Antike bis ins 19. Jahrhundert* (4th edn, Duncker & Humblot 2003)

Hofmann M, *Von der Transformation zur Kooperationsoffenheit? Die Öffnung der Rechtsordnungen ausgewählter Staaten Mittel- und Osteuropas für das Völker- und Europarecht* (Springer 2009)

Hofmann R, 'Die Rechtskontrolle von Organen der Staatengemeinschaft' (2007) 42 Berichte der Deutschen Gesellschaft für Völkerrecht 1

Hofmann R and Laubner T in Zimmermann A, Tomuschat C, Oellers-Frahm K, and Tams C (eds), *The Statute of the International Court of Justice: A Commentary* (2nd edn, OUP 2012) Art 57

Hong QL, 'Constitutional Review in the Mega-Leviathan: A Democratic Foundation for the European Court of Justice' (2010) 16 Eur L J 695

Hoss C, 'Satisfaction' in Wolfrum R (ed), *Max Planck Encyclopedia of Public International Law* <http://opil.ouplaw.com/home/EPIL> accessed 27 January 2014

Hoss C, Villalpando S, and Sivakumaran S, 'Nicaragua: 25 Years Later' (2012) 25 Leiden J Intl L 131

Howse R, *Enforcing International Trade Law: The Evolution of the Modern GATT Legal System* (Butterworth 1993)

Howse R, 'The Legitimacy of the World Trade Organization' in Coicaud J-M and Heiskanen V (eds), *The Legitimacy of International Organizations* (United Nations UP 2001) 355

Howse R, 'Membership and its Privileges: the WTO, Civil Society, and the *Amicus* Brief Controversy' (2003) 9 Eur L J 496

Howse R, 'A New Device for Creating International Legal Normativity: The WTO Technical Barriers to Trade Agreement and "International Standards"' in Joerges C and Petersmann E-U (eds), *Constitutionalism, Multilevel Trade Governance and Social Regulation* (Hart 2006) 383

Howse R, 'Moving the WTO Forward—One Case at a Time' (2009) 42 Cornell Intl L J 223

Howse R, 'A New Device for Creating International Legal Normativity: The WTO Technical Barriers to Trade Agreement and "International Standards"' in Joerges C and Petersmann E-U (eds), *Constitutionalism, Multilevel Trade Governance and International Economic Law* (Hart 2011) 383

Howse R, and Kalypso Nicolaïdis, 'Legitimacy and Global Governance: Why Constitutionalizing the WTO Is a Step Too Far' in Porter RB, Sauvé P, Subramanian A, and Zampetti AB (eds), *Efficiency, Equity, and Legitimacy: The Multilateral Trading System at the Millenium* (Brookings Institution Press 2001) 227

Howse R and Mavroidis PC, 'Europe's Evolving Regulatory Strategy for GMO's—The Issue of Consistency with WTO Law: Of Kine and Brine' (2000–2001) 24 Fordham Intl L J 317

Howse R and Teitel R, 'Delphic Dictum: How Has the ICJ Contributed to the Global Rule of Law by its Ruling on Kosovo?' (2010) 11 German L J 841

Hudec RE, 'The GATT Legal System: A Diplomat's Jurisprudence' (1970) 4 Journal of World Trade 615

Hudson MO, 'The Permanent Court of International Justice—An Indispensable First Step' (1923) 108 Annals of the American Academy of Political and Social Science 188

Hudson MO, *International Tribunals: Past and Future* (Carnegie Endowment for International Peace and Brookings Institution 1944)

Hudson MO, *Progress in International Organization* (Fred B Rothman & Co 1981)

Ioannidis M, 'A Procedural Approach to the Legitimacy of International Adjudication: Developing Standards of Participation in WTO Law' (2011) 12 German L J 1175

Ioannidis M, *Due Process and Participation Rights in WTO Law* (CUP 2014, forthcoming)

Ipsen HP and Nicolaysen G, 'Haager Konferenz für Europarecht und Bericht über die aktuelle Entwicklung des Gemeinschaftsrechts' (1964) 18 Neue Juristische Wochenschrift 339

Irwin DA and Weiler JHH, 'Measures Affecting the Cross-Border Supply of Gambling and Betting Services (DS 285)' (2008) 7 World Trade Rev 71

Jackson JH, *The World Trade Organization: Constitution and Jurisprudence* (Royal Institute of International Affairs 1998)

Jackson JH, 'The Case of the World Trade Organization' (2008) 84 Intl Affairs 437

Jacob M, 'Precedents: Lawmaking Through International Adjudication' (2011) 12 German L J 1005

Jacob M, *Unfinished Business: Precedent and Case-Based Reasoning in the European Court of Justice* (CUP 2014, forthcoming)

Jackson VC, 'Judicial Independence: Structure, Context, Attitude' in Seibert-Fohr A (ed), *Judicial Independence in Transition* (Springer 2012) 19

Jakab A, 'Probleme der Stufenbaulehre' (2005) 91 Archiv für Rechts- und Sozialphilosophie 333

Jellinek G, *Allgemeine Staatslehre* (3rd edn, Häring 1914)

Jenks CW, 'The Conflict of Law-Making Treaties' (1953) 30 British YB Intl L 401

Jenks CW, *The Prospects of International Adjudication* (Stevens & Sons 1964)

Jennings RY in Zimmermann A, Tomuschat C, and Oellers-Frahm K, (eds), *The Statute of the International Court of Justice* (OUP 2006) General Introduction

Jhering R von, *Der Zweck im Recht*, vol 1 and 2 (4th edn, Breitkopf und Haertel 1904)

Jhering R von, *Law as a Means to an End* (Isaak Husik tr, Boston Book Company 1913)

Jouannet E, 'Actualité des questions d'indépendance et d'impartialité des juridictions internationales: la consolidation d'un tiers pouvoir international?' in Ruiz Fabri H and Sorel J-M (eds), *Indépendance et impartialité des juges internationaux* (Editions A Pedone 2010) 271

Joannet E, *Vattel and the Emergence of Classic International Law* (Bellande G and Howse R trs, Hart 2012)

Joyce D, 'The Historical Function of International Criminal Trials: Re-Thinking International Criminal Law' (2004) 73 Nordic J Intl L 461

Junne G, 'Theorien über Konflikte und Kooperation zwischen kapitalistischen Industrieländern' in Rittberger V (ed), *Theorien der Internationalen Beziehungen* (Westdeutscher Verlag 1990) 353

Kaltefleiter W and Pfaltzgraff RL (eds), *The Peace Movements in Europe and the United States* (Croom Helm 1985)

Kamto M, Thouvenin J-M, Szurek Sin Corten O and Klein P (eds), *The Vienna Convention on the Law of Treaties: A Commentary*, vol 1 (OUP 2011) Arts 9–11

Kant I, *Critique of Pure Reason* (Guyer P and Wood AW trs/eds, first published 1781, CUP 1999)

Kant I, 'Idee zu einer allgemeinen Geschichte in weltbürgerlicher Absicht' in Vorländer K (ed), *Kleinere Schriften zur Geschichtsphilosophie, Ethik und Politik* (first published 1784, Felix Meiner 1964) 3

Kant I, 'Über den Gemeinspruch: Das mag in der Theorie richtig sein, taugt aber nicht für die Praxis' in Weischedel W (ed), *Werkausgabe*, vol 11 (first published 1793, Suhrkamp 1977) 125

Kant I, *Perpetual Peace: A Philosophical Proposal* (Buckland JH tr, first published 1795/1796, Sweet & Maxwell 1927)

Kapeliuk D, 'The Repeat Appointment Factor: Exploring Decision Patterns of Elite Investment Arbitrators' (2010) 96 Cornell L Rev 47

Keller H and Stone Sweet A (eds), *A Europe of Rights: The Impact of the ECHR on National Legal Systems* (OUP 2008)

Kelsen H, *Hauptprobleme der Staatsrechtslehre entwickelt aus der Lehre vom Rechtssatze* (2nd edn, Mohr Siebeck 1923)

Kelsen H, 'Wesen und Entwicklung der Staatsgerichtsbarkeit' (1929) 5 Veröffentlichungen der Vereinigung der Deutschen Staatsrechtslehrer 30

Kelsen H, *Vom Wesen und Wert der Demokratie* (2nd edn, Mohr Siebeck 1929)

Kelsen H, 'International Peace—By Court or Government?' (1941) 46 American J of Sociology 571

Kelsen H, *Law and Peace in International Relations: The Oliver Wendell Holmes Lectures, 1940–41* (Harvard UP 1942)

Kelsen H, *Peace Through Law* (The University of North Carolina Press 1944)

Kelsen H, *Introduction to the Problems of Legal Theory* (Litschewski Paulson B and Paulson SL trs, Clarendon 1992)

Kennedy David, 'Theses about International Law Discourse' (1980) 23 German YB Intl L 353

Kennedy David, 'The Move to Institutions' (1986–1987) 8 Cardozo L Rev 841

Kennedy David, 'The Politics of the Invisible College: International Governance and the Politics of Expertise' (2001) 6 Eur Human Rights L Rev 463

Kennedy David, *The Dark Sides of Virtue: Reassessing International Humanitarianism* (Princeton UP 2004)

Kennedy David, *Of War and Law* (Princeton UP 2006)

Kennedy Duncan, *A Critique of Adjudication: Fin de siècle* (Harvard UP 1997)

Keohane RO, Moravcsik A, and Slaughter A-M, 'Legalized Dispute Resolution: Interstate and Transnational' (2000) 54 Intl Organization 457

Keohane RO and Nye J, *Power and Interdependence: World Politics in Transition* (Little Brown and Company 1977)

Kingsbury B, 'Sovereignty and Inequality' (1998) 9 Eur J Intl L 599

Kingsbury B, 'Foreword: Is the Proliferation of International Courts and Tribunals a Systemic Problem?' (1999) 31 NYU J Intl L and Politics 679

Kingsbury B, 'International Courts: Uneven Judicialization in Global Order' in Crawford J and Koskenniemi M (eds), *Cambridge Companion to International Law* (CUP 2012) 203

Kingsbury B, Krisch N, and Stewart RB, 'The Emergence of Global Administrative Law' (2005) 68 L and Contemporary Problems 15

Kirchner C, 'Zur konsequentialistischen Interpretationsmethode' in Eger T and Schäfer H-B (eds), *Internationalisierung des Rechts und seine ökonomische Analyse: Festschrift für Hans-Bernd Schäfer zum 65. Geburtstag* (Gabler Edition Wissenschaft 2008) 37

Kissling C, 'Repräsentativ-parlamentarische Entwürfe globaler Demokratiegestaltung im Laufe der Zeit: Eine rechtspolitische Ideengeschichte' (2005) Forum Historiae Iuris < http://www.forhistiur.de/index_de.htm> accessed 19 September 2012

Klabbers J, 'Undesirability of Soft Law' (1998) 67 Nordic J Intl L 381

Klabbers J, 'Constitutionalism Lite' (2004) 1 Intl Organizations L Rev 31

Klabbers J, *An Introduction to International Institutional Law* (2nd edn, CUP 2009)

Klabbers J, 'Setting the Scene' in Klabbers J, Peters A, and Ulfstein G, *The Constitutionalization of International Law* (OUP 2009) 1

Klabbers J, 'Controlling International Bureaucracies' in *IILJ International Legal Theory Colloquium Spring 2010* <iilj.org/courses/documents/2010Colloquium.Klabberpp.pdf> accessed 19 September 2012

Klabbers J, Peters A, and Ulfstein G, *The Constitutionalization of International Law* (OUP 2009)

Klatt M, *Making the Law Explicit: The Normativity of Legal Argumentation* (Hart 2008)

Kleinlein T, *Konstitutionalisierung im Völkerrecht: Konstruktion und Elemente einer idealistischen Völkerrechtslehre* (Springer 2012)

Kneisel S, *Schiedsgerichtsbarkeit in internationalen Verwaltungsunionen (1874-1914)* (Nomos 2009)

Koch H-J and Rüßmann H, *Juristische Begründungslehre: Eine Einführung in die Grundprobleme der Rechtswissenschaft* (CH Beck 1982)

Kohler-Koch B, 'The Organization of Interests and Democracy' in Kohler-Koch B and Rittberger B (eds), *Debating the Democratic Legitimacy of the European Union* (Rowman & Littlefield Publishers 2007) 255

Kohler-Koch B and Rittberger B (eds), *Debating the Democratic Legitimacy of the European Union* (Rowman & Littlefield Publishers 2007)

Kolb R in Zimmermann A, Tomuschat C, Oellers-Frahm K, and Tams C (eds), *The Statute of the International Court of Justice: A Commentary* (2nd edn, OUP 2012) General Principles of Procedural Law

Komorowski A von, *Demokratieprinzip und Europäische Union: Staatsverfassungsrechtliche Anforderungen an die demokratische Legitimation der EG-Normsetzung* (Duncker & Humblot 2010)

Koroma AG, 'International Court of Justice, Rules and Practice Directions' in Wolfrum R (ed), *Max Planck Encyclopedia of Public International Law* <http://opil.ouplaw.com/home/EPIL> accessed 27 January 2014

Koselleck R, 'Staat und Souveränität III' in Brunner O, Conze W, and Koselleck R (eds), *Geschichtliche Grundbegriffe*, vol 6 (Klett-Cotta 2004) 25

Koskenniemi M, 'The Politics of International Law' (1990) 1 Eur J Intl L 4

Koskenniemi M, 'General Principles: Reflexions on Constructivist Thinking in International Law' in Koskenniemi M (ed), *Sources of International Law* (Ashgate 2000) 359

Koskenniemi M, *The Gentle Civilizer of Nations: The Rise and Fall of Modern International Law 1870–1960* (CUP 2002)

Koskenniemi M, 'Legal Cosmopolitanism: Tom Franck's Messianic World' (2003) 35 NYU J Intl L and Politics 471

Koskenniemi M, 'Global Governance and Public International Law' (2004) 37 Kritische Justiz 241

Koskenniemi M, *From Apology to Utopia: The Structure of International Legal Argument* (reissue CUP 2005)

Koskenniemi M, 'International Law in Europe: Between Tradition and Renewal' (2005) 16 Eur J Intl L 113

Koskenniemi M, 'The Ideology of International Adjudication and the 1907 Hague Conference' in Daudet Y (ed), *Topicality of the 1907 Hague Conference, the Second Peace Conference* (Nijhoff 2008) 127

Koskenniemi M and Leino P, 'Fragmentation of International Law? Postmodern Anxieties' (2002) 15 Leiden J Intl L (2002) 553

Krajewski M, 'Legitimizing Global Economic Governance through Transnational Parlamentarization: The Parliamentary Dimensions of the WTO and the World Bank' (2010) 136 TranState Working Papers < http://econstor.eu/dspace/handle/10419/41583> accessed 7 April 2014

Krajewski M, 'International Organizations or Institutions, Democratic Legitimacy' in Wolfrum R (ed), *Max Planck Encyclopedia of Public International Law* <http://opil.ouplaw.com/home/EPIL> accessed 27 January 2014

Kriele M, 'Grundrechte und demokratischer Gestaltungsraum' in Isensee J and Kirchhof P (eds), *Handbuch des Staatsrechts der Bundesrepublik Deutschland*, vol 9 (CF Müller 2011) 183

Krisch N, *Beyond Constitutionalism: The Pluralist Structure of Postnational Law* (OUP 2010)

Ku J, *Will the ICJ Have a US-Style Nomination Fight? (We Can Only Hope)* (3 November 2008) <opiniojuripp.org> accessed 20 September 2012

Kuhli M and Günther K, 'Judicial Lawmaking, Discourse Theory, and the ICTY on Belligerent Reprisals' in Bogdandy A von and Venzke I (eds), *International Judicial Lawmaking: On Public Authority and Democratic Legitimation in Global Governance* (Springer 2012) 365

Kumm M, 'The Cosmopolitan Turn in Constitutionalism: On the Relationship Between Constitutionalism in and Beyond the State' in Dunoff JL and Trachtman JS (eds), *Ruling the World? Constitutionalism, International Law, and Global Governance* (CUP 2009) 258

Lafaille F, 'L'identité catholique de l'Italie est-elle soluble dans l'État de droit constitutionnel (national et européen)?' (2010) 126 Revue du droit public et de la science politique en France et à l'étranger 771

Lagrange E, *La représentation institutionnelle dans l'ordre international: Une contribution à la théorie de la personnalité morale des organisations internationales* (Kluwer 2002)

Lambert E, *Le gouvernement des juges et la lutte contre la législation sociale aux États-Unis* (Giard 1921)

Lammasch H, 'Die Lehre von der Schiedsgerichtsbarkeit in ihrem ganzen Umfange' in Stier-Somlo F (ed), *Handbuch des Völkerrechts*, vol 5 (Kohlhammer 1914)

Lang A and Scott J, 'The Hidden World of WTO Governance' (2009) 20 EJIL 575

Latham R, 'Politics in a Floating World: Toward a Critique of Global Governance' in Hewson M and Sinclair TJ (eds), *Approaches to Global Governance Theory* (State University of New York Press 1999) 23

Lauterpacht E, 'Principles of Procedure in International Litigation' (2009) 345 Recueil des cours 387

Lauterpacht H, *The Function of Law in the International Community* (Clarendon 1933)

Lauterpacht H, *The Development of International Law by the Permanent Court of International Justice* (Longmans, Green and Co 1934)

Lauterpacht H, *International Law and Human Rights* (Stevens & Sons 1950)

Lauterpacht H, 'De l'interprétation des traités: Rapport et projet de résolutions' (1950) 43 Annuaire de l'institut de droit international, vol 1, 366

Lauterpacht H, 'Codification and Development of International Law' (1955) 49 AJIL 16

Lauterpacht H, *The Development of International Law by the International Court* (Stevens & Sons 1958).

Lauterpacht H, 'Kelsen's Pure Science of Law' in Lauterpacht E (ed), *International Law: Being the Collected Papers of Hersch Lauterpacht*, vol 2.1 (CUP 1975) 404

Leitner K and Lester S, 'WTO Dispute Settlement 1995–2010—A Statistical Analysis' (2011) 14 J Intl Economic L 191

Lepsius O, 'Was kann die deutsche Staatsrechtslehre von der amerikanischen Rechtswissenschaft lernen?' (2007) 7 Die Verwaltung, Beiheft 319

Lepsius O, 'Hat die Europäisierung des Verwaltungsrechts Methode? Oder: Die zwei Phasen der Europäisierung des Verwaltungsrechts' (2010) 10 Die Verwaltung, Beiheft 179

Lepsius O, 'Die maßstabsetzende Gewalt' in Jestaedt M, Lepsius O, Möllers C, and Schönberger C, *Das entgrenzte Gericht: Eine kritische Bilanz nach sechzig Jahren Bundesverfassungsgericht* (Suhrkamp 2011) 159

Lester A, 'UK Acceptance of the Strasbourg Jurisdiction: What Really Went On in Whitehall in 1965' (1998) PL 237

Ley I, 'Kant versus Locke: Europarechtlicher und völkerrechtlicher Konstitutionalismus im Vergleich' (2009) 69 Zeitschrift für ausländisches öffentliches Recht und Völkerrecht 317

Ley I, 'Zur Politisierung des Völkerrechts: Parlamentarische Versammlungen im Außenverhältnis' (2012) 50 Archiv des Völkerrechts 191

Ley I, *Opposition im Völkerrecht* (Springer 2014)

Lieber T, *Diskursive Vernunft und formelle Gleichheit: Zu Demokratie, Gewaltenteilung und Rechtsanwendung in der Rechtstheorie von Jürgen Habermas* (Mohr Siebeck 2007)

Limbach J, Villalón P C, Errera R, and others (eds), *Judicial Independence: Law and Practice of Appointments to the European Court of Human Rights* (Interrights 2003) <www.interights.org> accessed 20 September 2012

Lindblom A-K, *Non-Governmental Organisations in International Law* (CUP 2005)

Linderfalk U, 'Who Are "the Parties"? Article 31, Paragraph 3 (c) of the 1969 Vienna Convention and the "Principle of Systemic Integration" Revisited' (2008) 55 Netherlands Intl L Rev 343

Linton S and Kebede Tiba F, 'The International Judge in an Age of Multiple International Courts and Tribunals' (2009) 9 Chicago J Intl L 407

Liptow J, *Regel und Interpretation: Eine Untersuchung zur sozialen Struktur sprachlicher Praxis* (Velbrück Wissenschaft 2004)

Locke J, *The Second Treatise of Government* (first published 1690, The Liberal Arts Press 1952)

Loughlin M, *Public Law and Political Theory* (Clarendon 1992)

Loughlin M, *Foundations of Public Law* (OUP 2010)

Lübbe-Wolff G, *Rechtsfolgen und Realfolgen* (Alber 1981)

Luhmann N, *Legitimation durch Verfahren* (3rd edn, Suhrkamp 1993)

Luhmann N, *Law as a Social System* (Ziegert KA tr, Kastner F, Nobles R, Schiff D, and Ziegert R eds, OUP 2004)

Macdonald T, *Global Stakeholder Democracy: Power and Representation Beyond Liberal States* (OUP 2008)

Mackenzie R, 'The Amicus Curiae in International Courts: Towards Common Procedural Approaches?' in Treves T, Frigessi di Rattalma M, Tanzi A, and others (eds), *Civil Society, International Courts and Compliance Bodies* (Asser 2005) 295

Mackenzie R, Romano, CPR, and Shany Y, *The Manual on International Courts and Tribunals* (2nd edn, OUP 2010)

Mackenzie R, Malleson K, Martin P, and Sands P, *Selecting International Judges: Principle, Process, and Politics* (OUP 2010)

Madsen MR, '"Legal Diplomacy"—Law, Policy and the Genesis of Postwar European Human Rights' in Hoffmann S-L and Moyn D (eds), *Human Rights in the Twentieth Century* (CUP 2011) 62

Madsen MR, 'The Protracted Institutionalization of the Strasbourg Court: From Legal Diplomacy to Integrationist Jurisprudence' in Christoffersen J and Madsen MR (eds), *The European Court of Human Rights between Law and Politics* (OUP 2011) 43

Madsen MR, 'Sociological Approaches to International Courts' in Romano S, Alter KJ, and Shany Y (eds), *The Oxford Handbook of International Adjudication* (OUP 2014, forthcoming)

Miguel P Maduro, 'Courts and Pluralism: Essay on a Theory of Judicial Adjudication in the Context of Legal and Constitutional Pluralism' in Dunoff JL and Trachtman JP (eds), *Ruling the World? Constitutionalism, International Law, and Global Governance* (CUP 2009) 356

Maier ML, 'Normentwicklung durch WTO-Gremien am Beispiel von Handel und Gesundheitsschutz: Der SPS-Ausschuss' (2007) 68 TranState Working Papers 1

Malenovský J, 'L'indépendance des juges internationaux' (2010) 349 Recueil des cours 9

Malleson K and Russell PH (eds), *Appointing Judges in an Age of Judicial Power: Critical Perspectives from around the World* (University of Toronto Press 2006)

Mancini PP, 'Motion de M Mancini et son acceptation par le parlement italien' (1874) 6 Revue de droit international et de législation comparée 172

Manthey L and Unseld C, 'Der Mythos vom contra-legem-Verbot: Vom Umgang des EuGH mit einem Verfassungsprinzip' (2011) 64 Die öffentliche Verwaltung 921

Marks S, 'Reservations Unhinged: The Belilos Case before the European Court of Human Rights' (1990) 39 ICLQ 300

Marks S, 'The European Convention on Human Rights and Its "Democratic Society"' (1995) 66 British YB Intl L 209

Martineau A-C, 'La technique du balancement par l'Organe d'appel de l'OMC (études de la justification dans les discours juridiques)' (2007) 123 Revue du droit public et de la science politique en France et à l'étranger 991

Martinez J, 'Towards an International Judicial System' (2003) 56 Stanford L Rev 429

Masing J, *Die Mobilisierung des Bürgers für die Durchsetzung des Rechts: Europäische Impulse für eine Revision der Lehre vom subjektiv-öffentlichen Recht* (Duncker & Humblot 1997)

Matz-Lück N, 'Harmonization, Systemic Integration, and "Mutual-Supportiveness" as Conflict-Solution Techniques: Different Modes of Interpretation as a Challenge to Negative Effects of Fragmentation?' (2006) 17 Finnish YB Intl L 39

Maus I, *Über Volkssouveränität: Elemente einer Demokratietheorie* (Suhrkamp 2011)

Mavroidis PC, 'Amicus Curiae Briefs Before the WTO: Much Ado About Nothing' in Bogdandy A von, Mavroidis PC, and Mény Y (eds), *European Integration and International Co-ordination: Studies in Transnational Economic Law in Honour of Claus-Dieter Ehlermann* (Kluwer 2002) 317

Mayer FC, *Kompetenzüberschreitung und Letztentscheidung: Das Maastricht-Urteil des Bundesverfassungsgerichts und die Letztentscheidung über Ultra vires-Akte in Mehrebenensystemen* (CH Beck 2000)

Mayer M, *Die Europafunktion der nationalen Parlamente in der Europäischen Union* (Mohr Siebeck 2012)

Mayer O, *Deutsches Verwaltungsrecht*, vol 1 (3rd edn, Duncker & Humblot 1924)

Mayntz R, 'Governance Theory als fortentwickelte Steuerungstheorie?' in Folke Schuppert G (ed), *Governance-Forschung* (2nd edn, Nomos 2006) 11

McDougal M and Laswell H, 'The Identification and Appraisal of Diverse Systems of Public Order' (1959) 53 AJIL 1

McLachlan C, Shore L, and Weiniger M, *International Investment Arbitration: Substantive Principles* (OUP 2007)

McWhinney E, 'Law, Politics and "Regionalism" in the Nomination and Election of World Court Judges' (1986–1987) 13 Syracuse J Intl L and Commerce 1

McWhinney E, 'Judicial Settlement of Disputes: Jurisdiction and Judiciabilty' (1990) 221 Recueil des cours 9

Meinecke F, *Weltbürgertum und Nationalstaat: Studien zur Genesis des deutschen Nationalstaates* (6th edn, Oldenbourg 1922)

Mendes J, 'Participation and the Role of Law after Lisbon: A Legal View on Article 11 TEU' (2011) 48 CML Rev 1849

Mény Y, 'Can Europe Be Democratic? Is it Feasible? Is it Necessary? Is the Present Situation Sustainable?' (2011) 34 Fordham Intl L J 1287

Mérignhac A, *Traité théorique et pratique de l'arbitrage international: le rôle du droit dans le fonctionnement actuel de l'institution et dans ses destinées futures* (Larose 1895)

Merrills JG, *International Dispute Settlement* (5th edn, CUP 2011)

Meyer F, *Strafrechtsgenese in Internationalen Organisationen: Eine Untersuchung der Strukturen und Legitimationsvoraussetzungen strafrechtlicher Normbildungsprozesse in Mehrebenensystemen* (Nomos 2012)

Meyer-Ladewig J, *Europäische Menschenrechtskonvention: Handkommentar* (3rd edn, Nomos 2011)

Mitrany D, *A Functional Theory of Politics* (LSE 1975)

Möllers C, *Gewaltengliederung: Legitimation und Dogmatik im nationalen und internationalen Rechtsvergleich* (Mohr Siebeck 2005)

Möllers C, 'Expressive versus repräsentative Demokratie' in Kreide R and Niederberger A (eds), *Transnationale Verrechtlichung: Nationale Demokratien im Kontext globaler Politik* (Campus Verlag 2008) 160

Möllers C, 'Pouvoir Constituant—Constitution—Constiutionalisation' in Bogdandy A von and Bast J (eds) *Principles of European Constitutional Law* (2nd edn, Hart 2009) 169

Möllers C, 'Legalität, Legitimität und Legitimation des Bundesverfassungsgerichts' in Jestaedt M, Lepsius O, Möllers C, and Schönberger C, *Das entgrenzte Gericht: Eine kritische Bilanz nach sechzig Jahren Bundesverfassungsgericht* (Suhrkamp 2011) 298

Montesquieu C L de Secondat, de, 'De l'esprit des lois' in Laboulaye E (ed), *Œuvres complètes de Montesquieu*, vol 4 (first published 1748, Kraus 1972) 18

Monti M and Goulard S, *La democrazia in Europa: Guardare lontano* (Rizzoli 2012)

Moravcsik A, 'The Origins of Human Rights Regimes: Democratic Delegation in Postwar Europe' (2000) 54 Intl Organization 217

Moreno-Ocampo L, 'Preface' in Doria J, Gasser H-P, and Bassiouni MC (eds), *The Legal Regime of the International Criminal Court: Essays in Honour of Professor Igor Blishenko* (Nijhoff 2009) xv

Morgenthau H, *Die internationale Rechtspflege: Ihr Wesen und ihre Grenzen* (Noske 1929)

Mosler H, 'The International Society as a Legal Community' (1973) 140 Recueil des cours 1

Müller F, 'Richterrecht—rechtstheoretisch formuliert' in Hochschullehrer der Juristischen Fakultät der Universität Heidelberg (eds), *Richterliche Rechtsfortbildung: Erscheinungsformen, Auftrag und Grenzen* (CF Müller 1986) 65

Müller JS, *Perspektiven der Demokratie: Vom Nationalmythos Wilhelm Tell zur Weltsicht Immanuel Kants* (Stämpfli 2012)

Nanz P and Steffek J, 'Zivilgesellschaftliche Partizipation und die Demokratisierung internationalen Regierens' in Niesen P and Herborth B (eds), *Anarchie der kommunikativen Freiheit: Jürgen Habermas und die Theorie der internationalen Politik* (Suhrkamp 2007) 87

Nettesheim M in Grabitz E, Hilf M, and Nettesheim M (eds), *Das Recht der Europäischen Union: Kommentar*, vol 1 (CH Beck issue october 2011) Art 11 EUV

Neumann U, 'Zur Interpretation des forensischen Diskurses in der Rechtsphilosophie von Jürgen Habermas' (1996) 27 Rechtstheorie 415

Neumann U, *Wahrheit im Recht: Zu Problematik und Legitimität einer fragwürdigen Denkform* (Nomos 2004)

Neumann U, 'Theorie der juristischen Argumentation' in Brugger W, Neumann U, and Kirste S (eds), *Rechtsphilosophie im 21. Jahrhundert* (Suhrkamp 2008) 233

Neves M, 'La concepción del Estado de derecho y su vigencia práctica en Suramérica, con especial referencia a la fuerza normativa de derecho supranacional' in Bogdandy A von, Landa Arroyo C, and Morales Antoniazzi M (eds), *¿Integración suramericana a través del derecho? Un análisis interdisciplinario y multifocal* (Centro de Estudios Políticos y Constitucionales 2009) 51

Neyer J, 'Justice, Not Democracy: Legitimacy in the European Union' in Forst R and Schmalz-Bruns R (eds), *Political Legitimacy and Democracy in Transnational Perspective: Arena Report No 2/11* (ARENA 2011) 13

Nicolaïdis K, 'European Democracy and Its Crisis' (2013) 51 J Common Market Studies 351

Niesen P (ed), *Transnationale Gerechtigkeit und Demokratie* (Campus 2012)

Nollkaemper A, *National Courts and the International Rule of Law* (OUP 2011)

Nollkaemper A, 'International Adjudication of Global Public Goods: The Intersection of Substance and Procedure' (2012) 23 Eur J Intl L 769

Nolte G, 'Der Wert formeller Kontrolldichtemaßstäbe' in Frowein J Abr (ed), *Die Kontrolldichte bei der gerichtlichen Überprüfung von Handlungen der Verwaltung* (Springer 1993) 278

Nullmeier F and Pritzlaff T, 'The Great Chain of Legitimacy: Justifying Transnational Democracy' in Forst R and Schmalz-Bruns R (eds), *Political Legitimacy and Democracy in Transnational Perspective: Arena Report No 2/11* (ARENA 2011) 43

Nußberger A, 'The Reception Process in Russia and Ukraine' in Keller H and Stone Sweet A (eds), *A Europe of Rights: The Impact of the ECHR on National Legal Systems* (OUP 2008) 603

Öberg MD, 'The Legal Effects of Resolutions of the UN Security Council and General Assembly in the Jurisprudence of the ICJ' (2005) 16 EJIL 879

Oellers-Frahm K, 'Multiplication of International Courts and Tribunals and Conflicting Jurisdiction—Problems and Possible Solutions' (2001) 5 Max Planck YB UN L 67

Oellers-Frahm K, 'Souveräne Streitbeilegung? Überlegungen zu Art. 94 Abs. 2 und Art. 27 UN-Charta' in Frowein J Abr, Scharioth K, Winkelmann I, and Wolfrum R(eds), *Verhandeln Für den Frieden: Liber Amicorum Tono Eitel* (Springer 2003) 169

Oellers-Frahm K, 'Lawmaking through Advisory Opinions' (2011) 12 German L J 1033

Oellers-Frahm K, 'International Courts and Tribunals, Appeals' in Wolfrum R (ed), *Max Planck Encyclopedia of Public International Law* <http://opil.ouplaw.com/home/EPIL> accessed 27 January 2014

Oeter S, 'Chancen und Defizite internationaler Verrechtlichung: Was das Recht jenseits des Nationalstaates leisten kann' in Zürn M and Zangl B (eds), *Verrechtlichung—Baustein für Global Governance?* (Dietz 2004) 46

Oeter S, 'Zur Zukunft der Völkerrechtswissenschaft in Deutschland' (2007) 67 Zeitschrift für ausländisches öffentliches Recht und Völkerrecht 675

Oeter S, 'Federalism and Democracy' in Bogdandy A von and Bast J (eds) *Principles of European Constitutional Law* (2nd edn, Hart 2009) 55

Ogorek R, *Aufklärung über Justiz*, vol 2 (2nd edn, Vittorio Klostermann 2008)

Oraison A, 'Quelques réflexions générales sur les opinions séparées individuelles et dissidentes des juges de la Cour internationale de Justice' (2000) 78 Revue de droit international de sciences diplomatiques et politiques 167

Ortino F and Petersmann E-U (eds), The WTO *Dispute Settlement System 1995–2003*, (Kluwer Law International 2004)

Ossenbühl F, 'Öffentlich-rechtliche Entschädigung in Verfassung, Gesetz und Richterrecht' (1994) 109 Deutsches Verwaltungsblatt 977

Palmeter D and Mavroidis PC, *Dispute Settlement in the World Trade Organization: Practice and Procedure* (2nd edn, CUP 2004)

Palombella G, 'The Rule of Law Beyond the State: Failures, Promises, and Theory' (2009) 7 Intl J Constitutional L 442

Papa MI, *I rapporti tra la corte internazionale di giustizia e il consiglio di sicurezza* (CEDAM 2006)

Parlett K, *The Individual in the International Legal System: Continuity and Change in International Law* (CUP 2011)

Paulus AL, *Die internationale Gemeinschaft im Völkerrecht: Eine Untersuchung zur Entwicklung des Völkerrechts in Zeiten der Globalisierung* (CH Beck 2001)

Paulus AL, 'Subsidiarity, Fragmentation and Democracy: Towards the Demise of General International Law?' in Broude T and Shany Y (eds), *The Shifting Allocation of Authority in International Law: Considering Sovereignty, Supremacy and Subsidiarity: Essays in Honour of Professor Ruth Lapidoth* (Hart 2008) 193

Pauwelyn J, 'The Role of Public International Law in the WTO: How Far Can We Go?' (2001) 95 AJIL 535

Pauwelyn J, *Conflict of Norms in Public International Law: How WTO Law Relates to Other Rules of International Law* (CUP 2003)

Pauwelyn J, 'Bridging Fragmentation and Unity: International Law as a Universe of Inter-Connected Islands' (2004) 25 Michigan J Intl L 903

Payandeh M, *Internationales Gemeinschaftsrecht* (Springer 2010)

Pearson Z, 'Non-Governmental Organizations and the International Criminal Court: Changing Landscapes of International Law' (2006) 39 Cornell Intl L J 243

Pellet A in Zimmermann A, Tomuschat C, Oellers-Frahm K, and Tams C (eds), *The Statute of the International Court of Justice: A Commentary* (2nd edn, OUP 2012) Art 38

Perelman C and Olbrechts-Tyteca L, *The New Rhetoric: A Treatise on Argumentation* (University of Notre Dame Press 1969)

Perju V, 'Reason and Authority in the European Court of Justice' (2009) 49 Virginia J Intl L 307

Pernice I in Dreier H (ed), *Grundgesetz-Kommentar*, vol 2 (2nd edn, Mohr Siebeck 2006) Art 59

Peters A, *Das Gebietsreferendum im Völkerrecht* (Nomos 1995)

Peters A, 'Compensatory Constitutionalism: The Function and Potential of Fundamental International Norms and Structures' (2006) 19 Leiden J Intl L 579

Peters A, 'Dual Democracy' in Klabbers J, Peters A, and Ulfstein G, *The Constitutionalization of International Law* (OUP 2009) 263

Peters A, 'Rechtsordnungen und Konstitutionalisierung: Zur Neubestimmung der Verhältnisse' (2010) 65 Zeitschrift für öffentliches Recht 3

Peters A, 'Das subjektive internationale Recht' (2011) 59 Jahrbuch des öffentlichen Rechts der Gegenwart 411

Peters CJ, 'Assessing the New Judicial Minimalism' (2000) 100 Columbia L Rev 1454

Petersen N, *Demokratie als teleologisches Prinzip: Zur Legitimität von Staatsgewalt im Völkerrecht* (Springer 2009)

Petersen N, 'Braucht die Rechtswissenschaft eine empirische Wende?' (2010) 49 Der Staat 435

Petersen N, 'Determining the Effect of International Law through the Prism of Legitimacy' (2012) 72 Zeitschrift für ausländisches öffentliches Recht und Völkerrecht 223

Petersmann E-U, *Constitutional Functions and Constitutional Problems of International Economic Law* (UP Fribourg Switzerland 1991)

Petersmann E-U, 'The Transformation of the World Trading System through the 1994 Agreement Establishing the World Trade Organization' (1995) 6 Eur J Intl L 161

Petersmann E-U, The *GATT/WTO Dispute Settlement System: International Law, International Organizations and Dispute Settlement* (Kluwer Law 1997)

Petersmann E-U, 'Alternative Dispute Resolution—Lessons for the WTO?' in Weiss F (ed), Improving WTO *Dispute Settlement Procedures* (Cameron May 2000) 27

Petersmann E-U, 'Welthandelsrecht als Freiheits- und Verfassungsordnung' (2005) 65 Zeitschrift für ausländisches öffentliches Recht und Völkerrecht 543

Petersmann E-U, 'Constitutional Functions and Constitutional Problems of International Economic Law in the 21st Century' in *Collected Courses of the Xiamen Academy of International Law*, vol 3 (Nijhoff 2011) 155

Pfeiffer T, 'Die Rechtskontrolle von Organen der Staatengemeinschaft: Internatio nale Organisationen und ihre Rechtsgeschäfte mit Privaten' (2007) 42 Berichte der Deutschen Gesellschaft für Völkerrecht 93

Piacente N, 'Importance of the Joint Criminal Enterprise Doctrine for the ICTY Prosecutorial Policy' (2004) 2 J Intl Crim Justice 446

Pichon J, *Internationaler Strafgerichtshof und Sicherheitsrat der Vereinten Nationen: Zur Rolle des Sicherheitsrates bei der Verfolgung völkerrechtlicher Verbrechen durch den IStGH* (Springer 2011)

Pinto C, 'Iran-United States Claims Tribunal' in Wolfrum R (ed), *Max Planck Encyclopedia of Public International Law* <http://opil.ouplaw.com/home/EPIL> accessed 27 January 2014

Piovesan F, 'Fuerza integradora y catalizadora del Sistema Interamericano de Protección de los Derechos Humanos' in Bogdandy A von, Ferrer Mac-Gregor E, and Morales Antoniazzi M (eds), *La Justicia Constitucional y su Internacionalización: ¿Hacia un Ius Constitutionale Commune en América Latina?*, vol 2 (Instituto de Investigaciones Jurídicas 2010) 431

Pocar F, 'Criminal Proceedings before the International Criminal Tribunals for the Former Yugoslavia and Rwanda' (2006) 5 L and Practice of Intl Courts and Tribunals 89

Podlech A, 'Repräsentation' in Brunner O, Conze W, and Koselleck R (eds), *Grundgeschichtliche Grundbegriffe*, vol 5 (Klett-Cotta 2004) 509

Politis N, *La justice internationale* (Librairie Hachette 1924)

Porsch D, 'Die Friedens-Warte zwischen Friedensbewegung und Wissenschaft' (1999) 73 Die Friedens-Warte 39

Posner EA, *The Perils of Global Legalism* (University of Chicago Press 2009)

Posner EA and Yoo J, 'Judicial Independence in International Tribunals' (2005) 93 California L Rev 1

Postema GJ, *Bentham and the Common Law* (Clarendon 1986)

Proelß A, *Meeresschutz im Völker- und Europarecht: Das Beispiel des Nordostatlantiks* (Duncker & Humblot 2004)

Prott LV, *The Latent Power of Culture and the International Judge* (Professional Books 1979)

Putnam RD, 'Diplomacy and Domestic Politics: The Logic of Two-Level Games' (1988) 42 Intl Organization 427

Quaritsch H, *Souveränität: Entstehung und Entwicklung des Begriffs in Frankreich und Deutschland vom 13. Jh bis 1806* (Duncker & Humblot 1986)

Ralston JH, *International Arbitration from Athens to Locarno* (Stanford UP 1929)

Randelzhofer A, 'Zum behaupteten Demokratiedefizit der Europäischen Gemeinschaft' in Hommelhoff P and Kirchhof P (eds), *Der Staatenverbund der Europäischen Union: Beiträge und Diskussionen des Symposions am 21./22. Januar 1994 in Heidelberg* (CF Müller 1994) 39

Randelzhofer A in Maunz T and Dürig G (eds), *Grundgesetz: Kommentar* (64th edn, CH Beck 2012) Art 24

Randelzhofer A and Dörr O in Simma B, Kahn D-E, Nolte G, and Paulus A (eds), *The Charter of the United Nations: A Commentary*, vol 1 (3rd edn, OUP 2012) Art 2(4)

Rastan R, 'Testing Cooperation: The International Criminal Court and National Authorities' (2008) 21 Leiden J Intl L 431

Rawls J, 'The Idea of Public Reason Revisited' (1997) 64 U Chicago L Rev 765

Rawls J, *The Law of Peoples* (Harvard UP 1999)

Raz J, *The Authority of Law: Essays on Law and Morality* (Clarendon 1979)

Razzaque J, 'Changing Role of Friends of the Court in International Courts and Tribunals' (2001) 1 Non-State Actors and Intl L 169

Reinisch A, 'Verfahrensrechtliche Aspekte der Rechtskontrolle von Organen der Staatengemeinschaft' (2007) 42 Berichte der Deutschen Gesellschaft für Völkerrecht 43

Reinisch A, (ed), *Challenging Acts of International Organizations before National Courts* (OUP 2010)

Reisman M, 'Unilateral Action and the Transformations of the World Constitutive Process: The Special Problem of Humanitarian Intervention' (2000) 11 Eur J Intl L 3

Ress H-K, 'Die Zulässigkeit territorialer Beschränkungen bei der Anerkennung der Zuständigkeit des Europäischen Gerichtshofs für Menschenrechte: Anmerkungen zum Urteil des Europäischen Gerichtshofs für Menschenrechte im Fall Loizidou gegen die Türkei vom 23. März 1995' (1996) 56 Zeitschrift für ausländisches öffentliches Recht und Völkerrecht 427

Riecken J, *Verfassungsgerichtsbarkeit und Demokratie* (Duncker & Humblot 2003)

Riesenberger D, *Geschichte der Friedensbewegung in Deutschland: Von den Anfängen bis 1933* (Vandenhoeck & Ruprecht 1985)

Risse T, 'Transnational Governance and Legitimacy' in Benz A and Papadopoulos Y (eds), *Governance and Democracy: Comparing National, European and International Experiences* (Routledge 2006) 179

Robertson A (ed), *Collected Edition of the* 'Travaux Préparatoires' *of the European Convention on Human Rights*, vol 1 (Nijhoff 1975)

Röhl KF, *Rechtssoziologie: Ein Lehrbuch* (Carl Heymanns 1987)

Rojahn O in Münch I von and Kunig P (eds), *Grundgesetzkommentar*, vol 2 (5th edn, CH Beck 2000) Art 24

Rolin H, 'Has the European Court of Human Rights a Future?' (1965) 11 Harvard L J 442

Romano CPR, 'The Proliferation of International Judicial Bodies' (1998–1999) 31 NYU J Intl L and Politics 709

Romano CPR, 'International Justice and Developing Countries: A Quantitative Analysis' (2002) 1 L and Practice of Intl Courts and Tribunals 367

Romano CPR, 'A Taxonomy of International Rule of Law Institutions' (2011) 2 J Intl Dispute Settlement 241

Rorty R (ed), *The Linguistic Turn: Essays in Philosophical Method* (University of Chicago Press 1967)

Rosenau JN, 'Governance, Order, and Change in World Politics' in Rosenau JN and Czempiel E-O (eds), *Governance without Government: Order and Change in World Politics* (CUP 1992) 1

Rosenau JN, 'Governance in the Twenty-First Century' (1995) 1 Global Governance 13

Rosenne S, *The Law and Practice of the International Court 1920–2005*, vol 1 (4th edn, Nijhoff 2006)

Rosenne S, 'The International Court of Justice: New Practice Directions' (2009) 8 L and Practice of Intl Courts and Tribunals 171

Rothwell DR, 'The Contribution of ITLOS to Oceans Governance through Marine Environmental Dispute Resolution' in Ndiaye TM and Wolfrum R (eds), *Law of the Sea, Environmental Law and Settlement of Disputes: Liber Amicorum Judge Thomas A Mensah* (Nijhoff 2007) 1007

Ruffert M, 'Special Jurisdiction of the ICJ in the Case of Infringement of Fundamental Rules of the International Legal Order?' in Tomuschat C and Thouvenin J-M (eds), *The Fundamental Rules of the International Legal Order, Jus Cogens and Obligations Erga Omnes* (Nijhoff 2006) 295

Ruffert N in Calliess C and Ruffert M (eds), *EUV/AEUV Kommentar* (4th edn, CH Beck 2011) Art 9 TEU

Ruiz Fabri H, 'Drawing a Line of Equilibrium in a Complex World' in Sacerdoti G, Yanovich A, and Bohanes J (eds), The WTO *at Ten: The Contribution of the Dispute Settlement System* (CUP 2006) 125

Saavedra Alessandri P and Pacheco Arias G, 'Las sesiones "itinerantes" de la Corte Interamericana de los Derechos Humanos' in García Ramírez S and Castañeda Hernández M (eds), *Recepción nacional del derecho internacional de los derechos humanos y admisión de la competencia contenciosa de la Corte Interamericana* (Universidad Nacional Autónoma de México 2009) 37

Sacerdoti G, 'Appeal and Judicial Review in International Arbitration and Adjudication: The Case of the WTO Appellate Review' in Petersmann E-U (ed), *International Trade Law and the GATT/WTO Dispute Settlement System* (Kluwer 1997) 245

Sadurski W, 'Partnering with Strasbourg: Constitutionalism of the European Court of Human Rights, the Accession of Central and East European States and the Idea of Pilot Judgments' (2009) 9 Human Rights L Rev 397

Sampson GP, 'Introduction and Overview: Future Directions' in Sampson GP (ed), The WTO *and Global Governance: Future Directions* (United Nations UP 2008) 1

Sands PJ, 'The Independence of the International Judiciary: Some Introductory Thoughts' in Charnovitz S, Steger DP, van den Bossche P (eds), *Law in the Service of Human Dignity: Essays in Honour of Florentino Feliciano* (CUP 2005) 313

Sands PJ, McLachlan C, and Mackenzie R, 'The Burgh House Principles on the Independence of the International Judiciary' (2005) 4 L and Practice of Intl Courts and Tribunals 247

Sands PJ and Mackenzie R, 'International Courts and Tribunals, Amicus Curiae' in Wolfrum R (ed), *Max Planck Encyclopedia of Public International Law* <http://opil.ouplaw.com/home/EPIL> accessed 27 January 2014

Sarmiento D, 'The Silent Lamb and the Deaf Wolves' in Avbelj M and Komárek J (eds), *Constitutional Pluralism in the European Union and Beyond* (Hart 2012) 285

Sauer H, *Jurisdiktionskonflikte in Mehrebenensystemen* (Springer 2008)
Sauvant KP (ed), *Appeals Mechanism in International Investment Disputes* (OUP 2008)
Savarese E, 'Amicus Curiae Participation in Investor-State Arbitral Proceedings' (2007) 17 Italian YB Intl L 99
Scelle G, *Une crise de la Société des Nations: La réforme du Conseil et l'entrée de l'Allemagne à Genève* (Les Presses Universitaires de France 1926)
Schabas W, *An Introduction to the International Criminal Court* (3rd edn, CUP 2007)
Schachter O, 'The Invisible College of International Lawyers' (1977) 72 Northwestern U L Rev 217
Scharpf FW, *Demokratietheorie zwischen Utopie und Anpassung* (Universitätsverlag Konstanz 1970)
Schauer F, 'Precedent' (1987) 39 Stanford L Rev 571
Schermers HG, 'Election of Judges to the European Court of Human Rights' (1998) 23 Eur L Rev 568
Schermers HG and Blokker NM, *International Institutional Law* (5th edn, Nijhoff 2011)
Schill SW, 'Der Preis der Gerechtigkeit' in Dreier H (ed), *Rechts- und staatstheoretische Schlüsselbegriffe: Legitimität—Repräsentation—Freiheit: Symposium für Hasso Hofmann zum 70. Geburtstag* (Duncker & Humblot 2005) 9
Schill SW, 'International Investment Law and the Host State's Power to Handle Economic Crises: Comment on the ICSID Decision in LG & E v Argentina' (2007) 24 J Intl Arbitration 265
Schill SW, *The Multilateralization of International Investment Law* (CUP 2009)
Schill SW (ed), *International Investment Law and Comparative Public Law* (OUP 2010)
Schill SW, 'Deference in Investment Treaty Arbitration: Re-Conceptualizing the Standard of Review' (2012) 3 J Intl Dispute Settlement 577
Schill SW, 'System-Building in Investment Treaty Arbitration and Lawmaking' in Bogdandy A von and Venzke I (eds), *International Judicial Lawmaking: On Public Authority and Democratic Legitimation in Global Governance* (Springer 2012) 133
Schimmelfennig F, 'Legitimate Rule in the European Union' (1996) 27 Tübinger Arbeitspapiere zur Internationalen Politik und Friedensforschung 1 <tobias-lib.uni-tuebingen.de/volltexte/2000/150> accessed 11 June 2012
Schliesky U, *Souveränität und Legitimität von Herrschaftsgewalt* (Mohr Siebeck 2004)
Schlink B, *Abwägung im Verfassungsrecht* (Duncker & Humblot 1976)
Schmidt MG, *Demokratietheorien: Eine Einführung* (4th edn, VS Verlag für Sozialwissenschaften 2008)
Schmidt-Aßmann E, 'Die Herausforderung der Verwaltungsrechtswissenschaft durch die Internationalisierung der Verwaltungsbeziehungen' (2006) 45 Der Staat 315
Schmidt-Aßmann E in Maunz T, Dürig G, and others (eds), *Grundgesetz: Kommentar*, vol 3 (CH Beck 2012) Art 19(4)

Schmitt C, *Constitutional Theory* (Seitzer J tr/ed, Duke UP 2007)

Schneider AK, 'Bargaining in the Shadow of International Law: What the Normalization of Adjudication in International Governance Regimes Means for Dispute Resolution' (2009) 41 NYU J Intl L and Politics 789

Schneiderman D, *Constitutionalizing Economic Globalization* (CUP 2008) 25

Schomburg W and Nemitz JC, 'International Criminal Courts and Tribunals, Procedure' in Wolfrum R (ed), *Max Planck Encyclopedia of Public International Law* <http://opil.ouplaw.com/home/EPIL> accessed 27 January 2014

Schönberger C, 'European Citizenship as Federal Citizenship' (2007) 19 Revue européenne de droit public 61

Schönberger C, 'Die Europäische Union zwischen "Demokratiedefizit und Bundesstaatsverbot: Anmerkungen zum Lissabon-Urteil des Bundesverfassungsgerichts' (2009) 48 Der Staat 535

Schönberger C in Grabitz E, Hilf M, and Nettesheim M (eds), *Das Recht der Europäischen Union: Kommentar*, vol 1 (CH Beck issue October 2011) Art 9 TEU

Schorlemer S von in Zimmermann A, Tomuschat C, Oellers-Frahm K, and Tams C (eds), *The Statute of the International Court of Justice: A Commentary* (2nd edn, OUP 2012) Art 46

Schotel B, *On the Right of Exclusion: Law, Ethics and Immigration Policy* (Routledge 2012)

Schreuer CH, *The ICSID Convention: A Commentary* (2nd edn, CUP 2009)

Schreuer CH, 'From ICSID Annulment to Appeal: Half Way Down the Slippery Slope' (2011) 10 L and Practice of Intl Courts and Tribunals 211

Schücking W, 'Die Organisation der Welt' in van Calker W (ed), *Staatsrechtliche Abhandlungen: Festgabe für Paul Laband zum 50. Jahrestage der Doktor-Promotion*, vol 1 (JCB Mohr 1908) 533

Schücking W, *The International Union of the Hague Conferences* (Fenwick CG tr, Clarendon 1918)

Schulze-Fielitz H in Dreier H (ed), *Grundgesetz-Kommentar*, vol 3 (2nd edn, Mohr Siebeck 2008) Art 103(1)

Scobbie I, 'Une hérésie en matière judiciaire? The Role of the Judge ad hoc in the International Court' (2005) 4 L and Practice of Intl Courts and Tribunals 421

Scott JB, *The Hague Peace Conferences of 1899 and 1907* (Garland Baltimore 1909)

Scott JB, 'Editorial Comment' (1921) 15 AJIL 51

Seibert-Fohr A (ed), *Judicial Independence in Transition* (Springer 2012)

Seibert-Fohr A, 'Introduction: The Challenge of Transition' in Seibert-Fohr A (ed), *Judicial Independence in Transition* (Springer 2012) 1

Seibert-Fohr A, 'Judicial Independence—The Normativity of an Evolving Transnational Principle' in Seibert-Fohr A (ed), *Judicial Independence in Transition* (Springer 2012) 1279

Sen A, *The Idea of Justice* (Belknap Press 2009)

Shaffer G and Trachtman JP, 'Interpretation and Institutional Choice at the WTO' (2011–2012) 52 Virginia J Intl L 103

Shany Y, 'Toward a General Margin of Appreciation Doctrine in International Law?' (2006) 17 Eur J Intl L 907

Shany Y, *Regulating Jurisdictional Relations between National and International Courts* (OUP 2007)

Shany Y, 'No Longer a Weak Department of Power? Reflections on the Emergence of a New International Judiciary' (2009) 20 Eur J Intl L 73

Shany Y, 'Assessing the Effectiveness of International Courts: A Goal-Based Approach' (2012) 106 AJIL 225

Shany Y, and Sigall Horovitz, 'Judicial Independence in The Hague and Freetown: A Tale of Two Cities' (2008) 21 Leiden J Intl L 113

Shapiro M, *Courts: A Comparative and Political Analysis* (University of Chicago Press 1981)

Shaw J, 'Citizenship of the Union: Towards Post-National Membership?' (1995) 6 Collected Courses of the Academy of European Law 237

Shaw MN, *International Law* (6th edn, CUP 2008)

Shelton D, 'The Participation of Nongovernmental Organizations in International Proceedings' (1994) 88 AJIL 611

Shelton D, 'Form, Function, and the Powers of International Courts' (2008–2009) 9 Chicago J Intl L 537

Sheppard A, 'Arbitrator Independence in ICSID Arbitration' in Binder C, Kriebaum U, Reinisch A, and Wittich S (eds), *International Investment Law for the 21st Century: Essays in Honour of Christoph Schreuer* (OUP 2009) 131

Shklar JN, *Legalism* (Harvard UP 1964)

Simma B, 'Der Beitrag von Alfred Verdross zur Entwicklung der Völkerrechtswissenschaft' in Miehsler H, Mock E, and Simma B (eds), *Ius Humanitatis: Festschrift zum 90. Geburtstag von Alfred Verdross* (Duncker & Humblot 1980) 23

Simma B, 'From Bilateralism to Community Interest' (1994) 250 Recueil des cours 221

Simma B, 'Universality of International Law from the Perspective of a Practitioner' (2009) 20 Eur J Intl L 265

Simma B, 'Foreword' in Bogdandy A von and Venzke I (eds), *International Judicial Lawmaking: On Public Authority and Democratic Legitimation in Global Governance* (Springer 2012) V

Simma B, 'Human Rights before the International Court of Justice: Community Interest Coming to Life?' in Hestermeyer HP, König D, Matz-Lück N, and others (eds), *Coexistence, Cooperation and Solidarity: Liber Amicorum Rüdiger Wolfrum* (Nijhoff 2012) 577

Simma B and Kill T, 'Harmonizing Investment Protection and International Human Rights: First Steps Towards a Methodology' in Binder C, Kriebaum U,

Reinisch A, and Wittich S (eds), *International Investment Law for the 21st Century* (OUP 2009) 678

Simma B and Pulkowski D, 'Of Planets and the Universe: Self-Contained Regimes in International Law' (2006) 17 Eur J Intl L 483

Simpson GJ, 'Imagined Consent: Democratic Liberalism in International Legal Theory' (1994) 15 Australian YB Intl L 103

Simpson GJ, *Great Powers and Outlaw States: Unequal Sovereigns in the International Legal Order* (CUP 2004)

Slaughter A-M, 'International Law in a World of Liberal States' (1995) 6 Eur J Intl L 503

Slaughter A-M, 'International Law and International Relations' (2000) 285 Recueil des cours 9

Slaughter A-M, *A New World Order* (Princeton UP 2004)

Sohn LB, 'International Arbitration in Historical Perspective: Past and Present' in Soons AHA (ed), *International Arbitration: Past and Prospect* (Nijhoff 1990) 9

Somek A, 'The Argument from Transnational Effects I: Representing Outsiders through Freedom of Movement' (2010) 16 Eur L J 315

Somek A, 'Legal Science as a Source of Law: A Late Reply by Puchta to Kantorowicz' German L J (forthcoming)

Sorel J-M, 'International Courts and Tribunals, Procedure' in Wolfrum R (ed), *Max Planck Encyclopedia of Public International Law* <http://opil.ouplaw.com/home/EPIL> accessed 27 January 2014

Sorel J-M and Boré Eveno V in Corten O and Klein P (eds), *The Vienna Convention on the Law of Treaties: A Commentary*, vol 1 (OUP 2011) Art 31

Sornarajah M, 'Toward Normlessness: The Ravage and Retreat of Neo-Liberalism in International Investment Law' (2009–2010) YB Intl Investment L and Policy 595

Spiermann O, *International Legal Argument in the Permanent Court of International Justice: The Rise of the International Judiciary* (CUP 2005)

Spinelli A, *Una strategia per gli Stati uniti d'Europa* (Il Mulino 1989)

Staden A von, 'Democratic Legitimacy of Review Beyond the State: The Need for an Appropriate Standard of Review' (2012) 10 Intl J Const L 1023

Staton JK and Moore WH, 'Judicial Power in Domestic and International Politics' (2011) 65 Intl Organization 553

Steffek J, 'Accountability und politische Öffentlichkeit im Zeitalter des globalen Regierens' in Niesen P (ed), *Transnationale Gerechtigkeit und Demokratie* (Campus 2012) 279

Stein TL, 'Jurisprudence and Jurists' Prudence: The Iranian-Forum Clause Decisions of the Iran-U.S. Claims Tribunal' (1984) 78 AJIL 1

Steinberg RH, 'Judicial Lawmaking at the WTO: Discursive, Constitutional, and Political Constraints' (2004) 98 AJIL 247

Steinberger H, 'The International Court of Justice' in Mosler H and Bernhardt R (eds), *Judicial Settlement of International Disputes* (Springer 1974) 193

Steingruber AM, *Consent in International Arbitration* (OUP 2012)

Steinman AN, 'A Constitution for Judicial Lawmaking' (2003–2004) 65 U Pittsburgh L Rev 545

Stern B, 'A propos de la competence universelle.. . ' in Yakpo E and Boumedra T (eds), *Liber Amicorum Judge Mohammed Bedjaoui* (Kluwer Law International 1999) 735

Sterzel F, *The Inter-Parliamentary Union* (PA Norstedt & Söner 1968)

Stewart RB and Sanchez-Badin MR, The World Trade Organization and Global Administrative Law' in Christian Joerges and Ernst-Ulrich Petersmann (eds), *Constitutionalism, Multilevel Trade Governance and International Economic Law* (Hart 2011) 457

Stone Sweet A, 'Sur la constitutionnalisation de la convention européenne des droits de l'homme: cinquante ans après son installation, la cour européenne des droits de l'homme conçue comme une cour constitutionnelle' (2009) 20 Revue trimestrielle des droits de l'homme 923

Strijards GA in Triffterer O (ed), *Commentary on the Rome Statute of the International Criminal Court: Observers' Notes, Article by Article* (2nd edn, CH Beck 2008) Art 103

Suarez F, 'De legibus, ac Deo legislatore' in Scott JB (ed), *Selections from three Works: The Photographic Reproduction of the Selections from the Original Editions*, vol 1 (first published 1612, Clarendon 1944)

Suarez F, 'A Treatise on Laws and God the Lawgiver' in Scott JB (ed), *Selections from three Works: The Translation*, vol 2 (Williams GL, Brown A, and Waldron J trs, Clarendon 1944) 3

Sunstein CR, *One Case at a Time: Judicial Minimalism on the Supreme Court* (Harvard UP 1999)

Sunstein CR, 'Beyond Judicial Minimalism' (2008) 43 Tulsa L Rev 825

Suttner B von, *Lay Down Your Arms: The Autobiography of Martha von Tilling* (Holmes T tr, 2nd edn, Longmans, Green and Co 1908)

Swart M, 'Ad hoc Rules for ad hoc Tribunals? The Rule-Making Power of the Judges of the ICTY and ICTR' (2002) 18 South Africa J on Human Rights 570

Swart M, 'Judicial Lawmaking at the ad hoc Tribunals: The Creative Use of the Sources of International Law and "Adventurous Interpretation"' (2010) 70 Zeitschrift für ausländisches öffentliches Recht und Völkerrecht 459

Tallgren I, 'The Sensibility and Sense of International Criminal Law' (2002) 13 Eur J Intl L 561

Tega D, *I diritti in crisi: Tra Corti nazionali e Corte europea di Strasburgo* (Giuffrè 2012)

Teitel R and Howse R, 'Cross-Judging: Tribunalization in a Fragmented but Interconnected Global Order' (2009) 41 NYU J Intl L and Politics 959

Teitgen P-H, 'Presentation of the Report of the Committee on Legal and Administrative Questions' in A Robertson (ed), *Collected Edition of the* 'Travaux Préparatoires' *of the European Convention on Human Rights*, vol 1 (Nijhoff 1975) 264

Terris D, Romano CPR, and Swigart L, *The International Judge: An Inquiry into the Men and Women Who Decide the World's Cases* (OUP 2007)

Thiele C, 'Fragmentierung des Völkerrechts als Herausforderung für die Staatengemeinschaft' (2008) 46 Archiv des Völkerrechts 1

Thucydides, 'The History of the Grecian War' in Molesworth W (ed), *The English Works of Thomas Hobbes*, vol 2 (first published around 400 BC, tr Hobbes T, John Bohn 1843)

Thürer D and Burri T, 'Self-Determination' in Wolfrum R (ed), *Max Planck Encyclopedia of Public International Law* <http://opil.ouplaw.com/home/EPIL> accessed 27 January 2014

Tocqueville A de, *Democracy in America*, vol 1 (Alfred A Knopf 1980)

Tolbert D, 'The International Tribunal for the former Yugoslavia and the Enforcement of Sentences' (1998) 11 Leiden J Intl L 655

Tomuschat C, 'International Law: Ensuring the Survival of Mankind on the Eve of a New Century: General Course on Public International Law' (1999) 281 Recueil des cours 9

Tomuschat C, 'The European Court of Human Rights Overwhelmed by Applications: Problems and Possible Solutions' in Wolfrum R and Deutsch U (eds), *The European Court of Human Rights Overwhelmed by Applications: Problems and Possible Solutions* (Springer 2009) 1

Tomuschat C, 'International Courts and Tribunals' in Wolfrum R (ed), *Max Planck Encyclopedia of Public International Law* <http://opil.ouplaw.com/home/EPIL> accessed 3 April 2014

Tomuschat C in Zimmermann A, Tomuschat C, Oellers-Frahm K, and Tams C (eds), *The Statute of the International Court of Justice: A Commentary* (2nd edn, OUP 2012) Art 36

Torres Bernárdez S, 'L'intervention dans la procédure de la Cour internationale de Justice' (1995) 256 Recueil des cours 193

Treves T, 'Aspects of Legitimacy of Decisions of International Courts and Tribunals' in Wolfrum R and Röben V (eds), *Legitimacy in International Law* (Springer 2008) 169

Trevisanut S, *Immigrazione irregolare via mare: diritto internazionale e diritto dell'Unione europea* (Jovene 2012)

Triepel H, *Völkerrecht und Landesrecht* (Mohr Siebeck 1899)

Troper M and Grzegorczyk C, 'Precedent in France' in MacCormick N and Summers RS (eds), *Interpreting Precedents: A Comparative Study* (Ashgate 1997) 103

Tschentscher A, *Demokratische Legitimation der dritten Gewalt* (Mohr Siebeck 2006)

Tumlir J, 'International Economic Order and Democratic Constitutionalism' (1983) 34 ORDO 71

Tzanakopoulos A, *Disobeying the Security Council* (OUP 2011)

Uerpmann R, 'Internationales Verfassungsrecht' (2001) 56 Juristenzeitung 565

Ulfstein G, 'Institutions and Competences' in Klabbers J, Peters A, and Ulfstein G, *The Constitutionalization of International Law* (OUP 2009) 45

Ulfstein G, 'The International Judiciary' in Klabbers J, Peters A, and Ulfstein G, *The Constitutionalization of International Law* (OUP 2009) 126

van den Bossche P, 'From Afterthought to Centrepiece: The WTO Appellate Body and Its Rise to Prominence in the World Trading System' in Sacerdoti G, Yanovich A, and Bohanes J (eds), The WTO *at Ten: The Contribution of the Dispute Settlement System* (CUP 2006) 289

van den Hout T, 'Resolution of International Disputes: The Role of the Permanent Court of Arbitration: Reflections on the Centenary of the 1907 Convention for the Pacific Settlement of International Disputes' (2008) 21 Leiden J Intl L 643

van der Linden WH, *The International Peace Movement 1815–1874* (Tilleul 1987)

Van Harten G, *Investment Treaty Arbitration and Public Law* (OUP 2007)

Vattel E de, *Le droit des gens ou principes de la loi naturelle: Appliqués à la conduite et aux affaires des Nations et des Souverains*, vol 1 (Rey et Gravier 1838)

Vauchez A, 'The Transnational Politics of Judicialization: *Van Gend en Loos* and the Making of EU Polity' (2010) 16 Eur L J 1

Veeder VV, 'The *Lena Goldfields* Arbitration: The Historical Roots of Three Ideas' (1998) 47 ICLQ 747

Venzke I, 'International Bureaucracies from a Political Science Perspective—Agency, Authority and International Institutional Law' (2008) 9 German L J 1401

Venzke I, 'Making General Exceptions: The Spell of Precedents in Developing Article XX GATT into Standards for Domestic Regulatory Policy' (2011) 12 German L J 1111

Venzke I, *How Interpretation Makes International Law: On Semantic Change and Normative Twists* (OUP 2012)

Venzke I, 'The Role of International Courts as Interpreters and Developers of the Law: Working out the Jurisgenerative Practice of Interpretation' (2012) 34 Loyola of Los Angeles Intl and Comparative L Rev 99

Venzke I, 'Technical Regulation and International Standards: The EC-Trade Description of Sardines Case' in Cassese S, Carotti B, Casini L, and others (eds), *Global Administrative Law: The Casebook*, vol 2 (3rd edn, Istituto di ricerche sulla pubblica amministrazione 2012) 7

Venzke I, 'Understanding the Authority of International Courts and Tribunals: On Delegation and Discursive Construction' (2013) 14 Theoretical Inquiries in L 381

Verdross A, *Die Verfassung der Völkerrechtsgemeinschaft* (Springer 1926)

Verdross A, 'Forbidden Treaties in International Law' (1937) 31 AJIL 571

Verdross A, 'Jus Dispositivum and Jus Cogens' (1966) 60 AJIL 55

Verdross A and Simma B, *Universelles Völkerrecht: Theorie und Praxis* (3rd edn, Duncker & Humblot 1984)

Vergottini G de, *Diritto costituzionale comparato* (5th edn, CEDAM 1999)

Vierucci L, 'NGOs before International Courts and Tribunals' in Dupuy P-M and Vierucci L (eds), *NGOs in International Law: Efficiency in Flexibility?* (Edward Elgar 2008) 155

Vigil Toledo R, 'La contribución del Tribunal de Justicia de la Comunidad Andina al proceso de integración suramericana' in Bogdandy A von, Landa Arroyo C, and Morales Antoniazzi M (eds), *¿Integración suramericana a través del Derecho? Un análisis interdisciplinario y multifocal* (Centro de Estudios Políticos y Constitucionales 2009) 397

Villalpando S, 'The Legal Dimension of the International Community: How Community Interests Are Protected in International Law' (2010) 21 Eur J Intl L 387

Villiger ME, 'Das Urteil des Europäischen Gerichtshofs für Menschenrechte: Zustandekommen, Bedeutung und Wirkungen' (2008) 127 Zeitschrift für schweizerisches Recht 453

Villiger ME, *Commentary on the 1969 Vienna Convention on the Law of Treaties* (Nijhoff 2009)

Villiger ME, 'The Dialogue of Judges' in Hohmann-Dennhardt C, Masuch P, and Villiger ME (eds), *Durchsetzung und Verfahren: Festschrift für Renate Jäger* (Engel 2011) 195

Virally M, *L'organisation mondiale* (Librairie Armand Colin 1970)

Voßkuhle A, *Rechtsschutz gegen den Richter: Zur Integration der Dritten Gewalt in das verfassungsrechtliche Kontrollsystem vor dem Hintergrund des Art. 19 Abs. 4 GG* (CH Beck 1993)

Voßkuhle A, 'Der europäische Verfassungsgerichtsverbund' (2010) 29 Neue Zeitschrift für Verwaltungsrecht 1

Voßkuhle A and Sydow G, 'Die demokratische Legitimation des Richters' (2002) 57 Juristenzeitung 673

Waibel M, Kaushal A, Liz Chung K-H, and Balchin C (eds), *The Backlash Against Investment Arbitration: Perceptions and Reality* (Kluwer 2010)

Wälde TW, 'The Specific Nature of Investment Arbitration' in Wälde TW and Kahn P (eds), *New Aspects of International Investment Law* (Nijhoff 2007) 43

Waldock CHM, 'Decline of the Optional Clause' (1955–1956) 32 British YB Intl L 244

Waldock H, 'General Course on Public International Law' (1962) 106 Recueil des cours 1

Wallach L and Sforza M, *Whose Trade Organization?* (Public Citizen 1999)

Walter C, 'Die Europäische Menschenrechtskonvention als Konstitutionalisierungsprozeß' (1999) 59 Zeitschrift für ausländisches öffentliches Recht und Völkerrecht 961

Walter KF, *Rechtsfortbildung durch den EuGH* (Duncker & Humblot 2009)

Waters TW, 'A Kind of Judgment: Searching for Judicial Narratives after Death' (2010) 42 George Washington Intl L Rev 279

Weber A, 'Grundrechtsschutz in Europa—Kooperation oder Kooperationsverweigerung? Anmerkungen zum Verhältnis zwischen EGMR und BVerfG' in Akryük M, Baumgartner G, Jahnel D, and others (eds), *Staat und Recht in europäischer Perspektive: Festschrift Heinz Schäffer* (Manzsche Verlags- und Universitätsbuchhandlung 2006) 911

Weber M, *Economy and Society* (Roth G and Wittich C eds, University of California Press 1978) 212

Weber M, 'Science as a Vocation' in Lassman P and Velody I (eds), *Max Weber's Science as a Vocation* (John M tr, Unwin Hyman 1989) 19

Wehberg H, 'Friedrich von Martens und die Haager Friedenskonferenzen' (1910) 20 Zeitschrift für internationales Recht 343

Wehberg H, *The Problem of an International Court of Justice* (Fenwick CG tr, Clarendon 1918)

Wehberg H, *Grundprobleme des Völkerbundes* (Hensel & Co-Verlag 1926)

Weiler JHH, *The European Community in Change: Exit, Voice and Loyalty* (Europa-Institut der Universität des Saarlandes 1987)

Weiler JHH, 'The Transformation of Europe' (1991) 100 Yale L J 2405

Weiler JHH, 'Citizenship and Human Rights' in Winter JA, Curtin DM, Kellermann AE, and Witte B de (eds), *Reforming the Treaty on European Union* (Kluwer Law International 1996) 57

Weiler JHH, 'European Democracy and Its Critics: Polity and System' in Weiler JHH, *The Constitution of Europe* (CUP 1999) 264

Weiler JHH, 'The Rule of Lawyers and the Ethos of Diplomats: Reflections on the Internal and External Legitimacy of WTO Dispute Settlement' (2001) 35 Journal of World Trade 191

Weiler JHH, 'The Geology of International Law—Governance, Democracy and Legitimacy' (2004) 64 Zeitschrift für ausländisches öffentliches Recht und Völkerrecht 547

Weiler JHH, 'Law, Culture, and Values in the WTO—Gazing into the Crystal Ball' in Bethlehem D, McRae D, Neufeld R, and van Damme I (eds), *The Oxford Handbook of International Trade Law* (OUP 2009) 749

Wernicke S, 'Au nom de qui? The European Court of Justice between Member States, Civil Society and Union Citizens' (2009) 13 Eur L J 380

Wessel RA and van de Griendt WE, 'Offene Staatlichkeit: Niederlande' in Bogdandy A von, Cruz Villalón P and Huber PM (eds), *Handbuch Ius Publicum Europaeum*, vol 2 (CF Müller 2008) 177

Wet E de, *The Chapter VII Powers of the United Nations Security Council* (Hart 2004)

Wet E de 'The Prohibition of Torture as an International Norm of *jus cogens* and Its Implications for National and Customary Law' (2004) 15 Eur J Intl L 97

Wheeler R, 'Judicial Independence in the United States of America' in Seibert-Fohr A (ed), *Judicial Independence in Transition* (Springer 2012) 521

Wieser B, *Vergleichendes Verfassungsrecht* (Springer 2005)

Wildhaber L, 'A Constitutional Future for the European Court of Human Rights' (2002) 23 Human Rights Law Journal 161.

Williamson OE, *The Mechanisms of Governance* (OUP 1996)

Wilson RA, *Writing History in International Criminal Trials* (CUP 2011)

Winkler M, 'Die normative Kraft des Praktischen: Robert Brandom und die Rechtstheorie' (2009) 64 Juristenzeitung 821

Wittgenstein L, *Philosophical Investigations* (Anscombe tr, Basil Blackwell 1953)

Wolfrum R, 'Kontrolle der auswärtigen Gewalt' (1997) 56 Veröffentlichungen der Vereinigung der Deutschen Staatsrechtslehrer 38

Wolfrum R, 'Intervention in the Proceedings before the International Court of Justice and the International Tribunal for the Law of the Sea' in Götz V, Selmer P, and Wolfrum R (eds), *Liber amicorum Günther Jaenicke—zum 85. Geburtstag* (Springer 1998) 427

Wolfrum R, 'Concluding Remarks' in Wolfrum R and Kojima C (eds), *Solidarity: A Structural Principle of International Law* (Springer 2010) 225

Wolfrum R, Stoll P-T, and Kaiser K (eds), *WTO—Institutions and Dispute Settlement*, vol 2 (Nijhoff 2006)

Wood M, 'The International Tribunal for the Law of the Sea and General International Law' (2007) 22 Intl J Marine and Coastal L 351

Wood M, 'The Selection of Candidates for International Judicial Office: Recent Practice' in Ndiaye TM and Wolfrum R (eds), *Law of the Sea, Environmental Law and Settlement of Dispute: Liber Amicorum Judge Thomas A Mensah* (Nijhoff 2007) 357

Wright Q, 'Proposal for an International Criminal Court' (1952) 46 AJIL 60

Zagrebelsky V, 'Questions autour de Broniowski' in Caflisch L, Callewart J, Liddell R, and others (eds), *Liber Amicorum Luzius Wildhaber: Human Rights—Strasbourg Views* (NP Engel 2007) 521

Zarbiyev F, 'Judicial Activism in International Law—A Conceptual Framework for Analysis' (2012) 3 J Intl Dispute Settlement 247

Zemanek K, 'The Legal Foundations of the International System' (1997) 266 Recueil des cours 9

Zimmermann A, 'Die Zuständigkeit des Internationalen Gerichtshofes zur Entscheidung über Ansprüche gegen am Verfahren nicht beteiligte Staaten: Anmerkungen aus Anlaß der Entscheidung des IGH im Streitfall zwischen Portugal und Australien betreffend Ost-Timor' (1995) 55 Zeitschrift für ausländisches öffentliches Recht und Völkerrecht 1051

Zimmermann A (ed), *Deutschland und die internationale Gerichtsbarkeit* (Duncker & Humblot 2004)

Zimmermann A and Thienel T in Zimmermann A, Tomuschat C, Oellers-Frahm K, and Tams C (eds), *The Statute of the International Court of Justice: A Commentary* (2nd edn, OUP 2012) Art 60

Zimmern A, *The League of Nations and the Rule of Law 1918-1935* (Macmillan 1936)

Zoellner C-S, 'Third-Party Participation (NGO's and Private Persons) and Transparency in ICSID Proceedings' in Hofmann R and Tams CJ (eds), *The International Convention for the Settlement of Investment Disputes (ICSID): Taking Stock After 40 Years* (Nomos 2007) 179.

Zolo D, 'Hans Kelsen: International Peace through International Law' (1998) 9 Eur J Intl L 306

Zorn P, 'Die beiden Haager Friedenskonferenzen von 1899 und 1907' in Stier-Somlo F (ed), *Handbuch des Völkerrechts*, vol 3 (Kohlhammer 1915)

Zürn M, *Regieren jenseits des Nationalstaates: Globalisierung und Denationalisierung als Chance* (Suhrkamp 1998)

Zürn M, 'Vier Modelle einer globalen Ordnung in kosmopolitischer Absicht' (2011) 52 Politische Vierteljahresschrift 78

Zürn M, 'Internationale Institutionen und nichtstaatliche Akteure in der Global Governance' in Zürn M and Ecker-Ehrhardt M (eds), *Gesellschaftliche Politisierung und internationale Institutionen* (Suhrkamp 2014, forthcoming)

Index of Persons

Index of Subjects

Printed and bound by CPI Group (UK) Ltd, Croydon, CR0 4YY